# The Language of Law School

# The Language of Law School

*Learning to "Think Like a Lawyer"*

Elizabeth Mertz

OXFORD
UNIVERSITY PRESS
2007

# OXFORD

## UNIVERSITY PRESS

Oxford University Press, Inc., publishes works that further
Oxford University's objective of excellence
in research, scholarship, and education.

Oxford    New York
Auckland    Cape Town    Dar es Salaam    Hong Kong    Karachi
Kuala Lumpur    Madrid    Melbourne    Mexico City    Nairobi
New Delhi    Shanghai    Taipei    Toronto

With offices in
Argentina    Austria    Brazil    Chile    Czech Republic    France    Greece
Guatemala    Hungary    Italy    Japan    Poland    Portugal    Singapore
South Korea    Switzerland    Thailand    Turkey    Ukraine    Vietnam

Published by Oxford University Press, Inc.
198 Madison Avenue, New York, New York 10016

www.oup.com

Oxford is a registered trademark of Oxford University Press

Library of Congress Cataloging-in-Publication Data
Mertz, Elizabeth, J.D.
The language of law school : learning to "think like a lawyer" / Elizabeth Mertz.
p. cm.
Includes bibliographical references and index.
ISBN-13 978-0-19-518286-6; 978-0-19-518310-8 (pbk.)
ISBN 0-19-518286-3; 0-19-518310-X (pbk.)
1. Law—Study and teaching—United States.
2. Law—United States—Methodology.
I. Title.
KF279.M47 2007
340.071'173—dc22          2006045325

Printed in the United States of America
on acid-free paper

*For my daughters, Jenny and Becca*

# Preface

This is a study whose genesis dates back to the day I first took my seat in a Contracts classroom as a first-year law student, and that came to fruition as I for the first time taught Contracts to first-year law students. Having participated in both ends of the process has added depth to my understanding of the law school experience. As a first-year student, I took notes in my Contracts class in two columns; the first kept track of the concepts my professor was endeavoring to impress on us, and the second was a running anthropologist's commentary on the studies that someone should do to investigate the social and linguistic processes at work in contract law—and in legal reasoning generally. This work is an initial effort to investigate the distinctive shape of a core U.S. legal worldview, empirically grounded in the study of the language through which law students are trained to this new approach.

During the first year of law school, students are reputed to undergo a transformation in thought patterns—a transformation often referred to as "learning to think like a lawyer." Professors and students accomplish this purported transformation, and professors assess it, through classroom exchanges and examinations, through spoken and written language. What message does the language of the law school classroom convey? What does it mean to "think" like a lawyer? Is the same message conveyed in different kinds of schools, and when it is imparted by professors of color or by white women professors, and when it is received by students of different races, genders, and backgrounds? This study addresses these questions, using fine-grained empirical research in eight different law schools.

# Acknowledgments

In a fashion that ought to please followers of Carol Gilligan, I began composing the acknowledgments to this volume long before I started the book itself. This was because I have at all points felt deeply how much the work depends on a web of relationships, on the contributions of so many people to whom I feel profoundly indebted. Before I attempt to do justice to this rich relational context, let me thank two institutions, the American Bar Foundation and the Spencer Foundation, for the generous funding that made this project possible. Some of the material from Chapter 2 is reprinted by permission of *The Yale Journal of Law and the Humanities*, Vol. 4, pp. 168–173; portions of Chapter 4 appeared originally in *Natural Histories of Discourse*, edited by Michael Silverstein and Greg Urban (University of Chicago Press, pp. 229–249; © 1996 by The University of Chicago. All rights reserved). Chapter 6 contains material from *Language Ideologies: Practice and Theory*, edited by Bambi Schieffelin, Kathryn Woolard, and Paul Kroskrity (pp. 149–162, used by permission of Oxford University Press; © 1998 by Oxford University Press), as well as material that is revised by permission from *Democracy and Ethnography: Constructing Identities in Multicultural Liberal States*, edited by Carol J. Greenhouse (The State University of New York Press, pp. 218–232; © 1998 by State University of New York. All rights reserved). Thanks to the editors who worked on these materials with me as well as to those who helped with articles to which I retained copyright and from which I have drawn in this volume, which appeared in the *Journal of Legal Education* 48(1): 1–87 (with Wamucii Njogu and Susan Gooding), and the *John Marshall Law Review* 34(4): 91–117. I am also grateful to the many colleagues—anonymous reviewers as well as many who are named below—who have read and commented on parts of or all of the manuscript. Greg Matoesian and Stewart Macaulay graciously provided thorough reviews of the linguistics and contract law discussions; any errors that remain despite their efforts are of course my sole responsibility. Sincere thanks also to my wonderful OUP editors.

I wish to begin by acknowledging the team effort that goes into large-scale research projects of this kind. I have on numerous occasions reflected with some despair on the inadequacy of any mere acknowledgment to express my appreciation to the extraordinarily dedicated group of researchers who worked on this project. Readers who know this field will recognize among the names on this list gifted scholars who have gone on to make outstanding contributions in their own right. Despite the sometimes dreary and plodding character of the work, everyone carried through even the tougher moments with grace and energy, and with a sense of camaraderie and fellowship. I thank Nancy Matthews, the first project manager, for her vision, intellectual precision, and good humor in directing the nitty-gritty daily work as we began the process of gaining access, taping, and formulating coding categories, as well as for her own contribution to in-class taping and coding of one of the classes. Susan Gooding had the difficult task of taking over as project manager in midstream, a job she tackled with a high degree of commitment both to the people involved and to the project; her insights and conceptual rigor also greatly enriched the interpretation of the results as they emerged. Wamucii Njogu, who directed the bulk of the quantitative analysis, similarly insisted on careful and critical examination of the coding and data; her flexibility and intellectual curiosity in working across quantitative and qualitative aspects of the study brought a unique and exciting dimension to the results. And a heartfelt thanks to the exceptionally talented individuals who did the work of coding, inside and outside of the classrooms: Jacqueline Baum, Nahum Chandler, Janina Fenigsen, Leah Feldman, Christine Garza, Carolee Larsen, Mindie Lazarus-Black, Jerry Lombardi, Kay Mohlman, Robert Moore, and Shepley Orr. Steve Neufeld, Carlos de la Rosa, and Tom Murphy worked on the quantitative analysis. The tiring task of transcription was undertaken with care by Diane Clay, Leah Feldman, and Zella Coleman and her group.

I also thank the "subjects" of this research, the professors and students in the eight classrooms we studied. Inviting researchers with tape recorders and coding sheets into one's classroom takes guts, and the professors who did so deserve commendation for their willingness to take some risks in order to help advance our understanding of the teaching process. Having now taught law school classes myself, I have a better appreciation of the courage it took to allow us to observe and record in their classrooms.

I feel deeply grateful to the American Bar Foundation, my home since the project began and one of the major funding sources for this research. The Foundation has provided a uniquely congenial setting for this kind of work, with one of the premier groups of sociolegal scholars in the country. I have enjoyed and learned from my colleagues in that community, and I thank them for providing such an encouraging and intellectually rich context in which to do research. I am particularly grateful to the director of the Foundation during the time of this project, Bryant Garth, for substantial support and encouragement, and for the vision of interdisciplinary community that he has helped to make real. I owe much to all of my colleagues, past and present, at the ABF for their incisive critiques and their humor, and above all for their exercise of maturity, reason, and care in managing the ups and downs of institutional life. For colleagueship above and beyond the call of duty, I thank Carol Heimer and Bob Nelson, each of whom in different ways has provided highly valued support over many years now, as well as John Comaroff, Shari Diamond, Chris Tomlins, Mary Rose, William Felstiner, Susan Shapiro, Laura Beth Nielsen, Karyl Kinsey, Tracey Meares, Bonnie Honig, Annelise Riles, Steve Daniels, Bette Sikes, and Roz Caldwell, from each of whose expertise I have drawn in specific ways. And Joanne Martin, of course—an indomitable force at the heart of the ABF for years—provided her own eagle eye on our numbers as well as unflagging enthusiasm for the project. In the final stages of preparing the manuscript, I was very fortunate to have the assistance of Molly Heiler and Stephanie Lambert.

During the conclusion of the project, I had the good fortune to be invited to join the legendary law-and-society community at the University of Wisconsin Law School in Madison, for generations a leader among law schools in its insistence on the study and teaching of "law in action." I have learned a great deal from the perspectives and scholarship of my new colleagues, and from their insistence on uncompromising standards for bringing together legal and social scientific work. In particular, I thank Howie Erlanger and Stewart Macaulay for sharing their insights on law teaching and sociolegal studies as well as for their stalwart friendship and support, Jane Larson for the ongoing education I receive from our discussions, Art McEvoy for his encouragement and colleagueship, and a growing list of valued Madison compatriots for all that I am learning from them about sociolegal inquiry. Our dean, Ken Davis, and associate deans Alta Charo and Peter Carstensen have been generous in their patience and support as I've negotiated the completion of this project across institutions (and states!).

During several years of the project, I held in addition to my ABF appointment a position at the Northwestern University School of Law, where I had also been a law student. Much of the initial impetus for this study came from some of my observations as a student at Northwestern and from the insights of my fellow students there. In particular, I want to remember my classmate Cathy Novak, whose experiences during our first year challenged me to ask more about the process of legal education. My good friends Joe Margulies and Jonathan Turley learned with and taught me about the problems and possibilities of the law school environment, as did many other friends, including my Articles Office "family": Rick Sander, Krista Edwards, Sue Tuite Kirkpatrick, and Mark Challenger. As my third-year research supervisor, David VanZandt encouraged my initial interest in this project. While a professor at Northwestern, I also benefited from the intellectual insights and support of the short-lived but productive "Friday Faculty" group, including my friend and coauthor Cynthia Bowman, Jane Larson, Bob Burns, Clint Francis, Stephen Gardbaum, Ray Solomon, and Len Rubinowitz (known to generations of Northwestern law students and junior faculty, including me, as an exceptionally supportive colleague and friend). I warmly thank Michael Perry and Kathy Abrams, fellow NU departees, for sharing their perspectives in discussions pertinent to this work, and a number of other colleagues on whom I leaned for insights and advice, including Vic Rosenblum, Marshall Shapo, Theresa Cropper, Laura Lin, Charlotte Crane, Helene Shapo, Dick Speidel, Judy Rosenbaum, and Ron Allen.

To the inspiring groups of students in my Law and Language, Law and Anthropology, Legal Process, and Legal Profession classes at Wisconsin and Northwestern, my gratitude for their invigorating discussions and research on topics pertinent to this study. I have also gained fresh perspectives from the graduate students with whom I've worked, with particular thanks to Jonathan Yovel, Jason Freitag, Susan Gooding, Mark Goodale, Elizabeth Hoffman, Maud Schaafsma, and Scott Parrott.

Outside of my home institutions, I have drawn on a wealth of knowledge and support from a network of colleagues from whom I have been so fortunate to learn: Martha Fineman, scholar and mentor extraordinaire, to whom I owe a special debt of gratitude; David Wilkins and Joyce Sterling, my "legal profession" buddies; Martha Minow, who provided invaluable practical aid and encouragement at the outset of the project; and the gifted group of legal anthropologists, law-and-society scholars, and anthropological linguists from whom I continue to learn: Carol Greenhouse, Greg Matoesian, Sally Merry, Susan Hirsch, Charles Briggs, Marianne Constable, Susan Philips, Don Brenneis, Bambi Schieffelin, John Conley, Mindie Lazarus-Black, Ross Cheit, Lisa Frohmann, and many others. I owe a great deal of my trajectory as an anthropologist of language to my early teachers at Bryn Mawr and Duke—Judith Shapiro, Nancy Dorian, Jane Goodale, Frederica de Laguna, Virginia Domínguez, William O'Barr, Jim Boon, and Larry Rosen—as well as to the wonderful group of scholars who were part of the Center for Psychosocial Studies network during the time I was there. And I wish to acknowledge a special debt to Michael Silverstein, on whose pathbreaking work in linguistic anthropology I have drawn heavily.

I pause to express particular appreciation for the example set by my colleague Jane Larson, whose dignity and whose insistence on values that I respect, particularly regarding law and legal education, have pushed me and others to stand up for what we believe, at whatever cost. I also am grateful to Ian Macneil and Marshall Shapo, conscientious and sturdy voices in defense of academic freedom at a time when many of us thought that this freedom was very much imperiled.

At key turning points toward law in my career, I was fortunate to have the encouragement and support of two generous senior mentors. I thank Judge Richard Cudahy, who has stood strongly for a vision of justice in law while also insisting on meticulous and rigorous legal thought, for a clerkship experience that was the highest form of legal education. I also thank Barney Weissbourd, with whom I coauthored two of my earliest articles on language and law; if it weren't for our friendly but spirited battles over the proper interpretation of H. L. A. Hart's work, I might never have decided to go to law school.

Finally, I want to express my thanks to other friends and to family who have helped to make this work possible. To my mother, Barbara Mertz, a heartfelt thank you for all your help and support over the years, and for flying in to sleep on our couch during my law school exams so that I could study in peace knowing that Jenny had top-of-the-line attention. I am deeply grateful as well for the rich network of friends whose many kindnesses have greatly enriched my life and that of my family, often providing the missing pieces we needed to keep schedules and lives running smoothly: Eva, Karen, Joe, Jim, Kathy, Carol, Jeanne, Dave, Laurie,

Dean, Connie, Terry, Mary Jo, and the rest of the Skokie extended family who have been part of the "village" that has helped to raise my children. I will also always remember with appreciation and great affection the invaluable support I received from Katherine Shea, including her tireless renditions of Irish lullabies for my colicky newborn Becca as I struggled in that time to balance work and family.

And to my children, Jenny and Becca, I owe the debt of all working mothers—that they have shared me with my work, and that my connection with them continually brings renewal and joy to my life. Becca, born after I received my JD, knows the law school as one of the places where I work, and she is a veteran of many office visits, which she has weathered with characteristic good humor and artistic contributions. I have learned from her about resilience and resourcefulness in the face of change. Jenny was two years old when I began law school, and she experienced much of it with me, from Estates and Trusts class to the *Law Review* office. From her early willingness to last through the occasional Legal Writing class to her current vibrant concern about politics and injustice, I have learned alongside and from her about law and society. I dedicate this work to my daughters.

# Contents

Notes on Transcription    xvii

## I   INTRODUCTION

1.  Entering the World of U.S. Law    3

2.  Law, Language, and the Law School Classroom    12

3.  Study Design, Methodology, and Profile    31

## II   SIMILARITY: LEGAL EPISTEMOLOGY

4.  Learning to Read Like a Lawyer: Text, Context,
    and Linguistic Ideology    43

5.  Epistemology and Teaching Styles:
    Different Forms, Same Message    84

6.  On Becoming a Legal Person: Identity and the Social Context
    of Legal Epistemology    97

## III   DIFFERENCE: SOCIAL STRUCTURE IN LEGAL PEDAGOGY

7.  Professorial Style in Context    141

8.  Student Participation and Social Difference: Race, Gender,
    Status, and Context in Law School Classes    174

## IV   CONCLUSION: READING, TALKING, AND THINKING
LIKE A LAWYER

9.  Legal Language and American Law: Authority, Morality,
    and Linguistic Ideology    207

Notes    225

Bibliography    279

Index    301

# Notes on Transcription

(1.25)   Numbers in parentheses indicate length of turn (here, one minute and two and a half seconds). Turns are measured to .005, or half of a second.

(.)   Enclosed dot indicates a very short untimed pause.

// //   Parallel lines indicate overlapping speech.

[[laughter]]   Double brackets indicate backchannel sounds, laughter, etc. (Occasionally backchannel comments are indicated this way for ease of reading; more usually they are indicated using //parallel lines// to mark overlapping backchannels.)

emphasis   Underlining indicates emphatic stress.

()   Single parentheses indicate inaudible or barely audible speech.

*[says name]*   Italicized material in italicized brackets is descriptive commentary, summaries of omitted portions, and metacommentary from EM regarding transcript, as well as paraphrases and substitutes where necessary to protect confidentiality.

*[ . . . ]*   Ellipses in italicized brackets indicate omitted material.

*\*oh\* ((\*sarcastically\*))*   Italicized material in double parentheses describes aspects of speech delivery (intonation, etc.); asterisks mark the relevant transcript passage.

You-   Hyphen indicates a cut-off, usually one that is turn-internal.

I--

--you   Parallel dashes refer to coordinated speech, where one speaker stops before finishing an utterance, and another speaker begins speaking smoothly immediately thereafter (i.e., immediately latched utterances).

# I

## INTRODUCTION

*Law, considered as a science, consists of certain principles or doctrines. To have such a mastery of these as to be able to apply them with constant facility and certainty to the ever-tangled skein of human affairs, is what constitutes a true lawyer, and hence to acquire that mastery should be the business of every earnest student of law.*[1]

*The school is not a neutral objective arena; it is an institution which has the goal of changing people's values, skills, and knowledge bases. Yet some portions of the populations . . . bring with them to school linguistic and cultural capital accumulated through hundreds of thousands of occasions for practicing the skills and espousing the values the schools transmit.*[2]

This introductory section discusses the overarching questions motivating this study. It also provides the review of background concepts and literatures necessary for understanding the basic model of language used throughout the book. Put simply, this book is organized around two core questions:

* Is a common vision or language of law being taught to initiates across diverse U.S. law school classrooms? (And if so, what is it?)
* What kinds of differences among classrooms, students, and professors seem to be salient in creating any divergent refractions of a common vision?

Part II focuses on the first question (similarities among classrooms); Part III examines the second (differences). Part IV, along with other overall observations, concludes that both in content and form, U.S. law school classrooms are perpetuating a vision of law and human conflict that in effect erases certain key aspects of social experience. In sum, the language of U.S. law works to create an erasure or cultural invisibility, as well as an amorality, that are problematic in a society seeking to be truly democratic. Yet, at the same time, we can see a genius to some aspects of this at once abstract and concrete legal language.

We begin, in Part I, by setting the scene for the rest of the book. Chapter 1 outlines the central conclusions of the study and then takes the reader into the law school classroom, stepping into the shoes of law students who are beginning to learn legal language. Chapter 2 provides a more detailed statement of the study's research agenda and of the cross-disciplinary perspectives that inform it. Chapter 3 explains the methodology used and sketches an initial profile of the data.

# 1

## Entering the World of U.S. Law

Much has been written about the first year of law school. There have also been many attempts to define core aspects of U.S. legal reasoning. This book considers these two issues together, using a study of the initial law school experience to shed light on legal worldviews and understandings. One focus of this research is the content of U.S. legal epistemology (i.e., distinctively legal ways of approaching knowledge), as revealed in the training of initiates into the world of law. The study uses close analysis of classroom language to examine the limits that legal epistemology may place on law's democratic aspirations. It also asks whether legal training itself may impact the democratization of the legal profession—that "public profession"[1] that figures so prominently in the governing of our country.

An important corollary of this focus on language as the window to legal epistemology is the central role of discourse to law and other sociocultural processes. In particular, the ideas that people hold about how language works (linguistic ideologies) combine with linguistic structuring to create powerful, often unconscious effects. In recent years, linguistic anthropologists have made much progress in developing more precise analytic tools for tracking those effects.[2] In addition to studying spoken discourse, they have turned their attention to the impact of written texts on social interactions in ritual and institutional settings. This book uses linguistic anthropological analysis to uncover the ways microlevel processes in language embody and perpetuate powerful linguistic ideologies. These ideologies structure and reflect the social uses of language and text in legal contexts, and thus, I argue, provide a key foundation for "thinking like a lawyer."[3] In this sense, one thinks like a lawyer because one speaks, writes, and reads like a lawyer. Some would associate thinking like a lawyer with superior analytic skills in a neutral sense; I

3

would instead characterize the acquisition of lawyerly "thinking" as an initiation into a particular linguistic and textual tradition found in our society.

To develop a detailed picture of the epistemology and process of legal training, I obtained tapes and observational notes from a full semester of Contracts classes in eight different law schools. The law schools range in status from "top five" to "local" law schools; the professors were diverse in terms of gender, race, and legal training. Observers (including myself) taped and coded the interactions in these classes throughout the first semester of law school. Coders then worked with full transcripts of the tapes and in-class observational notes to quantify aspects of the turns in each class. They also qualitatively assessed aspects of developing classroom dynamics. The overall results provide our first detailed observational data on racial dynamics in law school classrooms; they also are the first to allow comparisons across a full range of diverse law schools. Although there has been more observational study of gender dynamics in law school classrooms than of race, previous studies of gender did not use methods that permitted fine-grained analyses of aspects of talk in classrooms beyond broad tallying of numbers of turns. Working from transcripts, we have been able to track both differences and similarities among a broad range of law school classes. A combination of qualitative and quantitative methods allows us to explicate in detail the language of U.S. law as it is taught in diverse law schools.[4]

The first part of this chapter presents, in summary form, the core argument of the book. The second part takes the reader inside the law school classroom, sketching more concretely the kind of discourse found in U.S. law teaching. Our focus is on the very first semester of law school, when students are initiated into a new way of thinking and talking about the conflicts with which they will be asked to deal as attorneys.

## Legal Epistemology and Law Teaching

Although much of this book deals with the nuances and complexities of analyzing U.S. legal language, its central conclusions can be stated in seven relatively simple propositions:

1. *There is a core approach to the world and to human conflict that is perpetuated through U.S. legal language. This core legal vision of the world and of human conflict tends to focus on form, authority, and legal-linguistic contexts rather than on content, morality, and social contexts.* We can trace this view through close analysis of the content and structure of the language found in law teaching and written law texts, as law professors inculcate this distinct approach and as law students learn to speak it. In the law school classroom, initiates to the legal profession take their first steps into a world in which the linguistic processes of combative dialogue and textual exegesis substitute for substantive, socially grounded moral reasoning.

2. *This legal worldview and the language that expresses it are imparted in all of the classrooms studied, in large part through reorienting the way students approach written legal texts. This reorientation relies in important ways on a subtle*

*shift in linguistic ideology.* We find this common approach across the many differences among teachers and classes. Thus, a key function of law school is actually training to a common language that lawyers use to communicate about the conflicts with which they must deal. An important part of this shift involves learning to read the "conflict stories" contained in legal cases in a new, more dispassionate way—guided by a new ideology about language.

3. *Although apparently neutral in form, in fact the filtering structure of legal language taught to students is not neutral.* Legal training focuses students' attention away from a systematic or comprehensive consideration of social context and specificity. Instead, students are urged to pay attention to more abstract categories and legal (rather than social) contexts, reflecting a quite particular, culturally driven model of justice. One aspect of this model is the idea that justice will emerge from a process that is heavily dependent on linguistic exchange or dueling, which moves back and forth between at least two positions. The social context of the exchange is less important than the form, and this form is echoed in role-play in class as well as in "legal reasoning" more generally (often taught as a form of internal dialogue). Another feature of the linguistic ideology that emerges in law school classrooms is an emphasis on layers of textual authority as neutral sources for legal decision making. Legal pedagogy perpetuates this model using a linguistic approach that combines attention to specific details of particular cases with the ongoing development of abstract categories for processing these details and contexts. Students learn to select those details and aspects of context deemed salient for the analogies that are used to bridge concrete cases and abstract doctrines. A standard legal reading conceals the social roots of legal doctrines, avoiding examination of the ways that abstract categories, as they develop, privilege some aspects of conflicts and events over others. Instead, the core issue is one of textual analysis—of parsing written legal texts for the correct reading, which is focused on issues of linguistic authority. A new orientation to the world is subtly conveyed through the filtering linguistic ideology implicit in law school training.

4. *There is a "double edge" to the approach found in U.S. legal language; it offers benefits but also creates problems.*[5] One benefit of this approach is that the language appears to ensure the same treatment for everyone, regardless of the specifics of their situation, and this appearance can sometimes become a reality. U.S. legal language also generates an enormously creative system for processing human conflict, one that can at times provide the flexibility needed to accommodate social change and the demands of different situations while also promoting some stability and predictability. However, there are also problems with this approach. In some cases, it obscures very real social differences that are pertinent to making just decisions; it can also create an appearance of neutrality that hides the fact that U.S. law continues to enact social inequities and injustices. Through an anthropological lens, we can identify these twin difficulties as a simultaneous problem of "cultural invisibility and dominance"; that is, some aspects of context and cultural viewpoints become invisible while others dominate (and this process itself is largely invisible, hidden beneath the apparent neutrality of legal language and approaches to reading written texts).[6]

Similarly, legal language in many ways discourages students from overt consideration of morality, while still packing a hidden normative punch.

5. *There is also a cultural invisibility/dominance problem in law school classroom interactions, where learning the apparently neutral language of the law appears to have different effects on students of different races, genders, and class backgrounds.* Some of these effects are common to many kinds of classrooms as well as to other speech situations in our culture, especially formal ones, and they reflect fundamental aspects of our social structure. However, these effects can have an impact particular to law school training when combined with peculiarly legal modes of talking and reasoning. The classroom is just one location, a beginning or foundational place, in which these different refractions initially emerge. The book's conclusion suggests lessons to be learned through a careful examination of this foundational moment.

6. *Although this study finds a shared underlying epistemology imparted in diverse classrooms, it also delineates significant differences among law schools and law teachers.* The conclusion also urges more fine-grained and contextual attention to the ways that school status and culture, as well as aspects of professorial style and classroom dynamics, may affect equality of opportunity in law training and subsequent practice.

7. *Both in terms of content and form, legal education and the language it inculcates mirror a "double edge" arguably found in capitalist epistemology more generally.* This double edge offers the possibilities but also the problems that come with moving to a particular form of abstraction, which can erase both those aspects of social context that lead to bias but also those that permit in-depth understanding of social inequalities. Facing this dilemma is a crucial task for any legal system with democratic ideals—as well as for the legal language through which such a system operates.

Note, then, that this research uses the study of language to track underlying cultural worldviews or epistemologies, drawing on anthropological linguistic approaches.[7] In particular, the analysis traces the contours of a distinctively legal epistemology, furthering attempts to uncover and explicate a basic structure to U.S. legal reasoning begun some time ago by scholars such as Edward Levi.[8] This part of the analysis is, in my view, distinct from the ensuing examination of the power dynamics and capitalist epistemology that I hypothesize as specific to U.S. law. Taken on its own, the linguistic analysis maps the way language interacts with and embodies social worldviews and institutional practices, and as such speaks to issues of language and epistemology apart from any consideration of power. When it focuses on the nonneutral character of legal language and reasoning, this study does move on to also consider the interaction of language with social power and democratic ideals, building from scholarship in anthropological, legal, and social theory. However, I also argue that the language of law has its own dynamics that are not transparently reducible to issues of power or social structures. In this sense, this analysis rejects visions of legal language as either an entirely autonomous arena, divorced from social impacts, or as a mere reflex of external social forces. Rather, combining both linguistic and social perspectives, we can find in the first-year law school classroom a fascinating prism through which to view a part of the world of U.S. law.

## Initiation: First Steps into the World of Law

Picture yourself entering a law school classroom on the first day of law school.[9] Although many law schools are now experimenting with smaller first-year classes, it is still common to find the bulk of a first-year student's time spent in larger classes of seventy to one hundred students. Traditionally, the first-year class is divided into sections to which students are assigned; these sections then stick together, taking all the same required classes. There is typically relatively little choice in the matter; all students must take a set of core first-year classes (e.g., Contracts, Torts, Property, Criminal Law, Civil Procedure, and, in some schools, Constitutional Law), and their section is assigned to particular professors for each of these courses. Students are also commonly assigned to smaller Legal Writing sections, which are often taught by non-tenure-track instructors (in much the way Freshman English is taught in many colleges).

So you have arrived at your first class, toting a back-breaking load of the heavy casebooks frequently used in the teaching of these core doctrinal courses. You look around the large room, filled with more than a hundred of your fellow classmates, and drop into the first empty seat you can find. If you were alert and fortunate, you noticed that there were already assignments to be read for the first day of class, and so you arrive having already tackled the casebook for this course. (If you were not clued in to this, you realize shortly after class begins that you were supposed to do reading, as the professor randomly selects students and asks them questions about the assignment—and you spend much of the time praying that you will not be one of the draftees.) The casebook, a heavy hardcover textbook that is over a thousand pages long, consists largely of excerpts from appellate court opinions, interspersed with brief commentary and notes.

The professor, clad in formal attire, strides into the classroom. As he climbs to the podium at the front of the rows of seats, the chatter of voices in the room suddenly hushes. The first order of business involves passing around a difficult-to-decipher seating chart, with little boxes for each of the more than one hundred seats in the room; you are instructed to enter your name in the box that corresponds with the seat you have chosen and to sit thereafter in the same place. You are informed that your grade for the entire semester will depend on one exam, graded anonymously, given at the end of the term. After a brief but somewhat ominous moment of silence, the professor looks up from his class list and calls out, "Mr. Chase?" (Although our set of classroom teachers contains a number of professors of color and white female professors, it is still the case that the first-year doctrinal classes are predominantly taught by white males. So, we will begin our story using the predominant profile.)

Relieved that your last name does not even resemble "Chase," you relax momentarily into your chair while the unfortunate Mr. Chase sits up anxiously, book opened to the first case assigned for the day, and prepares to answer the next question. The professor begins, in a reassuring voice, "Okay. I want to begin by trying to figure out- little bit slow- start by trying to figure out what the lower court decided in Hawkins's case. What became of that?"[10] And now your legal training begins, for the professor is not starting by asking you to tell the dramatic story of poor young Hawkins, who wound up with a terrible hand after trusting Dr. McGee to give him a 100 percent perfect hand, a good hand. It may be that the details of the evocative plot of this story, or the villainy or pathos of its central characters, were the main things that stuck in your head after reading the case. But here is the professor asking you to worry first about what the lower court did. Why? Who cares? Isn't what we care about here justice? Isn't the main thing whether young Hawkins was screwed over by an incompetent, uncaring, or generally vicious surgeon, and whether our society is going to do something about it? Or is the main issue whether we're going to be so hard on doctors that they'll never again try to help anyone with a bad hand?

But the professor's questions move methodically on, pushing Mr. Chase to dig up more than he ever thought he'd have to know about what the lower court did. And you realize that apparently, to the legally trained mind, a core aspect of this case you just read involves the layers of authority that come into play in reaching the decision. For example, in this case, it seems important that the text was written by an appellate court (i.e., not by the judge who actually oversaw the trial, but by a judge or group of judges whose job it was to review the decisions made by trial courts). This may not have been anything that particularly struck you in reading the case initially, and you begin to wonder if you were really cut out to be a lawyer. When Mr. Chase hesitantly volunteers that the lower court "decided in favor of the plaintiff" (which would be young Mr. Hawkins), the professor wants to know "in what respect" this was true. Mr. Chase then explains that "they" decided the plaintiff could get damages (translation: money), but that "they" reduced the damages. This sounds like a pretty specific response to you, but the professor interrupts and gets very picky about who "they" are. It turns out that the "they" who awarded the damages was the jury, but the "they" who reduced the damages was the judge.

This seems to matter a great deal to the professor, who, unsatisfied with this level of specificity, starts harassing Mr. Chase about whether it really was the judge who just decided on his own to reduce the damages. Before long, Mr. Chase finds himself explaining to the class that actually the defendant (the doctor) asked the judge to reduce the damages, that he "asked" the judge by filing something called a motion, and that the motion claimed the damages were too high. So now, you think to yourself, trying to be sure you have this all down, what really happened was this: there was a jury trial; Hawkins won and got lots of money; the doctor wanted to pay less money and filed a motion; the trial judge reduced the amount of money Hawkins could get; and Hawkins is appealing that decision by the trial judge. Far from focusing on young Hawkins's angst over his hand now, you are beginning to feel a bit annoyed at him for refusing to accept the offer for a lower amount of money, thereby causing you to have to twist your brain around these byzantine details. (You decide not to worry at all at this point about whether it was Hawkins or his father who actually made the contract with the doctor or about the fact that it was clearly not Hawkins but his lawyer who filed the motion. I mean, enough is enough.)

Throughout your classes in the early fall, your professors repeatedly engage in this irritating habit of dissecting the cases you've read, asking you to focus on the oddest aspects of these assigned texts. For example, in beginning a class discussion, one professor asks, "First of all, was anyone curious about what it means under the name of the case when it says, Supreme Court of Rhode Island, 1969, 105RI612249A second 414? Anybody curious about what that meant? Does anybody know?"[11] You feel relieved when a neighbor responds, "Well I understand the Supreme Court and Rhode Island, but I don't understand the numbers underneath," because you were afraid you were the only one in the class who hadn't yet deciphered the tangle of numbers and letters under the case names. The professor explains that these numbers and letters are citations to books called "reporters" in which cases are, well, reported. This sounds like one of the more reasonable things you've heard all week. She also describes how you can tell what kind of court wrote the opinion from the exact letters used for each citation, but you decide to worry about that later. The professor assures you that deciphering the case citations "will become second nature to you before you leave the law school." You begin to worry about the overall shape of your mental processes by then.

As the semester wears on, however, the professor's prediction turns out to be accurate. When handed a case to read, you now automatically check to see which court wrote the opinion in the case, what happened previously in the case, and what the court did in reaching its decision. Poignant, glaring, pitiful stories of human drama and misery begin to sail easily past you, as you take them expertly in hand and dissect them for the "relevant" facts. Just as a medical student has begun at a parallel point in her training to deal with body parts and incisions in a routine fashion, you are acquiring a certain distance in dealing with stories of human conflict. You are also learning other aspects of a legal reading, which train you to notice only certain parts of a story while discarding others (more on this in Part II). And so when, after buying a home, you discover a concealed leak in the floor of your basement, your first instinct is not to call the previous owner inventive names. Instead, you cheer and point happily to the fact that an obvious attempt had been made to hide the leak. "Look," you say to your baffled friends with glee, "concealment, active concealment." (You now realize that active concealment is one element you'll need to prove if you want to sue the previous owners.) Your friends think that finding out that someone deliberately tried to cheat you should be cause for gloom—an indication that we just can't trust anyone anymore—but instead it seems to make your day. They may comment admiringly on your new ability to approach such difficult situations with a somewhat removed and objective eye, but they also find themselves wondering at times if you're the same person you were before you started your legal training.

At one point in the semester, a classmate asks one of your professors whether a salesperson can get away with lying to a customer when making an agreement. The professor replies to her hypothetical, saying, "Well, if he's made an offer, he's revoked it and unless 2-205 is going to be applied and there has to be a signed writing, unless you could argue estoppel, if you're dealing with the code number 1-103, which opens the doors to the common law, you don't have that kind of protection, unless it's a consumer statute, or a federal trade regulation- regulation, you don't have that- that kind of protection."[12] The student, with rising indignation, asks, "I.e., salespeople can lie?" and the professor responds, "Huh? Not only, i.e., salespeople can lie, i.e., salespeople do lie, constantly." And when the student comments, "That's not fair," the professor underscores the point that fairness is not what they are actually discussing here: "No, no. Fairness is not something that I accept as a general proposition, and certainly not in my household." The class responds with laughter, and your vision is still further refocused to concentrate on this new legal frame, a frame your professors insistently put on the stories told in the cases you read, again and again, as they try to redirect your gaze from *what's fair* to *what the law says you can or can't do.*

At the end of your first semester comes exam time. Now you have a chance to demonstrate your newly acquired legal vision of the world. In exam after exam, you are asked to respond to hypotheticals, stories made up by your professors. These stories are often replete with pathos and drama. Your job is to ignore as much of the emotional content as you can while hunting for the details that are relevant to the legal tests and frames, steadfastly averting your gaze from the human perfidy, misery, justice, or injustice found in the story. Once you've done that, if you're very careful, you can throw in a little discussion of fairness, disguised as a "policy" argument, and sometimes get some extra points.

Your criminal law exam involves a hypothetical in which a woman is "beaten, raped, and killed in descriptions pornographically detailed."[13] If you have yourself been beaten or raped, you may find this question a bit difficult to answer. But your performance will depend on your ability to dispassionately analyze the details provided to you for traces of "facts" needed to satisfy one or another legal test. Your constitutional law exam requires you to read "the lengthy text of a hate-filled polemic" filled with racist slurs against African American and Jewish people, and then to argue why such a polemic should be protected by the First Amendment.[14] Again, if you are African American or Jewish (or someone with strong feelings about racism), this may require an internal struggle of some dimension, but only those students who can rise above such emotional reactions to the lofty heights of legal analysis will ace the exam. You may be able to succeed despite this internal struggle by putting aside your reaction for the moment and promising yourself that you will attend to it at some future time. You may even join a small group of students afterward in protesting the use of such questions on exams. But note that at the moment of demonstrating your newfound skill at legal thinking, you have found a way to put aside emotion and social context in order to fit facts to legal tests in dispassionate fashion.

You may find yourself feeling somewhat ambivalent about this newfound ability to rise above the heated details of social conflict. On the one hand, it gives you a very useful tool; in employing this somewhat removed vision, this legal frame, you can on some occasions rise above your own prejudices and predispositions. This new habit may actually force you to hear perspectives and ideas that you might previously have dismissed too rapidly. Before rushing in to take one side or the other, you find that you can stand back and weigh aspects of the problem at hand with an eye to realistic solutions and possibilities. Perhaps in a perfect world no one would ever cheat customers. But given that this happens, what level of cheating are we going to permit before we bring the full apparatus of the law to bear? Given that in the real world, it takes lots of time and money to go to court, and that courts make mistakes, do we really want the legal system to police this or that kind of injustice or unfairness? To what degree are we going to require a certain level of maturity, to respect individuals' rights to make their own choices—which also means expecting them to accept the consequences of their own decisions? On the other hand, when are we going to recognize that the playing field isn't always level, and that certain players lack the fundamental power required for their decisions to be truly voluntary? And so on. Sometimes you may feel pleased that your thinking now allows you to overcome initial passionate, but perhaps misguided, reactions. At other times, you wonder if, trapped in the maze of "ifs" and "thens" and "maybes," you've lost touch with some fundamental aspects of what brought you to law school in the first place: concerns with justice, fairness, or helping people.[15] You entered law school with the ambition of helping people and eventually performing public interest work aimed at improving poor people's access to justice. But more and more, you find yourself thinking that maybe you'll just start out in a lucrative job in a large law firm, at least for a little while—maybe just until you pay off some of your massive law school debt.[16]

To introduce the kinds of issues with which this study is concerned, I have painted a stark picture, omitting many of the nuances and complexities. Although this portrait does not do justice to the wide variations in emphases, teaching styles, and attitudes to be found in today's legal academy, it captures some core aspects of the initial law school experience and of the change required of law students during their initiation into the legal arena. The detailed discussions to follow provide more of the subtleties and complications needed for a fuller understanding of the law school process.

# 2

·———·

# Law, Language, and the Law
# School Classroom

In this chapter we survey the literatures and scholarship that provide the theoretical and empirical foundations for this research, focusing on issues of language
and law. It is through language that social problems are translated into legal issues.
At the broadest level, this study brings together two related inquiries: Is there a
distinctive approach to translation embodied in the canonical legal language taught
to law students? And if so, how do people learn to use that distinctive language as
they become legal professionals—in their first months of training to be the lawyers and judges whose voices and writings perform the act of legal translation? To
address these questions, we need to develop an understanding of how language operates in legal and other social settings. After all, it is through language that the law
works to shape our lives, and it is through language that people, including professionals, come to understand the world in particular ways.

Thus, in the law school classroom, a seemingly narrow domain, we actually
find a fascinating nexus of wider processes. This study uses a close analysis of law
school language to ask broad questions about the role of language in the constitution of selves, law, and society. It is obvious that an adequate reply to such questions would demand interdisciplinary investigations; accordingly, this research
bridges a number of divides. At the theoretical level, I draw on work in linguistics,
anthropology, legal theory, social theory, educational research, and psychology.
In terms of methodology, this study unites interpretive, linguistic, and quantitative analyses to uncover overarching patterns in the classrooms as well as the nuanced meanings that animate those patterns. This chapter provides a brief overview
of scholarship that has examined the role of language in society and culture, in
socialization practices, and in education; it concludes with a discussion of the role
of language in law, legal reasoning, and legal education. The resulting synthesis of

insights from multiple disciplines provides the foundation for the model of language in social context used in this study. We begin by delineating the central questions animating this project, and then proceed to locate these questions within frameworks provided by previous scholarship.

## Similarities and Differences

As noted in Chapter 1, this study focuses on Contracts classes in eight law schools from across the country. Included among the law schools were some of the most elite in the country and some with more local reputations, public and private, urban and rural, small and large, and schools with night classes for part-time students. The professors in the study also varied in background, philosophy, age, race, and gender, as did the students. Coders taped and took notes on interactions for an entire semester in these classes. To capture the initial stage of students' introduction to legal approaches, we always observed during the first semester. The tapes were then transcribed and analyzed both qualitatively and quantitatively. I asked two fundamental questions of the data we collected: What (if any) similarities are there across the widely variable classrooms of this study? And what is the shape of any differences among them?

### A Shared Vision of Law?

In asking about similarities, we can assess whether there is a shared worldview or cultural framework that cuts across the differing classrooms of this study. This is an empirical way of approaching a question with which legal scholars and philosophers have struggled mightily: Just what is "law"? How is it defined, how does it work? As an anthropologist, I would rephrase this question to take account of history and location, not assuming that law is the same thing in all times and places, or indeed that something we could call law is present everywhere.[1] And I would also be aware of the fact that there are many vantages from which to answer this question, even within one society.[2] Legal professionals are likely to view law differently than do laypeople, and there are also frequent divergences in vision among professionals and among laypeople.[3] In this book, my focus is on one version of the "expert" vision, the understanding of law imparted to students—initiates into the legal profession in the United States.

   The legal realist tradition and its modern cousin, the field of sociolegal studies, correctly insist that to achieve a meaningful understanding of legal processes, we must examine the face of law on the ground, as it affects and is shaped by the people it governs.[4] Scholars have often written of the difference between law "on the books" and law "in action," as if these were always opposed and distinct things.[5] And it is certainly true that written case law and legislation do little to capture the overall shape of legal interventions in our lives. Yet I would argue that a full inquiry into law on the ground requires us to study those who translate and administer the law—to examine the views and writings of experts such as judges and legislators.[6] If the formal frameworks of reasoning employed by lawyers and judges are only part of the story of how law actually operates, they nonetheless remain as a scaffolding on which much else builds: the linguistic structuring through which a great deal of legal decision making proceeds.[7]

Thus, we can rephrase the question a bit, asking: Is there a central vision or form of reasoning shared by those who have received legal training in the United States today, across their many differences? How does U.S. law, at the broadest level, conceive of the world and people with which it deals; is there an underlying worldview or epistemology that binds together the diverse ends of the legal profession by virtue of a similar initial socialization into legal language? There are, of course, multiple layers to consider in answering even this narrower question, for beyond any common expert understanding of legal categories and concepts, legal practitioners also share forms of practical knowledge and reasoning based on commonalities in the work they perform, on similar informal ideologies or folklore about law, and so forth.[8] Here we approach the question of a shared vision of law through an examination of the way that students are ushered into the world of legal thinking, treating the educational process of legal training as a window on that world, a place where the modes of thinking that characterize a legal worldview will be revealed as they are imparted to initiates. And indeed, this study does find that there are certain core understandings that are shared across the classrooms of this study, understandings that, when examined together, reveal a core orientation underlying U.S. legal reasoning.

### Differing Views of Law from Within?

At the same time as the study examines shared understandings, it also investigates how the classrooms we observed diverge from one another. In inquiring about differences among the classrooms, we ask: To what degree is any common vision refracted differentially through the experiences of students and teachers who come to the law from varying social backgrounds? If all law students must learn to speak roughly similar legal language, to use the same forms of reasoning, do some students take to this new language differently from others? Do some students approach or react to their new legal vision of the world in distinctive ways? Do some professors create—whether through deliberate design or not—different kinds of classroom settings within which this new worldview is inculcated, and if so, how do various students respond to these differences? And what is the impact of divergent law school cultures on the teaching and learning processes?

Here we enter the debate about social difference that is raging all over our culture today—and the legal academy is, predictably, no exception. Although fundamental legal categories and the methods used to teach them were for many years viewed as somehow neutral, above the social divisions found in society generally, powerful arguments have emerged to undermine this presumption of neutrality.[9] Not only is the administration of justice in the United States deeply skewed to favor those in power, scholars have suggested, but indeed the basic legal categories and forms of reasoning themselves set up an uneven playing field.[10] Hidden behind standard legal concepts such as the time-honored "reasonable man" standard, critics have argued, are deeply social visions of what kinds of experience count—and those visions privilege some members of the American public over others.[11] At the same time, when critics have attempted to specify how people differ from one another, they have encountered difficult dilemmas that arise from attempting to generalize using categories such as race and gender.[12] Often discussed under the rubric of "essentialism," these dilemmas emerge when we oversimplify based on a social label, assuming, for example, that all women share a common worldview that is different from that of all men, and forgetting that there is a great deal of variability among women. To continue the example, the notion that there is a homogeneous "essential" woman whose view of life is completely different from that of men also risks missing the large areas in which some women's and men's views overlap. As with so many intellectual developments (nature versus nurture, economic versus moral visions of human motivation), the choice when posed starkly seems a bit ridiculous: surely we can do better than to argue either that gender (or race, or class) makes no difference whatever, or that it is all-determining. Increasingly, researchers seeking to do justice to the complexities involved have sought models that take account of differences without ignoring similarities and complicated variations. The work of legal theorist Martha Fineman sets an important example for this, as when she uses concepts such as "gendered lives" to capture the idea that people can share orientations based on similar lived experiences rather than based on some common and uniform "essence."[13]

The results of this study suggest that differences among people (notably by race and gender) combine with differences across contexts (e.g., distinct kinds of schools, classrooms, and teaching styles) to create a complex patterning. Thus, *the law school classroom is indeed a different place for students of varying backgrounds.* Following Fineman, I argue for a complicated and grounded approach to analysis of this difference, one that looks carefully at varieties of shared experience and context, taking into account similarities as well as differences among students and professors.[14]

## Normative Implications

In presenting this work, I am often pressed for normative recommendations: Socratic method teaching should be abolished or kept; U.S. law school training and legal epistemology are good or bad, etc. Although I urge more careful contextual consideration of the issues involved than could be encompassed by such yes-or-no questions, this study certainly points out deeply problematic areas, areas that legal training and law itself need to address if our legal system is to live up to its central charge in a democratic state. At the same time, I hope to present a nuanced picture, one in which there are no simplistic answers, no obvious or overdrawn bad guys. This is not because I wish to evade analysis of injustices or problems in the existing systems (of law or of legal education). This study can be seen as contributing to a foundation for precisely such an analysis. However, I share the commitment of many with my training to the idea that it is through appreciation of the real complexity of social life that we can come to a better understanding of the weaknesses and strengths of particular social settings or configurations. Erasing the ambiguities and ambivalences only hinders genuine understanding and possibilities for change.

Thus, I take the view that there is a "double edge" to law and to legal education in this place and time: that the conceptual structure of U.S. law as it is taught today arose not only as part of an ongoing social process involving domination and power, but also as a not completely unsuccessful attempt to deal with difficult social dilemmas.[15] I argue, then, that there is something of value existing side by side with some highly problematic features of the solution suggested by this society's dominant forms of legal reasoning. Along with legal theorists who have sought to revive appreciation for the power and possibilities of the common law, I urge that we consider not only the failures but also the victories and freedoms that have been won using the language and procedures of Anglo-American law.[16] These victories and possibilities do not erase the substantial injustices and difficulties that still exist; there is clearly tremendous work yet to be done in moving to a genuinely democratic legal system in this country. And part of this failure to achieve truly democratic legal forms can be seen in crystallized fashion in the law school classroom. However, if we are to rise above essentialist and overly simplified approaches in envisioning reform, it is vital to take a nuanced view in which neither all of the vices nor all of the virtues of our system of legal thought are ignored.

In addition to exploring this double edge in legal reasoning and education, both sides of which are implicated in social power, I also argue that there are dynamics found in the law school classroom that do not directly translate into issues of power. Like others who have studied linguistic interaction in detail, I find aspects of these classroom exchanges that are contingent, spontaneous expressions of the particular people involved. Sometimes these linguistic exchanges are responses to structured aspects of the speech situation and institutional settings that are not easily reduced to power alone; sometimes these interactions create unique, individual linguistic footprints of the speakers themselves as they respond to one another. It is my goal in this study to balance analysis of these more speech-situation-specific characteristics of law school talk with careful attention to the aspects of speech that are clearly responsive to power dynamics within and beyond the classroom.

In the remaining sections of this chapter, I pause to outline key theoretical issues from the diverse disciplines that inform this research. Thus, we will look at existing scholarship on the role of language in social institutions, in socialization processes, in education, and in law and legal education. The resulting model of language, social process, psychology, and law will set the stage for subsequent discussion of what is happening in law school classrooms.

## A Framework for Studying Language and Law

So much of our social world is dependent on our use of language. How we talk turns out to be crucial in almost every imaginable context in which human beings participate: in raising our children, in negotiating relationships, in formulating policy, in passing judgment.[17] Many generations of anthropologists and linguists have studied the role of language in human societies, trying to formulate an accurate picture of the intricate interactions involved. I build on their work here in developing a model of how language works in the law school classroom, and in the law more generally.

## The Role of Language in Society

A number of traditions in linguistics, social theory, and anthropology converge on the study of language as an essential key to understanding human social life and psychology. These traditions insist that we study language in particular social settings, departing from the approaches that have focused on broad structural characteristics of language. Those previous approaches often attempted to use very abstract and general models of how Language (with a capital "L") works as the foundation for insights about human society or cognition. By contrast, this recent work in anthropology, sociolinguistics, and related fields investigates languages on the ground, in practice, as they are used by particular people in their daily lives. From a careful study of the way languages mediate social interactions, there emerges a quite different view of the role of language in human life, one in which language is valuable not because it affords insights into universal structures, but because it is particularly sensitive to different social settings, particularly imbued with the social life of which it is a part.

Perhaps one of the most famous formulations of the relationship between language and culture emerged from the works of language scholars Benjamin Lee Whorf and Edward Sapir and their followers.[18] Controversial from the outset, this school of linguistics examines the contribution of language structure to understanding the way speakers in different cultures think about and approach the practicalities of social life. Early on, the Whorfian approach was interpreted using rigidly determinist readings, in which the influence of language on thought and behavior was conceived as set in stone and painfully straightforward (e.g., a particular grammatical category is thought of as rigidly and single-handedly determinative of how speakers are capable of thinking about a certain aspect of the world).[19] Critics of this approach rightly rejected any implication that language categories could mold people's brains in so simple and rigid a fashion. However, recent reinterpretations of the Whorf-Sapir tradition have restored for us the more subtle vision inherent in Whorf's careful explication of the "habitual" character of language patterning.[20] Whorf did not intend to link differences in language with rigid limits on mental functioning—as if a speaker raised in one language could never learn different ways of talking and understanding. Rather, in his view, the regular use of the categories and ways of talking found in a particular language-and-culture broadly shape speakers' habitual understandings of the world.[21] These habitual understandings can be amended or shifted, and can fluctuate or vary through different uses, contexts, and parts of societies. However, Whorf teaches us that even these shifts will occur in and through language, and thus can be studied there.

Another contribution of this tradition is an insistence that we examine more than just words or concepts in studying language, so that we can capture the habitual patterning of cultural understanding that occurs through the use of whole systems of language (grammars) day after day throughout speakers' lives. Current work in anthropological linguistics warns against a focus on individual words, as if they could by themselves embody realms of thought, or as if meaning inhered in those segmented chunks of language rather than emerging from the active, creative use of a whole web of related sounds and meanings.[22] Thus, if we are to understand how language shapes our social world, our focus must be not on mere combinations of words, but on a complex linguistic structure that conveys meaning in multiple interconnected ways. In addition, we must take account of the fact that meaning is conveyed and created by the way linguistic structure is operationalized in the actual *use* of language every time we communicate. This adds yet another level to the analysis. Some schools of thought in essence throw up their hands when it comes to language use, by implication viewing it as too unsystematic or vast or unimportant to be included in a theory of language meaning. By contrast, research in anthropology and sociolinguistics has elucidated the regularities and processes at work in actual language use. I will briefly summarize key aspects of this approach.

We first visit the level of language structuring with which the Whorf-Sapir tradition concerned itself: that of a background grammar or structure to language categories. Building from work by Whorf and Sapir, Ferdinand de Saussure, Charles Sanders Peirce, the Prague School, Roman Jakobson, and others, recent scholarship by Michael Silverstein and other linguistic anthropologists has proposed an exciting reversal of the usual ideas about grammatical structure.[23] At the broadest level, this shift moves us to a greater focus on the centrality of pragmatic, or contextual, meaning in language.[24] Much previous work on grammar had proceeded as if the main point of language structure were to convey static concepts, propositional information, or meaning that exists apart from any particular context. (A noun, we can all recite in unison—paying homage to our grammar(!) school days— refers to a person, place, or thing.) However, Silverstein's work has clarified the many ways that the social and expressive functions of language—the contexts of culture and social relations, of prior texts and immediately surrounding language, of specific speech situations and uses—are actually pervasive in linguistic structure.[25] Grammatical structure is at every point responsive to the fact that it is a system created in use, for speaking, for carrying on social relationships and constituting cultures.[26] Far from being constituted solely of the static rules and abstract categories we associate with our old grammar books, grammatical structure can be conceptualized as the ever changing web of relationships between sounds and meanings immanent in the millions of uses to which speakers put their language every day.[27] It is the most social aspect of language, in the sense that it is the common structuring that brings us close enough that we can find some way to communicate our private meanings in a shared tongue. And that is precisely why a view of grammatical structure as constantly shaped and renewed in crucial ways by its use in social context makes such good sense.

This socially grounded grammar provides a reservoir from which flow the more and less predictable acts of speaking that constitute so much of our daily interaction. It is through the creative use of this shared structure that we can forge relationships, hurt someone's feelings, rupture the normal order of a meeting, or interpret precedent in a novel way. But we have, of course, only begun to understand these processes when we have analyzed grammatical structuring, even using this new heavily contextual approach. Much of the meaning we create when we speak depends on the subtle structuring of large stretches of discourse in particular contexts, and on the actual mobilization of many levels of language in each usage. Thus, we move to several other considerations that are important to our analysis.

In looking at the structuring of whole chunks of discourse, we move beyond the skeletal background framework of grammar to the richer, still more contextual domain that has been heavily studied by sociolinguists. Larger stretches of discourse are responsive to contexts of many kinds: social (e.g., we are people of unequal social power speaking in a classroom), generic (e.g., I am using the genre known as storytelling, building on a shared cultural sense of stories we both have heard), intralinguistic (e.g., I am playing this new image against the images of my immediately preceding utterance, or using poetic structure to convey meaning), speech-contextual (e.g., I am referring to previous contexts of speaking,[28] or to the one I am currently creating as I speak), and many more. Sociolinguist John Gumperz has analyzed how speakers rely on subtle "contextualization cues" to orient ongoing communication by pointing to these layers of context; linguistic anthropologists such as Brenneis, Duranti, and Goodwin have looked at wider social and metalinguistic structures and ideologies as also playing a crucial role.[29] This larger structuring of discourse is not always something of which speakers are consciously aware, so that conversation involves an astonishing coordination of background (often unselfconscious) cultural and linguistic knowledge with ongoing conscious language use.

Here, then, is a meeting place for individual creative language usage and socially shared structuring of language, at a level that is deeply cultural and only partially available to conscious awareness.[30] How intriguing it is that so many of the key political and ritual discourse forms in other cultures can structurally mirror, in very subtle and complex ways, the very model of society or language that they attempt to reinforce.[31] And, having recognized this link in "others," anthropologists have returned to analyze a similar connection between language and politics in the United States.[32] As we trace the ways that language and the polity mirror one another, the line between linguistic structure as a "model of" and a "model for" the social world can blur, so that our analysis reveals the mutually reinforcing role of political language and politics itself.[33] Taking this perspective into the legal field as it is revealed in the law school classroom, we would similarly want to investigate the general structure of "law school classroom speech." Is there a message conveyed by law school classroom discourses? What kind of relationship to different contexts, both inside and outside of the classroom, is set up by the structure of law school language?

Finally, even an examination of the contextual structure of discourse in the abstract is a step away from the study of actual language use—which is a form of action, of practice. What happens when speakers put these structures of grammar and discourse to use? Some language theorists have neglected this question altogether, perhaps viewing actual language use as entirely idiosyncratic or incapable of being theorized.[34] However, in current scholarship, anthropological linguists and sociolinguists are developing systematic ways to analyze linguistic performance, examining the moment when speakers translate language structures and regularities into everyday use.[35] Along with some social theorists, philosophers, and legal scholars, researchers studying language are stressing the centrality of social context and human creativity in the analysis of how the potentials inherent in language structures actually play out in everyday life. Previous work had, for the most part, investigated the aspects of language structure or usage that are in some sense presupposed when we speak.[36] We could concentrate, for example, on the fact that using a highly formalized register of speech tends to convey social distance and reinforce or create authority ("Yes, sir"). This is an aspect of meaning that is presupposed before and apart from any particular instance of speaking. However, as Silverstein's research has demonstrated, exclusive focus on this dimension of speech use can lead us to underestimate the creative, contextual, and contingent aspects of human social interaction and speech. So, to continue our example, use of a highly formalized register ("Yes, sir!") in a joking tone, suddenly, with someone you have just gotten to know a bit better, could actually convey and create intimacy. (Note that it would do so by pushing both of you to suddenly focus on dimensions of the context that cause the use of distant, formal language to seem anomalous—a context that is continually emerging in the ongoing interaction between you.) This aspect of meaning is contingent, created in the moment by particular speakers. Obviously, any adequate model of linguistic meaning would need to consider both presupposed backdrops and ongoing creativity in language use in order to achieve a thorough understanding of how we forge, rupture, and maintain social relationships in and through language.

Another interesting discovery emanating from the systematic study of language use is the growing interest in the reflexive, or *meta*level of language: the way language is pointing to itself as it is used. We see this, for example, when we examine indigenous speakers' own understandings of how language works, otherwise known as their "linguistic ideologies." As Kathryn Woolard and Bambi Schieffelin explain, summarizing several strands of thought in the field, the concept has been used in a number of ways:

> Linguistic/language ideologies have been defined as "sets of beliefs about language articulated by users as a rationalization or justification of perceived language structure and use" . . . with a greater social emphasis as "self-evident ideas and objectives a group holds concerning roles of language in the social experiences of members as they contribute to the expression of the group" and "the cultural system of ideas about social and linguistic relationships, together with their loading of moral and political interests" . . . and most broadly as "shared bodies of commonsense notions about the nature of language in the world."[37]

On the one hand, language ideology can operate at a broad, conscious level, as when a social group is consciously linked with a form of speech that is taken to mirror their identity (if a stigmatized subgroup of a population, for example, is linked with a "lower" form of speech). Susan Gal and Judith Irvine would characterize this as a form of iconicity or mirroring, one of several distinctive semiotic processes that they identify as part of the process of linguistic ideologization.[38] On the other hand, language ideology can also operate at a more subtle microlevel. It turns out that how we conceive of the details of speaking is a central part of the structuring of everyday discourse, not just an accidental or incidental aspect.[39] At all points, our ongoing language use depends on an equally ongoing assessment of what it is we are doing (e.g., having a fight, explaining a legal doctrine, giving testimony, using technical language to exclude nonexpert listeners). We draw on preexisting notions and categories of discourse (e.g., fighting, explaining, testifying), and these are also always up for reinterpretation or even contestation (e.g., "No, I won't fight with you" or "You're not explaining a legal doctrine, you're perpetuating the violence inherent in legal categorization!"). This framing of interlocutors' understanding of "what we are doing as we speak now" actually impacts the very meaning of the words we speak: I can say "Oh, the hell with you, then" and have it mean the end of a relationship, a moment of joking repartee, a crestfallen admission that I've lost an argument, a powerful moment of refusing to let someone bully me. And much of this meaning will be given by the multiple layers of context (where, with whom, how, why, with what background, etc. I am speaking) in combination with my (and my interlocutors') metalevel understandings of what it is we are doing when we are speaking. This is subject to continual negotiation, not set in stone. Large shifts in meaning may depend on small shifts in intonation, the raising of an eyebrow, or the use of one pronoun rather than another. Thus, there is presupposed, shared cultural knowledge but also ongoing social creativity always at work as we speak. And nothing less than the ongoing structure of our relationships, societies, and selves are at stake in this process.

This vision of language meaning—as multiple and overlapping, structured and contingent, shared and individual, presupposed and creative; as emergent from the use of language in context; as culturally forged and shaped in a practice of speaking that is different in different cultures and languages; as central to social institutions like schooling and law—is a vision that lies at the heart of much of the most exciting current work in linguistic anthropology.

### The Role of Language in Socialization

In studying how children are socialized to become members of their societies and cultures, scholars such as Bambi Schieffelin and Elinor Ochs have demonstrated that language use provides a central mechanism by which this process is accomplished.[40] It is through particular linguistic practices and exchanges that children form a vision of their world, acquiring key frameworks within which emotions, cognitive understandings, and fundamental notions of the self operate. To take one small example, in Samoa children are urged from very early ages to recognize and call out to other villagers by name; as they walk with children, caregivers engage in ongoing linguistic instruction designed to inculcate attentiveness to others and the beginnings of proficiency in complex greeting routines that indicate respect.[41] This and many other kinds of exchanges build "affective" or emotional competence in these small initiates, competence that they will need in order to take their places as mature and capable members of their society. Conceptions of who they are, their place in society, what range of emotionality is appropriate in given settings, and much more are formed in an ongoing stream of linguistic routines and interactions with adults.[42]

This process of language socialization is not confined to children's language. As we shall see in Chapter 4, the linguistic routines used by some law school professors have affinities with those used in socializing children among the Kaluli of New Guinea. Like the first linguistic socialization of children, the training of adults to a new social identity (sometimes spoken of as "secondary socialization") also involves the use of language to orient initiates to a social world.[43] For example, one study of training in medical school revealed the powerful reorienting effect of the first-year experience in the gross anatomy lab, an experience designed to impart the "'clinical attitude,' the attitude it is hoped students will master in order to behave intelligently and gracefully in the face of calamity."[44] Common cultural taboos centering on death and the body are violated in the work of the anatomy lab, and prior attitudes and opinions are jarred as medical students begin the transformative task of becoming doctors.

This process of breaking down prior beliefs and assumptions during a process of adult (or postprimary) socialization has been analyzed by scholars studying other kinds of rituals designed to move members of societies to new statuses.[45] In his analysis of rites of passage across a number of societies, Turner first describes a phase during which neophytes, or "initiands," are "stripped of status and authority . . . and further leveled to a homogeneous social state through discipline and ordeal."[46] The initiands are immersed in a new, separate social setting, and an effort is made to undermine normal perceptions and routines.[47] The separation phase is followed by a period of time during which the initiand remains at the margin of normal society, marked off in some way; Van Gennep refers to this as a "liminal" state.[48] Finally, there is a period of "reaggregation" during which, now reformulated as a person with a new social identity and status, the initiate reenters the "normal" social world.

In the first-year law school classroom, just as in the gross anatomy laboratory, students experience their first, often jarring confrontation with the worldview and practices of a new profession. To the degree that the first year of law school involves a breaking down of standard cultural assumptions and inculcation of new orientations, analysis of this process can reveal a crucial focal point of professional identity—one that differentiates members of this profession from members of others, and one that gives some sense of unity to otherwise diverse professional experiences. As we shall see, a key aspect of this focal point in legal education is precisely language itself, and a crucial rupturing occurs around expectations regarding language use. If students entering the medical profession must endure a breaking down of everyday beliefs about the body, physicality, and death, students entering the legal profession undergo a linguistic rupture, a change in how they view and use language. This transition is, of course, itself signaled and performed through language, the language of the law school classroom. As in other forms of language socialization, new conceptions of morality and personhood are subtly intertwined with this shift to new uses of language.[49]

## The Role of Language in Education

Bourdieu and Passeron have described the educational process as one in which a new relation to language and culture is transmitted, in an apparently autonomous institutional setting that nonetheless constantly contributes to the reproduction and legitimization of the established social order.[50] Similarly, anthropologists and sociolinguists working in classroom settings have frequently found in the language of the classroom a powerful orienting social practice.[51] Hidden beneath the apparent content of a lesson may be a deeper message about how the world operates, about what kind of knowledge counts, about who may speak and how to proceed— a cultural epistemology that is quietly conveyed through classroom language. Thus, we can see broader social patterns and struggles played out and transformed in the smaller-scale dynamics of classroom interaction. Insights from linguistics and sociolinguistics have been very useful in analyzing these dynamics.

Formal education typically takes place through linguistic exchanges in classrooms and through interaction with written texts. Sociolinguistic approaches to classroom education analyze these interactions as socially embedded linguistic practices, asking how the form and content of language work to accomplish (or, in some cases, fail to accomplish) the social transformation that is the aim of much formal education. Some of the central debates in this literature have centered on how to conceptualize the role of writing in formal education, asking, for example, whether written language achieves an "autonomy" or "rationality" not found in spoken language. Scholars have also examined the connection between the language of education and social structures or epistemologies, with a particular focus on whether the language used in classrooms might be linked with the wider goals of Western educational systems and states. In addition, research in this area has studied the relationship between identity, social class, ideology, ethnicity, race, culture, and gender, on the one hand, and the language of the classroom, on the other. (Chapter 8 examines studies on diversity in schooling in more depth, with a particular focus on research in the area of legal education.) This section gives a brief overview of scholarly work on language in education to set the stage for our consideration of the law school classroom in particular.

Early work on literacy suggested that written language is connected with peculiarly abstract and autonomous qualities of cognition.[52] However, anthropologists and psychologists have criticized the earlier focus on a particular linguistic medium (in this case, writing), without sufficient attention to the role of context.[53] Thus, in their study of Vai literacy, Scribner and Cole pointed out that writing in the context of schooling is quite different from writing in other contexts.[54] Studies of writing in classroom settings may not be capturing any essential quality of written language per se, but instead are likely to be tapping aspects of a particular setting in which writing occurs. Street took the critique one step further, arguing that even Scribner and Cole err in attempting to parcel out the effects of schooled literacy versus nonschooled literacy, as if the literacy itself were an isolable variable to be dealt with neutrally, apart from its social character and valorization as social practice.[55] Street's socially embedded approach to literacy has much in common with Bourdieu's treatment of education more generally as a social institution.

From these critiques of the "autonomous" view of literacy, there emerges a methodological caution: in analyzing spoken versus written discourse, or particular forms of spoken or written language, it is important to look at those discourses as they are situated in particular contexts. James Collins urges a focus on the role of "relativist or situated literacies, seen as diverse, historically and culturally variable practices" in creating, circulating, and interpreting written texts, as opposed to "a universalist or autonomous literacy, seen as a general, uniform set of techniques and uses of language."[56] Thus, rather than characterizing literacy in school settings as tantamount to a training to abstract logic, we must specify the kind of logics involved in various kinds of literacies, questioning whether lessons vary across different school settings, and asking how abstraction of a particular sort might serve institutional or wider social goals.[57] As Shirley Brice Heath documented in her classic research on training to "schooled literacy" by parents as well as schools, particular approaches to written texts and to reading can carry important social implications, demonstrating Collins and Blot's dictum that literacies are "inseparable from values, senses of self, and forms of regulation and power."[58] This approach directs our attention to the issue of cultural epistemologies: What socially constructed understandings of language and text do participants bring to or encounter in the classroom?

Ethnographic studies of classroom learning by scholars such as Jenny Cook-Gumperz, Sarah Michaels, Hugh Mehan, Susan Philips, Courtney Cazden, James Gee, and others have demonstrated that careful attention to the details of linguistic interactions provides important insight into these issues.[59] For example, studies of urban schooling have shown that some children bring with them into the classroom norms for organizing speech that differ considerably from those employed by their teachers.[60] Analysis of minute linguistic detail in one such case revealed (a) that the child's discourse structure differed radically from standard classroom discourse (but that it contained many rich and subtle techniques for conveying meaning);[61] (b) that specific differences between the child's discourse and that of her teacher made mutual understanding difficult; and (c) that imposition of the teacher's discourse norms resulted in a classroom structure that devalued differing, though complex and interesting, patterns of speech, thereby silencing the child. This and other similar studies indicate the advantage of detailed analysis of classroom language: it permits us to capture the actual process by which classroom interaction effects a transformation or reinforcement of linguistic patterns and epistemologies.[62] Observation of the results achieved through classroom language can also uncover the differential effects of social structure on different participants in classroom interaction, a point of interest to anthropologists studying the impact of Western schooling in colonial and postcolonial settings.[63] These issues are important in the study of law school classroom language as well. What cultural norms are conveyed or violated by the discourse pattern of the classroom, and would these norms affect different students differentially? How does the exercise of pedagogical power in constraining or shaping (or evaluating) classroom discourse accomplish a socializing process?

Sociologists studying education have focused on the way education can operate to reproduce and reinforce existing power relations and structures.[64] This "reproduction" approach represented a change from earlier, more neutral "functionalist" approaches.[65] A familiar debate emerged as scholars began to explore the relationship between social power and education. Some studies posited a relatively determinist relation between social structure and education, in which education is conceptualized as a reflex of existing class relations.[66] In reaction to this apparently determinist approach, scholars such as Apple and Giroux pointed out that schools serve as fora for struggle over social power, and thus are not mere reflexes of economic structure.[67] They took issue with determinist theories on two points: first, they argued that people who are disadvantaged in a particular society do not become passive receptacles of dominant culture, but instead retain their capacity to struggle; second, they insisted that social institutions such as schools are characterized by some measure of autonomy from economic structure, however small.[68] Carnoy and Levin further argued that if Western educational institutions provide a somewhat autonomous forum with a dynamic of its own, then an essential aspect of that dynamic is tension between preparing citizens for participation in democratic society (i.e., training them to know and fight for their rights under the law) and training workers who can function in relatively authoritarian work regimes.[69]

Functional conflicts of the sort described by Carnoy and Levin would obviously differ across subcultures and societies along with cultural conceptions of citizenship, with differing economic situations and needs for worker training, and with different roles for educational institutions themselves.[70] The work of Pierre Bourdieu on education incorporates this notion of culturally circumscribed educational practices and also recognizes a somewhat autonomous dynamic to educational organizations.[71] At the same time, Bourdieu thinks that schooling plays a key role in reproducing class structures, and that language is an essential part of that process.[72]

There is a continuing tension in this scholarly tradition between these more *macro*structural accounts that consider broader social and cultural patterns and less reductive *micro*level accounts that capture the complex and creative dynamics at work on the ground in educational settings.[73] As Yon explains, during the 1990s research in the area followed "an increasing move away from essentialism toward a view of race, gender, and class as social processes linked to competing interests in education and society."[74] One of the key conceptual tools in this antiessentialist move is the concept of "schooling as a discursive space," in which the *micro* and *macro* interact in complex, nondeterminist ways.[75] Scholars such as Stanton Wortham who are working in the area of language and education have pointed to the analysis of indexical structuring in discourse as an important tool for achieving this *micro-macro* synthesis.[76]

This study, then, examines underlying cultural and power dynamics at work in the language of the law school classroom, but also considers ways that legal training might transcend or gain some measure of autonomy from these dynamics. The analysis brings together two different approaches: psychologists' and linguists' focus on how the language of education interacts with the formation of social epistemologies and identities, and sociologists' and anthropologists' broader concern about the role of education in reproducing power relations. Drawing on a Silversteinian framework, we will pay careful attention to indexical structuring and the creativity of real-time discursive processes in an effort to bridge the *micro-macro* analytic divide. Thus, building from a strong tradition in anthropology, sociolinguistics, and linguistic ethnography of education, this study examines the details of classroom interactions to understand the larger dynamics at work in educational processes.

### The Role of Language in Law, Legal Reasoning, and Legal Education

The centrality of language and language structure to legal reasoning has long been recognized by legal theorists. From John Austin's conceptualization of law as the "command" of a sovereign through Ronald Dworkin's insistence on the centrality of interpretation to law, jurisprudence has grappled with the place of language in legal decision making.[77] Legal scholars investigating the structure of legal reasoning from a variety of angles seem inevitably to wind up asking questions about legal language or rhetoric and how it works.[78] In an interesting early attempt to map the language of an evolving doctrine, Edward Levi showed how phrases such as "imminently dangerous" and "inherently dangerous" took on a life of their own over time in legal reasoning, going through messy periods of linguistic evolution during which jurists themselves became somewhat unclear about the meaning of the obstreperous legal categories.[79] James Boyd White has suggested that in the language of judicial opinions, judges constitute communities and engage in conversations that can foster or discourage democracy.[80] And scholars like Patricia Williams and Duncan Kennedy have looked at the law school classrooms in which this language is taught as prisms through which we can see, in crystallized form, the language of law in action—though the landscape they discern is very bleak indeed, reinforcing existing power asymmetries, sexism, and racism.[81]

Indeed, over the years, a great deal has been written about law school education by legal academics, much of it taking the form of a debate over the relative benefits and detriments of particular approaches to law school education.[82] Ever since 1870, when Christopher Columbus Langdell introduced his new revolutionary approach at the Harvard Law School, law school teaching has had its own distinctive "Socratic method" genre of teaching. Langdell linked this method for teaching with an overall substantive theory of law, predicated on the idea that there are foundational legal principles, analogous to scientific law, that are discernable through analysis of the raw data of appellate cases. Although it is not clear to what extent people using the label "Socratic method" are actually talking about the same kind of speech genre,[83] commentators continue to speak of Socratic teaching as the signal approach to law school pedagogy.[84] The stereotypic picture of this genre is that professors question students on the cases assigned for a particular class, so that information is imparted not through lecture or explanation but through an ongoing stream of questions designed to challenge unquestioned assumptions and reveal underlying legal principles.[85] There have been numerous critiques of Langdell's formalist philosophy and pedagogical system—most notably from the legal realist school of the 1930s, which also pressed for more clinical education in law schools,[86] and more recently from critical scholars within the legal academy.[87] However, despite a number of arguably successful attacks on the substantive underpinnings of Langdell's approach, the method itself appears to have outlasted its theoretical rationale.[88]

Central themes in critiques of Socratic method teaching in law schools have been that it fails to impart moral values, that it imparts the wrong moral values, that it is not functionally adequate even for teaching doctrine, that it causes unnecessary and harmful stress, that it favors white male students, that it fosters incivility and overly competitive attitudes, and that it leaves students unprepared for the realities of practice. Johnson, for example, notes that as law schools adopted the Socratic method, there was a shift from the model of lawyers as moral decision makers to an image of law as a technical field of expertise.[89] Zemans and Rosenblum similarly note the move away from moral considerations involved in Langdellian scientism.[90] Critical legal theorists like Duncan Kennedy take this insight one step further, insisting that the shift to technical expertise itself embodied a morality, but in a negative sense.[91] In a somewhat different vein, James B. White characterizes current law school training, with its emphasis on "doctrine in a vacuum," as a failure, and proposes instead a more egalitarian and creative training.[92] Implicit in White's critique is also the notion of functional, as well as moral, failure: that the Socratic method and accompanying approaches to law school education, when losing the interest and destroying the confidence of law students, fail to effectively impart even the more abstract conceptual aspects of legal training.[93] Another long-standing criticism has been that law schools turn out lawyers not equipped to practice law.[94] This criticism, though it did not end the use of Socratic training, did contribute to a partially successful movement for clinical education in law schools.[95] Today, some of the most innovative ideas about improving law teaching can be found in the scholarship of clinical and legal writing law professors.[96]

Specific critiques of the Socratic method have emerged from psychological, sociological, and educational research. For example, psychiatrist Alan Stone used a combination of personal observation and interviewing to assess the advantages of this teaching method.[97] Although he concluded that there were some advantages for "channeling group emotions into structured academic inquiry," Stone also expressed concern about the negative effects of the Socratic method on students' interpersonal relations and sense of self-esteem, a theme echoed in current studies of psychological distress among law students.[98] Studies have also highlighted the limits of Socratic teaching in reaching students with diverse learning styles, personalities, and backgrounds.[99] Susan Daicoff connects the shift to more impersonal reasoning encouraged by legal training with lawyer dissatisfaction, lowered public trust in the legal profession, and declining professionalism.[100] In addition, Taunya Banks, Lani Guinier, and others have indicated ways that Socratic teaching might operate to differentially exclude women and students of color, results given support by an ABA report on the subject (see discussion in Chapter 7).[101]

In contrast, supporters of the Socratic method maintain that the method bears a special relationship with the style of reasoning required by lawyers, that it is efficient in large classrooms, that it stimulates active involvement on the part of students, that it prepares students for the adversarial debates and quick retorts required of practicing attorneys, that it is not necessarily more dominating and manipulative than the methods used in clinical teaching, and that it conveys at once the guiding principles and indeterminacy of the law in a way that lectures could not.[102] Elizabeth Garrett, for example, highlights the utility of Socratic teaching as a method for fostering active learning and critical thinking.[103] Along with Stropus and other defenders of Socratic teaching, she distinguishes the Socratic method itself from unduly harsh or uncivil classroom dynamics and suggests ways to encourage a less intimidating atmosphere in the law school classroom.[104] On the other hand, Vitiello repudiates the purported benefits of "gentle" pedagogical approaches in law schools, insisting that one of the virtues of true Socratic teaching is its acerbic edge, which prepares students for "demanding judges who are impatient with attorneys who are not well prepared or who do not answer their questions directly."[105] In this study, I present analyses that demonstrate a different potential congruence between the canonical Socratic method and legal thinking—not an argument for greater teaching efficacy, certainly, given other results of the study, but an argument for a strong resonance or linguistic fit.[106]

Some social science research has attempted to assess specifically what skills are imparted in law school by particular methods and how that might vary across law schools. Several studies found differences among law schools according to prestige ranking of the school, with elite schools less likely to emphasize rigid rules and more likely to emphasize analytical thinking and theory.[107] Interestingly, however, regardless of where they went to law school, lawyers in one study overwhelmingly agreed that "'ability to think like a lawyer' was the most important knowledge imparted by law schools."[108] This knowledge includes specific skills such as "fact gathering," "capacity to marshal and order facts to apply concept," and "ability to understand and interpret opinions, regulations, and statutes."[109] These results were confirmed in research by Garth, Martin, and Landon on current attitudes among urban and rural attorneys.[110] The one area that practitioners across the board agreed was important to practicing lawyers, and that they agreed was relatively well addressed by law school teaching, was legal reasoning: "There are some relative successes in teaching the specifically legal skills of legal reasoning, legal research, substantive law, and now also professional responsibility."[111] A question that remains is whether any particular teaching methods are important to attaining this reported success.

Studies of teaching method have often produced negative results; there is little, if any, relation found between the method used and the results. Thus, controlled experiments in which first-year classes were divided into separate groups, some taught Socratically and others not, resulted in generally similar performances.[112] When Bryden attempted to test the difference between first- and third-year abilities to perform functional analysis applying concepts to facts, to distinguish holding from dicta, and to construe ambiguous statutes, he found less difference than would be expected, given that third-year students had had a number of years of training using the Socratic method.[113]

From a linguistic standpoint, to bring our discussion back to its starting point, the Socratic method can be understood as an oral genre or speech style, and this study tackles the issue of teaching method from that standpoint. It may be obvious that children are learning new orientations when their parents and teachers teach them spoken and written language, but adults can also undergo similar transformations. Building on Whorf's insights about the orienting power of language structure, we can expand beyond the effects of grammatical categories on speakers' habitual perceptions to examine the effects of the contextual organization of language as a system in use. Viewed in this way, linguistic ideology and metapragmatic structuring can be understood as powerful influences shaping lawyers' orientations. As we will see, learning to read written legal texts is one key component of this orienting practice, conveyed in the process of the particular kind of language socialization that we find in legal education. Learning the language of law, then, involves a reorientation not only in how students speak, but also in how they approach written language. (See Chapter 4 for further discussion of how anthropologists approach the practices associated with written and performed texts.)

Linguistic anthropologists, sociolinguists, and others studying language in social context have developed a considerable literature on the social ramifications of different discourse styles or genres, and on the role of language in classrooms. In particular, linguistic anthropologist Susan Philips characterized what happens in law school classrooms as "acquiring the 'cant' ": as learning a new way of speaking.[114] Empirical researchers have also delineated the distinctive shape of legal language in courtrooms, law offices, and other legal settings. Recent books in the area by John Conley and William O'Barr, Susan Hirsch, Gregory Matoesian, and Susan Philips have shown that legal language plays a crucial, nontransparent role in mediating social conflict, social change, and the distribution of power in societies.[115] Matoesian and Conley and O'Barr clarify the ways social power affects and is translated through the language of law. They do not, however, depict legal language as a simplistic reflex of social structure, but analyze it as a complex resource with its own dynamics.[116] However, along with scholars like Charles Briggs, they do also stress that legal discourse can operate to reinforce social inequality, while essentially hiding its own tracks.[117]

Philips and Hirsch examine the impact of culture and ideology on how legal texts are differentially contextualized and used in court. Philips demonstrates the complicated ways that politics can be filtered through metalinguistic structure to affect judicial behavior, so that judges with different political ideologies operationalize the very same textual language quite differently. Hirsch combines analyses of the discourses of Islamic law, Swahili ethics, spiritual health, and Kenyan law in studying how marital disputes are discussed in a Kenyan court. In keeping with Philips's earlier research on Tongan law, Hirsch resists the idea that there is a single, uniform, state-enforced ideology regimenting Kenyan courtroom discourse. Instead, she stresses that legal negotiations involve multiple layers of language and ideology, which interact with one another in sometimes unpredictable ways.[118]

Sally Merry reached similar findings in her study of working-class plaintiffs in U.S. courts. She shows how the intertwining discourses of law, morality, and therapy interact to frame the claims that litigants bring to court, accepting some as valid and dismissing others as "garbage cases."[119] Paradoxically, litigants have to accept state intervention in their lives as they attempt to gain power through perceived legal entitlements. As Sarat and Felstiner have documented, in this process, the imposition of legal discourse requires that people separate aspects of their experience and selves from others; Merry explains that "the construction of some kinds of identity and effacing of others is a fundamental aspect of the power of the law in the present as well as the past."[120] We see this dynamic in the law school classroom as well. Greenhouse's landmark work among the Baptists of "Hopewell" took this issue of identity and law up to the level of community, tracking how legal discourse can mark the line between insider and outsider, between past and present, between acceptance and exclusion.[121] Thus, anthropologists have provided us with an in-depth picture of the complicated role of legal language in mediating between the wider social world that litigants inhabit and the narrower confines of legal institutions.[122]

## Summary

In the rest of this volume, I build from these literatures and from previous studies of law school classroom methods and discourse, as well as from research on texts and textuality, to develop a detailed analysis of law school classroom language.[123] The strands of scholarship that I have brought together in this chapter together provide a rich foundation for an analysis of law school classroom language. First, work on the social foundations of language urges us to examine the way language itself might embody a worldview or epistemology. This scholarship also indicates the importance of studying the interaction between discourse structures and patterns of language use. Second, studies of language socialization have uncovered the ways that linguistic routines and practices can shift children's and adults' understandings and orientations in the world. Studies of classroom language have revealed that distinctive cultural worldviews are at work in educational processes, and have inquired into the power dynamics at work when worldviews clash. Finally, scholarship on law school teaching has debated the relative value of distinctively legal teaching genres, most notably the Socratic method. In general, studies have suggested that law teaching is most successful in conveying legal reasoning, though commentators have disagreed as to whether that is a desirable result. And empirical researchers studying language in other legal domains have demonstrated the socially powerful effects of legal language in shaping legal results. The remainder of the book draws these strands together in an examination of similarities and differences in the language of eight Contracts classrooms. We begin with an explanation of the methodology involved.

# OXFORD
## UNIVERSITY PRESS

# Invoice

website: www.oup.com/us
Oxford University Press, Inc.
2001 Evans Road  Cary, NC 27513
SAN # 202-5892    FEI 23-7398718

| | |
|---|---|
| **Invoice No.** | 95609587 |
| **Invoice Date:** | 11/18/2011 |

**Bill-To Acct:** 5305886
RICHARD BOYCE
464 MOLIMO DR
SAN FRANCISCO CA  94127-1621

**Ship-To Acct:** 5305886
RICHARD BOYCE
464 MOLIMO DR
SAN FRANCISCO CA  94127-1621

| Payment Terms: **30 Days** | Due Date: **12/18/2011** | Page: 1 of 1 |
|---|---|---|
| Shipped via: **Mail (USPS)** | Delivery: **84459129** | PO Number: **BOYCE 11/17/2011** |

| QTY | ISBN | TITLE | AUTHOR | UNIT PRICE | DISC CODE | DISC % | NET VALUE |
|---|---|---|---|---|---|---|---|
| 1 | 9780195183108 | LANGUAGE OF LAW SCHOOL P | MERTZ | 14.00 | ND/06 | 0.0 | 14.00 |
| 1 | 9780195314076 | SHOW TUNES 4E C | SUSKIN | 21.00 | ND/01 | 0.0 | 21.00 |

| CUSTOMER SERVICE | 800-445-9714 | | SUMMARY | | |
|---|---|---|---|---|---|
| ORDERS | 800-451-7556 | FAX: 919-677-1303 | Delivered: | Subtotal(USD) | $ 35.00 |
| BUSINESS HOURS: | 8:00 AM - 6:00 PM EST, MON. - FRI. | | Qty:    2 | Shipping | $ 7.00 |
| CREDIT DEPARTMENT | 800-732-3120 | FAX: 919-677-8828 | Lines:   2 | Taxes | $ 2.98 |
| BUSINESS HOURS: | 7:30 AM - 4:45 PM EST, MON. - FRI. | | | Total | $ 44.98 |
| | | | | Prepaid Balance | $ 44.98 |
| | | | | Amount Due | $ 0.00 |

# 3

## Study Design, Methodology, and Profile

This opening section outlines the particular synthesis of methodological approaches used in this study. In addition, it describes the site selection process and the trajectory of the research as it developed. Finally, it outlines some of the complexities involved in coding turn-taking in law school classes.

## Design and Methodology

### Combining Methods

What method is adequate to the task of uncovering both similarities and differences across different law schools and classrooms? Being an anthropologist, I begin with a preference for actually observing what people are doing, rather than relying solely on their reports of what they do. Anthropologists pioneered the use of participant observation, a method that relies on researchers to immerse themselves as much as possible in the setting they wish to understand. The kind of study that is produced by this intensive and systematic observation over an extended period of time is called an ethnography, also developed primarily out of the discipline of anthropology, which has used this approach to study and understand cultures.[1] Anthropologists and linguists studying classroom settings have adopted the ethnographic method, providing rich accounts of the dynamics in classrooms—dynamics that form students' experiences.[2]

In addition to observing and interacting in the settings they study, anthropological linguists concerned with the details of language-in-use frequently tape interactions and then transcribe them to provide a basis for more exacting linguistic analysis. This method permits careful scrutiny of the ways that minute aspects of language operate to shape ongoing interactions and to enact social structures. In addition, sociolinguists have for some time used quantitative methods to track overall patterns in speech, counting and measuring salient features of discourse. Finally, scholars from these and other disciplines have combined other methods with the use of interviews to obtain better information about how the participants themselves make sense of what is going on. I drew on all of these methods in developing an understanding of law school classroom dynamics. This study, then, employed a combination of in-class observation, ethnography, transcript analysis, quantitative coding, and interviews. We observed and taped an entire semester of classes to get a fuller picture of classroom dynamics and to avoid capturing only one part of a semester-long process. We worked in eight different schools in an effort to catch differences that might exist across the status hierarchy of law schools. To include this number of classrooms in a study employing these kinds of methods was unusual (and at times daunting!). The level of in-depth work required for this kind of research has rarely permitted inclusion of a variety of schools in any single study; instead, classroom ethnographies have generally presented detailed data on the dynamics in one or two classrooms.

Building on a tradition of careful attention to the details of language from the closely aligned fields of anthropological linguistics and sociolinguistics, classroom ethnographies have provided compelling accounts of the powerful (and often not readily apparent) effects of spoken exchanges in school. Researchers have focused not only on the way language conveys ideas and content (often referred to as "propositional" or "referential" information), but also on how it functions socially and in expressing identity, asking questions such as: "How do patterns of language use affect what counts as 'knowledge,' and what occurs as learning? How do these patterns affect the equality, or inequality, of students' educational opportunities? What forms of communicative competence do these patterns presume and/or foster?"[3] This kind of careful work has helped to reveal how seemingly small linguistic differences among speakers of different class, age, and ethnic identities can contribute to failures in communication—failures that, in a classroom setting, can have a powerful impact on students' ability to learn and to absorb a sense of empowerment that might help them in future endeavors. Systematic comparisons across kinds of schools and educational settings have been fairly small-scale, or have involved bringing together results from different studies, given the labor-intensive methodology involved.[4] This study created a comparison set by including classrooms from eight different law schools that vary by status. Where possible, I also compare these data with results from other existing studies.

The method of transcript analysis employed here also builds on previous linguistic studies in other kinds of social and, in particular, legal settings. Thus, for example, O'Barr and Conley have analyzed the language of small claims courts, demonstrating the ways litigants' and judges' "voices" frequently clash because of differing orientations.[5] Their intriguing conclusion was that the very courts designed to help the layperson have become favored sites for business people, whose mastery of a more legal voice and orientation gave them a distinct advantage. Similarly, Sarat and Felstiner, in their study of the language used in divorce lawyers' offices, tracked the subtle process whereby lawyer and client negotiate and struggle

over the "reality" of the marriage and divorce at issue.[6] I build on these method-
ologies, adding quantified attention to race and gender, so that we can better track
the kind of patterning Conley and O'Barr indicated might be emerging from their
study.[7] In this I draw on the work of Matoesian, Merry, and Frohmann, who use
discourse analysis to trace class- and gender-based differences in orientations toward the law.[8]

   The resulting study, then, is a broader picture than could be obtained by studying one or two classrooms and permits us to begin to map possible patterning of
law school discourse. The classes are not to be viewed as a random sample, of course,
but as a set of in-depth case studies that can be compared with one another and
with other existing studies of law school classrooms.

## Access, Site Selection, and Project Process

The eight schools selected for the study were chosen in an effort to maximize diversity of school status and professor profiles. In many cases, a combination of the
issues involved in gaining access to classrooms and availability of proficient coders also shaped the choices. Access to classrooms was sometimes quite difficult to
obtain; in several instances, professors declined because they understandably felt
self-conscious about being observed, although the deans of the law schools involved
had granted permission. In one case, indeed, we were asked to provide a precise
description of the discourse features we'd be analyzing; this we declined to do because of possible reactivity effects (i.e., that professors who were aware we were
observing certain dimensions of classroom interactions might become self-
conscious and alter their approach to those aspects of the discourse). Another limiting factor was the availability of suitable coders; only coders who had graduate
training in linguistics, anthropology, or sociology were used for the study; in one
case we had to drop a particular location because we couldn't obtain coders who
met these requirements. The combination of selection for diversity, professor access, and coder availability shaped the choice of research sites.

   I personally observed and coded a full semester of classes in one of the schools
of the study; the remaining schools were handled by other observers. Each classroom
was covered primarily by one coder (although coders also arranged for coverage by
a backup person who could tape and code on days when they were ill or otherwise
unavailable). This ensured a high level of within-classroom consistency in coding
for each school; in addition, it raised overall coding accuracy. Perhaps not surprisingly, growing familiarity with the students' identities and professorial style meant
that coders with more experience in a particular classroom could follow rapid-fire
exchanges without missing a beat. Thus, in several cases, when I flew in to perform
intercoder reliability checks (I independently coded classes alongside the coders and
then cross-checked our results), I found that despite having pioneered the coding
method myself, I missed a turn or two that the regular coder for that classroom caught.
(Fortunately, subsequent cross-checks of all coding using tapes and transcripts ensured that we would in any case eventually catch any missed turns.)[9]

   I also conducted interviews with small focus groups of students from the classroom that I coded and interviewed six of the eight professors who participated in

the study. In addition to performing in-class coding and observation, the other coders carried out group interviews with students in several of the schools.[10] To avoid possible variation by subject matter, we studied only Contracts classes. I chose to study first-semester, first-year classes to catch the socialization process at a critical moment; it is during this first semester that students receive their primary initiation into distinctively legal language and thought. The Contracts course in these eight schools was a required class, and students were assigned to sections, so that their own preferences and choices were not an influence on their selection for a particular class. Although there was one exception, we generally included only professors with significant amounts of teaching experience at their law schools, so as to maximize any influence the institution might have on teaching norms and styles.

As noted, the classes were first taped and coded by in-class coders. The in-class coders noted the identity of each speaker in terms of race and gender, whether a turn was called on or volunteered, and any other particularly salient aspects of the interaction that might not be captured on tape. For example, in one case a student responded to a professor's question by putting her head down on her desk; this nonverbal response would be noted on the coding sheet. Coders also tracked any notes the professor put on the board.

The tapes were subsequently transcribed at the American Bar Foundation in Chicago. Using tapes, transcripts, and in-class coding sheets, each turn in each class was then coded for the following information:

1. Speaker identity (students were assigned numbers in order to track repeat players across classes).
2. Speaker gender.
3. Speaker racial identification.
4. Order of appearance number (for each class, students were assigned a number based on the order in which they spoke in that class).
5. Linguistic type (turns were coded in terms of the kind of speech occurring: monologue, various kinds of dialogue).[11]
6. Kind of turn (called on without volunteering, volunteered and called on, spoke without being called on, etc.; spoken, nonverbal, or silent turn).
7. Length of turn (timed to half of a second).
8. Evaluation (whether the turn contained a positive or negative evaluation of the preceding turn).
9. Speaker transition type (for turns that overlapped but did not interrupt previous speech, we coded whether they were facilitative backchannels [as when someone comments "right," or "mmm hmm" in the background while a primary speaker is talking], or other kinds of background comments).

As with the earlier, in-class phase of the project, the transcript coding for each school was overseen by a single coder.[12] Extensive cross-checking of the coding was performed by proofreaders who checked the coding sheets, data enterers who entered the coding sheets into the computer, quantitative analysts who performed the data cleanup and statistical analyses, and the two project managers.[13] We could and did, on multiple occasions, go back to the tapes and transcripts to double-check the coding decisions. The professor and student interviews were transcribed as well. Coders also drew together in-class coders' notes and their own reports of the tapes and transcripts to form short written ethnographic accounts of each class.[14]

## Coding Complexities: The Trouble with Turns

Although this sounds like a great deal of work, nevertheless my description to this point is deceptively straightforward in comparison with the actual process. Here I give just a few examples of the complex nuances involved in coding these classroom exchanges. As with most quantitative analysis, there is frequently a trade-off involved when we sort the messy stuff of human social interaction into the unrealistically neat, but more easily manipulable, categories required for this kind of work.

For some time now, the field of language studies known as "conversation analysis" has relied heavily on the "turn" as a unit of analysis.[15] By breaking down exchanges into turns, conversation analysts have been able to discern crucial aspects of the sociology of turn-taking and the overall structure of discourse. In the law school classroom, this approach should be relatively easier to apply than in ordinary conversation, because the structure of turns in these classrooms is, in general, relatively formalized. With the professor controlling most of the interaction, there is a clearer division of labor than in many conversational situations, and the back-and-forth usually follows a relatively set pattern in which the professor either speaks or designates a student to speak. However, even in this relatively structured speech situation, ambiguities arise.

Let's start with a fairly common example, an exchange between a professor and student (both white males). We enter the conversation at turn 20:[16]

*Transcript 3.1 [1/5/20]*

| 20 | Prof.: | I can't (), okay, all right, that doesn't help me much but // what- but what // is an offer? |
|---|---|---|
| 21 | Class: | // [[Laughter (.01)]] // |
| 22 | Student: | It's a commitment or a promise, which satisfies the intentions of individuals embarking on a () agreement. |
| 23 | Prof.: | All right, so, it's a commitment, and the reason it has to be a commitment is? |
| 24 | Student: | So someone can rely on it. |
| 25 | Prof.: | Okay, in other words, we're trying to enforce reasonable expectations, and if I'm making a commitment or promise, there is a basis for your reasonable expectations. Right? Okay, so an offeror is the person who makes the offer, and the offeree, obviously, is the person who accepts it, right? |
| 26 | Student: | Right. (.01 pause) |
| 27 | Prof.: | All right. Now, do I have to know about an offer before I can accept it? |

Note that at the very beginning of this excerpt we could characterize the turn structure in at least two different ways. As mapped in Transcript 3.1 (following the coding structure we adopted), the class laughter simply overlaps one single turn by the professor. This turn is also coded (under "speaker transition type") as a background comment.[17] In another version, shown below, the sequence is coded as three distinct turns (despite the fact that the professor never actually stops speaking). Class laughter, which occurs in essence in the background, in the midst of the professor's turn, is coded as a form of interruption. The professor's turn up until the episode of class laughter is coded as one turn. The "interrupting" class turn of laughter is counted as an intervening turn. And then, when the professor renews his speech, we have a third turn in this sequence:

*Transcript 3.1.1*

20   Prof.:   I can't (), okay, all right, that doesn't help me much but, //what-
              but what--//

21   Class:              // [[ Laughter (.01)]] //

22   Prof.:                                                               -is an
              offer?

This latter approach would obviously create more, and shorter, turns. (So, former turns 20 and 21 now occupy turns 20–22.) This approach captures the positioning of the turns more accurately in the sense that the class turn is located neither before speech that it follows nor after speech that it precedes. However, it creates a nonexistent interruption. Another approach might be to ignore class laughter or "insignificant" background speech entirely. We took a middle route, neither ignoring the background nor giving it so much prominence that it overshadowed the flow of foregrounded speech. If the professor, on the other hand, were addressing the class as a whole, asking it questions and receiving lengthy laughter in response, the class laughter would then be counted as an individual turn, as in the following example:

*Transcript 3.2 [1/5/08]*

08   Prof.:   *[ . . . end of lengthy monologue on test preparation . . . ]* What we test is
              how you apply it. And as you may be able to tell at this point, that
              takes a lot more effort than learning words, and rules. Any questions?
              Feel better?

09   Class:   [[Laughter (.04)]]

10   Prof.:   You should start outlining some time in the near future. I don't want
              to see your outlines, and I'm not going to ask you for your outline
              *[ . . . continues monologue . . . ]*

Here turn 9 is a response to the professor's question, the second part of a question-answer adjacency pair,[18] and does not overlap with the professor's speech. Hence, it takes a demarcated spot in the turn-taking structure and is recognized as such in the coding. Taking one more example from the same class, we see a bit more of the complexity involved in coding turns:

*Transcript 3.3 [1/5/33]*

33  Prof.:      Okay, uhh, are oral contracts enforceable?

34  Student:  Yes.

35  Prof.:      All right. Do you have an example of that?

36  Student:  [[silence (.04)]]

37  Prof.:      The helicopter case, wasn't that an oral contract?

38  Student:  Yes, it was.

Turn 36 is an entirely silent turn. If we think of turns as composed of speech, then this is an odd coding decision. However, the logic of the conversation makes clear that this space in the speech belonged to the student, and the professor's subsequent turn responds to the silence as clearly as it might have responded to a spoken answer.[19] Again, we could choose to simply omit this kind of turn, but then we would miss an important phenomenon in these classrooms: the no-answer response to professorial questioning. Distinct codes under the coding category "kind of turn" distinguished nonverbal and silent turns from spoken turns, so that we could, for purposes of some analyses, remove all silent turns.

A law student from abroad once told me that she found mastery of turn-taking to be one of the most difficult aspects of language learning when she came to the United States. It was far easier to pick up the vocabulary—and to learn how to string this vocabulary together into intelligible utterances—than it was to figure out when another speaker was really finished talking and an acceptable moment for beginning one's own speech had arrived. This skill turned out to be, as several generations of conversation analysts could have told her, essential to participating in communicative interaction in a way that permitted mutual comprehension and also social connection. Thus, we see how complex and difficult it is to pin down the nuances of the back-and-forth of conversation—and how important it is to undertake that task, despite the challenges involved.

## Project Profile

The entire population of students in the eight classrooms of the study was 705. Of this group, 41.8% were female and 15.9% were students of color. In 6 (75%) of the classrooms, men outnumbered women. In individual classes, percentages of students of color ranged from a high of 46.9 (school 8) to a low of 6.6 (school 3). Table 3.1 provides a basis for comparing these figures with national statistics. The student sample profile is close to national averages in terms of gender distributions and in terms of percentage of African American students; it is slightly lower than the national average in terms of percentage of Latino/a students and slightly higher than the average in terms of Asian American students.

In terms of professors, this sample was purposely high in diversity, as is evidenced by the comparison with national averages in Table 3.2. There are indications that the national statistics for full-time faculty are likely to include more professors of color and white female professors than are first-year teaching faculties. Thus, the

TABLE 3.1

Student Race and Gender Distribution Comparison
of Study Sample with National Averages

|  | Total Study Sample | National Statistics on First-Year Law Students: 1990–91[1] |
|---|---|---|
| Women | 41.8% | 42.6% |
| Men | 58.2% | 57.4% |
| African American | 6.2% | 7.2% |
| Asian American | 6.1% | 4.6% |
| Latino/a American | 2.7% | 4.8% |
| Other* | 0.8% |  |
| Total Minority | 15.9% | 17.2% |

*Other includes Native American, Arab American, Pacific Islander students, and otherwise not specified students of color.

1. American Bar Association, *Review of Legal Education.*

overrepresentation of female and minority professors in my study is still stronger than even the above comparison would indicate.[20] For this reason, I do not present aggregate figures for the data set as a whole, because to the degree that professor race and/or gender affects classroom dynamics, aggregate figures from this data set are likely to be misleading. However, in Chapter 7, I provide profiles for classrooms of various types to give a background for qualitative assessments of the impact of various characteristics of the students, teachers, and overall classroom interactions on the teaching in those classes. The study includes three classes from the elite/prestige categories of law schools, two from regional schools, and three from local law schools.

TABLE 3.2

Faculty Race and Gender Distribution Comparison
of Study Sample with National Averages

|  | Total Study Sample | National Statistics: 1994[1] | |
|---|---|---|---|
|  |  | Full-time | Full- and Part-time |
| Women | 37.5% | 26.0% | 35.3% |
| Men | 62.5% | 74.0% | 64.7% |
| Minority | 25.0% | 12.0% | 13.9% |

Note an alternative statistic: in six of the top-tier schools, women taught fewer than 20% of the first-year courses.[2]

1. American Bar Association, *Review of Legal Education.*
2. American Bar Association, *Unfinished Business.*

## Summary

In sum, this study combines multiple methods in assessing the first-year law school classroom experience. The set of classrooms studied contains more diversity in race and gender of professors than is found in the average first-year law school classroom and spans the range of law school status rankings. We turn now to examine similarities that bridge these diverse classrooms.

# II

·———·

# SIMILARITY: LEGAL EPISTEMOLOGY

*Therefore it appears that the kind of reasoning involved in the legal process is one in which the classification changes as the classification is made. The rules change as the rules are applied. More important, the rules arise out of a process which, while comparing fact situations, creates the rules and then applies them.[1]*

*The task . . . then, is not to discard rights but to see through or past them so that they reflect a larger definition of privacy and property: so that privacy is turned from exclusion based on self-regard into regard for another's fragile, mysterious autonomy; and so that property regains its ancient connotation of being a reflection of the universal self.[2]*

In this section we trace the common thread that binds the quite divergent classrooms of this study together, an underlying approach or worldview that I call U.S. legal epistemology. In Chapter 4 we examine the shared underlying approach to reading (i.e., to written texts and their contexts) that is conveyed in first-year law school training across otherwise diverse classrooms. We begin with a close study of the discourse for which law school is famous: classic Socratic method teaching. We ask: In its most highly structured form, what does this discourse style "do," how does it teach? This analysis reveals some core metalinguistic traits of legal epistemology, traits that are encoded in Socratic pedagogy. The chapter moves on to demonstrate that, throughout the classrooms of this study (all of which vary to some degree from the most rigid form of Socratic teaching), there is still an approach that shares many of the underlying tenets of the classic Socratic method, conveying the same core metalinguistic features through a variety of discursive styles. Thus, in the second half of Chapter 4, we trace these features as they emerge in the universally shared "internal" categories of a legal reading: the labels that natives to the system themselves use in describing the genre, such as "facts," "law," and "policy arguments." Learning to think like a lawyer, I suggest, is in large part a function of learning to read, talk, and write like a lawyer; all this involves a distinctive approach to written texts and textual interpretation.

Having examined this distinctive approach exhaustively in Chapter 4, in Chapter 5 we focus more explicitly on the divergent teaching styles found among the classrooms of this study. Here we examine the variety of ways that a similar message about legal language is conveyed in today's law school classroom, ranging from a class dominated by lecturing to modified Socratic teaching to a style characterized by shorter student-professor exchanges. This gives us an opportunity to examine the nuances of discourse structure across different classes. Although surface features of classroom discourse differ among these classrooms, we find some interesting resonances in other structural features of classroom language. These resonances provide subtle structural support for the underlying message about legal epistemology (and accompanying metalinguistic orientations) that is being conveyed to students.

Finally, in Chapter 6, we consider what kind of person is created through the talk of the law school classroom, and along with this we ask about the larger view of the world, of human selves and motivations, and of social context that are entailed in this creation. Chapter 6 concludes by considering the broader social implications of the underlying legal epistemology outlined in the chapters of Part II. Here I turn to contemporary social theory to draw connections between U.S. legal language and the wider social system in which it is embedded.

# 4

## Learning to Read Like a Lawyer: Text, Context, and Linguistic Ideology

*"Mr. Karlin!" Perini cried sharply.*

*Nearby, I heard a tremendous thud. . . .*

*"Mr. Karlin," Perini said, ambling toward my side of the room, "why don't you tell us about the case of* Hurley v. Eddingfield?*"*

*Karlin already had his notebook open. His voice was quavering.*

*"Plaintiff's intestate," he began. He got no further.*

*"What does that mean?" Perini cried from across the room. He began marching fiercely up the aisle toward Karlin. "In-tes-tate," he said, "in-tes-tate. What is that? Something to do with the stomach? Is this an anatomy class, Mr. Karlin?" Perini's voice had become shrill with a note of open mockery and at the last word people burst out laughing, louder than at anything Perini had said before.*

*He was only five or six feet from Karlin now. Karlin stared up at him and blinked and finally said, "No."*

*"No, I didn't think so," Perini said. "What if the word was 'testate'? What would that be? Would we have moved from the stomach"—Perini waved a hand and there was more loud laughter when he leeringly asked his question—"elsewhere?"*

*"I think," Karlin said weakly, "that if the word was 'testate' it would mean he had a will."*

*"And 'intestate' that he didn't have a will. I see." Perini wagged his head. "And who is this 'he,' Mr. Karlin?"*

*Karlin was silent. He shifted in his seat as Perini stared at him. Hands had shot up across the room. Perini called rapidly on two or three people who gave various names—Hurley, Eddingfield, the plaintiff. Finally someone said that the case didn't say.*

*"The case doesn't say!" Perini cried, marching down the aisle. "The case does not say. Read the case. Read the case! Carefully!"[1]*

43

*If Socrates really used this method, he wasn't given the hem-
lock soon enough.*[2]


In the first excerpt, we see depicted for popular audiences the classic genre of law
school teaching: the infamous Socratic method, by some accounts dreaded by
law students across the United States (and across generations). This passage captures many of the features often mentioned as core aspects of Socratic method teaching: extended questioning of a single student about a case assigned for that particular
day, frequent interruption, few (if any) answers provided, an insistence on close
attention to the language of the cases, a challenging, if not hostile, tone.

Following an initial section in which I provide some theoretical background,
this chapter begins the actual language analysis in the second section, which takes
as its starting point the classic form of Socratic method law school teaching, asking what this method does when performed in the traditional style. As we will see,
there are law teachers now who vary considerably from the traditional style in a
number of ways. But just as we might begin an exploration of a literary genre by
asking about the classic or canonical form it has taken, I start by examining the
Socratic method in its most highly structured form.[3] As it turns out, a key feature
of Socratic method teaching is the new relationship with language that it creates
for the students. An important part of forging this new relationship with language
is the inculcation of new conceptions or ideologies of language. And when I say
"language," I mean not only spoken language but also written language, the written texts of the cases that are the primary focus of most class discussions in the
typical first-year classroom.

After examining the classic Socratic discourse form and the metalinguistic
ideology it conveys, this chapter moves on in the third section to analyze how this
ideology is inculcated in the primary classrooms of this study (which all vary in
one degree or another from the classic form). In particular, I focus on the internal
categories of the case law genre. We will see how, in the process of introducing these
fundamental categories (facts, law, etc.), professors inculcate a distinctive, legal
metalinguistic orientation, an orientation that is broadly shared across all of the
classes in the study. A close examination of classroom discourse structure reveals
not only a shared underlying orientation, but also intriguing resonances in subtle
aspects of linguistic structure despite some very obvious divergences in professors'
discourse styles. However, before moving on to the language analysis itself, the first
section of this chapter provides a background, reviewing developments in analyses of texts and their social contexts with a particular focus on recent work in linguistic anthropology that addresses this topic.


## Text, Context, and Ideology

Because law school teaching in the first year is very much focused on written legal
texts, we are drawn to the question of such texts and their use in social contexts

generally, an issue on which anthropologists and linguists have focused a great deal in recent years.

### Text as Process

Just as research on language structure has led to an emphasis on the crucial role of context and language use in organizing how language in general conveys meaning (see Chapter 2), studies of the ways written texts carry meaning in human societies have similarly demonstrated the importance of contextual analysis to understanding the significance of these texts. However, following initial work that simply emphasized the importance of context to textual interpretation, recent work is "in the midst of a radical reformulation wherein 'text,' 'context,' and the distinction between them are being redefined."[4] As part of this reformulation, researchers like Bauman, Briggs, and Silverstein have questioned a clear-cut division between text and context, casting doubt on the utility of such a reified and static conceptualization. Rather, building from a new framework centered on language pragmatics, scholars analyzing written and other texts now focus on processes, analyzing "contextualization" of texts rather than "context," "entextualization" (the process by which texts are created) rather than "text."[5]

The action discussed under the rubric of entextualization is a first step in the process by which text is recontextualized; it is simply "the process of rendering discourse extractable, of making a stretch of linguistic production into a unit—a *text*—that can be lifted out of its interactional setting. A text, then, from this vantage point, is discourse rendered decontextualizable."[6] It follows that the word "text" in this sense can refer to units derived from spoken as well as written discourse, as with a myth that is passed down through oral tradition. Silverstein distinguishes between the "*text-artifact*, such as a graphic array on the printed page" (i.e., the physical object),[7] and the varieties of more *abstract text* connected with these text-artifacts, for example, the "denotational text" (roughly, what this stretch of discourse "means" in a denotational or semantic sense), which can be differentiated from the "interactional text" (again roughly, what this stretch of discourse "means" as an instance of social interaction: what it "does" socially).[8] In this book, I generally distinguish the text-artifacts of legal cases by referring to them as "written texts," as opposed to discussions of text or textuality, or of the "meaning of texts" in a more abstract sense.

This new approach to the study of textuality allows researchers to examine the dynamic process through which interpreters invoke features of texts in creating and shaping their contexts of use. Here text does not exist entirely apart from context, as something that is then acted upon by contextual factors; rather, features of the text influence and form a part of interpretive context. This new approach problematizes the creation of texts as detachable chunks of discourse, asking about the process by which speakers segment discourse into texts that can then be removed from one context (decontextualized) and put into another (recontextualized). Note, as well, that the move to examine process also highlights human agency to a greater degree, reminding us always that texts are created and recreated through people's actions and interpretations.

One need only think of the process by which legal texts become precedents to understand this approach. An important aspect of the authority of the legal opinions issued by U.S. courts is their appeal to prior cases as precedents. Thus, a judge writing a new legal opinion will commonly draw on previous cases; each citation or quote is essentially a claim that this new decision rests on previously established principles and law.[9] It would be possible to understand the text of a case that is invoked as precedent as a statically conceived entity that exists apart from context—a chunk of case law easily extracted and placed in various settings. This kind of static model might indeed proceed to consider the role of context, but it would begin by assuming the unit of analysis—the precedent—as prefigured, defined apart from its contexts. Even if the meaning of that static text is thought to depend on some aspects of context—typically the "original" context of its writing—the precedent would nonetheless be thought to exist apart from any subsequent invocation. Instead, the new reformulation emerging from linguistic studies would understand the creation and use of precedent as a complex interactive process wherein our very perception of the original text as a precedent depends on a segmentation of some part of the precedential text that removes it from its setting in the prior case and recontextualizes it in a subsequent legal case. It is in a very real sense not a precedent until it is reconstituted as such. In this creative process, the precedential text as it is now conceptualized is in one sense recreated and reconfigured.[10] At the same time, aspects of the precedential text (including features of the prior context it is deemed to carry with it) now shape the new textual context in which the prior text is being invoked. There is a blurring of the line between text and context. Interestingly, legal actors' self-understanding of this process vacillates between a fairly naïve conception (in which the new opinion is really just taking a set precedent from the older case) and one that accepts the idea that invocation of precedent involves an inevitable transformation at some level.[11]

The linguistic anthropological framework, as we have seen, also points to the centrality of ideology, of metalevel understandings of what it is we are doing when we use spoken language (see Chapter 2). This is no less the case when the language in question involves written texts. Here as well, researchers have come to see the ideologies of text and language at work in particular settings as crucial to the interpretive process.[12] The ideas that speakers and readers have about spoken and written language are not neutral, and they shape how that language is understood and used. Through analyses of the use of written and oral texts across societies, scholars have isolated a core ideology that has governed much of Western thinking about textuality, an approach that could be characterized as a "referentialist" or "textualist" ideology. This ideology, which is explored below in greater depth, views written texts as in a sense self-contained, as carrying determinate meaning that inheres in the written words themselves. What is central about texts, in this view, is their referential or semantic content, and that content or meaning exists within the writing, the written text.

Anthropological linguists and sociolinguists have demonstrated, however, that when written texts are mobilized for human use, they necessarily depend on and create context in order to have meaning.[13] This has drawn increased scholarly attention to the way written texts connect with their contexts of use, as, for example, when the written script of a play is performed. In performances, it becomes quite clear that the meaning of written text is conveyed not only through the semantic content of the words, but also through myriad linguistic features connecting the text to contexts[14] (frequently to prior contexts as well as to the current one). These features can be as subtle as a shift in intonation patterns or as an attitude conveyed through facial expressions. We can all think of examples in which the "same" word can carry quite divergent meanings in different recontextualizations; thus, it becomes vital to examine the different social functions that the "same" text might be serving.

To make the point more vivid, let us take as an example several possible readings of a seemingly identical written text—in semantic terms, the same words. Imagine, for example, a high school teacher intoning with reverence to his class in 2006 the phrase "We hold these truths to be self-evident: that all men are created equal." Here the performance of an important written political text in the United States conveys a meaning that is only partially dependent on the abstract meaning or content of the words.[15] Who, for example, is the "we" here? What does the use of the present tense "hold" and "are" mean when repeated in this way in this time? The meaning of the written text in this context depends in part on the role of the speaker (teacher), the situational context (a classroom), the purpose of the speaking (didactic, and in a sense political), and on many verbal cues indicating that the utterance is to be taken seriously—not to mention many other aspects of the context as well. It also depends on a relationship between this context and prior contexts—minimally, the context in which the original version of this political text was written, but also the ongoing contexts that contributed (through history and in the audience's lives) to its current cultural valence. Implicit in the way that the context of the first writing is invoked (or indexed), there may be a profound message about a perceived continuity between the original authors and the current readers, an assumed mingled identity in the word "we."[16] (There are likely also many other assumptions invoked here about the relationships among text and various contexts: for example, about the relationship between elites and all of "the people," and about the use of written text to embody timeless political ideals.) Through his performance of the text, the teacher may be viewed as attempting to impart core values of the polity to which he and his students belong.

Imagine now the identical words being repeated by a professor of history whose great-grandparents were slaves and who has just described to her graduate students aspects of slaves' lives on plantations in the southern United States; picture her repeating these words with angry irony, perhaps, or as an impassioned plea. Do the words mean the same thing as when they were uttered in our first example? Now who is the "we," and what does the phrase "all men" mean? What are the messages about the authority of the original authors, about inclusion or mingled identity, about atemporal ideals embodied in political texts, about the just or noble character of the polity, about democracy?

In one sense, we could say that the words say the same thing in both of these contexts, that a reduced core meaning is arguably conveyed in both cases. The words may in each case be understood to express a core aspiration for the American polity, and that aspiration could be roughly summarized as a democratic one: that all

members of the polity should be regarded as equal, accorded the same level of respect, treated with the dignity owed all others. This could be viewed as a "residual"
semantic or referential meaning, a portable meaning that is carried from context
to context with this phrase. (We can locate this kind of residual meaning even in
the most context-dependent words, words such as "this" and "that," for example.
The word "this" standing alone conveys little to us without more knowledge of the
context in which it was uttered, and yet we know that it probably referred to an
object that was closer to the speaker than any object introduced by the word "that."
This sense of reference to something closer rather than farther is a residual semantic, or context-independent meaning that is part of our interpretation of the word
"this" wherever it is used, despite its heavily indexical or pragmatic character.
However, to understand the meaning of any particular use of the word "this," we
need to know a great deal more about the context in which it is being used.)

In similar fashion, we can point to a core semantic meaning carried by the
phrase "all men are created equal." However, this residual acontextual meaning
does little to elucidate the full-blown import of the words as spoken in the two
contexts described above, and focusing on this context-independent meaning
would leave us with little understanding of what each utterance actually "meant"
to its speaker or audience. A textualist or referentialist ideology would focus our attention on such residual, decontextualized aspects of meaning, to the exclusion of
the more contextually dependent aspects of meaning. However, anthropological linguists and sociolinguists have convincingly demonstrated that such an approach
cannot accurately map how language conveys meaning; language is always relying
on both semantic (decontextual) and pragmatic (contextual) features to accomplish
this. Thus, it is necessary to combine attention to the meanings that are carried across
contexts through use of written texts with attention to the fact that textual meaning
is always dependent on context. This requires that we take account of the continual
process of extraction and recontextualization of the meaning of those written texts,
a process wherein what appears to be the same text changes and takes on somewhat
different meaning by virtue of new connections with novel contexts (i.e., through
heavily pragmatic or contextual aspects of meaning).

This view of textuality and written texts leads us to ask not only about the stability of written language across contexts, but also about how chunks of text become
extractable from their foundation in a particular written version, decontextualized
and recontextualized, in a highly social and somewhat destabilizing process. Through
what kind of process can judges extract phrases and portions of previous case texts?
Can they pick any old words out; can they transpose or alter the words; do all sets
of words from previous cases carry similar weight? And what is the overall ideology
of texts, writing, and language that gives any weight at all to some extracted chunk of
verbiage derived from a text written at a previous time under different circumstances
by certain judges? At the same time as they have argued for studying the detachabil-
ity of texts from previous contexts, however, language scholars like Richard Bauman
and Charles Briggs have also stressed that we should pay attention to the material
that "the recontextualized text bring(s) with it from its earlier context(s)."[17] Thus, in
addition to maintaining some decontextualized *general* meanings that are more
readily detached from specific historical contexts, ongoing recontextualizations of

written texts may also continue to rely on aspects of their previous contexts of origin and use for the more *specific*, context-dependent meanings they convey in subsequent contexts. In reusing the phrase "all men are created equal," for example, some subsequent authors might intend to invoke features of the social context in which these words were originally written. Rather than expressing a general aspiration for the polity, they might say, perhaps this phrase should be taken as stating quite specifically that only men (and not women) are created equal. How and whether aspects of previous or current contexts should form part of the meaning of texts when they are recontextualized through subsequent use is obviously a highly ideological matter, as anyone following the debates over so-called original intent and the U.S. Constitution can attest. Thus, our analysis of the processes by which texts are reused and reconfigured in new contexts inevitably brings us to a fuller consideration of ideologies of language and text.

## Ideologies of Text

Chapter 2 introduced the idea that ongoing spoken linguistic interactions are shaped by ideologies of language (i.e., the ideas that speakers hold about how language works). My sense that what is happening is a conversation (or an argument, or a lecture) affects how I behave in a linguistic interaction, and this sense, in turn, is based on ideas about what a conversation is, what it is we are doing when we interact through language, and so forth. Subtle norms of communication, often operating somewhat reflexively rather than consciously for speakers, are everywhere at work when we convey meaning through spoken language, and these norms are deeply imbricated in the sociocultural systems in which speakers live.

Linguistic ideology plays a formative role with written language as well, as we noted in pointing to the centrality of a referentialist or textualist ideology in Western society. One domain in which the importance of this kind of ideology becomes particularly obvious is that of schooling, a setting in which children receive their formative training in reading written texts. Studies of the initial years of socialization in U.S. educational institutions have identified a shared textualist ideology that underlies the dominant orientation imparted to schoolchildren.[18] In U.S. classrooms, teachers approach the meaning of written texts as fixed and transparent, as universally available. Furthermore, early schooling in many U.S. schools employs a conception of literacy as technique, under which interpretation of written texts is a skill to be publicly displayed and evaluated in a context-independent, quantifiable (i.e., measurable by grades) fashion.[19] Not only the written texts that are read, but even the performances of those texts in class come with their own entextualization preordained, for the institutional context of the schoolroom puts a premium on the extractability of text and performance from context. The goal of the recontextualization of written texts in reading class performances is precisely the decontextualization of the performance in an individual-focused assessment of ability or skill. The key official function of the recontextualizing performance is to demonstrate mastery of this underlying skill. This institutional framing of students' recontextualizing performances is an exercise of social power with profound consequences.[20]

Through his study of elementary school classrooms, anthropologist James Collins discerns two different approaches to reading written texts: a relatively more fragmented approach focused on the pragmatics of pronunciation, and a more "orderly" approach stressing the extraction of referential content through a focus on semantic interpretation. So-called low-ability reading classes are typically more characterized by the former, where the more empowering pedagogy in high-ranked reading classes pushes children to move beyond merely pronouncing the text correctly, to discussing and extracting its content. Notice that in these more advanced classes, written texts are about their content, about the stories they tell; literacy consists in "decoding autonomous (fixed, transparent, universally available) text" that means the same thing to everyone.[21] Collins observes that this orientation obscures the social power at work in these readings of text, missing the ways that the reading lessons themselves are part of systems of inequality and social reproduction (as James Gee and others have also documented).

From this foundation in studies of written texts and textuality, we move on to examine the ideologies of text and the schooling practices that characterize legal education in particular. We begin with a close look at the canonical style long associated with law school teaching: the so-called Socratic method.

## The Canonical Form: Classic Socratic Method Teaching and Legal Pedagogy

*Transcript 4.1 [7/1/1]*

Prof.:   Okay. I thought I'd start telling you how I used to start the course of contracts. I used to wait about five minutes after an hour just to start. And then, () the students were wondering if they were in the right place, everyone's afraid to ask (). So, I'd come storm to the front of the room, slam books down on the desk, and shout out, "The course is Contracts and the name's Kingsfield!"

Class:   [[laughter]]

Prof.:   Well, I didn't do that this year. I don't feeling like slamming anything this year, uh, besides that, a couple of years ago I almost lost three people in the second row to cardiac arrest.

Class:   [[laughter]]

From the ideology of law school pedagogy there emerges a stereotypic image of the Socratic method as a highly stylized teaching genre, depicted vividly in the excerpt from the popular book *One L* that was quoted at the beginning of this chapter.[22] Although, as Transcript 4.1 attests, this cultural stereotype still casts a shadow in today's law school classrooms, the degree to which the popular image mirrors actual practice is to date largely unstudied.[23] Some aspects of the broader structure of many of the classes in this study are aptly captured by the stereotype of law school teaching that is described in legal academics' as well as popular accounts. Professors frequently begin class by calling on a student, who may then be expected to participate in dialogue with the professor for as long as an entire class period. Typically, the professor questions the student about aspects of legal cases assigned for class that day, with often painstaking attention to linguistic details. Although the answers that a student gives may lead the conversation in unexpected directions, this can happen only if the professor chooses to incorporate students' answers in his or her subsequent discussion. Thus, even potentially creative aspects of the exchange are carefully channeled and controlled.

In their work on graduate school education in France, Bourdieu and Passeron noted a number of ways in which the formal European lecture method enforced professorial authority:

> The lecturer finds in the particularities of the space which the traditional institution arranges for him (the platform, the professorial chair at the focal point on which all gazes converge) material and symbolic conditions which enable him to keep the students at a respectful distance. . . . Elevated and enclosed in the space which crowns him orator, . . . the professor is condemned to a theatrical monologue and virtuoso exhibition by a necessity of position far more coercive than the most imperious regulations.[24]

The discipline of the law school classroom, with regulations that require more than respectful distance and silence, can in a sense be seen as still more authoritarian. Duncan Kennedy describes this discipline as a loss of autonomy, for although students have freedom to drift away from the professor's message during a lecture, if they so choose, law students must always be ready to be called on and to perform in front of the large audience that is their law school cohort.[25] This emphasis on performance—on discipline to perform rather than just listen—contributes to professorial authority in a new way. For if, as Bourdieu and Passeron would have it, the college professor in lecturing imparts "the Word" much as a religious figure would, the law school professor requires students to divine and repeat back the Word as revealed to students through submission to the flow of professorial questioning.

This method requires students to remain in conversation with the professor, while never modifying the demand that they conform to certain stylistic requirements. This is one important way that the imposition of discourse style in a law classroom setting imparts a quite different message about power than is discernable in the working-class and so-called low-ability classrooms studied by scholars like Collins and Gee. For in law school, students are often forced to assume the new style; they are not generally permitted to give up, as the African American child of the Gee study was.[26] In one sense, the power imposed in the law school classroom is more authoritarian; yet, it is empowering also, in the sense that students are often not allowed to disengage without at least making a good attempt to respond. In this sense, they are pushed to remain in and master the dialogue. The law school professor is thus at once giving students no choice and telling them that they are capable of performing this genre.

## Teaching Precedent: A Traditional Socratic Classroom

The class on which we now focus conformed fairly closely to the stereotypic highly regimented traditional law school classroom.[27] The students in this class had received their initial reading assignment before their first class. It was posted on a student bulletin board in the student area of the law school, and there was an expectation that they would arrive in class the first day with their book bought and first assignment read. Subsequent assignments were posted on the board throughout the semester. Much of the knowledge about these expectations had been imparted or reinforced through informal student networks.

Like many first-year students in other law schools, students in this classroom were assigned to a cohort that would remain together through almost all of their first-year classes. After the initial class, the professor circulated a seating chart, and the students filled their names in. The professor then had a larger chart constructed, with a picture of each student's face and corresponding name in the appropriate seating slot. He used this when calling on students in class each day. The physical setting was a large classroom, seating around one hundred students. The seats rose in height from front to back along three sides of the center of the classroom. In the center was a small platform on which the podium rested, with a desk beside it. Behind the podium were blackboards.

Class began when the professor called it to order and delivered a brief exposition of a problem or question derived from the readings. The professor then posed a question, looked down at his seating chart, and called out a name. Address was formal, using surnames prefaced by "Mr." or "Ms." This professor typically asked each selected student a series of questions and occasionally continued speaking with the same student for the entire class hour. More often, however, he called on two or more students for extended exchanges through the course of one class hour. When dissatisfied with an answer, he often asked for volunteers and selected students who raised their hands, returning then to the designated student after other students had answered that particular question.

At no time during this pilot study did a student in this class respond to being called on by saying that he or she had not done the reading for the class. The professor had a daily sign-up sheet for students who were unable to do the reading; each student was permitted a limited number of "unprepared days" each semester. On other days, the students were expected to be prepared. The marked, almost ritual structuring of student language characteristic of the law school classroom can be analogized to other kinds of rituals designed to resocialize members of society to new statuses. As I've noted, the linguistic discipline of the first-year law school classroom in some respects transcends variation in professors' pedagogic styles and political philosophies; it can be viewed as part of an initial process through which previously learned linguistic conventions and conversational expectations are broken down.[28]

### The Process of Teaching Legal Reading

The first excerpt that follows was taken from the written text of an appellate opinion, traditionally found in official books known as reporters that publish the decisions of appellate courts (and now increasingly also obtained by attorneys from one of the online services that publish the opinions electronically). Portions of these opinions are excerpted in the casebooks used in law school classes, a process linguistic anthropologists would talk about as recontextualization because the portions of written text originally issued as parts of complete opinions by courts are taken from their original contexts and put into a new context.[29] The new context is formed by other case excerpts, notes on cases, occasional excerpts from articles or books, and the casebook author's commentary, typically bound together in a heavy book devoted to one area of law (contracts, for example, or criminal law). So, now let us turn to one such excerpted piece of written text:

SULLIVAN v. O'CONNOR

Supreme Judicial Court of Massachusetts, 1973.
363 Mass. 579, 296 N.E.2d 183.

KAPLAN, J. The plaintiff patient secured a jury verdict of $13,500 against the defendant surgeon for breach of contract in respect to an operation upon the plaintiff's nose. The substituted consolidated bill of exceptions presents questions about the correctness of the judge's instructions on the issue of damages.

The declaration was in two counts. In the first count, the plaintiff alleged that she, as patient, entered into a contract with the defendant, a surgeon, wherein the defendant promised to perform plastic surgery on her nose and thereby to enhance her beauty and improve her appearance; that he performed the surgery but failed to achieve the promised result; rather the result of the surgery was to disfigure and deform her nose, to cause her pain in body and mind, and to subject her to other damage and expense. The second count, based on the same transaction, was in the conventional form for malpractice, charging that the defendant had been guilty of negligence in performing the surgery. . . . *[paragraph omitted]*

As background to the instructions and the parties' exceptions, we mention certain facts as the jury could find them. The plaintiff was a professional entertainer, and this was known to the defendant. The agreement was as alleged in the declaration. More particularly, judging from exhibits, the plaintiff's nose had been straight, but long and prominent; the defendant undertook by two operations to reduce its prominence and somewhat to shorten it, thus making it more pleasing in relation to plaintiff's other features. Actually the plaintiff was obliged to undergo three operations, and her appearance was worsened.

If you have never read a legal opinion before, imagine how you would recount what you have just read to someone. Quite frequently, those without legal training focus on the story of the surgeon and the professional entertainer. By contrast, law professors insistently focus students' attention in a somewhat different direction. In the following transcript segment, a professor questions a student about the case, utilizing standard Socratic method teaching:

*Transcript 4.2 [PS/1/1/1]*

Prof.:    What errors were alleged in the appeal of *Sullivan v. O'Connor* ( ) Ms. [A.]? ( ) What errors were alleged in the appeal of *Sullivan v. O'Connor*?

Ms. A.:   Um the defense claimed that um the judge failed in allowing the jury to take into account for damages anything but a claim for out-of-pocket expenses.

Prof.:    Well that's a rather general statement. How did this get to the appellate court?

Ms. A.:   Well the um the the patient was a woman who wanted // a //

Prof.:                                                      // How // did this case get to the appellate court?

Ms. A.:   The defendant disagreed with the way the damages were awarded in the trial court.

Prof.:    How did this case get to the appellate court? The Supreme Court once ah- I think this is true- they asked some guy who'd never argued a case before the Supreme Court before, they said to him- he was a Southerner- and they said to him ah "Counsel, how did you get here?" [[laughter]] "Well," he said, "I came on the Chesapeake and Ohio River." ((*imitated Southern accent*)) [[louder laughter]] How did this case get to the supreme judicial court?

Ms. A.:   It was appealed.

Prof.:    It was appealed, you say. Did you find that word anywhere except in (the) problem? [ + positive uptake]

Note that here we have yet another recontextualization of one portion of the original written text from *Sullivan v. O'Connor*.[30] This time the text excerpt is recontextualized in a classroom discussion, its new discursive context. If we were to tell the story of this case, we might begin by talking about a woman, a professional entertainer, whose nose was deformed during the course of plastic surgery by a physician who had promised to "enhance her beauty and improve her appearance." In her first response to the professor's question, "How did this get to the appellate court?," Ms. A. attempts to recount this story: "Well the um the the patient was a woman who wanted a- ." The professor, however, is after a different reading of the case excerpt and immediately interrupts to repeat his question, "How did this case get to the appellate court?"[31]

In repeating the question, the professor in essence notifies the student that her previous answer was on the wrong track. Linguists studying classroom speech have analyzed this kind of response as an example of "zero-uptake" (or "nonuptake"). "Uptake" in a question-and-answer sequence is measured by whether subsequent questions incorporate any referential material from an immediately preceding answer. Thus, if a professor, in framing a question, includes some reference to the student's previous answer, we would say that there is uptake. The subsequent question takes up some portion of the previous answer, thereby indicating that the questioner heard and took note of that answer. Repeating the original question is perhaps the purest form of nonuptake possible, as it contains no referential acknowledgment of any intervening answer.[32]

From studies comparing high- and low-status elementary classrooms and groups, we know that nonelite classrooms are more likely to involve authoritarian control on the part of teachers, characterized by, for example, more frequent interruption of children's narratives, more frequent correction of perceived mispronunciations, more emphasis on the text as something to be pronounced rather than read for meaning, and, finally, less uptake.[33] Uptake could be viewed as one measure of control, for even in very structured exchanges, a student whose answer is acknowledged in subsequent questions is having some impact on the direction of the conversation. However, a comparison of these studies with the law school example demonstrates that the significance of uptake is highly contextual, so that a straightforward reading of linguistic structure as an index of relative social power is highly problematic. Understanding the social significance of discourse structure, predictably, requires contextual analysis.

If we examine carefully several excerpts from law school classroom exchanges, we see that, as in the lower-status elementary school reading group, the law school discourse is predominantly characterized by nonuptake:

*Transcript 4.3 [PS/1]*

Prof.:　　　[ . . . ] on March 1. (.) B promises to pay Seller ten thousand dollars for Whiteacre March 1. March 1 comes and goes (.) B now sues Seller for breach (.) of Seller's promise to deliver the title to Whiteacre on March 1. Seller defends saying, "It is true that I did not deliver title on March 1 but B did not tender ten thousand dollars on March 1." That is a good defense. Would you explain how the law goes about saying that it is a good defense (.) Ms. A.?

Ms. A.:　　Well the- it's a concurrent condition that in order for the Seller to tender title Buyer must pay ten thousand dollars and that the Buyer pay ten thousand // dollars //

Prof.:　　　　　　// Well // all right now you y- I just wanted to talk about this one (thought) all right for the moment (.) it's correct, what you said, but let's just talk about this- this is: B is entitled- now I asked you in this assignment to describe e-exactly how- what the condition is that will make this defense good.

　　　　　　*[- negative uptake]*

Ms. A.:　　That Seller could say- he could have transferred title to a Buyer (for) ten thousand dollars.

Prof.:　　　Well now there are two parts (). It doesn't make any sense to talk about one half of it without the other half; what are the two parts?
　　　　　　*[- negative uptake]*

Ms. A.:　　Seller would have to tender title if Buyer tendered the ten // thousan- //

Prof.:　　　// Well // n-name the two parts, would you, because people have a lot of trouble with this.
　　　　　　*[- negative uptake]*

Ms. A.:　　(.03 silence)

Prof.:　　　When you describe a condition what two things do you have to talk about?
　　　　　　*[- negative uptake]*

Ms. A.:　　<u>Oh</u> (that one) the duty it's conditioned on and the event constituting the condition.

Prof.:　　　Okay. The duty and an event. And the event is the condition. You can describe that event without talking about the duty but there's no sense in doing it because uh- it's going to sound () (it's not going to mean anything). All right. Now the duty in this case that we're talking about is (.)

in this case (.)

*[+ positive uptake]*

Ms. A.:    Um- the Buyer's duty to tender the ten // thousand- //

Prof.:                                                      // no //

*[- negative uptake]*

Although there was one instance of uptake in this excerpt, the exchange is over-whelmingly characterized by nonuptake, and thus resembles more closely discourse in the lower- rather than higher-status classrooms of the elementary school stud-ies. And this particular exchange is taken from a Socratic dialogue with a virtuoso student who was able to sustain the dialogue with only minimal interruption for the entire class hour. Although there was some variation among the professors in this study, professors frequently interrupted students, and they generally main-tained tight control of the discourse. Indeed, professors who differed widely in philosophy and style of teaching still controlled classroom discourse to the point that students were almost never permitted a verbal exchange among themselves that was not mediated by the professor. (For example, rather than permitting one student to respond to another directly, professors would interject comments such as "Mr. X., what is your response to Ms. Y.?")[34] Use of uptake structure to focus students' attention on particular aspects of the text varied by law school classroom in this study but was found in most of the classes.

If we stopped our analysis at this point, we might conclude that the uptake structure of classic Socratic law school classroom exchanges resembled that of low-ranked reading classes rather than high-ranked ones. However, a more detailed look at the pragmatic structure reveals some key differences. Although these law school exchanges are largely characterized by nonuptake, there is uptake, and it does not come at random points. In Transcript 4.3 above, uptake occurs when the student produces a pair of technical terms. Nonuptake occurs when the student attempts to produce a narrative that tells us a story about two people (albeit Buyer and Seller). We saw a similar pattern in the exchange centered on *Sullivan v. O'Connor*, in which the professor interrupted an attempt to give us the story of the woman and the surgeon. If we examine that first exchange (Transcript 4.2) from the point of view of uptake structure, we see a very similar pattern, with negative uptake through-out until the student produces a procedural term ("appealed"), at which point the professor responds with positive uptake. A pattern with only one uptake for every four exchanges between professor and student appears in both examples, in each case highlighting and picking up on students' appropriate invocation of legal cat-egories. In this subtle way, stories of human conflict, complete with their social contexts and moral overtones, are inexorably supplanted by new readings focused on layers of textual and legal authority.

## Ideologies of Text in Socratic Legal Pedagogy

What model of text is being conveyed by this tightly controlled turn-taking? In both of the examples above, uptake, pointing to (or indexing) a successful response, occurs when students produce technical terms. And these are not just any technical terms. In each of the examples, the professor is using the structure of Socratic questioning to highlight pragmatic aspects of legal texts, in particular, the ways that the texts become authoritative through the invocation of legal contexts. The text itself is highlighted here, rather than the story (reversing the common understanding of texts as mere vehicles for telling the story). Read in this light, these legal cases could be viewed as telling quite distinctly legal kinds of stories: tales of prior legal decisions at various levels (which are thus metalevel stories that reflect on the storytelling itself).

In Transcript 4.2, the professor sought a procedural term, "appealed," which drew attention to the history of the case as it was presented in the opinion the students read. Before a case reaches the state (or U.S.) supreme court level, it typically has moved through several levels, advancing from the trial court through an intermediate appellate court to the ultimate decision by a supreme court, and each move involves the invocation of various legal procedures.[35] In more complex cases, particularly criminal ones, the case can move up and down these levels a number of times, as, for example, when an appellate court rules that a lower court's decision was in error and sends the case back for reconsideration or retrial, or when a prisoner, having exhausted appeal procedures in the state system, attempts to receive redress in the federal system.

The procedural history of a case frames and delimits the current text's authority. The words in the opinion have force only because the case was formulated and reformulated in a particular way through successive procedural stages, and they have only the force that is prescribed by the procedural stance of the opinion. Thus, the technical term that the professor is training the student to notice in our example links the text to previous linguistic contexts, to courts and opinions that were part of its procedural development. If the case was not appealed properly from the court below, then the appellate court may lack the authority or jurisdiction to rule on it at all. Or some specific issues may not be properly before the appellate court if there was some defect in the procedure by which they were appealed.

The uptake structure of classroom discourse is pragmatic in the sense that it conveys meaning by virtue of its contextual grounding, referring both to the written text assignment and to the unfolding linguistic context provided by the teacher-student exchange. This contrasts, for example, with a lecture, which can be characterized as conveying meaning through a far greater reliance on semantic content, independent of any particular context or set of listeners. And if the uptake sequence is a pragmatic structuring of classroom discourse, the technical term it highlights in Transcript 4.2 is a key to the pragmatic structure of the written text—a structure by which the legal opinion takes on authority in the current context, a contextual connection that provides social power. In other words, depending on the manner in which the case was appealed, this court is empowered to decide on some things but not on others, and the words of the court have effect only within that framework. Here the pragmatic structure of law classroom discourse is used to train students to read written legal texts through the lens of their legally specified pragmatic structures.

Transcript 4.3 provided a slightly more complex case. There, the technical words to which the professor directed students' attention were not procedural but doctrinal concepts, derived from past cases, which structured the authority of the text in a different way. Legal doctrines emerge from courts' decisions on similar issues over time, in a process by which legal precedents develop. For example, in his classic essay on legal reasoning, Edward Levi traced the development of a legal doctrine that held manufacturers liable for injuries caused by "inherently danger- ous" objects.[36] The logic guiding the evolution of this doctrinal category, as Levi demonstrates, was anything but clear at times; however, it certainly drew on the language and reasoning of previous cases involving injuries caused by manufac- tured items. Judgments as to which injuries, items, and situations could properly be deemed analogous to one another are crucial to this process of doctrinal rea- soning and development. Doctrinal categories provide conceptual presuppositions that allow subsequent texts to speak authoritatively, as, for example, "On what authority can the judge say this is a good defense?" The judge's authority in this case rests on correct deployment of the doctrinal categories, which themselves derive their authority from their genealogy through previous cases perceived to be in some way similar (and decided by courts properly situated in the hierarchy).

Once again, then, the technical vocabulary to which the professor directs stu- dents' attention involves reference to previous legal language: to the language of earlier cases, distilled into doctrinal categories and concepts. Again, there is a prag- matic reflexivity: legal language referring to previous linguistic contexts to achieve authority. And again, this aspect of the text is conveyed to students using a similar reflexivity: the language of the classroom referring to the language of the case, which provides the context that gives it meaning.

Toulmin has used the term "warrant" to talk about the background informa- tion that allows us to make assertions.[37] In this case, the professor is focusing stu- dents' attention on the pragmatic warrants that give legal texts their authority, and is doing so using the pragmatic structure, rather than the semantic content, of class- room speech.[38] This isometry may account for the pervasive sense that the Socratic method is better suited to law school teaching than lecturing, despite studies that show no appreciable difference in results.

The approach to text inculcated in the law school classroom, then, differs considerably from that conveyed in lower-status reading classes. There, nonuptake blocks students from narrative control so that the text remains language to be re- peated or pronounced. In the law school classroom, uptake is part of a structure designed to break down a straight semantic reading of texts, at the same time as it undermines the norms of normal conversation.[39] Instead of approaching written texts as stories and classroom exchange as a chance to tell these stories, students are trained to focus on those texts in terms of layered legal authority. The levels of authority in legal texts are indexed through the successful deployment of techni- cal terms, which the students must identify through their readings—at the same time as the students must themselves successfully deploy technical terms in a dis- ciplined classroom discourse. The content of the texts—stories of human conflict and pain, of moral dilemmas and social injustices—is subtly subjugated to the struc- tures and strictures of law.

Thus, the ideology that is quietly conveyed here privileges levels of legal au- thority in the deciphering of texts, rather than the emotional or moral force of the story involved or the various potentially relevant social contexts. In searching the text for these layers of legal authority, students learn a style of reading that filters and frames the story of the case in a new way. Now the core messages for which they search the written text focus on relationships with previous legal texts, with authoritative authors—usually courts or legislatures—and with the legal actors who guided this particular case through earlier stages of the legal process (the trial judge, the jury, the attorneys on either side who shaped the arguments now at issue). A legal reading is first and foremost about textual and legal authority—about pragmatic warrants—and often that authority is to be deciphered from unpacking metalinguistic connections among legal texts and authors. When these connections have been established to frame the discussion, then the teaching of legal reasoning can proceed within this frame. The core questions and issues become ones dictated by the legal warrants, and students are taught to reason and speak using the categories and analogies that are salient within this legally delimited view of the conflict at issue in a particular case.

Another obvious and ubiquitous feature of Socratic method teaching is its insistence on a dialogic or argumentative form from which, eventually, legal truth emerges. This has some very obvious parallels with courtroom discourse and with the U.S. legal system's overall dependence on procedure as a guarantor of justice.[40] (As long as both parties get their day in court, represented by attorneys who will engage in vigorous linguistic combat on their behalf, justice is done.) The classic Socratic dialogue in law teaching, then, both indexes and mirrors a core legal model not only of how knowledge or truth is obtained but also of how justice is achieved. This powerful combination of epistemology and morality carries with it implications for conceptions of self, defining the contours of relevance that also shape legal conceptions of identity and personhood.[41] In one sense, we could question whether the classic law school teaching method really is a dialogue embodying two distinct voices, because its goal is to herd unruly interlocutors into a single, uniformly legal discursive approach. On the other hand, a defining feature of that approach is a continual shifting between adversarial positions, which are quite clearly defined as distinct and opposed voices. As we will see, this apparent contradiction is resolved when we pay close attention to footing in law school discourse. A close examination reveals that law teaching very commonly combines a division between sharply demarcated and distinct voices with ubiquitous elision of footing.[42]

Through our examination of Socratic pedagogy, we have begun to discern some distinctive aspects of legal readings. In particular, we have seen that legal reading relies on a contextual framework with layers of legal and textual authority. To provide a more comprehensive and in-depth understanding of this legal-textual framework, we now turn to a broader overview of the core features defining a distinctively legal reading of U.S. law texts.

## Fundamental Aspects of Legal Readings and the Case Law Genre

As we have seen, law school classroom discussions provide a kind of prism through which we can discern core features of legal readings and texts. Although there are, of course, many interesting variations and differences in the legal tradition regarding how to approach particular kinds of legal texts, there are also points of commonality, discernable across the classrooms of this study. I discuss different kinds of legal texts as "genres," meaning that there are distinctive aspects of the texts that identify them as cases, statutes, regulations, and so on, just as we might distinguish between a short story and a novel. There are also somewhat different norms and frameworks guiding legal readings of these distinct genres.

One feature of first-year legal education that is immediately apparent is a focus on case law, on the written opinions that courts produce to explain the results reached in individual legal cases. Much of the first year in U.S. law schools concentrates on reading cases, as did most of the discussion in the classes of this study. The textbooks assigned for typical law school classes are called casebooks and consist for the most part of a series of edited appellate court opinions, interspersed with excerpts from relevant statutes, academic articles, and other pertinent materials. Because learning to decipher the cases in many instances calls for an understanding of relevant constitutional provisions, statutes, or regulations, an adequate understanding of the case law genre often requires proficiency in other genres as well. If we analyze the opinions reproduced in law school casebooks as instances of a genre, we can begin to trace the outlines of an ideology of text and language that is quite different from the textualism and schooled literacy found in other arenas of U.S. culture.[43]

### The Process of Reading Cases

Each written case law text reports a decision by the authoring court, a determination as to the outcome of a conflict on which that court has been asked to rule. Thus, these legal texts have a peculiar character. In one sense, they report on a decision made by the judge or judges, but at the same time the texts themselves actually *are* the decisions: the words of the texts constitute or "perform" the decisions. Philosophers and linguists have talked about this kind of language as "performative": it performs or enacts the action that it names.[44] For example, when an official vested with the appropriate authority utters the words "I now pronounce you man and wife," she not only describes what she is doing (marrying two people) but also actually performs that act. Similarly, the written text that describes a court's disposition of a legal case also performs the act of deciding that case. Thus, the language in legal texts can be said to carry social power.

Legal readings of these case law texts are carefully structured around deciphering this powerful language, which decides often hotly contested social conflicts.[45] We have already encountered two key aspects of the case law genre: (a) cases invoke legal *precedent* to justify their decisions; that is, they rely on language from previously decided cases; and (b) a case law text typically points to the *procedural history* of the legal case in question. We will now explore how these two features of case law texts are intertwined with other distinctive facets that, together, define the genre. As we will see, the structure for legal reading created by this case law genre attempts to limit and shape the socially powerful implications of textual language. One constant feature of this limiting structure is a continual invocation or indexing of layers of legal authority, focused in large part on the question of who gets to decide what.

## READING PRECEDENT

For example, in drawing on precedent, courts follow an interpretive doctrine known as "stare decisis":

> To abide by, or adhere to, decided cases. Policy of courts to stand by precedent and not to disturb settled point. . . . Under doctrine a deliberate or solemn decision of court made after argument on question of law fairly arising in the case, and necessary to its determination, is an authority, or binding precedent in the same court, or in other courts of equal or lower rank in subsequent cases where the very point is again in controversy.[46]

The precedential authority of a case text depends on the hierarchical position of the court from which it issues as well as on the topic in question, so that on matters of federal law, U.S. Supreme Court opinions are deemed "binding" on lower federal courts and all state courts. Conversely, on matters of state law, opinions issued by the supreme courts of the individual states are viewed as authoritative. Appellate courts at times explicitly overrule their own precedents, or they may "limit" prior decisions by imposing narrow interpretations on precedential texts. Of course, a case operates as precedent only when it is drawn on in subsequent opinions.

To invoke precedent, authors of legal cases have to build analogies between the case before them and earlier cases. There are several steps required to create (or decipher) these analogies: one needs to identify which legal issue or issues are at stake, to understand and use the technical legal concepts involved in analyzing those issues, and to select particular "facts" that are relevant to the issue. Once these facts are selected, it is possible to make analogies between them and the relevant facts in previous cases. This deceptively simple-sounding set of tasks is at the heart of the legal reading that many scholars have struggled to describe and dissect.

Note, then, that there is a legal story that must be told of the events in question in order for this process of analogizing to proceed. However, the particular aspects of those events (crystallized into facts) that form the core of a legal story are quite different from the usual narrative that might be told by laypeople. As I have indicated, the facts selected for a legal story are structured by the legal issues at stake in this particular conflict. These issues in turn are defined by categories generated from statutes or other similarly formalized rules, and/or (via precedent) from earlier cases. Thus, for example, if we know from previous cases that courts will deem a contract to be formed only if there is an "offer" and an "acceptance" of the offer, we will look at previous cases to determine what sorts of words or actions counted as offers and acceptances, and then attempt to find similar words or actions in the case at hand. Arguments as to whether a contract was formed will then center on whether the words or actions in this case were analogous to those in previous cases, with opposing parties arguing for and against. At times, it may be that there isn't really much of an issue on this point. Perhaps it is quite clear that there was an offer and acceptance, and the only really arguable point is whether the contract thereby formed was breached, or broken. Part of what students must learn is when to fight over an issue, and when to concede: when is there a debatable point over analogies, and when is it a waste of time? This is a very important part of their training, for attorneys who pursue frivolous issues can in extreme cases actually be formally sanctioned. (A more common disincentive is that frivolous arguments waste valuable space in briefs, in addition to trying the presiding judge's patience.)

READING PROCEDURE

We have discussed one kind of framework for reading cases, that of the textual context provided by precedent.[47] We now turn to examine the framework provided by the procedural history of a case.[48] Just as the authority of a case as precedent is in part a function of the position (in a clearly demarcated status hierarchy) of the court from which it issued, the authority of a case as a decision on the immediate conflict at issue depends on its "procedural history." By the time a case has reached an appellate court, it has been shaped by the procedures of the trial court below and by the procedures invoked during the appeal, so that there is a strong semiotic framing of the issues to which an appellate court may speak. Issues not raised at trial or on appeal may generally not be addressed by an appellate court, and the appellate court may not rule on issues that would be raised by a different factual situation. When the text of an appellate court opinion addresses such out-of-bounds issues, that part of the opinion is called "dictum" and is deemed not authoritative or binding. Only that part of the opinion that speaks to issues "properly before the court" is thought to be authoritative; this part is called the "holding" of the case. Of course, the distinction between holding and dictum opens a great deal of room for semiotic maneuvering of various kinds. A crucial part of reading legal opinions, then, if one wishes to understand them as socially powerful texts, is discerning the frame that is imposed by prior oral and written contextualizations of the same conflict in courts below and by the semiotic frame imposed by the litigants as they chose particular issues to appeal. Once again, the dictates of a legal reading provide limits to the social power of any particular case law text, building a careful consideration of layers of legal and textual authority into the core reading habits of legal professionals.

## *Legal Ideology through a Linguistic Filter:*
## *Hierarchies of Legal and Textual Authority*

We have seen a common thread that runs through these fundamental aspects of case law texts and readings thereof. This thread involves a shared focus on hierarchies of legal and accompanying textual authority. Written texts are to be read within a series of nested questions about the authority of various courts deciding the case at issue, and also of the courts that authored precedents. At the same time, there is more to this linguistic filter (or, more accurately, metalinguistic filter). If we are to connect a current text with precedent, we must work with the language of this and previous cases, distilling legal tests and issues from previous texts to guide our delineation of facts, carefully parsing descriptions of factual situations to build analogies, cleaving holding from dictum through close analysis of the authoring court's words and authority. Layers of linguistic form and legal authority are intertwined in this process, creating a kind of linguistic filter through which a core legal worldview is conveyed.[49] What, then, is the worldview or ideology buried in this approach to language, reading, and text?

First, where a textualist ideology regards the text as fixed, the U.S. case law tradition depends on a conception of texts as subject to changing interpretation, as fundamentally reconstitutable through the process of recontextualization in subsequent cases. This is not to say that cases are not also given authoritative, determinist readings. But the cultural constitution of cases as precedent has a double-edged quality; subsequent interpretation at once creates the authoritative meaning of a precedential case, and yet is constrained by the framing discourse of the language used in that precedential case. What a case means emerges only as it is interpreted as precedent in subsequent cases. At the same time, because subsequent discourse is constrained and framed by the terms of argument set up in precedential cases, any subsequent authoritative interpretation relies in a fundamental way on the authority of the prior text. In terms of meaning and authority, these legal texts are mutually constitutive.

Thus, it is the very capability of a text to be reconstituted when it is recontextualized as precedent that makes it powerful in the textual tradition; case texts are "fixed" and "refixed" in the continual process of ongoing legal opinion writing and reading. A clear explanation of this process turns out to be oddly elusive. As noted, Edward Levi provides a description in his astute analysis of this sort of legal discourse: "The kind of reasoning involved in the legal process is one in which the classification changes as the classification is made"; it is at once "certain" and "uncertain."[50] James Boyd White similarly defines legal reasoning as "an organized and systematic process of conversation by which our words get and change their meaning."[51] An often invoked adage emerging from the ideology of law school teaching is that there are no right answers to questions asked about case law in class. This is somewhat puzzling, for observation of law school classroom exchanges makes clear that at one level there are, if not right, then certainly wrong answers. But the "no right answers" ideology is a response to the essentially contestable character of case law texts; meanings may be refixed, new interpretations may be forged, and attorney adversaries in practice will argue vastly different interpretations of the same cases in efforts to harness powerful case law precedent for their purposes. Students may give wrong answers when they fail to observe the canons for reading legal texts, or fail to discern the limits to contestability. But to accept the notion that a legal text is sufficiently fixed that it contains right answers is precisely to miss a key canon for reading legal texts.

Embedded in the concept of precedent is also a reworking of temporality and history. Casebooks present "lines" of precedent using cases from disparate times and places; the principle of selection is the logic of precedent development. Thus, if a court in one place extends a principle of liability beyond the point developed by a previous case, drawing on the reasoning of that previous case while also expanding in a new direction, the two cases will be brought together across time and place as part of a developing line of precedent.[52] This approach collapses historical time and social context in the service of a new legal framework whose organizing principle is a genealogy of texts. Vast differences in the cultural meaning of particular kinds of actions or items are elided and translated into a common legal language; a defective coffee urn, mislabeled poison, a loaded gun, and defective hair wash become analogous as "inherently dangerous" objects.[53] At the same time, a defective carriage and a bursting lamp wind up in the "not-dangerous" category.[54] This legal logic defies common everyday understandings, making partners of people and objects that would ordinarily not be mentioned in the same conversation, let alone sentence. They are brought together in a legal genealogy that binds plaintiffs, defendants, and causes of action across time and space. This is another aspect of the performative character of legal language: it creates new temporalities and contexts, while translating and eliding others.

Legal approaches to textuality also depart from everyday understandings in another way. We can recall that the broadly shared textualist approach to texts, found elsewhere in U.S. education, views language as transparent, so that texts are to be read for literal, referential meaning that is universally available. Here again there is a sharp contrast with the case law tradition. It is perhaps not surprising to find that much legal writing is characterized by the inaccessible expert language found in many professions. But there is a more profound inaccessibility, for even were all the technical vocabulary to be somehow transformed into more accessible language, the meaning for which lawyers read the text would remain elusive to those reading for referential content. A legal reading of case law focuses rather on the metapragmatic structure of the text, in which lies the key to its authority. This metapragmatic structure is (at least) twofold, indexing both the context of prior cases in the textual tradition (now reanimated as precedent for this particular case), and the procedural context of this particular case in its prior transformations.

To train students in this new kind of reading, as we have seen, law school classroom discourse undermines a standard referentialist approach to text. Instead, professors introduce students to a new legal storytelling, in which the landscape is defined by other legal texts and by legal warrants for textual authority. In Chapter 6 we will explore further how the people and social contexts in this legal landscape are defined. In this chapter and the next we focus on the overall structure of these legal narratives and on the ways that this structure is taught to students.

## A Shared Message: Constructing Legal Accounts of Conflict from the Inside

We have unpacked the structure of the case law genre from the vantage of metalinguistic warrants and structure, from categories that are external to a legal worldview. Let us now approach the genre from a slightly different vantage, viewing the ordering of case law narratives as they are unfolded in law school classes, using categories internal to a legal worldview. We will explore the logic of the case law structure outlined in previous sections, but as it is enacted in classroom recitations. Although the classes diverge in style, there are some striking commonalities among them, much as English teachers might instruct their students about English grammar in a variety of ways, but still be imparting some basically identical messages regarding language structure.

Most of the professors' turns in the classrooms of this study can be characterized as falling into one (or several) of the following indigenous categories: (a) clarifying facts; (b) applying legal principles to facts, which entails identifying the legal issues raised by the case and linking them to particulars of the case; (c) clarifying law, from doctrine to technical terms; (d) parsing the effects of legal procedure; and (e) discussing policy or social implications of legal decisions, including consideration of strategic concerns. These aspects of a case law reading, found in all of the classrooms, are classic components of the genre as it is understood "from the inside" and thus become core organizing principles. In addition, some turns could be described as giving general clarifications and comments (this includes explanations of the conventions behind a legal reading of texts, warnings regarding the realities of legal practice, discussions of class or law school requirements, and, interestingly, discussions of social and emotional contexts).

Several additional features are worth mentioning. First, we find frequent deployment of hypothetical examples at various points in classroom discussion. Hypotheticals can be used to push students toward further clarity in applying law to facts, or toward better articulation of legal principles, or toward sharper delineation of competing policy or social interests. Second (and this is discussed in detail in Chapter 6), most of the professors make use of role-playing to locate students as characters within the new legal landscapes and narratives created by legal texts and readings. Another feature that is delineated further in Chapter 6 is the simultaneous mention and marginalization of social contexts, moral considerations, and emotionality. Finally, sprinkled throughout all portions of the discussion are speculations as to strategy and motive: the judges' motives for ruling as they do, the litigants' motives for behaving or arguing as they do, the lawyers' motives for pitching the arguments they make in particular ways. These speculations further highlight the sense of legal narratives as contingent on power and metalinguistic maneuvering.

Quite frequently, class discussions of a case began with a recitation of the facts, during which students were called on to select and correctly recount those details of the events in question most pertinent to the legal issues raised in the case. Recitations of facts thus often merged into applications of law to facts, as professors guided students to select the particular details required by legal tests. Once the facts had been clearly enunciated, professors frequently moved onto legal analysis, asking students to state explicitly the connections between particular facts and the requirements of legal tests. If procedural issues affected which issues could be raised and therefore which facts were pertinent, they would also be addressed at some point in the discussion. (A number of professors began case discussions by stressing procedural issues to a greater degree early in the semester, when students were still learning to parse procedure in legal texts.) Professors also asked students to spell out the legal tests, which commonly required students to repeat particular words and phrases distilled from their readings of this or prior cases. At times, it would be necessary for professors to pause over this task, reminding students of the structure of the test, which might have several prongs or parts. Finally, discussion would typically move to consideration of the social or policy implications of the legal approach taken by the court. An alternative structure found in some of the classes began with a recitation of the arguments for the plaintiff and defendant, which requires application of facts to law. This discussion would be interspersed with a careful delineation of the facts, further discussion applying facts to law, clarifications of the law, and discussions of social policy. Interestingly, these orderings found in classroom discussion can also be discerned in the structure of case law texts themselves, which often (but not invariably) begin with a recitation of facts and then move on to legal analysis and finally policy discussions.

As is apparent from this description of typical structures of classroom recitations, there was frequent blurring of boundaries. For example, a short policy discussion might arise during applications of fact to law, or clarification of a particular legal test might briefly interrupt a statement of the facts. At some points, professors would encourage this boundary blurring to point out the interconnectedness of all of these aspects of a legal reading. By contrast, at other points, professors would carefully police the boundaries, to make sure that students understood important distinctions. In addition, this typical structuring of classroom discussion was at times interspersed with humorous asides, comments about class or law school requirements, consideration of social or emotional contexts, and so forth, although these kinds of comments were peripheral both in terms of qualitative features (professors marking these comments as marginal through the content of what they said) and quantity (they were a small percentage of total turns). In the discussion below, we explore in more depth each of the main content-based categories for law school discussions outlined earlier, as well as examining examples of both blurred boundaries and carefully drawn distinctions among these categories.

## Just the Facts, Please

One crucial aspect of a legal reading, taught in all of the classrooms of this study, is the selection of facts to create a new, legal narrative of the conflict at the heart of the case. The word "facts" itself is an indication of the new legal framing: the judges who write legal opinions will accept particular versions of what actually occurred in the case, depending on the procedural stance of the case. If, for example, the person being sued (the defendant) files a motion to dismiss the case before it has actually gone to trial, then the question for the court is whether, under any version, there is actually a "live" legal issue. Thus, in such cases, the court is supposed to accept the version of the case that is most favorable to the person bringing the legal action (the plaintiff). The statement of facts in an appellate opinion in such cases, then, is not supposed to be a rendition that can be certified as factual in the usual sense. Rather, the legal story told in such cases is a collection of the plaintiff's allegations that, taken together, would give him or her the best shot at making a supportable legal claim.

Correct readings of such cases require a suspension of disbelief, an epistemological hedging that is quite different from the underpinnings of the "conflict stories" generally found outside of legal fora. When average speakers tell stories of conflicts in which they suppose themselves to be somehow wronged, they may put emphasis on the actual truth of their account of events. This emphasis can be seen in linguistic markers designed to assure listeners of the epistemological strength of speakers' claims. In addition, speakers draw on a wealth of cultural warrants through which blame and responsibility are allocated, which include moral claims and emotional contexts.[55] These cultural warrants dictate to a large extent which details will be selected in telling the conflict story.

By contrast, as we have seen, legal accounts of conflict are centered on warrants derived from layers of legal authority. This not only directs the reader to different details in recounting events. It also means that the very epistemological status of the facts as recounted depends on layers of legal authority. On the one hand, there is a far more modest claim as to the factual authenticity of these recounted events than in everyday trouble telling. The claim is not a strong assertion that these events actually occurred. Rather, the claim is that this version of what occurred is to be accepted as true, based on the legal status of the case. If the case has already gone to trial, and a jury has accepted one party's version of the facts, then that is the version we must accept in reviewing the case at an appellate level. The jury may have been mistaken in its weighing of the evidence. But unless there is a very blatant indication that it overstepped its prerogatives, we are to adopt the version of the facts accepted by the jury.[56] Just as in cases involving motions to dismiss, the status of the story told in the facts is thoroughly hedged and defined by issues of legal authority.

At the same time, a statement of legal facts contains a highly determinative epistemological claim. More than would be possible in everyday discourse, a court, in stating the legal version of what has occurred, is rendering an authoritative account. Whether or not events actually occurred in this way, this is the version of what occurred that has been declared to be legally accepted. It is therefore the version of the story on which any legally sanctioned action will be taken. From this vantage, we see that the selection of the word "facts" to describe legal storytelling is an apt index of the definitive social power entailed in this process. In each case, a combination of procedural and doctrinal or similar legal warrants delimits which versions of what occurred (and indeed, which aspects of the events in question) will be included in a set of legal facts. When students are called on to recite these facts, they are learning to create a new, legally defined narrative of "what occurred." This narrative is at once quite modest and highly authoritative as to epistemological certainty, and students must undergo a quiet but radical reorientation in their readings. In one sense, it really doesn't matter what occurred, because all we can know is what the legal decision maker has accepted as fact for certain purposes. In another sense, an accurate reading of the facts, replete with quite particular, legally relevant details, gives students a new power. They now know how to construct versions of conflict stories that can be understood by legal authorities and given legal effect.

These aspects of fact construction can be seen in classroom exchanges. On the one hand, professors will push students to enunciate details that seem picky in the extreme. In the following exchange, an otherwise well-prepared student bogs down when asked for such a detail, one that is important to the resolution of the case but that might easily escape the eye of an average lay reader attempting to tell the story of a conflict between people:

*Transcript 4.4 [3/3/7]*[57]

| | |
|---|---|
| Prof.: | Wait, wait, was there a contract for a delivery of wheat? No, for sale of wheat, right? A contract for the sale of wheat? |
| Student: | Right. |
| Prof.: | Okay, and so what was the price of wheat? |
| Student: | Well, the delivery to- (price at the) time of delivery (.) |
| Prof.: | When was the time of delivery? |
| Student: | Specifically? Ah (.03 pause) |

Similarly, in the next example, a professor stops the student's recitation of facts to probe his understanding of what might appear to be a small detail—one which a nonlegal reader could skip over with impunity.

*Transcript 4.5 [5/34/4]*

| | |
|---|---|
| Prof.: | Now, tell me about this mortgage that the defendant held on the plaintiff's land. What kind of a mortgage was it? In a minute we'll try to figure out what the mortgage is. |
| Mr. K.: | Um (.07 pause) What do you mean what kind of mortgage? |
| Prof.: | What does it tell us in the case? What is it called? |
| Mr. K.: | Um (.14 pause) Well, it said that uh (.) it was a third mortgage (). |
| Prof.: | What does that mean? |
| Mr. K.: | I have no idea. |
| Prof.: | Third mortgage. That means there must have been three mortgages, right? |
| Mr. K.: | Right. |
| Prof.: | What's a first mortgage and what's a second mortgage; what's a third mortgage? You're lucky, Mr. K., you haven't yet had to have first, second, and third mortgages. [[laughter]] You haven't yet had to face the problem. Someday you may. Maybe you won't. Maybe you'll become a high-priced lawyer and this will never bother you. But there are folks out there dealing with third mortgages. (You) probably will never see a third mortgage, but this person strangely enough did. What's a third mortgage? Let's- uh, let's ask around a little bit. |

Note that here, as in many of the classes, the professor uses humor to soften the effects of this detailed questioning. Thus, although the exchange in many ways mirrors that with which we opened this chapter, taken from Scott Turow's vivid (and horrific) account of Socratic teaching at Harvard Law School, the overall tone here is somewhat different. There is a similar attention to detail. There is also a parallel, quite strong suggestion to be gleaned from this line of questioning: that a good legal reading of facts might entail some background investigation of pertinent legally relevant features. It is not good enough to simply gloss over or guess at the meaning of key features of important facts. The message is delivered with humor, and the professor moves quickly off the student when it becomes apparent that he has bogged down. However, a very similar message about the requirements of a good legal reading is conveyed. And though he is not grilled mercilessly, the student is for a moment caught in a Socratic spotlight without all of the necessary equipment, with almost one hundred fellow first-year students looking on. The general message is succinctly expressed by another professor, when advising a student who was unable to answer this kind of detailed background factual question: "Look it up, and do some thinking" (1/4/10).

At the same time as they focus in on very detailed exegetical discussion of some facts, professors also pass lightly over others. This again retrains students' vision, teaching them to hover carefully over some quite particular details while painting large parts of the story with a very broad brush.

*Transcript 4.6 [3/3/3]*

Prof.:     Hi. Um, can you start developing for us the arguments for the plaintiff and the defendant. (.) Um, Ms. N.?

Ms. N.:    Um, that the plaintiff was a young, youthful man // with //

Prof.:                                                  // great // the plaintiff was a beautiful man (). [[class laughter]] Is that what you said?

The professor breaks in on the student's attempt to tell the story of the case in a traditional narrative frame, directing her away from details of the plaintiff's appearance that are legally irrelevant, but that might be of great interest in a popular telling of the story. Rather than focus on detailed descriptions of the characters in the drama, the professor urges the student to skip to a discussion of the two possible legal approaches that might apply to the facts in this case: "Okay, all right, so there's a lot at stake in the choice of which branch of this rule to apply in this particular fact situation. And all I'm interested in, Ms. N., is what the arguments are, um, for cost of completion, which is what the plaintiff wants in both cases, and what the arguments are for diminution in value, which is what the defendant wants in both cases, all right? I want the argument, okay?" (3/3/4).[58]

As they urge students to focus on some details while ignoring others, professors also underscore the peculiarly circumscribed epistemological status of the facts in legal texts:

*Transcript 4.7 [4/1/8]*

Prof.:     Does the court ever say- does the New Hampshire Supreme Court ever say, "And then we know for a fact that Dr. McGee said, quote *[professor writes quote on blackboard]*?" Does the court ever say that?

Student:   No.

Prof.:     No. What does the court say? How does the court characterize what the doctor said? (.09 pause) What's the best we can say about these statements?

Student:   That there's some likelihood that they had been spoken (.)

Prof.:    Okay, that's inferring from the fact that um we don't have any counterevidence, presented by the Supreme Court, but (). The court says, specifically, something about these statements. The court doesn't say, "We know for a fact that these statements were made." (.075 pause) It's a little less definitive than, "We know for a fact that-" (.10 pause) Um, yes?

Student:  Um he says um, "There is evidence to the effect that the quoted operation was performed on the plaintiff in ()--"

Prof.:                                                          --Yes, several times, the court says "There's evidence to the effect," or "Evidence was presented," or "There was evidence that." We're dealing with () appellate opinion, which takes us back to the trial court. The trial court takes us back to the witnesses' documentary evidence, sometimes physical evidence. (.065 pause) The facts as they actually happened and the facts as reported in the appellate opinion, well, very often they're two quite different things.

The professor moves on to further discussion of how procedure affects the delineation of facts. Although the discourse structure here is somewhat different from that in our earlier examples taken from a more strictly Socratic classroom, there is a very similar focus on the role of procedure in shaping and limiting legal narratives and epistemological validity. In both instances, we are dealing with classes early in the semester; professors more commonly focus on these aspects when students are still new to legal reading. As the semester moves on, these core underpinnings to the reading of facts appear to become part of an understood background, mentioned if an unusual wrinkle in the case—or a forgetful student—brings them back to the foreground briefly.[59]

## Applying Law to Facts: Issues, Arguments, Analogies, Holdings, Hypos

Transcript 4.8 [6/13/16]

Prof.:    All right, next. *Hamer v. Sidway*, we're not done with that. What- where is the consideration?

Student:  In that the nephew forebore, what he had a legal right to do. He didn't drink, he didn't smoke, he // didn't //

Prof.:                                      // Exactly // the consideration here was in the detriment to the promisee. *[sequence followed by positive uptake, then by further question as to what the benefit was to promisor]*

Another key step in legal readings of cases is the application of general legal categories to the particular facts involved in the case at hand. As we have seen, this process has already begun implicitly whenever there is a recitation of facts, because the very definition and selection of those facts is guided by legal categories and issues. The backbone of legal doctrine comes more explicitly into view when students are asked to match specific facts with relevant legal categories and to explain the fit between them. In the excerpt above, the professor calls on the student for an explicit delineation of the facts in the case that would fit with the legal category "consideration" (one of the requirements for contract formation).

This process may require excursions into other cases that the students have read or into precedent cited by the court. These other cases provide analogical templates, because in them, the fit between specific fact and legal category has already been established. Whether or not a legal claim can be established in the new case, then, will depend in part on whether these facts are arguably similar to those in previous cases where legal claims were upheld.

*Transcript 4.9 [7/4/13]*

Prof.:   [ . . . ] Why does the court say there is no consideration in this promise? Yes, Ms. S.?

Ms. S.:   Because there was no- no exact agreement to forbear at this time, there was no exact reason to forbear.

Prof.:   Right. So the court, the court acts as a (). What would we call this kind of promise?

Ms. S.:   An illusory promise.

Prof.:   It's an illusory promise. This is an illusory promise. [ . . . ] Now, could his promise of forbearance have constituted consideration? Is the money- it's very important to understand what this case stands for. Is it standing for the proposition that there's no way that a promise to forbear by a person in the plaintiff's position () constitute consideration for the- for the wife's promise? Or is it simply that on these facts, it simply didn't happen? Which one? In other words, could there have been adequate forbearance of a promise? Could there be a promise of forbearance to constitute consideration? Mr. H.?

Mr. H.:   Well, yeah. Certainly, I mean, if it were bargained for that would- he would have said, "If you sign, if you endorse this, I will forbear for two years. I give you that promise." If it was nothing bargained for then it (wouldn't) be a consideration.

Prof.:   Well, forbearance of a certain, for any legal right- and that was a clear lesson of *Hamer v. Sidway* and *Fiege v. Boehm.* But forbearance (of) a certain legal right constitutes- can constitute consideration. Now, it did not in this particular case, because to do so he must give up something. And he worded it in such a way that he still retained total discretion, and Mr. H. is exactly right (). If he's going to make her promise, and through that promise, have (a) bargained for exchange, (if) it's going to be forbearance to assert the demand for payment, you're going to have to put a time on it. No matter how long it's got to be in there because otherwise he's still got the right to demand payment immediately. So they didn't do it that way. It was not consideration on the facts in this case because he did not agree to forbear for any certain period of time. He still retains total discretion. [ . . . ]

First, note here the professor's emphatic repetition of a technical category, "illusory promise." In a sense, teaching the students how to apply the law to facts and teaching them the technical doctrine itself are here elided. This is not at all uncommon throughout the transcripts. One important way law is taught is through its application, by example.

Returning to our primary point, we can also notice that in this excerpt the professor urges the student to compare the facts in the case being discussed to those of other cases. In the previous cases, a promise to forbear had been found to constitute adequate consideration, so that a valid contract was formed. A promise to forbear in the case now being discussed was not viewed as adequate. The professor is pressing the student to examine the facts in each case to discern the legally definitive difference. A first pass reveals one difference: the promise here did not actually limit the promisor's discretion. The professor then goes on to push the contrast still further, saying of the case at hand, "Well, in fact he actually did forbear for two years after the promise. So why wasn't that consideration? Certainly good enough in *Hamer v. Sidway*. Why weren't the actual two years of forbearance, to insist upon paying the note, consideration?" (7/4/14). Here the professor is demonstrating to students that there are multiple possible points of analogy and that each must be examined for key similarities and differences.

This excerpt also highlights the way particular cases come to "stand for" legal principles, through this process in which law is applied to facts. The professor stresses the point here in order to ensure that students take the right lesson from the case. On the one hand, it could be that a promise to forbear would never suffice for contract formation. On the other hand, the case could stand for a more limited legal principle: that when a promise to forbear actually leaves the promisor with total discretion, it will not suffice for contract formation.[60] Figuring this out requires careful parsing of the backbone of law as it is applied to facts through several cases, as well as examination of the potential analogies among them. Of course, when courts engage in this process, law is not only applied but also created. Students follow their professors' lead, engaging as well in this process of analogical parsing:

*Transcript 4.10 [6/22/3]*

Prof.:   You said it's a form letter and that indicates it's not an offer. Why not? Ed?

Ed:      I'd say it's similar to the advertisement () more people could accept it than there are numbers to pass out. So there's only one property, and if it's a form letter more people could accept it, if it was an offer. So that makes it unreasonable to think that is an offer.

*Transcript 4.11 [8/20/15]*

Student:   Well, I mean, I would say the biggest differentiation here between this and the painting contract was the immediacy. I mean, if I made a threat to you right now, then it's probably much more likely to be enforced than if I say, call you up on the phone and threaten you, I mean.

Notice that a similar parsing process is necessary to discern the holding of any particular case; students must glean which legal principles are at issue, which facts from previous cases were most pertinent, which facts in this case are most pertinent, and exactly what the court has decided regarding the issue on these facts. (This also requires them to push aside irrelevant issues and facts.) It is worth noting that the fundamental semiotic choices as to what aspects of two events render them analogous involve deeply cultural perspectives. These perspectives are not neutral or given, but rather emerge from particular vantages. For example, people of different genders or social backgrounds might diverge considerably in how they interpret threats or understand the implications of form letters. Yet these social and cultural roots to analogizing are "naturalized," hidden, rendered as natural and therefore unproblematic, indeed invisible, in the form of this Anglo-American legal reading.

Professors also teach this parsing process using hypothetical situations. These hypotheticals can provide fine-grained exercises in analogizing.

*Transcript 4.12 [3/22/7]*

Student:   Umm, this other one says that it's a real promise, that the father was making up this case of the mortgage and that the deed was really just a symbol of what he was actually going to do. And then when he died, he didn't um upkeep his promise, so that when he died the mortgage wasn't paid. So that, um, if he's trying to protect his daughter, then he didn't keep up his end // of the promise //

Prof.:                         // but, well //  actually let me clarify, that wouldn't be enough. In other words, we will enforce promises against a mistake. So, the fact that he died without completing the promise would not be- would not be a factor in determining whether or not this is a umm gift. *[ . . . ]* Um, so that that wouldn't indicate the seriousness, or not, uh, would it? I mean, what if he'd been struck by lightning? [[class laughter]] Hit by a truck?

*Transcript 4.13 [7/20/14]*

Prof.:   *[ . . . omit most of 1.51 min. turn . . . ]* Well, this, uh, you know, () have hypothetical brief case, I like to use the hypothetical flagpole case. Uh, what's this thing? Here's- here's the conflict in the (). I promise to pay you one hundred dollars if you climb to the top of the flagpole and touch the golden eagle at the top, and you want a hundred dollars, and you start up there and just, you know, when you're at the top and you're- when you're at the top and you're- just as you're reaching to touch the golden eagle I yell at you, "I revoke!" [[class laughter (.04)]] And then laugh at you.

In this last example, the professor is varying the level to which someone has performed before the person with whom she or he contracted revokes an offer. The discussion begins with the general principle that when someone makes an offer— in particular, an offer that can be accepted simply by doing something rather than by saying something—then that person should in theory be able to revoke the offer up until performance of the deed.[61] The clear-cut hypothetical proffered by the professor highlights the case of revocation right at the instant before the deed is complete, thus throwing into sharp relief the problem of the injustice that might result. In the subsequent discussion, the professor then proceeds to explain how the law has "jiggled" with the general principle in order to prevent injustice. Use of hypotheticals can in essence provide the students with a speeded-up process of legal reasoning which, in actual court cases, might take years; the courts must wait for real life to vary the parameters, presenting them with situations in which problematic (or unclear) aspects of legal principles are laid bare by the facts in the case.

Thus, we see how complex and yet crucial this process of applying law to facts (and facts to law) is to the semiotics of deciphering case law texts. Upon it depends discerning the central import of legal decisions, textually packaged as holdings. It also guides the central semiotic process through which analogies (and their close relatives, hypotheticals) help to elucidate and create precedent, arching between diverse written legal texts and social times to create a kind of continuity. Around this linguistic backbone, the muscles and flesh of legal arguments and the social issues they address can move fluidly while maintaining some form of structure.

## Clarifying the Law

As we have seen, the law is taught not only through explicit discussion, but also in the selection and recounting of facts and in instruction as to applying facts to law. Indeed, a great deal of learning is through examples, analogies, hypotheticals, and other kinds of applications. This is necessary because the legal categories themselves rely on application to specific situations for their (often shifting) definitions: Levi's process "in which the classification changes as the classification is made." At times, however, professors or students will exit the process of application in order to explicitly discuss the legal tests that are being distilled from class discussions, generally with the goal of clarifying potentially confusing points.

*Transcript 4.14 [8/40/1–2]: SPECIFIC PERFORMANCE*

Prof.:  All right. All right, yesterday- yesterday we were talking about specific performance and the *American Brands* case and if you notice the standard, that the person has to satisfy, is that there is something unique, right, non-fungible, something unique, () all right. *[ . . . ]* Do notice something, the uniqueness test is still there in the Restate-ment, if you- and you should have read that- and in the UCC *[part of 3.20 turn omitted: mini-lecture on specific performance, professor then raises question about phrasing in the UCC]* But it goes on to say there is one class of cases for which it really should be the preferred remedy. Anyone read it, the note? There's one classic- yeah?

Student:  Wait a minute, there's one class where you said specific performance remedy?

Prof.:  Yeah.

Student:  When it's- uh (.) when substitute goods aren't available--

Prof.:                                                         --are not available, okay, and what's the phrase before "the substitute goods are not available"? Notice we have a presumption usually that markets substitute goods.

Conceivably if you really have to go out there and prove scarcity, which starts, though, trying to look like what? Real scarcity.

Class:       (.03 turn) *[multiple students speaking, individual utterances inaudible]*

Prof.:       —sort of uniqueness. A slightly broader definition of uniqueness, all right. ( ) be my mother's diamond ring, it can be very rare potatoes, but– all right. But what else, what other class of cases?

Student:     Damages aren't compensatory? Or --

Student #2:                                   --right.

Prof.:       All right, where damages aren't compensatory, but I guess if you look at the phrase before, it suggests: outputs in requirements contracts. Remember when we did them?

Here the professor summarizes across various textual sources, pulling out and explaining key defining legal points that constitute part of the doctrine of specific performance.

In these kinds of exchanges, professors make visible a logic uniting lines of cases that have been read by the students. As in this example, teachers also draw on sources in which legal principles are explicitly enunciated, most notably the Restatement and the Uniform Commercial Code, but also various state and federal statutes or regulations, and so forth. At these moments, sometimes involving mini-lectures, the professors step back from detailed dissection of individual cases to point out a thread that runs through disparate cases, examples, and hypotheticals. In the process of explaining legal doctrines, professors are also highlighting for students the specific issues on which nit-picking factual analogies or distinctions will have to rest. The resulting outline lays bare the backbone of legal structure that is organizing factual comparisons, and it is a structure centered on legal authority, using legal texts as the key filters of that authority.

## Parsing Procedure

We have already extensively discussed the crucial role of deciphering legal procedure in shaping legal readings. Particularly during classes early in the semester, but also at later points, professors repeatedly remind students of the crucial role of legal procedure in delimiting the relevant facts and the application of law to those facts. This is, again, a lesson in legal reading found throughout the classrooms of this study.

## Social and Policy Implications

In an interesting contrast with the emphasis on precision in other aspects of the legal reading taught to law students, class discussions of cases also frequently include wide-ranging discussions of the possible social and policy implications of legal doctrines. These discussions are at times peppered with speculation as to causation, strategy, and motives: the motives of legal decision makers when ruling (or legislating) in particular ways, or of people subject to law when behaving in certain ways.

*Transcript 4.15 [8/17/13]*

| | |
|---|---|
| Prof.: | Organs, all right, organ transplants and stuff. Now, you might or might not agree with it and it might or might not happen, all right. But there are- there's at least some concept that there (is) some things that are beyond the pale to be allocated through private resources. (.03 pause) Well, is *Batzakis* that- or isn't it, and should it- (.03 pause) and what should the court do with it? Yeah? |
| Student #1: | See, I don't see organ, like donating an organ for money as the same thing as *Batzakis*- like they're in a war-torn country and the only way for them to get the money is to give up an organ, in that sense I could see them being similar. But if you're a rational person living in America and just one day decide you want to give up your organ, I think that should be allowed more so than a situation where you have no choice. |
| Student #2: | But the only reason people give up their organs is when they're under extreme duress, they're so poverty-stricken that they say, "All right, I'll sacrifice one of my two kidneys to this person who's much richer and can afford to buy it because I need the money in order to feed my kids." |
| Prof.: | That's the supply side of it, and what's the problem with the demand side of it, and by the way if you would say this is somewhat hypo-critical because I don't see the difference between this and milk, on the demand side I'd say, "Yeah, I think we are drawing lines and some of it does look very hypocritical, but we are drawing lines and have to"- what? |

In this example, as in many policy discussions, students and professor tell stories to illustrate the possible moral and social underpinnings for the intricate legal apparatus that forms the core of a legal reading.

There is an intriguing paradox to be found here. On the one hand, this kind of free-ranging commentary on fairness would not be a correct move during the actual parsing of a legal text, and that parsing forms the core of the classroom lessons. A correct legal reading requires strict submission to layers of legal authority discernable in the text: the question is not what any reader thinks is fair, but what the court says or what the law permits. (See excerpt from 1/7, in Chapter 1, pp. 9–10.) However, after a text has been properly read, there is quite broad latitude for consideration of possible social or moral implications. The degree of latitude here contrasts interestingly with that in a social science discussion, in which it is likely that professors would focus attention on the evidence required to support gener-alizations as to the social class of organ donors. This focus would require parsing of social science data and studies, in which there are stringent requirements for demonstrating generalizations regarding social impacts. By contrast, law profes-sors focus students' attention on the kinds of evidence and proof required for legal assertions. This focus requires deciphering of legal texts and layers of legal author-ity and of the legally accepted facts formed by legal filters. When classroom dis-course moves to consideration of social causes and impacts, a much more free-form discussion occurs in law schools. Implicit in this movement is the sense that one can discern social and moral implications through unraveling a cultural logic that is obvious or transparent.

Thus, when law professors speak of policy considerations, a great deal is packed into their conception of policy. In effect, the questions of whether law operates in a just manner, whether certain legal decisions were motivated by class interests or other extralegal concerns, whether particular social conditions caused or resulted from specific legal decisions—all these are encompassed in the broad-ranging inquiry into policy. And in answering these questions, students do not need to consult studies or other evidence, although professors may indeed throw in casual cites to what "studies show" from time to time. Rather, students need to unravel cultural logics through the telling of persuasive stories: of poor people who must sell their organs, of judges or juries who may well have been racially biased in particular instances (or who may have been attempting to achieve certain social results through their decisions). Most of this discussion is anecdotal or speculative, and indeed lapses into the use of hypothetical storytelling at times. Not surprisingly, one can also find this form of policy discussion in the explicit language of legal opinions themselves—although in classroom discourse, reading for policy considerations frequently requires moving beyond the explicit language of the text in an attempt to intuit underlying motives and implications.[62] However, both in the legal texts themselves and in policy discussions of those texts, this move to a broad grab bag of social and moral considerations is a brilliant, if problematic, stroke. Were the system of textual exegesis to remain mired at the tightly constructed surface, it might lack the flexibility and openness needed to retain credibility. Instead, this approach maintains a tight, technical center, but also permits an expansive periphery of policy considerations. In this way, the legal reading taught in law school classes at once closely limits the kinds of warrants permitted for legal conclusions (to layers of legal-textual authority) and at the same time encompasses virtually any kind of social data or issues deemed culturally relevant.

Furthermore, these broader policy discussions are often accompanied by closely related speculative storytelling regarding the motivations of the people who are players in the case being dissected. After all, if a person is motivated by greed or racial hatred, it is possible that in ruling for or against him or her, a court can be encouraging or discouraging such behavior. So, side by side with speculations about the real underlying policy motivations for legal decisions, one can find speculations about why people behaved as they did in the underlying dispute (or in the tactics they pursued when bringing legal claims). These speculations can also serve to sharpen students' sensibilities in a number of other ways. First, they alert the students to a loose realist idea that there is much going on beneath the surface of a legal text—that it is important not to accept legal rulings at face value. Second, they push students to be mindful of the strategic effects of proceeding in one way or another when bringing legal cases. Third, they initiate students into an unofficial genre of legal storytelling that is reportedly quite common in practice: the cynical recounting of the so-called real motives for formal legal maneuvers.[63] Finally, they continue the brilliant opening up of legal readings to virtually all kinds of cultural stories about why things happen or what really mattered in an interaction—

without threatening the carefully disciplined core focus of legal translations, which remains centered on textual authority and precedent.

*Transcript 4.16 [5/8/14]*

Prof.:    So we're talking about a time, thirty years later. Thirty years after the fighters' prime, thirty years after their prime, they meet. It's unlikely they're going to fight thirty years later. I mean it's unlikely that they'll move very easily. [[class laughter]] And in the case of modern boxers, it's the last- they can't even talk, let alone fight [[class laughter]], at this point in their careers. Now, what's going on here, why does it take thirty years for Dempsey to meet Wills? Now there are all kinds of overtones, racial and otherwise in this case. But I think there's a pretty simple explanation for why Dempsey doesn't want to fight Wills. And I don't think- I could be wrong about this- that it has anything to do with matters of race. I think it's a bit simpler than that. Take a wild guess, Ms. U.

Ms. U.:    He was afraid to lose?

Prof.:    He was afraid that he was going to get maimed by Wills, the "Brown Bomber" who was probably the greatest boxer of the world, indeed of the universe at that point, and Dempsey wants to stay away from him, okay? Now there are a lot of people who want to try to get him to fight Wills, but there is, alas, a problem with the color bar in a lot of places and there are a lot of promoters who won't touch that fight and there are a lot of people who are worried about the future of the sport. *[ . . . ]* my guess is he's worried about losing the battle. And maybe he finally realizes that that's what's going to happen. He signs the contract and he tries to back out. Now what do you do with the fact that he's backed out of this contract? *[This question marks the transition to the core case analysis, and the remainder of the discussion centers on issues of contract breach and legal remedies]*

Here one aspect of social context—racial prejudice—is touched on briefly, and then we are told an alternative story centered on strategic concerns, on a fear of losing. Note that there is no careful weighing of the evidence supporting this story, nor is there a basis in the text for these speculations. Rather, the epistemological foundation for this discussion lies in common sense, a cultural logic shared by the speakers. If we know that one fighter backed out of a fight, and we are told that he was probably a weaker fighter, then it makes sense that he may have backed out to avoid losing. The relative honor and shame entailed in backing out as opposed to losing, common understandings of human motivation, the primacy of strategic concerns— these are the kinds of warrants on which this speculative attribution of motive rests.

In sum, there are rich data in the discussions of policy. They alone could form the basis of an entire volume, which could trace the cultural logics and assumptions underlying such conversations about policy and society while also noting how and when they flirt with legal analysis. In these policy discussions, we find tales about human motivation, about trust and trickery, about poverty and free will. Grand stories are told about the role of markets in ordering societies, about competing visions of justice, and more. These broadly painted backgrounds surround the nitty-gritty dissection of fact, law, and procedure with which law students and their professors are centrally occupied. They add humanity, humor, and purpose to an otherwise highly technical, removed discourse. However, they stand in marked contrast to the central legal discussion, marginal not only in terms of discursive structure, but also because these policy discussions never impart any real analytic standards for assessing one story against another. (Arguably, one would need to teach some form of social science to accomplish this.) When social context comes in the door, structure, standards, and rigor exit.

### Policing the Boundaries: Ordering Legal Narratives

At the same time as students are learning to read case law texts in terms of these new categories, they must also absorb the proper deployment of the categories. Professors repeatedly remind students to keep different components separate, instructing them in the conventions surrounding correctly structured legal narratives. This proper structuring, in contrast to conventions ordering some other genres, does not always require a set order of components. Indeed, as we will see, it is at times necessary to mix components or blur boundaries to create an integrated legal reading. But first it is important to understand where the lines are drawn: which components cannot be put in front of or mixed with others, which parts of the story must be in place before certain conclusions can be discussed or drawn.

For example, in the following excerpt, a professor interrupts a student in the act of mixing fact-recitation with legal argument:

*Transcript 4.17 [1/9/23]*

Student:  But in any case, before the Board made the ultimate decision to accept her resignation or not, she goes on to argue // that //

Prof.:                                                  // See // but what you're doing is you're just jumping ahead here. You're stealing the knockout punch. You've got to wait. But it's okay. Let's work with this. Okay, all right. So the next thing that happens is you've got this school reacting by having her thrown off and kept off the property? Is that right?

Here the professor wants to make sure that the student has laid out all of the important facts of the case before moving on to consider the legal arguments developed from those facts. Certain factual details need to be in place for these arguments to be comprehensible; therefore, it will not work to move too quickly to the punch line.

This theme can be seen even more clearly in the following excerpt, in which a professor overtly instructs a student on the art of legal storytelling:

*Transcript 4.18 [6/4/1–2]*

Prof.:    Okay. Why don't you tell us the story of *Mills v. Wyman*.

Student:  Sure. Uh, in this case, Levi Wyman is () years old and long emancipated from his family, returned from a sea trip and took ill, the plaintiff in this case () Mills took Levi in and cared for him until his death on

> February 20, 1821. The defendant wrote a letter to the plaintiff on February //() //

Prof.:             // Wait // now, who is the defendant?

Student:    The defendant in this case is Levi Wyman's father. He wrote a letter to the plaintiff on February 24th of the same year after all these charges had been incurred for taking care of this man's son, promising that he would pay all expenses related to such care. No consideration was given for the promise // () //

Prof.:                    // Well // now wait a second. When you're stating the facts you don't want to be using- you want to minimize your legal conclusions. So in the facts, instead of saying "no consideration was given for the promise," what might you say instead?

Student:    Well the uh--

Prof.:                    --I mean that, the consideration aspect would be more appropriate in your holding, or your issue, or your analysis.

The professor interrupts the student twice in this passage: once to seek a clarification while also ensuring that the story was told in the right order (clarifying who the defendant was before moving on to describe what he did), and a second time to stop the student from mixing legal conclusions with recitation of facts. Although the selection of relevant facts is highly dependent on the legal categories to be used, the professor wants the student to strongly separate the recitation of facts from overt legal analysis. Application of the technical word "consideration" by definition moves the discussion into legal conclusions, which the professor wishes to avoid before the facts have been thoroughly reviewed.

Aside from the need to have all the requisite facts before proceeding to legal analysis, there is another message conveyed by this careful boundary maintenance. By placing the factual storytelling first, both teachers (in class) and judges (in written opinions) create a structure that contains a metalinguistic signal. "Before we come to any conclusions," we are told, "let us (both readers and the courts writing the opinions) carefully review what happened in a dispassionate manner." The boundary maintenance between statements of facts and legal conclusions permits the classroom discourse (or written legal text) itself to send a signal about law's impartiality and fairness.[64] The ways that law has already shaped the facts become less visible, and the facts themselves take on a stronger epistemological status by virtue of the wall dividing them from legal conclusions and assessments.

We have seen that there is a trick to telling legal stories: one cannot simply jump ahead or mix different segments of the storytelling together. Understanding acceptable orderings of the fact pattern, separating facts from law—an adequate legal reading must respect these boundaries. At the same time, professors constantly elide boundaries as well.

### Putting the Pieces Together: Blurred and Distinct Boundaries in an Integrated Legal Account

Throughout this discussion, we have seen a number of examples of blurred boundaries, where professors mixed recitation of facts with application of law to facts, or application of law to facts with clarifications of law. Obviously, this takes some skill, for an incorrect mixing of boundaries can cause readers to miss the central message of a case. However, when professors blur the boundaries, they teach their students the interconnectedness of all these various facets of legal reading.

*Transcript 4.19 [2/20/14]*

| | |
|---|---|
| Prof.: | This is an incredibly- this is, as you know [[class laughter]], () probably interesting area. Not only that, but very hard thoughts in areas, in the real very intense struggle going on in our courts over this issue. And not only in the courts, but in the legislature it's a very (high) issue. Okay. Well, still, I know you know a whole lot about employee-at-will. But- [[class laughter]] If you don't say anything in a contract for instance about employment at will, and you get into some, sort of, relationship and I don't say anything about the length of the relationship. What do you assume? |
| Student: | That either party can get out of the contract at any time. |
| Prof.: | Right. Either party can get out of the contract, and can get out of the arrangement at any time, be terminated at any time. Just suppose I say that (.) you have a job for the rest of your life if you come work for me. What's the relationship, what happens then? |
| Student: | Then you say- I'm not sure () how it would work out. That means it would be vague, and it would be considered vague and ()- |
| Prof.: | Any takers on that? I say, "Come work with me, I'll pay you. You have a job for life. And I'll pay you, you know, a certain amount every year." What's the status of that? |
| Student #2: | It seems like a definite time, I mean, there is a () about time. When a person dies, () is over. When the person dies, his term is over and that's ()- |
| Prof.: | Any other takers on that? And it seems probably a perfectly logical, in that as long as you live, you know, that definitely has a termination date unless you get too metaphysical about it. Um- [[class laughter]] Any other comments on this issue? Yes? Way in the back. Yes? |

This excerpt exemplifies the way exegetical descriptions of legal principles frequently slide into and depend on application to particular fact situations, here using hypothetical examples. The professor frames the hypotheticals using role-playing and reported speech: "Just suppose I say that (.) you have a job for the rest of your life if you come work for me." As we will see in Chapter 6, these techniques have the effect of placing the professor and student for a moment in the position of the parties, as, for example, in this transcript excerpt, where the classroom interlocutors take the places of bargaining parties in a contract-formation scene. Legal principles are enacted in dialogic discourse, in which there are two parties, two sides, and numerous possible arguments and strategies and outcomes. As professors and students in essence perform repeated dramas in class, they enact and embody the intricate dance in which law constrains and shapes, yet also emanates from, facts. These performances make vivid the complicated combination of boundary maintenance and boundary blurring required for a full legal reading, in which all of the distinct aspects of a legal reading are at once fully respected but also synthesized and brought together.

Similarly, discussions may merge a presentation of the arguments on each side (applying facts to law as it explicates legal principles) with a discussion of the policy arguments supporting each position. Some doctrines almost require this kind of merger, because they rely more explicitly than most on overt policy or fairness rationales. One such doctrine is that of "unconscionability," which permits the courts to refuse to enforce contracts in which a person with grossly disproportionate bargaining power has foisted manifestly unfair contractual provisions on the other person.

> Transcript 4.20 [8/40/6]
>
> Prof.:     Well, that's one side of it, and the other side of it is the one that says "No, we won't uphold it, because it's not fair"- what kind of argument?
>
> Student:  Unconscionability.
>
> Prof.:     It's an unconscionability-style argument [ . . . ]

In a sense, these kinds of doctrines test students' ability to develop a keen sense of boundary deployment: they bring policy arguments right into the heart of doctrinal categories. And yet, students must still remember that the measure of whether a contract is unfair enough to merit unconscionability status is not their own sense of outrage, or that of an average person on the street. Even here, it is necessary to look to prior legal decisions and patiently work out legally permissible analogies or distinctions. Thus, a full legal reading of text involves constant calculations regarding the boundaries between fact telling and legal application, between explication of law or procedure and policy discussions—at times clearly distinct from one another, yet at others wound together to form a complete legal narrative.

## Summary

We have now reviewed two different vantages on the structure of a legal reading. From the perspective of anthropological linguistics, we have seen the crucial role of a peculiarly legal metalinguistic structuring in shaping how students are trained to read written legal texts. From an internal vantage, we have seen how indigenous metalinguistic categories function to organize written legal texts and readings thereof. Throughout it is clear that this complicated structure continually reinforces a focus on legal warrants and layers of authority, translated generally through the lens of a characteristic textual analysis. To be sure, there is also an exciting openness invited at the edges of this legal reading of text, one in which all kinds of social and moral considerations can be imagined, stories of all sorts can be told, virtually any experience or event can be made relevant to some kind of legal question or test. This sense of drama is heightened by role-play in class, with professor and students standing in the shoes (or, more accurately, speaking in the voices) of players on the legal stage.

At the same time, a very stringent set of guidelines for unpacking legal texts is conveyed, through overt instruction but also through a subtle redirection of attention. As students tell and listen to the facts, they begin to notice different aspects of the conflict story encompassed in the written case law text. As they apply facts to law, they learn rules for building appropriate analogies between cases. These rules are as often gleaned from the way a professor retells the story, or redirects discussion to students who are on the right track, as from explicit admonitions. Professors also clarify the law to be applied, pushing students to identify the tests and standards to be found in lines of cases (or statutory language). At times, the limiting structure of legal procedure becomes a focus as well, when professors remind students of the effects of procedure on the establishment of facts or on the overall stance of the case. It is only when the professor is sure that students know how to package the events in question into these narrow legal boxes that classes engage in wide-ranging policy discussions. These discussions open the door to a variety of social and moral issues, which can be connected with some freedom to the legal questions at hand; however, the class has now exited the core legal analysis.

Thus, at two levels, a legal reading appears to be capable of translating virtually any event or concern. First, *any* events involved in a conflict that winds up in a legal forum can be translated as facts fitting into the narrow categories of a legal reading, whether they involve the building of a church, agreements among family members as to the care of an ailing relative, disputes between manufacturers and buyers, franchisers and franchisees, and on and on. Second, discussions of policy that surround these readings permit legal readers to speculate on almost any social or moral aspect of the situation involved. Thus, a legal reading combines a nearly universal translating mechanism with a narrowing filter that sharply constrains which factual details and which policy concerns can actually affect legal outcomes. This focus is profoundly metalinguistic in character: it runs events as well as social and moral concerns through a complex filter structured around the interrelation of precedential texts, text-based analogies, repetition of key phrases and terms from text to text, and layers of legal authority relayed through and in layered legal texts. Although professors may vary in how they convey these facets of legal reading, we can nonetheless trace the same basic approach across all of the classes in the study.

# 5

Epistemology and Teaching Styles:
Different Forms, Same Message

In this chapter, I discuss how the shared message identified in Chapter 4 was conveyed across variations in the teaching styles used by the law professors we observed, focusing now on the diversity of discursive formats found in these classrooms. The chapter concludes with a programmatic outline of the peculiarly legal approach to texts and human conflict conveyed to all of the law students in the study, across these divergences.

## Different Forms: Lectures, Modified Socratic Exchanges, and Classroom Conversations

*Transcript 5.1 [6/24/16]*[1]

Prof.:   *[ . . . ]* Why is this far more than ( ) ad and actually an offer, Daniel?

Daniel:  Due to the specific language that the ad was in, uh, for example, the promise is very definite, a hundred pounds reward will be paid by the Carbolic Smoke Ball Company--

Prof.:                                              --And we're even depositing that money in a certain account right now.

Daniel:  I was just getting to that.

Prof.:   I'm sorry? Oh, I'm sorry.[2]

Class:   [[laughter]]

*Transcript 5.2 [3/3/5]*

Prof.:  By the breach of contract. Okay. The plaintiff rented this land to the uh
        defendants in exchange for money, all right? And, in addition to getting
        one hundred thousand dollars or whatever it was he got, re-leasing the
        land, he also asked for the land to be returned to the uniform grade, okay?
        So the first argument- and that the um plaintiff, or the court really relies
        on behalf of the plaintiff um, is- it's not the first one, it's actually the
        second one on page eleven, um- and this is the one I assume you're
        referring to, paragraph number two, second full paragraph on page eleven,
        um, the law aims to give the disappointed promisee what he was promised,
        and then the court wanders into a discussion of a- of a case, but that
        argument is an argument that we saw in *Hawkins* and *Sullivan v.
        O'Connor*, namely a claim that the purpose of contract damages is what?
        All together now?

Class:  Com // pensation //

Prof.:       // Compensation, comp // ensation. The purpose of contract
        damages is compensation. Now, that statement is going to turn out to be
        the most problematic issue of the evening. The purpose of contract
        damages is compensation. And so the plaintiff says, "I want my expecta-
        tion compensated. I thought I was gonna get a uniform grade for my land,
        how can I get that if you don't give me the money I need? So if you're
        really going to compensate me for breaching the contract, you didn't do
        the grading; I can't get the grading done unless you give me the money for
        it." The purpose of contract damages is compensation, so he again relies
        on the purpose of contract damages, which is to compensate, right? But
        there's another additional argument that is made a part of the general
        claim of compensation [ . . . ]

As these excerpts indicate, a tightly controlled Socratic style of turn-taking
is by no means the only form of discourse found in the classrooms of this study.
In Transcript 5.1, we hear a professor apologizing to a student for interrupting
him; in Transcript 5.2 the professor invites the class as a whole to chime in mid-
way through a lengthy monologue about the purpose of contract damages. Even
in more Socratic classrooms, it is not uncommon for the professor to break into
this kind of mini-lecture, taking off from a particular point to explain an issue at
some length to the class. There was a wide range of variation among the eight
classes in the degree to which professors used lecture, focused Socratic dialogue,
and more diffuse styles of discursive interaction with the class. In this section we
explore these differences in terms of an underlying similarity: despite stylistic
differences, we can find across all of these classrooms the same fundamental
approach to text, reading, and authority that is so clearly delineated in Socratic
teaching. In Chapter 7, we will focus more on dissimilarity, exploring these divergent teaching styles in terms of the differing patterns of student engagement
and participation that appear across the classrooms of the study. But here we focus
on a shared message to students found across all of these otherwise differing
classes.

Saving a more detailed description of the variations in teacher style for Chapter 7, here it will suffice to note that three different, broadly defined styles of teaching are discernible in the classes of this study. First, one professor (Class #7) used largely lecture. He spoke 95% of the time and spent 91% of the time in monologue, or lecture. This is in marked contrast with all of the other professors of the study, who spent more time in dialogue with the students and far less time lecturing. This was the class in which the professor exercised the most control over the classroom talk. Next in line along the spectrum of professorial control were the classes in which professors utilized some Socratic dialogue. None of the classes conformed as strictly to the Socratic style of teaching as did the classroom from the pilot study, analyzed in Chapter 4. However, a number of teachers used what could be called a modified form of Socratic teaching, in which there was a relatively high proportion of dialogue focused on one person (focused dialogue). These professors spent between 45% and 60% of class discussion in focused dialogue with individual students. These classes are also identifiable as Socratic in terms of qualitative features of the professor-student exchanges. Finally, we can identify classes in which there was a higher percentage of shorter professor-student exchanges (nonfocused dialogue), with professors spending only between 21% and 29% of the time in the more extended focused dialogue exchanges. In the subsections that follow, we will see how a similar message about legal readings is imparted despite these differences in teaching styles.

### Lectures on Legal Texts, Doctrines, and Authority

We begin with a class in which a lecture format predominated (Class #7). Recall that this professor's turns constituted 95% of the total class time, and that 91% of his time speaking was spent in monologue, or lecture.

*Transcript 5.3 [7/3/11–12]*

Prof.:    *[First portion of 10.45 turn omitted]* For thirty-seven years with Mrs. Feinberg () *[a case discussed in class previously]*, there is no case, that's a gratuitous promise. There is no way to say there's consideration there and make a plausible argument. This one, there's ways to argue it both ways. It seems to- that is part of the process of identification is to recognize what's () and also to recognize what's a close issue. You get a close issue like this and say, "Look, here is competing considerations, I would favor it for the following reasons," and then lay it out. Demonstrate to me that you understand that this is a much closer call, a close question. And that there are an awful lot of areas involved that are close questions. But there are also a lot of changes that are very definitive. So you have to learn to discriminate. Well, okay, what- I think we were still back- we have played with this characterization. I think we have to advance the understanding a little bit further about how we are going to go about, on a case-by-case basis, to distinguish bargained-for exchange from a gratuitous promise subject to a condition. You cannot tell exclusively by the format of the language. This is a tough case, this is a tough determination. Because what's happening, it's stating the condition as he's stating it here. He's asking for her to do something first. "If you do this, I'll do this." That's exchange, that's starting to look like exchange, isn't it? Particularly when he is saying to do something that will come back to benefit him, something that will come back to him. So, in an exchange, you are going to always see that, you are always going to have that type of () be implicit. You do this for me, I'll do this for you. But that language alone does not make it in and of itself a bargained-for exchange, because it could be a situation: "If you do this for me, I will give you this gift." In which case it is a condition to gratuitous transfer. So, it is not the language itself; what we are faced with is a very difficult characterization problem. What it is really coming down to is intent (). What lies behind all of this? Gratuitous intent or bargain intent (). In other words, what must be- in order to constitute consideration, it has to be sought in a bargaining context. It must be returned as part of a bargain. That kind of circular statement, that's what's involved. Now sometimes the context is very obvious. Let me give you a real simple illustration. I tell you, "If you break your leg in the football game this weekend, I'll pay you fifty bucks. If you break your leg in a football game this weekend, I will pay you fifty dollars." Now is that a condition of gratuitous promise, or is that a bargained-for exchange? Um-huh.

Student:    It's a bargained-for exchange.

Prof.:    Yeah, I think this is very obvious. *[Intonation markers indicate a shift to a new hypothetical here]* I (), at least sometimes. I'm not really bargaining for you to go out there and bust your leg on Saturday. Instead, I am saying, "Hey look, if you play hard and you get hurt, I'll (see) you're paid something." But I said, "I'm not going to give you fifty bucks if you don't come out with a broken leg either." I don't think there is much question there that that is a (gratuitous) situation subject to condition. But when I start posing the condition that you have to give something back with some benefit () me, particularly if it is a direct economic benefit, now we start looking at things that are much- and of course I () with the characterization. Now, what we have here is essentially a question of fact. A question of fact. And it is somewhat difficult, but I will introduce the subject for the first time, and within contract formation analysis we can look at it much more extensively. *[Remainder of 5.05 turn omitted]*

In this passage, the professor explains and clarifies a legal principle distinguishing enforceable contractual agreements from gratuitous promises. Along the way, he applies this principle to several specific fact situations, using examples to demonstrate the doctrine. The beginning of the excerpt specifically points to a case previously discussed, involving "thirty-seven years with Mrs. Feinberg." It contrasts the situation in that case (where "there is no way to say there is consideration there and make a plausible argument") with the situation in the case currently being discussed ("this one, there's ways to argue it both ways"). Thus, the passage also involves application of law to the specific facts of several cases and synthesis of these cases in terms of an overarching legal principle. (And indeed, the professor moves on immediately to discuss and apply the facts of the case at hand in more detail.)

In the process of bringing the two cases together, the professor highlights for students the facts on which they must concentrate if they want to use analogies to argue for the validity of the agreement in the case before them. He is also demonstrating how legal principles depend on and develop from factual situations—at the same time as they constrain the telling of new legal stories.

In one sense, this is but a rather marked extension of structures found in other classes of the study. All of the professors at times launch into mini-lectures, especially when clarifying legal points. And though this professor does rely heavily on lecture, he also asks the students questions, and then often incorporates their answers into the ongoing lecture. However, the overall proportion of lecture far exceeds that in other classes, and the professor does a great deal more of the work of discussing all aspects of the cases, from factual exegesis to policy considerations. By calling on the students at particular moments, the professor retains a much attenuated version of the dialogue found in other classes. This, at least to some degree, conveys a sense that this dialogic process is an important part of thinking through and discussing legal texts. However, because he is taking on so much more of the discursive load, the professor will also carry on the dialogue himself, internally to his turns. By asking rhetorical questions ("That's starting to look like exchange, isn't it?" and "What lies behind all of this?"), the professor can retain something of a dialogic structure while limiting actual exchanges with students. Here, as well, there is some continuity with the other classrooms, in which the other professors also frequently ask questions that they answer themselves, albeit within the span of much shorter turns.

Note also that the professor is conveying a number of metalinguistic messages. First, he is instructing the students on how to order their own legal texts (i.e., examination answers) and arguments: they must "demonstrate" to him that they understand when there is a "closer call, a close question." Some fact situations pose no-brainers; in these instances, there is really no credible way to argue two different positions. Understanding when this is the case involves a highly developed sense of which kinds of analogies work in legal settings and which would be considered frivolous. And this entails making metalinguistic judgments about the limits of legal categories, evolving in their ever changing genealogies through lines of cases and of fact patterns.

Second, the professor directs students' attention to forms of reported speech, the talk that forms the basis of contractual agreements. He urges students both to pay attention to the precise wording of agreements made between parties and to look beyond the wording to find aspects of the situation that would indicate intent. In the remaining portion of that turn (not included in the excerpt here), the professor proceeds to spell out still further the metalinguistic rules governing this kind of analysis, noting that the law will not attempt to divine the "subjective intent" of the speaker. Instead, the law will focus on the "reasonable expectations" that could be generated from a particular speech act, on "intent that you measure from the objective manifestations." Embedded in this instruction is a theory of the relationship between language, context, and speaker intent filtered through shared cultural assumptions about which kinds of language, in which contexts might reasonably be interpreted to constitute a bargained-for exchange versus a gratuitous promise.[3] Thus, students' education in the techniques of legal reading contains an abundance of subtle lessons in metalinguistics, always reorienting their gaze away from the more accustomed warrants underlying a standard semantic deciphering of stories, while creating new layers of filtering dictated by legal warrants and texts.

## Modified Socratic Exchanges: Lessons on Authority in Discourse Form and Content

In three of the classrooms of the study, professors spent a considerable percentage of time in the focused dialogue typical of Socratic exchanges (Classes #1, #4, and #5). I would not characterize any of these professors as "strict" Socratic teachers; they spent only between 45% and 60% of the time in this kind of dialogue, and they supplemented the dialogic exchanges with lectures that overtly clarified doctrine, an approach not associated with the classic stereotype of Socratic teaching.[4] Indeed, in two of these three classes, the professors spend 49% and 47% of the time in monologue or lecture, far more than would be found in the archetypical Socratic classroom. In the third classroom (Class #1), which had the highest amount of focused dialogic exchanges (60%), only 17% of the time was spent in lecture. This might lead us to conclude that the professor was conforming closely to a strict Socratic model; however, this class had a much higher amount of nonfocused dialogue (i.e., short exchanges with multiple students) than was found in the other two modified Socratic classes (24% as compared with 5% and 6%, respectively). This higher percentage of nonfocused, more free-ranging dialogic exchange between professor and multiple students is actually more typical of the short-exchange classes, where it occupied from 13% to 46% of class time. However, because there was a substantial amount of focused dialogue in Class #1, I categorize it as a "modified Socratic" classroom.

The bulk of the textual examples used in previous chapters came from either the modified Socratic or the short-exchange classrooms, so that we have already encountered numerous examples of the ways that a shared message about legal texts is imparted across these differently structured classes. Recall that in Transcript 4.5, a modified Socratic form of dialogue was used to focus students' attention on the details (and accompanying background research) needed for a competent statement of facts ("What kind of a mortgage was it?"). In Transcript 4.7 we found the professor conveying the peculiar epistemological status of legal facts through use of modified Socratic exchange (characterized by combined questioning and very brief interspersed lecture-style commentary). Transcript 3.3 demonstrated the use of modified Socratic method to teach the application of law to facts in different cases (at the same time as it demonstrated the integral role of analogizing fact patterns to the development of legal doctrine). Transcript 3.1 provided a wonderful example of the use of dialogue to clarify doctrine. And in Transcript 4.17, we heard a modified Socratic teacher interrupt a student to correct an inapt blurring of generic boundaries in an attempted recitation of facts.[5]

Unlike the lecturer, then, professors in modified Socratic classrooms generally seek to convey their points to a large extent through extended interactions with individual students. During these exchanges, professors push students to move further into case analysis. The dialogue here arguably attempts to mirror a thought process, an idea captured in the popular description of law school education as "learning to think like a lawyer." In Socratic classrooms, this process of thinking like lawyer is taught through dialogic speech in which students are by example encouraged to ask themselves a series of questions about the case and to consider the arguments on both sides in answering those questions. (In Chapter 6 we will consider other ramifications of this dialogic form.)[6] Typically, the most canonical Socratic teachers avoid giving direct answers or summaries, leaving it to the dialogic process and the student's diligence in following it through to do the teaching. This pure form is not common in the transcripts from this study; it is more often the case that professors step back and provide answers, if not immediately, then at the end of a particular case or doctrinal discussion—or as class is concluding. However, we can find some whispers of the canons of strict Socratic teaching at points in the modified Socratic classes.

*Transcript 5.4 [1/4/10]*

| | |
|---|---|
| Prof.: | Well, let's go back to Mr. H. *[Returning to selected Socratic dialogue participant]* What is the good involved in the transaction? |
| Mr. H.: | I would say that it () service. |
| Prof.: | Is there a good in that transaction? Is Article 2 applicable at all? Come on now, I don't want to (). Yes or no. |
| Mr. H.: | No, it's not. |
| Prof.: | Is that a "no" that you believe in, or is that a "no" that you're just wimping out? [[Class laughter]] Are you sure? |
| Mr. H.: | I am sure. I would say that it is "no"-- |
| Prof.: | --No. No good in that transaction. UCC, no. Common law, yes. |
| Student #2: | So they, they're- the UCC presents a point that isn't a good. |
| Prof.: | For you to discern a difference between the two. And to wonder, and be concerned about, lose sleep. That's what this is all about. Okay? *[ . . . ]* |

In this rather elliptical exchange, the professor is focusing on a key distinction in U.S. contract law: whether the contract involved goods or services. Contracts for goods are covered by the Uniform Commercial Code (UCC); contracts for services are not, and must be dealt with under common law rules.[7] Although the professor's question and subsequent comment presuppose that the students understand this distinction, Student #2 seems to be indicating that this is a new insight and attempts to clarify the point. Despite his apparent refusal to respond at the end of this excerpt, the professor has actually already provided the answer to the student's question in a previous turn. Note also that, as in Transcript 4.1 at the beginning of Chapter 4, these comments by the professor at times approach a satiric level, operating at a metalevel to make fun of traditional conceptions surrounding law teaching. (Yet, in each case, there is arguably some double-voicing in which the satiric tone both mocks and subtly invokes the stereotype.)

Through Socratic questioning (but also through departures from traditional Socratic teaching such as mini-lectures and giving answers), teachers in modified Socratic classrooms push students to perform all of the steps required for an adequate legal reading as outlined in Chapter 4. Arguably, there is a slightly more attenuated mirroring relationship here between authoritative classroom talk and a canonical legal reading focused on authority. However, there is still a strong family resemblance in both the structure and content of the message. As we see in Transcript 5.4, professors use negative uptake not only to press for technically correct responses, but also to push students to adopt appropriately authoritative tones of voice. During the substantial amount of class time spent in extended exchanges, they prod students to decipher correctly the authoritative form and content of legal discourse.

## Shorter Law Class Conversations: Authority in Sheep's Clothing

Finally, four of the classrooms of the study spent less time in the classic, extended Socratic dialogues than was found in our modified Socratic classes, and less time in lecture than in Class #7. Instead, these four, less conventional classrooms were characterized by a higher proportion of the shorter, nonfocused professor-student exchanges (Classes #2, #3, #6, and #8). Some of these classes also at times adopted a more relaxed, conversational style of interaction. Of course, this is all relative; there were still major differences between the structure of these classes and ordinary everyday conversation. Turns at talk here were still closely controlled by the professor, and unmediated exchanges among students were a relative rarity. Nonetheless, there was far less focused Socratic dialogue in these classes than in the modified Socratic classrooms (focused exchanges being those involving more extended dialogue with one student, whereas nonfocused exchanges entail only one or two turns with a given student). Interestingly, three of these four classes were taught by women professors (and, indeed, there are only three women professors in the study).[8] In all but one of these four classrooms, the shift away from extended dialogue was accompanied by a marked rise in the time spent on shorter exchanges, with more students speaking for briefer periods of time (from 22% to 46%). In the other school (Class #3), there are still more of the shorter, nonfocused student-professor exchanges than in the modified Socratic classes (13% as compared with 5% and 6% of class time). However, this percentage is substantially lower than is found in the three other short-exchange classes. Instead, there is more time spent in lecturing (63% as compared with 29%, 33%, and 50% in the other short-exchange classes). Thus, this class falls at the less interactive end of the continuum, with some affinities to a lecture format, whereas the other three short-exchange classes involve more overall discursive interaction between professors and students.[9]

Despite these divergences in style, professors in all four of the short-exchange classes teach the same canons of a standard legal reading that we have already identified in other classrooms. Once again, we have encountered numerous examples from these classrooms in previous discussions. Some of these previous transcript excerpts help to underscore the point that all of the teachers in this study at times use lecture as well as Socratic exchanges of one kind or another. Thus, in Transcript 4.4, we heard a professor in one of the short-exchange classes utilize a fairly standard Socratic method of questioning in her effort to clarify a student's statement of the facts (involving the timing of a delivery of wheat). This was also true in Transcript 4.6, where the same professor interrupted a student who began her turn by describing the plaintiff as a "youthful man" rather than using a legal frame. In both cases, the professor called on a student to explicate the case assigned for the day and continued in dialogue with that student for some time, in an exercise designed to sharpen the students' understanding of fact construction in legal narratives. Transcript 4.8 showed us a short-exchange professor pushing a student to apply law to facts (asking him to select which facts constituted consideration), and in Transcripts 4.10, 4.11, and 4.12 professors from these kinds of classes work with students to develop skills in analogical reasoning. Transcript 4.14 used an exchange from a short-exchange classroom to exemplify the process by which professors clarify law (here, the doctrine of specific performance), and here we see how a similar pedagogical message to that conveyed in formal, more Socratic classrooms can be delivered in a more informal kind of exchange. (In Transcript 4.14, the student began a request for clarification by saying "Wait a minute," the class interrupted with multiple speakers talking at once, and a second student chimed in to approve the first student's answer, a privilege usually reserved for the professor in more formal classrooms.) Interestingly, students were still using a vigorous turn-taking structure to clarify aspects of a legal reading focused on authoritative case law language and the practice by which it can be de- and recontextualized.[10]

Thus, when nonfocused exchanges are doing much of the work in a class, the same core pedagogical message is conveyed in a somewhat different form. With lectures, professors do much of the discursive work, whereas in focused dialogues individual students must stay in the spotlight for extended periods of time, laboriously uncovering the legal story as they respond to question after question. In nonfocused exchanges, multiple students may chime in to help one another and the professor in constructing an acceptable legal narrative, adopting a more conversational style. The same rules for reading apply, but they are learned in a somewhat different form.

*Transcript 5.5 [6/6/23]*

Prof.:      What do- what constituted the promise, that's a very good question? What was the promise? Where do you get it from the materials? I think it's pretty clear. You've got her saying, "He promised I'd be beautiful" and you've got him saying, "I didn't promise anything." Fill that out a bit more and tell me how you can come to the conclusion that he- she wins in terms of he did promise her a beautiful nose?

Student #1:  Well, he promised her something in two surgeries. I mean, um, he was specific enough to say it's gonna take two surgeries to do this, whatever it is, and considering that he's a plastic surgeon and she's in the entertainment business and that she went to him because she wanted to look more beautiful, I think, it's- it can be (but) implied that in two surgeries, "I'm going to give you a beautiful nose."

Prof.: You think that from what you've read of the record and what you know of the case, that the transaction between them was one in which he promised her to improve her appearance. She wouldn't have undergone the surgery had he not made that promise?

Student #1: Mmmhmm.

Student #2: Under that theory, though, anybody could sue any plastic surgeon under, under an implied promise because if you imply that I'm going to the plastic surgeon to be- to become more beautiful, if that doesn't happen then I would have grounds to sue then.

Prof.: Well, one- one way that, that doesn't happen is the physician is just really // exceptionally //

Student #2:          // right // clear in having you sign I didn't-wasn't promised any particular results. But [ . . . ] Why do you have the clear proof here?

Student #3: Because of the picture he said was stolen.

Prof.: That was helpful?

Student #4: I thought it was the fact that you had two surgeries. If there was just one--

Prof.:          --apparent- well, it's questionable as to whether they said in the first place she was supposed to have // two; // I think, that the testimony is conflicting on that, she ended up having three.

Student #4:                              //Okay//

Student #5: I think, she looked at the analysis they have under the remedy for the breach of contract. [Rest of .23 turn omitted]

Here the professor is teaching the students to identify the particular facts that are legally relevant to the question of how to define the actual promise underlying the contract in this case. This line of questioning prompts the professor, at a later point in the exchange, to take the students back to the jury deliberations, reminding them that the facts as accepted by the appeals court are those approved by the jury below. In Transcript 4.7, we saw this identical point made through a combination of focused dialogue and mini-lecture by the professor. Thus we see, over and over throughout these transcripts, identical lessons taught through varying pedagogical means. The same set of tools—from recitation of facts through policy discussion—are imparted in every class, with the same metalinguistic message attached regarding the centrality of legal-textual authority. And note that although here we have primarily focused on the discursive differences among the classrooms, we also are repeatedly reminded of considerable continuities. All employ some form of dialogue, all use lectures for clarification, and there is a similar deployment of question-answer sequences in deciphering texts, whether internal to a professor's turn, or between professor and one designated Socratic partner, or among professor and students with several interlocutors chiming in. Socratic dialogue may provide a more precise mirroring of the message in discursive form (i.e., it has simultaneous iconic and indexical features), but the message is imparted in all of these classes, and often with some echoes of this Socratic mirroring of pedagogical message in discursive form.[11]

## Summary

A shared message about legal reading is conveyed across diverse classrooms, professors, and teaching methods. This is not surprising, for the students are being trained to a common language: a new kind of reading, writing, and talking. The tales of conflict that they might have read for plot, character, and moral are now being dissected using new metalinguistic rules. In Chapters 4 and 5, I have delineated the core structure and features of this new legal reading, concentrating on the reading of cases across diverse classrooms.

In Chapter 4, we learned that professors reorient students' gaze to the pragmatic warrants that give legal texts authority. These warrants involve several kinds of legal-textual lineages: the line of previous cases and other legal texts that a court (or lawyers, or law students) can cite as authorities in deciding the case at hand, and the procedural lineage of the case, traceable through opinions of lower courts, the record in the case, and so forth. This new focus on pragmatic warrants is perhaps most visible in the strict Socratic classroom, where the new structure of reading is mirrored in the structure of classroom discourse.

However, the refocusing occurs in other kinds of classrooms as well. Even in the classroom most heavily dominated by lecture, there are vestiges of a Socratic teaching style, for example, the use of some dialogic structuring to convey the logic of this new reading. This can occur either between professor and student or internally within the professor's own turns, as he poses himself questions and answers them. There is obviously nonetheless a vast difference in style between this class and canonical Socratic method teaching. Yet despite this divergence, we find an identical message conveyed about the structure of legal reading.[12]

That structure relies on constant filtering of conflict stories through the lens of legal-textual authority. We have now explored the fundamental aspects of this kind of filtering. First, courts look to lines of precedent that provide legal genealogies for the case before them, accepting or rejecting analogies to similar facts in previous cases. An intricate set of metalinguistic understandings governs the process of building analogies. As we've noted, courts also parse other kinds of relevant legal texts: statutes, constitutions, administrative regulations, uniform codes (such as the UCC), Restatements, and so forth. Second, courts consider the ways that legal procedure, inscribed in legal documents, circumscribes which facts to accept, which legal issues to address, and what kinds of conclusions can be reached. The transition to a new legal reading pulls students away from referentialist approaches, which treat the text as transparent and view its core meaning as its referential content. Instead, here the text is understood as a repository of power, whose core meaning centers on legal-textual authority.

We have also taken a closer look at aspects of the metalinguistic filter through which legal-textual authority is deciphered and constrained. These aspects are taught in every classroom of the study. Students learn that the very construction of the facts on which legal conflict stories are based involves legal filters: only certain details will turn out to be legally accepted or relevant, and the determination of which details depends on the complex calculus of textual constraints and metalinguistic warrants described earlier. The ability to decree the legal construction of reality through delineation of facts gives legal language enormous, but essentially invisible, power over social generalities. (And this power is expanded further through the semiotics of policy discussions.) Legal categories are explicitly matched with particular facts, so that students learn how to make a successful fit. When courts make this match, new law is constantly being formed; thus, law both emanates from and creates fact patterns. Professors also explicitly enunciate—or bring students to enunciate—the backbone structure of legal principles shaping the use of facts. In addition, professors point out the effects of legal procedure on both fact construction and the development or application of law. Throughout, and across a fascinating diversity of pedagogical styles, professors are conveying a linguistic ideology centered on the crucial structuring role of layers of authority, discernable in the text. Emotion, morality, and social context are semiotically peripheralized in this process. At the same time, professors occasionally open up a wide panorama of social and moral and personal stories that could arguably be relevant to legal decisions at the fringes of the core legal reading. The lack of careful analysis and substantiation in these wide-ranging discussions only furthers the sense of legal power over social life. Although professors carefully marked boundaries between the different aspects of legal texts, they also at times encouraged boundary crossing. When and how to blur boundaries among these components of a legal reading itself becomes part of learning to read legal texts.

We have also specifically focused on the ways these facets of a legal reading could be conveyed via quite different pedagogical means, from more heavily lecture-oriented classrooms, through quasi-Socratic teaching, through classroom discussion organized around shorter exchanges. Despite this diversity in form, we saw that an identical set of strictures regarding reading legal texts is emphasized in all classes. These strictures focus attention on pragmatic warrants while peripheralizing or erasing "extraneous" contexts such as social-historical settings, emotions, and moral considerations. The result is a language that appears to be able to effect a nearly universal translation of events, people, and actions into a common language. This process renders disparate material equivalent or commensurable, but through the narrowed gaze of legal-textual warrants.

Thus, a core feature of U.S. legal epistemology, vividly visible in law school classrooms, is the new relationship created for legal readers with language and text. We know things because this legal text says so, and we can only accept certain things as important under this textual proof, while rejecting others. The overall linguistic framework naturalizes and conceals any social, cultural, political, or ideological skewing, hiding these kinds of influences behind the complex veil of intertextual layerings. Susan Philips has analyzed the political implications of a hidden "intertextual gap" between spoken and written law, demonstrating the ways this creates a functionally invisible opening for political maneuvering in courts.[13] In this chapter we have seen how the same legal text could be read with different meanings, creating an open texture that in some ways belies the semblance of precision and certainty given by other aspects of legal reading. This core aspect of legal metalinguistic framing contributes to the possibility of what Philips calls "ideological polysemy": "I argue that the discourse has multiple meanings at the same time but that these meanings differ in the degree of consciousness with which the judges as speakers recognize or acknowledge them."[14] We have seen that the fundamental metalinguistic principles guiding legal readings and orientations to language have built into them both a receptivity to ideological polysemy and a mechanism for concealing this phenomenon when it occurs. This structure permits social power to affect legal discourse in more or less covert ways. Having examined the structure of legal conflict stories and readings thereof, ringed around with layers of legal-textual authority, we turn now to ask about the legal landscapes and personae created by a distinctively legal form of reading and creating texts.

# 6

## On Becoming a Legal Person: Identity and the Social Context of Legal Epistemology

In the previous chapter, we saw that a distinctive approach to reading written legal texts is inculcated in law school classrooms. *Reading* like a lawyer turns out to be an essential ingredient in the transformation to *thinking* like a lawyer. And, of course, the way that professors determine whether students are learning to read like lawyers throughout the semester is by assessing how they *talk* about legal texts. In this chapter we move further into an analysis of the transformative process in first-year law school classrooms, turning now to ask about the contours of the legal personae revealed in talk about legal texts and about the spaces these people inhabit. In other words, what kind of people are revealed and created through legal readings—not only the people in the texts, but also the speakers in the classrooms? And what are the points of reference, the landscapes, within which they operate? We will find that as students shift to thinking like lawyers, they at times speak from an analytical distance, while at other times they actually stand in the shoes of new, legal personae. As students and professors speak from these positions, we can discern the outlines of a distinctively legal drama, with its own characters and settings made real as they are discussed and enacted in law school settings. In this chapter, we focus more carefully on metalinguistic features such as reported speech, footing, framing, role-play, deixis, and pronominal usage to understand this process in detail.

Using this approach, I delineate a somewhat different, more complicated understanding of the law school process than is usually indicated by those who characterize it as learning to think like a lawyer.[1] Although I will not constantly use quotation marks to mark this particular framing of the concept "thinking like a lawyer," I would ask that this more complex understanding of the phrase be assumed wherever it appears in my text. First, this has long been an established catchphrase used by the

97

legal profession (and those studying or writing about it) to describe the essence of law school training.[2] It represents, in a sense, a distillation of indigenous ideology, a summary of how the process is viewed from within.[3] However, to unpack or analyze this ideology, we find that we have to understand more than a mere acontextual outline of cognitive processes. Instead, we must examine what it means to read or talk like a lawyer, and this means that we are analyzing metalinguistic norms and ideologies: we are looking at a new relationship with language that is created for lawyers. As I have already argued, embedded in this new relationship is a hidden epistemology, one with significant moral dimensions.

Numerous writers have commented on the ways that thinking like a lawyer pulls law students away from altruistic, public interest goals.[4] Robert Granfield's study of legal education characterizes this change as a shift from a "justice-oriented consciousness" to a "game-oriented consciousness."[5] Being able to argue either side of a case or to concoct a legal argument by "testing facts against . . . legal doctrine" replaces concerns with substantive justice.[6] But it is through the filter of legal language, written and spoken—as well as of metalinguistic structuring and ideology[7]— that this change is effected. The change definitely includes these shifts to more strategic, adversarial, and doctrinal approaches, but it is even more profound: it alters how stories are constructed and read, which contexts are salient, how people are categorized and conceived, how selves are constructed. In sum, there are entirely new views of reality and authority, new landmarks and ways of speaking, altered conceptions of themselves and others (and their relations to the world around them) packed quietly into the reading lessons students encounter in the first-year law school curriculum.

Metalinguistic structuring is performing powerful work here, carrying with it tacit (and not so tacit) linguistic ideologies, not the least of which is a strong, almost isomorphic relationship implied between how people talk and how they think. And so my conscious bracketing of the phrase "thinking like a lawyer" not only indicates that it is a well-worn indigenous saying or adage, but that the saying itself glosses over the degree to which what is changing is as much how students read and talk as how they think. Indeed, language operates as more than a filter here; it not only mediates the shift in students' perceptions, it is the stuff of which the change is made, the backbone of the new legal approach they must learn if they are to be fluent in the law.[8] When legally trained professionals speak of this alteration as a sharpening of thought, they are often implying that it involves a honing of general analytic ability rather than a shift into a very particular, culturally laden *kind* of thinking and talking. This *kind* of approach may indeed be more demanding than others as to some parts of the problem put before attorneys, but, as we are seeing, it is most certainly less demanding as to other parts. The phrase "thinking like a lawyer" is often used in a way that naturalizes this process, characterizing lawyers as possessors of an overarching and superior analytic ability rather than as experts in one profession's specialized way of processing relevant information. Like all professional epistemologies (and accompanying discourses), legal thought is socially and institutionally grounded in specific practices and power relationships. It asks some kinds of questions while neglecting others and makes sharp demands for proof in some places where elsewhere it accepts unproven assumptions. The first-year classroom is a key location for examining the shift to this particular pro-fessional language.

This study provides an anatomy of that change in law students' relationship with language, demonstrating that it is in the minute linguistic details that we can locate both a profound moral shift and the cover-up that often conceals this shift from view.

## Legal Personae

We have seen that law professors systematically focus their students' attention on layers of textual and legal authority when deciphering the conflict stories at the heart of legal cases. But what happens to the people in these stories? What aspects of their identities and lives remain important when refracted through this legal lens? We can ask as well: What aspects of the law students' and professors' lives and experiences are considered to be salient during the conversation?

As a legal reading tightens students' gaze on certain specific facts of each case, it focuses their attention on certain people, and on particular aspects of those people and their lives. When beginning their training, law students may attempt to discuss the people who appear in legal texts using different, lay conventions. For example, one might expect to introduce a person in the story by describing his appearance (Transcript 4.6) or general character. Some, especially those with social science backgrounds, might wonder about aspects of social context such as race, class, or gender. Or, drawn by the moral dimensions of the conflicts discussed in legal cases, students might want to begin by asking about what is fair, raising ethical issues about the people and their situations (see Chapter 1, pp. 9–10). How-ever, as we have seen, law professors insistently return their students' attention to the framework given by legal categories. They do so for obvious reasons: they are teaching first-year students a distinctive approach to language and reading. Only certain facts are relevant to this reading. If students fail to grasp this, they will not be able to write legal briefs, read legal opinions, or successfully shape legal argu-ments in court. If professors fail to convey this, they are in essence committing a form of pedagogical malpractice. The problem is that as students are drawn into this new discursive practice, they are drawn away from the norms and conventions that many members of our society, including future clients, use to solve conflicts and moral dilemmas. The seeds of citizens' dissatisfaction with the law, of clients' dissatisfaction with courts and lawyers, are sown already; already we can begin to understand the schism that divides a distraught divorce client, who is pouring out what she deems to be crucial emotional details, from her impatient attorney, seek-ing to shut down the stream of time-wasting, irrelevant material.[9]

### Individual Strategists, Economic Optimizers, and Standard Average Farmers: "Character"izing Legal People

How, then, do professors "character"ize the people we find in the legal landscapes of first-year Contracts classes? There is obviously a double meaning involved here.

On the one hand, professors attribute particular qualities to these people, thus "characterizing" them in quite specific ways. At the same time, these people actually become "characters" in narrated stories, legal personae who speak to us through reported speech. In this process, they are stripped of some of the characteristics that they themselves might deem important to their personalities and selves and are objectified in a process that highlights features important to their construction as actors in a legal drama, as characters in legal stories.

We can identify from the study data at least three kinds of influence that the norms surrounding legal readings exert on the conceptualization of legal personae. First, a core trope organizing legal readings is that of argument, particularly where the case law genre is concerned. When they write legal texts or opinions, judges are deciding which of two competing sides and arguments has won, and in doing so are presenting arguments of their own. When professors discuss the people who appear in legal narratives, they frequently present them in terms of the arguments they must make, could make, are making, and so on, whether the people are parties involved in the case, attorneys, or judges. Notice that in the process, legal narratives convert people into speaking subjects whose primary identity is defined by their location in an argument (plaintiff, defendant, appellee, appellant, party, plaintiff's attorney, judge, public defender, prosecutor, drafter, etc.). With this focus comes a concomitant, often tacit characterization of people as strategists: as organized around a strategic calculus regarding which arguments or actions will put them in the best position to win. Thus, professors will often invite students to speculate about what a particular person must have been thinking when she drafted the contract using certain words, or when he behaved in a particular way. They also initiate the students themselves into these identities, inviting them to take the positions of different parties or to make strategic arguments. Through role-play and hypotheticals, students themselves become people defined primarily by their ability to argue and strategize.

These two influences of a distinctive legal reading on conceptualizations of the person would hold true regardless of which kind of subject matter or doctrine was under discussion. However, there is a third kind of influence that is likely to take different forms depending on areas of law (i.e., depending on whether we are dealing with contracts, criminal law, torts, etc.): the definition of people in terms of doctrinal requirements. In Contracts class, we are focused on economic transactions that lie at the heart of capitalist exchange, and thus, arguably, at a very interesting nexus of law and social structure. That the people who emerge from the texts of contracts cases are characterized as economic maximizers, or in terms of their occupational status or worldly belongings, is hardly surprising. On the one hand, the language of economics has gradually infiltrated many other areas of law, moving beyond cases dealing with strictly economic transactions to use an "economic maximizer" calculus when analyzing family relationships and other interactions formerly thought to center on noneconomic principles. This move has, obviously, been the subject of a great deal of debate. Anthropologists might argue that it is not at all surprising; just as a capitalist calculus has managed to work its way increasingly into domains once considered relatively more autonomous from the economic system, so an economic logic is (in ever more overt ways) colonizing areas of law once deemed independent.

The wildly successful introduction of economics into law school teaching overall may well mean that what we observe in the Contracts classroom will be generalizable to other classes. However, it is important to note that we can expect somewhat different nuances to appear depending on the central features of pertinent doctrinal developments. In Criminal Law classes, for example, students will have to learn what features of an individual's behavior might suffice as evidence that crimes were committed intentionally, or in the heat of passion, and so forth. In Family Law, students will begin to untangle the unwieldy mess surrounding legal attempts to discern the "best interests" of a child. In all of these cases, what is important about people is dictated by legal doctrine, as deciphered through a genealogy of analogies. Each area of law will pose its own dilemmas for students, requiring them to separate some things that might otherwise be assumed to be linked in standard cultural accounts (someone's prior behavior, perhaps, from one's assessment of how he acted in this particular instance).

I want to stress again that this is a double-edged process: the very same legal norms that may strip a story of arguably important social context may also require that we set aside biases against people based on background or past behavior that should not be part of the judgment in a particular instance. But in either case, students must prioritize doctrinal definitions of the person, setting aside other kinds of information and approaches. As we will see, some kinds of cultural information will be let in, in somewhat sneaky fashion, through the analogical process of doctrinal definition; others will not. Not surprisingly, it will be easier for the cultural assumptions of the dominant group in society to make their way into a legal calculus than it will be for other viewpoints. Nonetheless, to avoid any overly simplistic mischaracterization of the process of legal reading being taught, it is important to note that there is still an open texture to this reading that allows competing information to enter at times, and yet also a rigidity to the frame that can discourage some forms of open prejudice. At the same time, the effects of other forms of covert social prejudice and power are disguised through a focus on layered legal-linguistic frames.

## PEOPLE WHO ARGUE AND STRATEGIZE: REPORTED SPEECH, FOOTING, AND FRAMES

We begin with the first two approaches to delineating legal personae, those that cross doctrines and areas of law. These approaches define people's central identities in terms of their roles as sources of argument and strategy. One of the most ubiquitous characterizations of the people occupying the legal landscapes discussed in law school classrooms involves their capacity to make arguments and to strategize. The parties, or people, whose disputes are described in the cases, the lawyers who bring the cases, the judges deciding the cases, and the students discussing the cases all share this central characteristic. They may make better or worse arguments, may strategize with more or less acumen, but these activities are central to who they are in legal narratives. Predictably, one common method of focusing students' attention on the centrality of strategic argument is to invite them to occupy the roles of attorneys, judges, and parties—to make these characters' arguments for them. We will return to this aspect of characterization later, in the discussions of role-playing and legal landscapes.

Not coincidentally, given the centrality of argument to defining legal personae, we also find that reported or quoted speech is a tool used ubiquitously by professors in their characterizations. The speech being quoted is frequently fictional or imputed, and may be either talk that would have been spoken out loud, or alternatively, can be talk that is uttered internally, to oneself. The following example is typical:

*Transcript 6.1 [4/32/14–15]*

Prof.:    [ . . . ] But of course it does put Ever-Tite Roofing in an excellent situation. They draft the terms of the offer and they decide whether to accept it or not, you know. They're like, "You want a deal? Sure. Maybe not." They- they're playing both sides. Now, um, how long after the offer is given from the Greens to Ever-Tite Roofing, uh, do we get the commencement of performance in the case? I think it's nine days, right?

Mr. M.:   Right.

Prof.:    Then nine days later, Ever-Tite Roofing packs up the truck and heads for the Greens. But what happens when they get there?

Ms. L.:   Someone else is there ().

Prof.:    Someone else is already on the job. Okay? The Greens' arguments are really two, it seems to me. One: "Our offer expired. It lapsed. There's nothing out there to accept anymore. You waited too long." The court doesn't buy that one. Uh, two: "The offer's still valid, but you haven't accepted yet." That second argument, Ms. L., was really an argument about what that phrase means in the offer, "commencement of performance," isn't it? According to the Greens, what would commencement of performance have been?

Ms. L.:   Um, well, after showing up at the house, saying, "Okay, you can start" --

Prof.:    --and actually nailing some nails, you know, or pulling out some asbestos. Right? Actually commencing the roof. What they did looks an awful lot like what the carpenter, builder, did in the *White* case, *White against Corlies*. The owner in this case, the Greens, would certainly argue that's true. They argue that there's been no commencement of performance. But the court doesn't agree with that, right? The court construes commencement of performance as including loading up the truck with the material and heading out there. Okay? [ . . . ]

Notice that in this excerpt, both professor and student put words in the mouths of the characters in the story. The professor first discusses Ever-Tite Roofing's role as drafter, or author, of key terms in this contract. Thus, Ever-Tite already occupies one crucial linguistically defined place: it is the producer of written language that has a great deal of legal salience. The professor then presents this corporate protagonist's thinking, explaining that it is "playing both sides," and represents this strategic thinking in terms of reported speech: "They're like, 'You want a deal? Sure. Maybe not.'" Ever-Tite's ability to occupy two powerful discursive spaces—

drafter and "accepter"—with an accompanying power to choose whichever out-come it wants (deal/contract or no deal/no contract), is dramatized through this imagined reported locution. It does not appear to matter that this is a company rather than a person; legal personae are most importantly interlocutors occupying various positions in a legally defined discursive interaction. When characterized in this way, corporations become exchangeable with human beings, for both are capable of speaking in the legal argument that is under way. Ever-Tite emerges, then, as a character in the story who can speak, whose speech reveals the domi-nance of strategic thinking, and whose position vis-à-vis written and spoken lan-guage gave it a good location from which to strategize.

Immediately switching sides, the professor proceeds to consider the thoughts of the people on the other side of this conflict, the Greens: "The Greens' arguments are really two, it seems to me. One: 'Our offer expired. It lapsed. There's nothing out there to accept anymore. You waited too long.' The court doesn't buy that one. Uh, two: 'The offer's still valid, but you haven't accepted yet.'" Just as in the folk ideology that equates legal education with learning to think like a lawyer, thought and speech are here vividly intertwined, and thought is transparently enacted in dialogic speech. This structure allows the professor to speak in the voices of the Greens, imaginatively enacting now the opposite side of the conflict-laden dialogue that he began in a previous turn. The student in this exchange (which occurs in mid-November, after several months of classes) adopts a similar discursive strat-egy: "Um, well, after showing up at the house, saying, 'Okay, you can start.'" We see that the student, as she imbibes the guidelines for making legal arguments, is also adopting this feature of the form used by her professor; instead of simply de-scribing what might have counted as commencement of performance (which in this particular instance would probably have been the preferable response), she attempts to enact it through reported speech.

On the one hand, direct quotation gives the semblance of reproducing speech verbatim, as it actually occurred. A direct quotation purports to repeat an utter-ance precisely as it would have been uttered, using the same verb tense, pronouns, and other spatiotemporal (or, more technically, "deictic") markers. Compare a direct quotation, "She said, 'I'm leaving now,'" with the equivalent indirect quo-tation, "She said that she was leaving then." In the indirect quotation, the speaker changes the tense from present to past, the pronoun from "I" to "she," and the temporal adverb "now" to "then." Linguistic scholars such as Bakhtin have ana-lyzed this difference in terms of the relative penetration of the reporting speaker's speech framework into the reported speech.[10] It is certainly the case that the shift to direct quotation carries with it a metalinguistic signal: the very maintenance of tense, pronouns, and other deictics seems to tell the listener that the reported speech is being reproduced precisely as it was spoken. This is obviously a more vivid ren-dition, more dramatic and immediate, bringing the speaker and hearer imagina-tively into the reported context itself. Conversely, the shifting of these same features in indirect quotation overtly reminds the listener that this piece of speech is being reported by someone who is not the same person (shift in pronoun), not speaking at the same time (shift of verb tense and adverb), and perhaps not standing in the same place (e.g., if there is a shift of spatial deictics).

However, as a number of scholars have noted, it is also possible for the reporting speaker to infiltrate the reported speech even using direct quotation.[11] When this is achieved the process is arguably somewhat covert, because the overt metapragmatic signal that accompanies direct quotation does not alert us to this process of infiltration. As Greg Matoesian has noted in his analysis of discourse in rape trials, use of direct quotation is a powerful and complicated tool in creating changes of discursive frame and footing:

> Although direct quotes purport to represent an exact wording of speech, they function more accurately as a way of constructing drama in talk, as a method of marking the speaker's emotional involvement with an issue, and as an evidential device for gauging, or better still constructing, the authenticity of the statement. . . . Thus, they index the reporting speaker's footing and moral agenda through stylistic variation in talk, while appearing to maintain a strict separation between quoting voice and quoted utterance.[12]

As we have seen, the way reported speech functions to construct "drama in talk" is quite evident in law school teaching, where frequently the quoted speech is clearly fictional. In these cases, the direct quotation obviously functions as a vivid device for representing general arguments, thoughts, or positions rather than as a purportedly accurate rendition of actually occurring speech.

Matoesian draws on work by Erving Goffman, which examines the different kinds of footing that a person may occupy in any given segment of speech.[13] For example, Goffman distinguishes among a number of distinct positions occupied by producers of language: the person doing the actual speaking is the "animator," the person who composed the words spoken is the "author," the person ultimately responsible for the position expressed by the utterance is the "principal." This concept of footing permits us to analyze the way speech contains signals about speakers' positions, relationships, and social power. Goffman refers to a shift in footing as "a change in our frame for events."[14]

What, then, can we make of the way direct quotation is used in law school classes? In Transcript 6.1 above, we could view both professor and student as occupying the footing of mere animators; that is, by using direct quotation, they give the semblance of merely speaking the words that were actually authored by characters in the story.[15] However, it is also relatively clear that both professor and student are putting words into these characters' mouths, and thus are in fact authors as well as animators. On the other hand, this authorship is hidden (albeit thinly) by the metalinguistic signals that accompany direct quotation. As we have seen, direct quotation retains the deictic markers of an original speech setting: of a reported speech setting that is distinct from the current, reporting context. There are a number of subtle ideological messages conveyed by the ubiquitous use of this kind of fictionalized reported speech in law school classrooms:

   (1) First, the effortless elision of animator and author footings through the use of reported speech in this setting conveys a subtle message about the power of legal discourse to put words in people's mouths—indeed, to literally create reality through discourse. As we saw in previous chapters, the rendition of events as facts in legal narratives actually creates an authoritative ac-

count of truth (under the terms of the discursive system's own ideology). In the law school classroom, use of imagined direct quotation has already begun to loosen the anchoring of reported speech from its original speaker and context, substituting instead the primacy of legally relevant strategic renditions in this kind of translation of events.[16] In developing the background characterizations of the personae who make legal arguments, it is strategic reasoning (which locates them in terms of those arguments) that becomes most important. The process of figuring this all out involves proceeding as if these strategic considerations were already part of the characters' internal or external dialogue as events unfolded. In unpacking the legal story, professors in essence move their characters around in a strategic landscape, trying them out (and allowing them to speak) in this location or that to see how their different positionings might affect the shape of the arguments they can make.

Interestingly, this free attribution of fictionalized locutions to characters in the story exists side by side with a demand for great precision about what was actually said, for certain purposes. As Matoesian has pointed out, precise repetition of previous utterances is highly valued as a means of impeaching witnesses who produce "inconsistent" renditions of the same events.[17] Similarly, in law school classrooms, professors will at times insist that students reproduce with precision aspects of written or spoken language that are legally crucial (e.g., to establish whether there was "acceptance" of a contract). As noted in Chapter 4, a hallmark of legal readings is this combination of blurred and precise boundaries, of obsessive attention to detail and yet also a permission to generalize freely without any substantiation about some matters. Here we find another such combination, bewildering to the layperson but entirely explicable within the bounds of legal epistemology: if the precise wording of a document or utterance is doctrinally important, then a proficient legal reader will be careful to focus on the exact phrasing involved. However, if we are developing a legal characterization of the players in the story, moving them about to locate them strategically and in terms of possible arguments they might make, we can freely imagine what they might have said. After all, it is precisely what strategies and arguments they can or might have developed that centrally define them as characters in this story. (And it is the attorney's job to figure this out and put the appropriate words in the characters' mouths.)

(2) When they employ direct quotation, law professors are also presenting the case through other people's voices, just as attorneys do in court (albeit with a somewhat different linguistic apparatus). In court, the process by which an authoritative version of the facts is created involves presentation of competing stories through the utterances of witnesses. Attorneys attempt to shape these utterances, selecting particular witnesses and rehearsing them in an effort to present the story that is most favorable to their side.[18] Although the witnesses often give the appearance of being both authors and animators of the stories they tell, the attorneys in fact share the author role, not only through coaching witnesses, but because they actually coproduce the narrative as they elicit testimony from witnesses through questioning. However, notice that this

coproduction is somewhat covert, because overt metalinguistic signaling frequently points to the witness as the main author of the narrative; the attorney's questions often appear as mere prompts and the answers as the "real" narrative. (This is obviously much more the case with well-prepared direct examinations of friendly witnesses than with overtly hostile cross-examination of the opposing side's witnesses.) Just as with professors' use of direct quotation, lawyers' authorship is at times hidden behind a thin metalinguistic veneer. In court, the witnesses produce their own direct locutions, which the attorney may then repeat as direct quotations in subsequent questions, a process that conceals the role the attorney played in producing the witnesses' utterance in the first place. Thus, there is a quiet linguistic ideology that emerges from deployment of direct quotation, one that foregrounds an inauthentic authorship and hides the complex play of social power and discursive maneuvering that are really involved in the utterance. This linguistic ideology surrounding the use of direct quotation in legal settings, as Matoesian has pointed out, plays a role in obscuring and naturalizing "how the law-in-action tacitly incorporates forms of social power, and how it constructs claims to knowledge, truth, and facticity in the details of discursive interaction."[19]

(3) Another subtle message conveyed through use of direct quotation by professors is the primacy of the dialogic (and/or question-answer) form in legal discourse. Dialogue is central in courtrooms—between attorneys and witnesses in direct and cross-examination, between judges and opposing attorneys when attorneys make objections. Indeed, attorneys may use dialogic form to tell competing stories in opening and closing arguments. Even in written opinions, judges create dialogues between two opposing arguments or sides as a way of tracing the steps that led to their decisions. And in law school classrooms, professors not only enter into dialogues with students, but also, as we see here, create dialogues within their own speech turns through use of direct quotation:

*Transcript 6.2 [2/16/12]*

Prof.:    Okay, okay, or to put it more simply, the company in Indiana is saying, "Listen, we got this law in Indiana that is essentially for the benefit of the commonwealth of Indiana; it says that people who do business here can be made subject to Indiana's law." And, the plaintiff is saying, "This Florida company is doing business here in Indiana." Right? And the defendant Florida company is saying, "Forget that, I don't do business here in Indiana, I don't even have () shop in Indiana." And it's a little bit unclear, actually, as to the way the court sort of smooshes together its statutory analysis and its constitutional analysis. What the court means to say is, "One. The statute does not seem to apply. Indiana says that companies that do business in Indiana are subject to Indiana's jurisdiction, but, it doesn't seem as though this statute applies given the facts of this case because this doesn't seem to be a company doing business in Indiana." The court then cites to a whole bunch of federal Supreme Court cases and uses the term "due process." And, what

> the court really means to say there is, "Even if a judge were to view Indiana's statute as giving jurisdiction to a court under these circumstances, that statute itself would be unconstitutional; it would be unfair to make this Florida cor() answer to this Indiana corporation in Indiana since this Florida corporation, you know, didn't have any- wasn't really doing business in Indiana." Okay. Let's just- okay. Then, after having discussed that stuff and again () that's due- just a jurisdictional issue, statutory, constitutional. Then the court says, "But, that doesn't end the issue for us," right? There may be another basis on which- there may be another basis on which the court can exercise jurisdiction in this case, and what's that other basis? Yeah.

Student:  Well, the plaintiff, the seller (con)tends that "because there is no contract, allow the personal jurisdiction because, there is a separate clause and additional term that says that in any dispute, that Indiana has jurisdiction over Florida."

Fully analyzing the wealth of intertextual references in this short excerpt could occupy almost an entire chapter itself. In the initial portion of the professor's turn, we see the characteristic use of turn–internal dialogue to vividly summarize the core arguments on each side. Again, the professor glides easily between the opposing sides, taking first one voice and then the other.[20] The footing in this passage is somewhat unclear. On the one hand, this is not wholly fictional dialogue; it is a translation of arguments presented in the text of the opinion. Thus, the professor can more credibly appear as a mere (re-)animator here than in the previous excerpt. On the other hand, it is clear that the translation is not an exact one, and so we have a peculiar exactitude given by this use of direct quotation to what is at best a very loose rendering of what was actually said or written. The footing becomes still more complicated when a third interlocutor, the court, enters the discussion. Because the professor views the court's text as somewhat confused, he proceeds to put words in the court's mouth as well, telling the students what the authoring judge "means to say." In a sense, the direct quotations here seem to signal that the professor is giving us the "real" message encoded in the confused language of the opinion, in an interesting inversion of the usual metapragmatic convention under which direct quotation would replicate the form rather than the gist of the message with exactitude. Note also that this move highlights the interesting potential fluidity of attributed footing that can be produced (with varying degrees of transparency) by this subtle displacement of discursive responsibility ("I am merely re-animating here, in direct quotation, what the court was really *saying* [possibly implying the court's role as quasi- or coauthor], and simultaneously I am conveying the court's underlying meaning [court as principal]"). At the end of the exchange, we find the student responding using a fabricated quotation to loosely represent the plaintiff's argument-based perspective.[21]

In addition to using direct quotation to create turn–internal dialogue, professors at times talk to themselves within their own turns, first asking and then answering their own questions. They may also employ a mix of the two, asking themselves a question but answering using reported speech. The following excerpt contains examples of both of these alternatives:

*Transcript 6.3 [7/20/8]*

Prof.:   What's- what's a very reasonable alternative interpretation of the first term, "first come, first served"? "As the entire metropolitan area lines up to purchase coffee at forty-nine cents a tin, we will wait on you and take your money in the same order of which you appear." So that's why that's not going to- that's not going to change it. That's not an indication [ . . . ] Okay, how 'bout if it says, everything that we've suggested previously, says "One per customer, one per customer"? Offer or no offer? Now, again, you cannot answer the question without measuring it against the legal rationale. Is there still a potential for theoretical unlimited demand in this type of problem? Yes. It's not as easy knowing you can come in there and start ordering it by the carload and trainload. [ . . . ]

At the beginning of the turn, the professor poses himself a question about reasonable alternative interpretations of a (directly quoted) term. He responds to himself with an unframed quotation, which is nonetheless recognizable as such by virtue of the shifts in pronouns and tense ("we will wait on you" rather than "they would wait on first-comers"). Here he appears to take on the voice of a business that may or may not have made an offer to customers, speaking to the entire metropolitan area in the second-person plural ("you"). This is, however, clearly another voice as well: not the professor's own, but that of one possible interpreter of the written text, who is not necessarily rendering the meaning of the text as the author would. The professor then proceeds to vary the facts, creating a small hypothetical ("how 'bout if it says . . . 'one per customer'"), and poses himself another question, "Offer or no offer?" This question is followed by a brief metapragmatic injunction about how to answer these kinds of questions, and then by another question ("Is there potential . . . ?"), which he answers ("Yes").

These excerpts give a sense of how professors convey the primacy of dialogic and/or question-answer form in legal language and thought (thought and language, again, remaining thoroughly intertwined in the indigenous, legal/linguistic ideology). Not only must lawyers respond to and initiate argumentative dialogue with others, but they should proceed when analyzing legal texts using internal dialogue structured around the posing of a series of questions. By midsemester, we see the students begin to adopt the format (albeit with some interesting and creative variations) in their responses. One tacit epistemological lesson that is conveyed along with the discourse format is that legal truth emerges through argumentative dialogue, the privileged discursive form in this domain. Take one side, pose the appropriate questions, then take the other side. From this ongoing debate will emerge legal analysis.

When I refer to a possible distinction between dialogic and question-answer forms, I am indicating an interesting issue raised by possible differences between "genuine" dialogue, in which there are distinct voices, and a mere question-answer adjacency pair form (which may or may not instantiate differentiated voices). Silverstein would characterize the original Socratic dialogues as actually a form of monologue: "Plato writes dialectic monologue but distributes it to multiple participants, frequently in the form of adjacency-pair structures like Question/Answer, or Remark/Counter-Remark."[22] To the extent that this is replicated in law school classrooms, Silverstein notes, the discourse could be said to "inculcate a sense that legal dialectic is a procedure, an algorithm of interrogation for generating Q-A pair part investigation of issues-that-matter, seeking a telos."[23]

As noted previously (note 42 in Chapter 4), the smoothest instances of Socratic questioning found in this study most closely approximate this "monologue in the form of dialogue."[24] However, as we have seen, there are many sources of variation on this prototypical form. First, a number of the classrooms in the study use shorter, more informal exchanges, sometimes approaching almost conversational style, in unpacking the case law genre. This varies from being an occasional feature of class discussion in the more formal classes (often during policy discussions) to being a central organizing characteristic of the classroom discourse. Second, the unruly student voices frequently break out of the constricting frame of even the more tightly controlled Socratic exchanges, so that we can identify genuinely independent footing and voice. Third, at many points professors are attempting to teach students to take opposing positions in legal arguments; in these instances they are actually coaching the students to create and occupy distinct voices (for example, through role-playing). Finally, one fascinating feature of law school classroom discourse is the ubiquitous use of reported speech to represent different perspectives or voices, right alongside a frequent blurring of footing and elision of boundaries in the construction of the legal self. (The blurring of footing, of course, relies on there being a distinction in the first place.)

Thus, we can distinguish a number of kinds of exchanges, all of which might be characterized as Socratic: (a) monologue in pair-part form, produced in exchanges between one or more students and the professor (the classroom analogue, perhaps, of direct examination in the courtroom, where ideally attorney and client together construct one narrative through their question-answer exchanges, keeping in mind that the actual performance often falls interestingly short of the ideal);[25] (b) multiple kinds of two-part dialogue in pair-part form (including one in which the professor and student respond to one another in their own voices, and others in which professors and students take on alternative voices or roles or make arguments, based on the exigencies of legal argument; here, the closest legal analogue might be the dialogue between judges and attorneys during oral argument at the appellate level); (c) discussions in which the class as a whole or multiple students chime in, either mediated through the professor or (very rarely) unmediated, but nonetheless using distinct voices (though generally this still occurs in pair-part structures); and (d) an interesting interstitial category of coproduced speech in which the professor acts much as a parent does when coaching a child who is not yet proficient in a new verbal routine (so that the learner's distinct voice is still apparent in the back and forth between interlocutors).[26] Some of these categories can overlap in a single exchange, producing very interesting patterns of footing and voice. Note that Silverstein's point about inculcating an algorithm of interrogation still holds whether the pair-part structure instantiates a monologue in search of a telos, or a dialogue whose purpose is the uncovering of legal truth.

(4) An obvious, but important, correlative pedagogical message is the constant metalinguistic emphasis on language form as the actual source of epistemological certainty: that it is in and through speech that cases unfold, arguments emerge, and legal truth is discovered. Matoesian has correctly argued that this process conceals how law "constructs claims to knowledge, truth, and facticity in the details of discursive interaction,"[27] because the message is conveyed through tacit metalinguistic structuring and ideology and is therefore naturalized. In other words, students are never explicitly told that epistemological certainty lies in dialogic form. Instead, they are gradually tutored in a way of reading and speaking, at the same time as they are slowly reoriented to conceptualize people as above all producers of argument and strategy. From this position, it appears natural to accept that the facts emerging from the nested authoritative levels of discourse in legal settings will be the basis for definitive legal findings, just as it seems unremarkable that we would understand people who could be characterized quite differently (as distraught, in conflict, behaving emotionally) as constantly motivated by their best possible strategic positioning in an argumentative territory defined by legal outposts. Thus, the same metalinguistic process that Matoesian identifies as concealing the construction of legal epistemology and facticity *is* the process by which these tasks are accomplished.

The use of direct quotation in law school classrooms moves even further, beyond presenting the arguments of opposing parties, of courts, of lawyers, or of internal dialogue in service of legal analysis. Professors also at times recount abstract theories in dialogic form, often after assigning a theoretical article by a legal philosopher. These theories could be thought of as optimally suited for presentation in third-person, descriptive format. And that does happen. But in the following excerpt, we see the dialogic alternative, as the professor presents the theories of two (of course, competing) legal scholars on the issue of "specific performance":

*Transcript 6.4 [8/40/11]*

Prof.:  His argument is: "Look, the very fact that a person goes in there and says, 'Well, after all this has happened, I want specific performance,' all right, is itself an indication that there is not substitute," all right. He starts off with the position, "Hey, both undercompensation and overcompensation are bad, really bad," all right. Then he says, "Look, specific performance, is it something people are going to really want? Because, in order to harass the other person, which is the main reason given for why people will want it, you're gonna pay a big price

yourself." Before we get- is there a difference between the way
Schwartz looks at compensation and Scott looks at compensation?
What is it that Schwartz says about specific performance that Scott
probably would not say? Does Schwartz say that specific performance
undercompensates or overcompensates? This is important because it
goes to the fundament- again, of what we think it's about. What we
think damages are about. What's his argument about specific
performance?

So, once again, the world is configured around argument, and we can best
understand even abstract theories by pitting them one against the other in argumentative dialogue. There is no question that in pedagogical terms, this
creates a vivid tableau for students seeking to learn these theories. And one
can imagine professors in other disciplines employing a similar strategy. However, this pedagogical tool arguably has particular resonance and impact in
the context of the overall epistemology and form of reading that is characteristic of law training. And in the process, the people in legal landscapes, even
the philosophers who theorize about law, are defined by their positions in
dialogic argument.

An obvious extension of this logic is the characterization of legal actors
in terms of these opposed positions in a philosophical argument, especially
when they are conforming to the logic of a particular philosopher:

*Transcript 6.5 [8/14/8]*

| | |
|---|---|
| Prof.: | Now what would a more fierce judge- a generous judge says to you, "Okay, they're trying to manipulate you, all right, into relying." Okay? What might a fierce- Holmes, Hand- judge do? |
| Student: | () |
| Prof.: | "Hey, don't sit around relying." Do- what? |
| Student: | "Get a contract and make a bargain." |
| Prof.: | "Get the bargain. Make the contract. By relying, you're doing what?" |
| Student: | Being unreasonable. |
| Prof.: | Hmmm? |
| Student: | You're being unreasonable, the reliance is not reasonable, because the other person doesn't know that you have decided to rely. |

This excerpt provides a marvelous example of the complexities of direct quotation when used both for characterization and for pedagogy at the same time.
The professor begins with the predictable dialogic opposition between two
conflicting philosophers and philosophical positions: the person and the position are elided as they are voiced together through the direct quotations
"Okay, they're trying to manipulate you, all right, into relying" and "Hey, don't
sit around relying." The direct quotation form begins to break down under
pressure from pedagogical function as the professor formulates the next question: "'Hey, don't sit around relying.' Do- what?" The phrase "Do- what?" is

no longer clearly a direct quotation, as the professor slides more clearly into an intriguing mix of voices. The student supplies the missing direct quotation in his answer, and this pattern is repeated in the next exchange ("by relying, you're" *doing what?* "Being unreasonable"). Notice that the professor's initial invitation had placed the student directly into a dialogic exchange with the two judges ("a generous judge says to you"), but by the final student turn in the excerpt, the student is speaking to himself in the judge's voice ("You're being unreasonable"), an intriguing use of the pronoun "you"! Here the interaction of the imagined dialogue between judges and student with the actual pedagogical dialogue between student and professor creates a fascinating and complex layering of voice and footing. In the process, the student is unmoored from even the once-removed self created by the imagined role-play. The quickly shifting footing elevates fluency in speech-participant roles over the anchoring of self in any particular position.

The professor goes on to describe the "fierce" judge's position as the "market" or "business" position, which she opposes to the "generous" or "bleeding-heart" position. This neatly packages characterization into catchphrases centered on identity as defined by discursive position in an argument. The student is invited to imagine himself caught between these two conflicting ideologies/interlocutors, responding to a judge who is berating him for his approach to the bargain. The issue is triply contextualized in a single, vivid move: we have at once the context of the abstract legal subject bargaining, of conflicting political-philosophical traditions in Anglo-American jurisprudence, and of the student as role-player in a classroom drama.[28]

(5) Finally, use of direct quotation and dialogue to define and characterize legal personae in this way also stresses the essential contestability of any story or account of events, reminding students always to look to the other side, to ask what could be said in rebuttal. In a sense, each person becomes (minimally) half of a pair-part structure, whose salience and location are defined by discursive position in an argument. (Of course, there can be more than two positions in more complicated cases.) The only limit to contestability lies in the chain of authoring authority whereby legal facticity and guiding principles are established. And this chain itself is composed of nested sets of arguments and interlocutors.

Thus, we see that a great deal of power is packed into the positioning of legal personae as competing interlocutors in arguments. From a metalinguistic standpoint, it is actually a speaker's discursive position that turns out to be that person's key defining attribute in this system. And this position is a function of strategic considerations. Note that this is quite a reductive understanding; it reduces the vast complexities of personality, motivation, and the construction of self to the easily summarized contours of discursive position. Just as we saw in Chapter 4, a legal reading takes very complicated social events, issues, and people and uses the simplifying filters of doctrine, procedure, and, here, argumentative/strategic position, to translate complexity into manageable propositions. These propositions—the holding of the case, for example, or the position taken by the plaintiff or appellate judge—are generally summarizable in a single sentence. As we will see below, outside the precision of this legally defined frame, students are free to imagine whatever attributes they want to in speculating about characters in legal dramas, just as they are encouraged to freely imagine the policy implications and social contexts surrounding the cases they read. Additionally, through the process of characterization in legal training, law students become increasingly comfortable with the elision of animator, author, and principal footings as they prepare for a career in which they must put words into people's mouths without too obviously appearing to do so. We have already seen that this involves speaking in the voice of parties to the case, creating characters in a drama, in addition to characterizing those people in particular ways. Later in this chapter, we will return to the question of how role-play of this kind influences the conceptualization of people and self conveyed to students through legal education.

### ECONOMIC MAXIMIZERS AND STANDARD AVERAGE FARMERS: READING PEOPLE THROUGH DOCTRINAL CATEGORIES

We turn now to those aspects of a legal reading, as it is taught in these classrooms, that frame people in more doctrine-specific ways, ways that may in large part be responsive to the subject matter of Contracts classes. These are the characterizations that focus on people as economic maximizers—or that emphasize their occupational or other economic roles. As I mentioned earlier, the successful exportation of economic models across doctrinal areas has meant that these kinds of characterizations are unlikely to be limited to Contracts classes or to other classes dealing with more obviously economic domains (e.g., Corporations or other business law classes). Perhaps, given the analysis in the previous section, this is not surprising: a general legal understanding of people as strategic, as maximizing their position in a legal argument, has some obvious affinities with a view of people as economic maximizers.

A great deal of the doctrinal framework in the field of contracts centers on the issue of economic exchange, on bargains and business transactions. Thus, characters in the conflict stories told in Contracts classes are frequently identified in terms of their occupations or economic positions. In the following excerpt, the professor draws on a common stock figure in contracts tales: the "standard average" farmer who must decide about whether to breach a contract based on various strategic considerations:

*Transcript 6.6 [8/10/18]*

Prof.:     All right. If you think about what we're worried about is, on the one hand, the farmer is going to go out there as soon as the price rises, all right, make more money off his wheat, all right, thinking that he'll be hedged, all right, he's trying to make a profit out of his wheat, okay. And I suppose in that particular case, what might the farmer be hoping, assuming that- and this is part, my problem when I start talking like this. I have a problem with it because, of course, I'm assuming the farmer- that the farmer will know the law, all right, but in fact, you don't need to know the law. What might the farmer be hoping would happen? In fact, the law might favor the farmer on this one. Notice, why is it the farmer doesn't perform? One reason is, the market's gone up, but you say, "But wait a minute, what good does it do? He still has to pay the damages." What might the farmer be hoping? Yeah?

Student:    The buyer'll find cover.

Prof.:    To find a substitute and what else?

This excerpt includes a realist commentary, pointing out that the average citizen may not know the law. But note also that the farmer is not situated in terms of time or place. We are working here with a stereotypic, abstract individual whose main characteristics are a set of economic considerations given by his occupational situation and the market. Even the differences between small farmers and large agricultural enterprises, regional and cultural differences among farmers, the influence of long-term relational (or other kinds of) ties within communities and between participants in markets are not salient here.[29] However, professors do make sure that students pay careful attention to the stereotypical effects of occupational identity and economic position (with their implications for legal strategy) on litigants' probable thoughts and expectations (as in the excerpt above).

Students quickly pick up on the importance of fixing the characters in contracts stories in terms of their general economic and occupational identities:

EXAMPLES: STUDENTS STATING THE FACTS OF THE CASE,
INTRODUCING THE CHARACTERS

*Transcript 6.7 [2/12/11]*

Student:    All right, the plaintiff, B., is the landowner and the defendant, K., is the realtor.

*Transcript 6.8 [4/32/1]*

Student:    The plaintiff is the builder's () carpenter, and in September the defendants, who I guess are like businessmen [ . . . ]

*Transcript 6.9 [6/5/2]*

Student:    The plaintiff was a courier and he was supposed to go- he was hired to go on a trip with um the defendant and right before um the trip the defendant canceled the arrangement and said that he would not- that he was not making the trip and did not- no () no longer using the plaintiff's services.

As one professor explained:

Um, one of the things that I find useful to do is to think about the people who are suing each other in terms of their classification. So remember I've said that there are three kinds of contract cases that we tend to take up, um, there are contracts for uh, construction contracts, there are contracts for uh, employment, and there are contracts for the sale of goods, all right. So one of the things that may be useful is to trigger that: so are we dealing with a buyer and seller; are we dealing with an owner and a contractor, are we dealing with an employer and an employee? All right, so that it may be useful simply because- remember you may find that the rules are going to differ depending on which category you're in, okay? (3/3/6)

This succinctly summarizes how legal categorizations that emanate from rules governing economic transactions can shape what will be foregrounded about people's identities in subsequent legal analysis.

At times, this abstract individual loses even the specificity of occupational categories and becomes simply a buyer or seller, an offeror or offeree, a party to the transaction:[30]

*Transcript 6.10 [3/3/6]*

Student:    Ah, the plaintiff, uh the buyer is suing the () seller.

*Transcript 6.11 [1/9/5]*

Student:    I disagree. That- if the- it would be the offeree knew that the car was burned up, the car was sold, or that the offeror had changed his mind and said, "Hey, I'm not going to sell this"; if the offeree knew that, or should have known that, I think that's revocation of the offer.

*Transcript 6.12 [5/24/21]*

Prof.:    No, he doesn't have to buy the land, but if he does, he has to sell it to the other party.

Here people and problems are located in and as individuals operating against the odd acontextual context of a legal geography, two contracting parties interacting with one another, even speaking in the first person singular ("Hey, I'm not going to sell this"), against the backdrop of legal rights and doctrines. One wants to buy something, the other wants to sell: except for (presumably reflexive unmarked usage of) gendered pronouns, we have no sense of these actors as people beyond their postulated attitudes toward property and their bargaining interaction with one another. Just as initial medical school training moves students away from a personalized understanding of the human beings whose bodies they will treat, legal education pushes law students to place people in legally crafted categories, using abstraction to distance themselves from human dimensions of their clients' problems. The medical student's eye begins to narrow on anatomical parts and systems, losing a view of the body as a person. Likewise, the law student's vision locates people involved in conflicts using categories that define them in terms of doctrinal and argumentative positions.

### At the Edge of Legal Categories: Identity and Social Context, Emotion and Morality

What about other aspects of identity, aspects often made central in nonlegal storytelling? Readers might want to know about a person's character or personality, emotions, social background or status, and many other culturally identifiable features. As we have seen, a legal reading has room for almost any facet of social context or identity—but at the margins. After the basics of doctrinal and procedural framing are established, or before moving into the serious and systematic legal analysis, there is room for social specifics, framed as humor, place setting, or courtroom strategy. The professor may mention in an aside that even if doctrinal requirements have not been met, judges or juries may sometimes be persuaded by the particular circumstances of a case to overlook doctrinal difficulties, perhaps to avoid manifestly unjust results. Alternatively, the professor may mention in passing that social context or prejudice against certain kinds of people can at times affect legal outcomes. When a case outcome seems to fly in the face of prevailing legal doctrine, social context and emotion often emerge as wild cards that can explain these apparent anomalies. In general, discussion of these sorts of factors in the classrooms of this study rely on stereotyping and generalizations about "kinds" of people or situations. Interestingly, there is often speculation about underlying motivations packed into these discussions. The professors of this study exhibited a considerable amount of variation in the degree to which they mention such extralegal factors when discussing the people in legal texts. What all of the professors shared was an insistent return to the core of a legal reading, using various kinds of discursive markers to indicate the marginality of other factors.

IDENTITY AND SOCIAL CONTEXT

Consider, for example, the jump from ethnic stereotype to characterization of a person and his motives in the following excerpt, all presented as ancillary to the real guts of the legal reading under way:

*Transcript 6.13 [5/10/2]*

Prof.:    Mr. S. Is [student's last name] Greek, by any chance?

Mr. S.:   No, it's Polish, sorry.

Prof.:    All right.

Class:    [[laughter]]

Prof.:    Well, for the moment we're going to assume that it's Greek. Go on.

Class:    [[laughter]]

Mr. S.:   Okay, Mr. Ganas was a Greek and he uh was a waiter on-

Prof.:    Is it significant that Mr. Ganas was a Greek?

Mr. S.:   I don't think it is. It shouldn't be.

Prof.:    Well, let's decide which it is.

Class:    [[laughter]]

Prof.:    Is it significant, or is it that you think it shouldn't be?

Mr. S.:   Mmm (.) I think it shouldn't, he shouldn't- shouldn't matter.

Prof.:    It shouldn't matter.

Mr. S.:   No.

Prof.:    What a wonderful, absolutely American perspective. Just like a World War I movie. It shouldn't matter, you suggest, where you come from. It shouldn't matter what your ethnic group is. Let me disillusion you just a little.

Class:    [[laughter]]

Prof.:    One of the wonderful rules in interpreting common law cases is, whenever you have a party whose name ends in a vowel, rule against that party.

Class:    [[laughter]]

Prof.:    Watch carefully, see if that doesn't work out in practice. There is something rather interesting going on here. Okay, he's a Greek, it shouldn't make a difference.

The class discussion moves on from this humorous introduction to focus on questions pertinent to doctrinal issues: Had the Greek servant's amorous feelings for his employer's wife constituted a breach of contract between servant and employer? Could the employer's estate use the servant's behavior as a defense to the servant's eventual request for restitution damages? Did it matter whether the amorous feelings had actually interfered with the servant's performance of his duties, and so on? Ethnicity is presented as a stereotypic background factor that might affect the reaction of the court if it were to depart from a standard legal analysis, but this is tangential to the systematic legal reading with which the class is centrally occupied:

*Transcript 6.14 [5/10/3]*

Prof.:    *[ . . . ]* Why did they tell us he's a Greek?

Mr. S.:    I don't know. I guess they were just interested in that.

Class:    [[laughter]]

Prof.:    Why are they interested in that? Why tell us that he's a Greek? What if he were French, what if he were Polish, would it make a difference? What is it about Greeks? Yes, uh, Ms., uh?

Ms. C.:    "C" *[states last name]*

Prof.:    Ms. C.

Ms. C.:    After reading *Zorba the Greek,* I would say maybe because of their reputation as lovers or--

Prof.:                              --There's this zest for life (.) There is something going on and there's all kinds of hideous things about the Greeks that the Americans sometimes think. Indeed, there are horrible things to think about virtually every ethnic group you can name. At least that was in the good old days when you admitted that sort of thing. We don't do it anymore. But this court involved in the casebook, seems to feel it necessary to tell us that Ganas is Greek. And you can bet that it was plastered all over the opinion, right? There is this thing, we'll say for the moment, putting as neutral a face on it as possible, about Greeks in love. Go on.

There is no attempt to deny that a person's social background might be decisive in legal outcomes; indeed, this particular class provides one of the best examples in the study of a direct discussion of the potential impact of such factors. In other classrooms in this study, professors covered similar cases with no mention what-ever of ethnicity, stereotypes, or prejudice. At the same time, we can see that even when these kinds of factors are mentioned, there is no sustained or systematic analysis of them.

Later in the same class, as the professor turns to another case, there is another allusion to ethnicity, this time simply as humorous punctuation:

*Transcript 6.15 [5/10/13]*

Prof.:   Here we are, by the way, with another interesting ethnic group. Swedish Evangelical Lutheran. What do we know about them? The answer: absolutely nothing! But they want a church, apparently. Go on.

The class then moves on to a systematic consideration of legal issues: whether the builder's failure to construct a church to meet certain specifications constituted a breach of the contract, justifying the church's decision not to pay the builder; whether defects in construction provided the church with an adequate defense against having to pay the builder damages. The cotextual reference to the previous discussion about Greeks ("another interesting ethnic group") underlines the spo-radic and seemingly haphazard effect of social context on legal results.

This pattern can be found even when questions of race or gender are raised as directly pertinent to legal results, whether by professors or students. For example, one case studied in many of the classrooms involved an interracial boxing match that gave rise to a contractual dispute. Notice how the impact of race is at once acknowledged and peripheralized:

*Transcript 6.16 [3/12/8]*

Prof.:   I think, it was one of the first occasions in which there was gonna be an interracial fight, and, therefore, one of the reasons clearly not articulated, clearly not arguable to the court, would be some racism that would enter in- ah some concern on the part of the court that ah maybe people wouldn't pay, that they would boycott such a fight or maybe that they would- maybe they would pay more. Racism is not the kind of thing you would argue in the court, but it may have been a factor certainly in the court's refusing to let the issue go to the jury.

After acknowledging the possible impact of racial identity and prejudice, the pro-fessor proceeded to focus the students' attention on the "real" legal problem: the "damage issues arising under *Dempsey*," which were discussed as a distinct, and more central, matter. As we saw in Chapter 4, a different professor also mentioned race at the beginning of the discussion of *Dempsey* but dismissed its importance in the development of the case:

*Transcript 6.17 [5/8/14]*

Prof.:   So we're talking about a time, thirty years later. Thirty years after the fighters' prime, thirty years after their prime, they meet. It's unlikely they're going to fight thirty years later. I mean it's unlikely that they'll move very easily. [[class laughter]] And the case of modern boxers, it's the last- they can't even talk, let alone fight, [[class laughter]] at this point in their careers. Now, what's going on here, why does it take thirty years for Dempsey to meet Wills? Now there are all kinds of overtones, racial and otherwise in this case. But I think there's a pretty simple explanation for why Dempsey doesn't want to fight Wills. And I don't think- I could be wrong about this- that it has anything to do with matters of race. I think it's a bit simpler than that. Take a wild guess, Ms. U.

Ms. U.:    He was afraid to lose?

Prof.:    He was afraid that he was going to get maimed by Wills, the "Brown Bomber" who was probably the greatest boxer of the world, indeed, of the universe at that point, and Dempsey wants to stay away from him, okay? Now there are a lot of people who want to try to get him to fight Wills, but there is, alas, a problem with the color bar in a lot of places and there are a lot of promoters who won't touch that fight and there are a lot of people who are worried about the future of the sport. [ . . . ] Now maybe Dempsey is worried about the future of the sport; my guess is he's worried about losing the battle. And maybe he finally realizes that that's what's going to happen. He signs the contract and he tries to back out. Now what do you do with the fact that he's backed out of this contract? What do we do with that? We know there's a breach of contract, at least the court tells us there's a breach of contract. What does the promoter here, the Chicago Coliseum Club, want to recover? Let's start with the first item. [ . . . *rest of professor turn, focusing on lost profits, omitted* . . . ]

A third professor covered the *Dempsey* case with no mention of race whatsoever (4/7/8).

We also find this kind of approach to social context and identity in a class-room taught by an African American professor, when an African American stu-dent raises the question of whether the racial identity of one of the parties might have influenced a case outcome:

*Transcript 6.18 [2/3/37]*

Prof.:    It could have. Th- and it may have been complicated. It could have been important to the decision-making. And, in fact, I mean you could imagine that all of this legal gobbledegook is simply a cloak for, you know, an- racial animus. It's a possibility. On the other hand, it could have been this person simply put down the fact that the, ah, this is a quote, Negro, simply out of a reflex. Out of a, you know, this race being important for the moment (.) a reflex. And it really didn't have anything to do with the ultimate outcome of the case- that in fact if this guy Skinner had been white, same result. Tough () sort of get beneath the- the um the ah (.) the materials at hand. It's not, I mean it could have been important, then again it might not have been important. Tough to tell.

Here the professor is, of course, completely correct that it is hard to tell much about this aspect of social context from the materials at hand, whether from the case ex-cerpts themselves or the accompanying casebook commentaries and additional read-ings. But then again, that is because elision and erasure and lack of precision on such matters are intrinsic aspects of the legal approach that is being taught in these class-rooms—and being enacted in actual case law decisions. Notice that in previous examples, there is no attempt to hide or deny the possible effects of racial or ethnic identity on legal outcomes; indeed, any such attempt might risk rendering the system implausible. Instead, there is a fascinating combination of a complete willingness to accept the impact of social identities on case results, with an ongoing evasion of any systematic inclusion or analysis of those impacts. Where a social science class would focus on the ways we can trace or know about such impacts, law school training reserves certainty for the core story uncovered through legal readings and discursive practices. At the same time, random social and other aspects of people's identity dance freely at the margins. Perhaps people's race or social situation affected the outcome; probably they do sometimes. But we really can't know for sure. We can speculate as freely as we like, developing likely scenarios, imagining possible motives. And then we must return to the core aspects of a person's identity in any legal story: those features defined by the relevant legal doctrine or procedure (offeror or offeree? plaintiff or defendant?). We do not ask whether someone is a generally reliable person. We ask whether she or he showed up at the time and place specified in the contract, and with the goods as agreed upon. We ask whether someone precisely mirrored a contractual offer in accepting it, not whether he or she has dreams of being a novelist. We may ask about the relative power the two parties had in making a contractual bargain, but that inquiry will be very narrowly circumscribed by the legal definition of what an unconscionable contract is; we will not, for example, conduct a sociological examination of the way race, class, gender, educational background, the structures of neighborhoods or companies or the capitalist economy, or a number of other factors may impact power. Social identity and context do sometimes enter contract doctrine, but in broad categories: consumers versus merchants, for example. Even when race or gender becomes relevant, as they do in constitutional law, they are extracted from particular social contexts and personal histories, and once again, a legal reading will require that people step back from the usual coordinates by which such identities are understood and look instead to the doctrinal categories.[31] It should be noted that in the realm of Contracts teaching, there is one approach that might yield a somewhat different picture, and that is the "relational contracts" approach. This approach attempts to focus on the relational matrix surrounding contractual relations, and thus tends to give social analysis a more systematic place in legal discourse.[32]

## EMOTION AND MORALITY: ROLE-PLAY, LINGUISTIC IDEOLOGY, AND THE LEGAL SELF

We have seen that legal pedagogy pushes students to read for the metapragmatic structuring of text and authority, as well as the discursive positions of legal personae. These moves toward more pragmatic readings of texts, and translations of people's stories, generally require students to suspend, at least temporarily, their judgments about the emotional or moral aspects of events. Whether someone was right or wrong, moral or immoral, reprehensible or ethical is not part of the central structure of this pragmatic (and metapragmatic) approach to reading. If emotion and morality become relevant, they will only do so through the carefully filtered reading yielded by doctrine, procedure, and strategy. In one class, a student confronted her professor about whether salespeople had to be honest in negotiating with customers:

*Transcript 6.19 [1/7/9]*

Student:    The salesperson tells you something that is completely opposite to // what //

Prof.:                                                                          //At //
            the auto parts store?

Student:    At the auto parts store. I'm, you know, I like your voice or whatever--

Prof.:                                                                      --not
            my face anymore?

Class:      [[laughter]]

Student:    They do this, doesn't tell you if there is no money back guarantee, or anything like that. You got it, okay. And then the owner calls back, and goes "Well, you know there's a mistake," but you've already written the check, or whatever.

Prof.:      Well, if he's made an offer, he's revoked it and unless 2-205 is going to be applied, and there has to be a signed writing, unless you could argue estoppel, if you're dealing with the Code number 1-103, which opens the doors to the common law, you don't have that kind of protection, unless it's a consumer statute, or a federal trade regulation- regulation, you don't have that- that kind of protection.

Student:    I.e., salespeople can lie?

Prof.:      Huh? Not only, i.e., salespeople can lie, i.e., salespeople do lie, constantly.

Student:    That's not fair.

Prof.:      No, no. Fairness is not something that I accept as a general proposition, and certainly not in my household.

Class:      [[laughter]]

The clear message here, as it is throughout the classes of this study, is that a legal reading is primarily focused on *what the law says you can or cannot do* rather than on *what's fair*. This is simply an accurate rendition of the metalinguistic norms surrounding a competent legal reading; professors may vary in their attitudes about whether this is a good thing, and may even convey a distancing from this approach at times through metalinguistic commentary or signaling, but they uniformly stress this focus on layered textual authority. In the excerpt above, we see that the professor in fact jovially embraces the tacit ethics (or lack thereof) involved in this kind of approach. His response also models for students the nested series of textual resources through which they should mentally check in answering a question such as "Can a salesperson lie?" Just as medical training requires a hardening and distancing of students' sensibilities from empathic reactions to death and human bodies, legal training demands a bracketing of emotion and morality (as it is commonly understood) in dealing with human conflict and the people who appear in legal conflict stories.

Students do struggle with this shift, and occasionally vocalize their discomfort, as with one student, who finally protested, "Is all we do as lawyers think of ways to get out of contracts we've made?" (2/6/146). This exchange highlights the marginalization of both emotion and unmediated concerns about ethics and morality. The student leads into this ethics question with a statement of emotion:

*Transcript 6.20 [2/6/16–18]*

Student:    Thank God you brought that up! [ . . . ] Does anyone else feel angry? [[laughter]] I mean, I'm just furious. I mean, I'm the only one in the room?

Prof.:      I missed something, I missed something, I don't- why are you angry? () You're angry at me?

Student:    I'm- [[laughter]] I'm angry at the whole class. [ . . . ] all we can do is try and think of ways to worm out of *[the contract we just made]*? Is that what we're trying to do as lawyers?

The professor's somewhat startled response here signals the perceived incongruity of this level of emotional response to the issue. In subsequent turns, the professor first invites discussion of the issue, leading into a hypothetical involving the concept of efficient breach, which generates some role-play and joking. He then broadens the discursive frame (although setting clear limits in terms of time) by asking a practicing lawyer in the class to comment and subsequently opening up the floor with the comment, "We're going to have a few minutes on this issue" *[of lawyer ethics]*. In the ensuing discussion, a practicing lawyer gives a view from the trenches, stating that he generally just goes along with the system (the implication being that this is in fact realistically how the system runs). Another student says that she is worried about the emotional student, characterizing him as being "innocent." At the end of the exchange, the professor suggests taking a class vote on the issue, but backs off when a student asks whether it would be appropriate to do so in such an emotionally charged atmosphere. The professor closes off discussion with the following comment: "About (.) quite frankly, I mean I have my own views on issues like this which at some point I'll express. But as a general matter on issues like this, in terms of our Contracts class, we'll find it mainly pretty agnostic the way I see this; I don't know what the ultimate views are and what you all do in the world." In conclusion, he notes that he sees his job as training the students to be "masters, black belts of contract argumentation" (2/6/30). By the close of this exchange, the emotion with which it began has been capped off, although backchannel rumblings in the class indicated that a number of students were not satisfied with the outcome. The professor has modeled for the student a split between the selves with which he approaches these problems: there is the personal opinion, which he holds in abeyance and over which he exercises control, and there is the professional response, which is "agnostic" and whose primary goal is honing the students' discursive power (quite literally; note the "black belt" metaphor). This approach is somewhat reminiscent of the way a medical student might be taught to hold emotional responses in abeyance while treating a badly injured patient, and then to deal with personal responses later, putting them away while exercising professional judgment and responsibility. In the lawyers' case, that responsibility involves formulating the best possible argument for their clients, seeing the issue from all angles, and bracketing emotional responses that might limit their ability to analyze the issue clearly. Analysis requires running the factual situation through metalinguistic filters, mentally standing on each side of each argument and imagining the other side's response, and asking oneself a set of nested questions derived from the filters of doctrine and procedure (organized as discursive strategy). We can see the double edge here. There is a power to bracketing off emotion when it helps to obtain for a medical patient or legal client the full benefit of dispassionate professional judgment, but there is a disempowerment in permitting only part of the patient's or client's full experience to be considered.

As the semester proceeds, classroom discourse insistently channels ethical questions and emotional responses into doctrinal channels:

*Transcript 6.21 [3/26/6]*

Prof.:  That's good. All right. Why did the borrowers win? What is the court's explanation for why the borrowers should be permitted to recover on this counter claim?

Ms. M.:  Because of the injustice.

Prof.:  No. Not because of the injustice. In other words, what you're doing now is struggling with the application of the promissory estoppel rule and the three elements? We'll come back to that. Ms. T.?

Later in the dialogue, the professor returns to the question, telling the student, "Now, here's how you answer this question, all right?" She proceeds to outline the doctrine:

*Transcript 6.22 [3/26/8]*

Prof.:  What is the rule of promissory estoppel? The rule of promissory estoppel is that if a promise is made, which is A. intended to induce reliance, and B. if the promisee relies on that promise to his or her detriment, then, C. the promise may be enforced to the extent justice requires. Where am I getting this rule? It's articulated in *Allegheny College*. It's articulated in *East Providence v. Geremia*. It is articulated in both of the cases that we read for tonight. And it is also articulated in section 90 of the Second Restatement, which is on page 270 of the text. So, three elements of the rule. What that means is, that when you want to make an argument for promissory estoppel, you're going to take the elements of the rule, promise intended to induce reliance, detrimental reliance has occurred, justice required the enforcement of the promise, and you are going to apply the elements of the rule to the facts of the case: first, on behalf of the promisee and then you're going to have to anticipate what the promisor would say in response. Okay? So that's you, Ms. M. What you want to do is now say, "Was there a promise made intended to induce reliance?" What was the promise?

In the contrast between the professor's first answer ("No, not because of the injustice") and her second (which overtly includes "justice" as a part of the legal picture here), we have a powerful example of the crucial role of screening texts and doctrines in legal reading. It is not that the student shouldn't include some calculation regarding injustice in solving this problem. That calculation is in fact appropriate here because the legal doctrine calls for it. But a reply in which "injustice" appears unmediated by doctrinal screens is rejected; the solution lies in filtering the issue of justice through layers of doctrinally delineated tests. Note that the professor also goes on to make explicit the role of textual genealogy in creating these legal filters. It is also worth observing that the professor again here urges on the student a particular form of thinking about problems by advocating that she ask herself a question from doctrinal categories and answer it through application of facts. Thus, there is (at least) a double mediation here: first, running the facts through layers of doctrinal filtering, checking for the relevant issues (which may or may not include justice); second, performing that doctrinal check through a question-answer pair-part form. Unmediated ethical analysis of injustice is not the point, and indeed flies in the face of doctrinal analysis.

This doctrinal filtering is one of several ways in which students are tacitly encouraged to adopt a new, more distanced attitude toward morality and emotion. Another pedagogical technique that furthers this shift is an insistence on the primacy of ongoing argument or dialogue (or, at times, just ongoing pair-part responses). If students express discomfort or emotion, a common professorial response is to urge them to channel their feelings into "arguments" (generally, of course, framed in terms of doctrinal categories). Again we find some students struggling as they are pushed to engage in this discourse:

*Transcript 6.23 [5/8/8]*

Student:   The contract, the original contract itself had a provision in it for prices that change due to an advance in case of the rise in the wages, which actually happened causing the forward contract to be much more expensive. So, if we're looking at expectation damages, then the point that- I mean, in his contract that he would have, his original contract that the coke would have been subject to rise as well, would it not?

Prof.:   I don't know. What's the relevance of that to--

Student:                                        --well--

Prof.:                                        --how we solve the problem?

Student:   (.) *[rising intonation]* It just bothers me. I-

Class:   [[laughter]]

Prof.:   What bothers you?

Student:   *[smiles, silent, looks down]*

Prof.:   What bothers you, I take it, is the parties thought about the problem of labor and increased price in labor. And you're suggesting this is something they recognized. Now, do you want to go from there to say, "If they recognized that (.) there was a problem with the cost of labor (.) if there was going to be a stunningly disturbed market, they should have said something about it," is that what you want to say? If that's what you want to say, where does that leave you?

Student:   *[again, silence, looks down]*

By the end of the exchange, the professor has essentially adopted the student's voice, using indirect speech ("you're suggesting this was something they recognized"). The student has refused to budge from her chosen register ("It just bothers me") and has indexed that refusal with silence. And so the professor speaks for her, taking her place in the dialogue, and in the absence of any cooperation from her, imbuing her with the correct voice. This is a voice that produces arguments from a particular discursive position, not a voice that expresses emotion. His insistent continuation of the dialogue, even without help from his interlocutor, forces on this segment of speech the metapragmatic interpretation he seeks to impose: that this instance of speaking is an event of a particular discourse type (Socratic dialogue with its accompanying metapragmatic rules). One key rule of this type of discourse is that people keep talking, keep coming up with reasons and justifications for articulated and antagonistically defended positions ("Where does that lead you?"). Her silence can be read as inserting a competing interpretation into the exchange: this chunk of speech is an exchange in which she wishes to express a felt dissatisfaction with a case outcome. The power differential between the two interlocutors is perhaps evidenced by the fact that the final interpretation goes to the professor. Yet her strongly maintained, smiling silence is a resistance that is not ultimately overcome by him. The timing of the class's laughter obviously reinforces the professor's signal that her response was inappropriate.

The technique of taking a student's place in the dialogue when the student does not respond as desired is used in many of the classrooms of this study. More unusual but dramatic illustrations of the general metapragmatic struggle at work here are instances in which the professor literally dictates to the student which words to use. In one particularly vivid example of this, the professor actually instructs a student who has answered "no" to "try 'yes' ":

*Transcript 6.24 [5/24/21]*

| | |
|---|---|
| Prof.: | Let's put it slightly differently. Is the party making the promise, "if I buy the land, I'll sell it to you," surrendering any legal right? |
| Student: | No. |
| Prof.: | What do you mean, "no"? Try "yes." |
| Class: | [[laughter]] (.02) |
| Prof.: | <u>Say</u> (.) "<u>yes.</u>" |
| Student: | Yes. |
| Prof.: | Why? |
| Class: | [[laughter]] |

In this excerpt we see a movement from more implicit metapragmatic indicators that a student's answers were unsatisfactory to a breakthrough into very explicit regimentation when all else failed. This more explicit metapragmatic regimentation, directing the student to repeat ("Say 'yes'"), is identical in form to the metalinguistic formulations found across many cultures in child language socialization routines, which typically take "the form of explicit prompting by the caregiver or other member of the group. . . . The prompting routine is itself marked by characteristic linguistic features. For example, the routine is usually but not always initiated by an imperative verb form meaning 'say' or 'do,' followed by the utterance to be repeated."[33] The modeling of correct language use in the Socratic routine above, then, invokes one of the more powerful linguistic socialization techniques available in the human repertoire. There is a particularly apt comparison between this kind of law school exchange and the routines used to socialize Kaluli children.[34] The exchange in this transcript is also a marked example of what conversation analysts call "repair," in which the professor is inviting (indeed, ordering) the student to correct a prior response.[35] This seemingly banal invitation to repair, and other, more subtle versions of it throughout these classrooms, actually contains a correlative invitation to reformulate the self of the student into whose mouth new words are put. This new self is first and foremost a "black belt" of legal argument, distanced and separated from the emotional, socially situated personal or nonprofessional self. This separation is subtly reinforced through multiple aspects of classroom discursive form, including elevation of argumentative positioning as a top priority for legal speakers, an insistence on primacy of legal filters for making sense of legal stories and characters, the ubiquitous elision of footing, and frequent use of role-playing.

During role-playing exchanges, professors push students into new conceptualizations of the person by literally placing them in the shoes of legal personae, demanding that they speak in this new voice. In these exchanges, the socialization process comes still closer to home for students. Here, in a sense, the development of legal personae for students becomes more personal, for they are asked not only to describe people in certain terms, but to imagine themselves as those people, to speak in their voices. And because of the elision of footing often found in these exchanges, the boundary between those other voices and a student's own voice blurs. The strategic arguer who is the buyer/plaintiff speaks in the same voice as the plaintiff's attorney, and in the same voice as the student articulating (animating? authoring?) the possible arguments in light of the array of available discursive positions. The scenarios can be derived from the actual events of cases the students read or from hypotheticals created by the professor; the difference becomes unimportant as parallels in argumentative positioning are foregrounded. At the same time, emotion and morality become background, mobilizable to the degree that strategic interests demand.

We have already seen a number of examples of role-playing in previous transcript excerpts. Recall that in Transcript 6.5, the professor places the student in the role of an interlocutor in an exchange between legal parties and a fierce judge, culminating in a shift where the student admonishes himself in the judge's voice. In Transcript 4.13, the student is placed near the top of a flagpole as the professor cruelly revokes an offer at the last minute. Transcript 4.19 found a professor speaking in the voice of an employer, inviting the students in the class into the role of employees. As we will see in the rest of this chapter, role-playing in law school classrooms repeatedly locates students in a new legal landscape, where the important compass points are features of discourse. In the process, the students themselves move out of accustomed frames to speak in the voices of personae defined by the demands of that legal discourse. In the following exchange, a professor is apparently attempting to guide a student into playing the role of herself—but it is an interestingly abstract "standard average law student" from whom he wants to hear:

*Transcript 6.25 [5/7/24–26]*

Prof.:      Tell me. Why are you in law school, Ms. C.? Why are you studying the law? Don't tell me "to become a lawyer;" I understand that.

Ms. C.:   It interests me.

Prof.:      Because it interests you. What a quaint way to put it. Why aren't you in business school? Where every sensible person probably ought to be now.

Ms. C.:   I'm thinking of changing right now.

Prof.:      A possibly wise move. But why didn't you go directly to business school?

*[Several turns omitted in which the student reiterates that law school interests her, and the professor repeats his question about her motivation for choosing law school.]*

Ms. C.:   To do something different.

Prof.:      What is it that's different about the law, from business?

Ms. C.:   It's not certain; it's ever-changing.

Prof.:      Well, it is that. It is ever-changing. Or is it just that you like variety? Come, Ms. C., you're not that shallow a person. Let's be honest. Let's force you to say something maybe you don't really mean. Let's psycho-analyze you. You're in law school rather than business school because you find it at bottom more deeply satisfying or at least you thought you could, to study the law than to go to business school. You may be right, however, to be a lucre-seeking monster at the present time in history, but that's not what you are. There is a deep emotional fulfillment that you are supposed to be getting from the law school. That is why you came here.

Here the student is actually put in the position of giving "incorrect" answers about her own inner thoughts and motivations. The professor, in supplying the "correct" answers, imports for her not only a way of talking but also an entire persona and set of normative orientations. These orientations oppose the purely money-seeking motivations of those who attend business school to the alternative, more lofty goals of those who pursue law. The student is being trained to play herself in a drama defined by the professor, to discern in strategic terms what discursive position is required to carry this drama forward, and then to speak in the voice of that "I."

As we've noted, the message conveyed through this fluid reanchoring of footing across sides of legal arguments is one that privileges language structure over content, ability to shift discursive positions over fixed moral or emotional anchors. Indeed, the self that emerges from the prism of this linguistic ideology is above all else defined by an ability to make arguments. This new self can rise above the distracting pulls of emotion and common cultural judgments by means of an ongoing internal and external dialogue based in legal doctrines and categories. Competence in this dialogic discourse form becomes a measure of one's ability to be and think like a lawyer. Achieving reason is possible through discourse. If one is so angry that one cannot make the arguments on the other side (perhaps feeling such righteous indignation that it is difficult to contemplate that there *is* any other viable side to the discussion), one will very likely lose to some-one who can take either side of the argument. And arguably, the ability of the legal system as a whole to rise above emotion and set-in-stone moral frameworks is a cornerstone of its legitimacy in a liberal society. On the other hand, the dialogic self that emerges from the formative discourse in law school classrooms must learn to take a somewhat agnostic position concerning matters about which many people in society care passionately, must be able to let go of set moral standpoints and deep emotions—at least while speaking and reading and writing the language of the law. This might well differentially disadvantage students who have difficulty doing so.

## Legal Landscapes

We turn now to an examination of the odd geography in which these distinctively legal personae are located. Across the different classrooms of this study, we can discern two commonly occurring features of the legal landscapes within which students are taught to operate. First, interestingly, the most frequent spatial referent seems to be geographical: students are asked to remember the state or country in which the action is located.[36] Second, and more ubiquitously, professors locate students in a landscape composed of argumentative positions, discourse frames, and participant roles or footing.

### We're Not in Kansas Anymore—or Are We?

A focus on particular states or locales follows from two different legally framed dictates. First, the doctrinal focus on occupational categories brings with it an occasional pedagogical attempt to invoke related geography, asking, for example, if anyone in the class is from a farm or has worked in a certain locale that is relevant to the occupation in question. Second, differences between states are relevant to jurisdictional rules, which determine whether a particular court can decide the issue and which state's law it must apply. Finally, apart from its use inside strict legal frames, geographical context may occasionally be invoked in much the way other kinds of social context are: at the margins of legal discourse, as professors invite students to imagine what kinds of "nonlegal" considerations might be affecting decision making.

In the following excerpt, we find geography raised as part of an inquiry into jurisdiction:

*Transcript 6.26 [4/13/16]*

Prof.:     Put it like this, is it the only mortgage on the cottage?

Student:   We don't know.

Prof.:     We don't know, it could be a second. But, where is it? Where is the cottage?

Student:   In Michigan.

Prof.:     In Michigan. Where are we in the case?

Student:   We're in Wisconsin.

Prof.:     We're in Wisconsin. Does that raise any problems?

Notice how voice and footing work in this passage. The first "we," introduced by the student, asserts a shared position based on a common predicament as readers of a text that gives only limited information. The second "we," used by the professor, moves into the shared reader role, accepting the footing and adopting the voice proffered in the previous turn. The third "we" (also from the professor) goes further, to a position defined by the legal institutional setting from which the written case text was generated (asking the student the location of the court that wrote the opinion: "Where are we in the case?"). Note what use of "we" accomplishes here:

1. It again unites professor and student, as readers and also as legal professionals who read the text for certain (contextual, pragmatic) technical framing information, of which the location and kind of court issuing the opinion count among the more important.
2. It places the student and professor *in* the case, as it were, uniting them now with the authoring court, creating a momentary equation that allows the student to imagine himself as an authoritative legal source. (Note also that it elides the case as written and the case as enacted in court, "in the case" referring to both; a wonderful example of how salient and vivid written contexts are in legal epistemology.)
3. It foregrounds the location of the court, as opposed, for example, to other places that are loci for the story unfolding in the case.

In focusing on the location of the court, the professor's questions highlight a potential problem: the laws in Michigan might vary from those in Wisconsin. Additionally, where several locales are involved, difficulties can arise over whether a particular court has authority or jurisdiction to hear the case. Legal training transforms geographic and sociopolitical locations into "jurisdictions," where the crucial borders are defined by the boundaries of legislatures' and courts' authority.

Just as characterization in law school classrooms produced a kind of abstract individual, the reliance on geography just described results in an oddly acontextual context. In one sense, we are given spatial coordinates for the narrative that is unfolding. But the context thereby configured is understood in typified or abstract dimensions, in tropes of jurisdiction or economically delineated geography (farms, homes, businesses). This is even more the case when we move into a landscape defined purely in terms of legal argument.

## The Landscape of Argument and Discourse Frames

We have already seen many examples of the most ubiquitous form of contextualized identity found in these classrooms: professors invite students to play the roles of legal professionals, of lawyers and judges, and to make legally relevant arguments. Also, at times, arguments that would actually be made by lawyers are put into the mouths of parties or litigants. The most salient aspect of identity in these scenarios, as we've noted, is students' location in a legal landscape, situated in a geography of strategies and argument:

*Transcript 6.27 [4/23/16]*

Prof.:    All right, now the strangest part of all, I guess, uh Mr. H., let's say you know damn well that this potential infliction suit is a piece of garbage, all right. But, you get a settlement out of me anyway. [ . . . ]

*Transcript 6.28 [1/3/9]*

Prof.:    Well, if I say I intend to give you five thousand dollars if you climb to the top of the Sears Tower, is that an offer?

*Transcript 6.29 [1/3/25]*

Prof.:    So, in other words, if I give you five thousand dollars this year for your tuition, (is) part tuition, and five thousand dollars next year, () your tuition (.) All right? And, depending on how you do in school for the next two or three years, five thousand dollars. I'm wondering whether or not if I renege you can sue me for breach of contract.

Notice that there is a sense of spatial and relational coordinates in these passages, but again of an oddly abstract-contextual variety. In the first passage, the student is described as getting a settlement "out of" the professor; in the second we imagine the student catapulted to the top of a very tall building in return for five thousand dollars; in the third we picture the student doggedly pursuing college studies at a "standard average" college. In all three passages, use of the pronouns "I" and "you," as well as use of the present tense, foreground a speech situation in which the operative locutions are crucially defined by legal (and linguistic) concerns. Professors place students in the shoes of people occupying legal positions, located in landscapes whose key referents are legal requirements. The primary relevant context becomes that provided by legal argument and strategy. Places and related occupational characteristics become relevant spatial referents only through the filters of legal jurisdiction and doctrine. Each time a professor places a student in this landscape, the student must learn to focus on the details needed to shape a legal argument: to convert social and spatial coordinates into legal categories. People and problems are located in abstract individuals operating against the odd acontextual context of a legal geography, two contracting parties interacting with each other—even speaking in the first-person singular—against the backdrop of legal rights, jurisdictions, and doctrines.

## Summary: Learning to Think—and Talk—Like a Lawyer

As we will see in the next chapter, there is some striking variation among the professors in this study in terms of discursive format, as well as in terms of their own political and pedagogical philosophies regarding the proper role of law. It is therefore all the more intriguing to find strong continuities in metapragmatic structuring beneath these apparent differences. These continuities express a more subtle ideology about language, one that is part of the larger system to which law students are being socialized, of the written texts they are being trained to read, and of the way of speaking-and-thinking that their professors urge on them.

This language ideology stresses a transparency of metapragmatic form to social result. This is the case on several levels. Let us first consider the effect of role-play, whether between professor and student or internally within professor turns (when professors report the speech of various protagonists in dialogue with each other, playing each role in turn). The metapragmatic form of at times coercive dialogue is ideologically represented as transparent to the social result of a transformed social identity (learning to think like a lawyer, conveyed through classroom dialogue, being a crucial step on the way to becoming a lawyer). However, metapragmatic form is also understood as transparent to the social results of cases that are won by speakers able to hold up their end of similar dialogues—those who are able to take on and speak roles fluidly.

"Taking a position" as an interlocutor in a dialogue is a necessary part of gaining power for legal actors. This taking of a position is most vividly enacted through role-playing, and it doesn't matter which role is played as long as some role is played. Professors take roles themselves, speaking for various characters in the cases and even in legal philosophical texts, as they unfold a dialogic drama in classroom speech. At times, professors also push students to take these roles themselves and to play them with certainty. Lack of assurance, breakthroughs of genuine affect, indexing through tone and gesture a failure to play the role, and silence are gaps in the dialogue—or worse, refusals to acquiesce in the ongoing metapragmatic structuring of discourse.

That structuring is a key ideological message of law school socialization. It prepares students for a legal world that constantly effects a translation of people into their roles (plaintiff, defendant) and actions into their legal categories (tort, breach of contract). This translation occurs in a system in which either of two opposing results is initially possible (guilty, not guilty) and in which effectual and "correct" metapragmatic regimentation (in courts, in legal documents, in lawyers' talk) yields powerful social results. A key presupposition of the legitimacy of those results is the untying of the drama as legally translated from its usual social moorings, the putative objectivity of the story once told in the apparently dispassionate language of the law. As the people in the cases become parties (i.e., strategic actors on either side of a legal argument), they are stripped of social position and specific context, located in a geography of legal discourse and authority. Their gender, race, class, occupational, and other identities become secondary to their ability to argue that they have met various aspects of legal tests. These contextual factors do sometimes become salient to the discussions, but only as ammunition in just this way—as fodder for metalinguistic legal filtering.

Thus, not only through the immediate modeling of role-play but in other ways as well, we can say that the linguistic ideology of legal pedagogy represents metalinguistic form as transparent at a third, even deeper level, for the metapragmatic structure conveyed in law school classrooms also mirrors a broader legal epistemology. This legal epistemology undergirds the U.S. legal system, which derives its legitimacy in part from an act of translation of social events and actors into their corresponding legal categories and roles. These categories and roles, like the legal texts re-entextualized in new legal opinions, are always part of an oppositional discourse in which one of two opposing parties, and interpretations, will "win." The linguistic ideology conveyed through this metapragmatic structure pushes social context and emotion to the margins, except when they have been abstracted and processed through legal categories (as, for example, with the concept of "provocation" in criminal law).[37] Otherwise, emotion and context enter only through the backdoor, as when the professor warns the students that the "equities" of the situation can skew legal results. (An example of this would be if a legal requirement has not been strictly met, but the judge or jury finds for the party anyway because of sympathetic feelings for an individual plaintiff.) Role-playing in the classroom attempts to bring students to the level of actual people,[38] but the specific roles that are played omit many of the social particulars that shape not only normal social interactions themselves, but also moral assessments of those interactions. The bracketing of social context, along with the translation of people and events into legal categories and roles, is deemed to be a crucial way in which law achieves objectivity and lawyers achieve dispassionate professional competence. And, as we have seen, the means to this objectivity is through language: through insistent dialogic exchange and questioning, taking each side, trying on different positions and roles.

This removed approach to the person and to human conflict feeds into an ideology of universal translatability in which legal language serves as a discursive medium of exchange across all areas and levels of society.[39] In converting virtually every possible event or conflict into a shared rhetoric, legal language generates an appearance of neutrality that belies its often deeply skewed institutional workings. The classroom experience initiates law students into this new language using an approach that encourages them to push aside the emotional and socially embedded particulars of the conflict. Instead, law professors direct their students' attention to the oddly abstract conceptions of people and contexts provided by layered readings of legal texts. The people in these landscapes, as well as the landscapes themselves, are configured around points of legal argumentation, around strategically structured dialogue. Students begin to learn a process of translation that they will eventually take for granted. This legal translation is a key ground from which they will operate when performing their role as lawyers; it embodies an epistemology that is the background grammar for all legal discussion.[40] When students speak this language, they operate in a world in which important aspects of social context and identity have become invisible. This is the phenomenon I refer to as "cultural invisibility." At the same time, other aspects of dominant culture and assumptions become highly visible: the logic of capitalist exchange, for example, in Contracts classes, and the focus on an abstract, strategizing individual as the central figure in legal narratives. Thus, a cultural dominance for some aspects of context accompanies a cultural invisibility for others. And so when professors translate human conflict into this legal language, they drain away much of the sociocultural specificity, along with many emotional and moral dimensions. In doing so, they subtly erase a great deal of the context and detail on which most laypeople would rely in forming ethical judgments. At the same time, they strongly insist that students focus on details pertinent to doctrinal, statutory, and procedural require-ments delineated by layers of legal texts and legal authorities. And they model a question-answer form of dialogue as the canonical means to legally acceptable conclusions.

There is an interesting combination of abstraction and specificity involved in this process. To connect each new conflict story with legal precedent, students must focus on detailed aspects of the stories, if they are to categorize the new facts as instances of general, legally specified types. For example, a student might argue that a particular act or event in this new conflict story constitutes a breach of contract because it is arguably the "same" as an action or an event in a previous case where the courts found a breach. Yet, this apparent concern for specificity wrenches de-tail from its particular social and (nonlegal) narrative contexts in ways that can obscure or erase the features of the story to which laypeople look when reaching moral judgments. One could argue that there is an attraction to the apparent neu-trality of this kind of categorization; it conveys the idea that no matter who you are, you will be dealt with similarly. By running the facts of the conflict or case through the filter of legally relevant categories (guided by and invoking forms of legal authority derived from legal texts), any individual may be able to escape the prejudices and inequities of socially embedded moral judgments. Indeed, we can point to cases where this has been the case: in which appeal to more formal and abstract legal categories and procedures has permitted socially stigmatized victims to be heard. However, there is a double-edged character to this legal mediation, one that social theorists have found in the commodity form more generally.

For example, building from the Frankfurt School, Moishe Postone describes a complex "double character" to capital, labor, and time in capitalist societies. In particular, he notes that labor has both an abstract and a concrete character in capitalist societies. Labor has a concrete character because, for society to survive, some kinds of work must be physically performed. However, in capitalist societ-ies, concrete labor is mediated by an abstract level in which "individuals are com-pelled to produce and exchange commodities in order to survive."[41] Postone calls this "abstract labor."[42] This new kind of social mediation is "impersonal, abstract, and objective."[43] It creates a form of domination and alienation that is quite dif-ferent from those found in other kinds of societies. However, this does not mean that capitalism is necessarily worse than other, previous social forms, which em-ployed other kinds of domination. For example, in feudal society, precisely because labor was not taken away in such an impersonal and abstract way, Postone argues that "expropriation . . . [by the elite, nonlaboring classes] was *and had to be* based [more] upon direct compulsion."[44] The move to abstraction in capitalist society therefore carries both a liberating potential and increased opportunity for conceal-ing the alienation of concrete labor through an illusion of freedom.

Although we must proceed cautiously in drawing parallels at this broad level of social analysis, it is interesting that the legal language taught in the United States also has a double edge. On the one hand, the approach to legal reading found in law school classrooms offers students a potentially liberating opportunity to step into an impersonal, abstract, and objective approach to human conflict. On the other hand, erasing (or marginalizing) many of the concrete social and contextual features of these conflicts can direct attention away from grounded moral under-standings, which some critics believe are crucial to achieving justice. Moreover, this step out of social context and emotion provides the law with a cloak of appar-ent neutrality, which can conceal the ways that law participates in and supports unjust aspects of capitalist societies. This approach also gives the appearance of dealing with concrete and specific aspects of each conflict, thereby hiding the ways that legal approaches exclude from systematic consideration the very details and contexts that many would deem important for making just moral assessments.

As a result, the alienation experienced by some law students during legal train-ing may be an unavoidable consequence of a process in which increasingly instru-mental and technical appeals to legal authority blunt moral and context-sensitive judgment. Such technical appeals lie at the heart of U.S. legal epistemology and are an important part of the legal system's very legitimacy. As we have seen, the people and landscapes that result from this new legal approach to reading and composing conflict stories are defined by their positions in legal arguments, con-stituted in and through dialogue. Taking a step back from any emotional response, the legal reader uses question-answer pair-parts to create a discursive distance that nonetheless allows him or her to simultaneously actually enter into the conflict as well, standing in the shoes of the people involved. Just as legal translation into putatively objective categories gives the legal system a veneer of legitimacy, the ability to take either position in this ongoing dialogue also conveys a sense of ob-jectivity and fairness. All points of view are ostensibly under consideration; all sides of the conflict will be given voice. In this sense, role-playing and question-answer dialogic form are features of the metapragmatic regimentation of discourse that takes institutionalized ideology to the heart of the speaking that constitutes the legal arena. As Matoesian[45] has noted, domination is well concealed and indeed natu-ralized through metalinguistic ideology and structure in legal settings, and the law school classroom offers a prism through which to see this process in action.

In her study of the language of judges, as we've already noted, linguistic an-thropologist Susan Philips also stresses the role of legal discourse in naturalizing and concealing the enactment of politics and power in court:

> The judges in this study are conscious to varying degrees of the ideological dualisms and oppositions identified in legal, political, and everyday control ideologies. But it is striking that ideology and conflict are most acknowledged where they are consid-ered peripheral. Ideological conflict is displaced from the political and legal into the everyday "nonlegal" discussion of courtroom control in a way that furthers the im-age of the law as ideologically monolithic.[46]

There is an obvious parallel here to the way professors acknowledge the potential impact of racism or politics on legal decisions, but push it to the margins of discourse. Philips also demonstrates that judges vary systematically, by political orientation, in how they approach hearing guilty pleas. However, they characterize what they do in the courtroom as above politics, as legal and professional: "Judges in fact repudiate the enactment of political ideology in their courtroom behavior."[47] Politics are at once enacted in the metalinguistic structure of courtroom discourse and concealed through the fiction that this discourse is "legal" rather than "political."

As we have seen, the putative safeguard provided by legal discursive structure relies on a metalinguistic filter. This filter has a number of dimensions: the characteristic layering of legal texts and legal authority,[48] translation into doctrinal categories, the metapragmatic warrants provided by legal procedure, the insistent shifting between positions in an oppositional dialogue, the distancing provided by ongoing technical questioning. To successfully master this discourse, students must be able to speak in an "I" that is not their own self, to adapt their position to the exigencies of legal language. Arguably, most professionals must do this, yet the fluidity of footing and role taught in law school classrooms stands out as more similar to, say, acting school than to medical school. In both law and theater, the fluidity of footing and role, submerging self into the discourse itself, are central to a new chameleon professional "I." It is not just one new professional self that must be learned and voiced; rather, there is an ongoing multiplicity of perspectives and voices (although they are bound together by a common metapragmatic foundation). Of course, in law school, the act of submersion in multiple voices is part of a linguistic process by which state power interacts with individual citizens' lives, giving it a different character from training in, for example, theater.

Law students, then, are undergoing a quiet process in which their very selves are decentered through and in speech, as they take on the voices and perspectives pushed on them by the demands of legal discourse. A poignant comparison can be made between this process in law school training and discourse in courtrooms. Recall for a moment the exchange in Transcript 6.25, in which the professor corrects a student's attempt to describe her own motivations for attending law school:

> Come, Ms. C., you're not that shallow a person. Let's be honest. Let's force you to say something maybe you don't really mean. Let's psychoanalyze you. You're in law school rather than business school because you find it at bottom more deeply satisfying or at least you thought you could, to study the law than to go to business school. [ . . . ] There is a deep emotional fulfillment that you are supposed to be getting from the law school. That is why you came here.

As we noted, this exchange highlights the process by which students are encouraged to separate their inner opinions and feelings from the discursively defined legal personae they are learning to embody. A core facet of this embodiment, of course, is the shift to a new voice, so that students engaging in dialogue with their teachers begin to speak as players in a legal drama. In the process, they move away from emotion, morality, and context as they create new selves anchored in legal discourse. This makes sense of the otherwise nonsensical situation we find in this exchange, where the professor can actually situate himself as more expert regarding the student's own motives than she herself is.

Let us now compare that law school dialogue with the following exchange reported by Philips in her study of courtroom discourse:

*Philips text:*[49]

Judge:        (Show) the defendant in custody. Uh as I informed you gentlemen in chambers, I have reviewed the uh defendant's record and I cannot go along with the plea agreement with you. If I were to

|  | sentence him I would sentence him to the (uh) state prison and certainly give him more than time served. The plea agreement provides that the defendant may withdraw his plea uh. |
| Defendant: | I don't wanna withdraw my plea. |
| Judge: | All right (let) the record show that the defendant has withdrawn his plea and the court orders that the matter be set for trial um – |
| Defendant : | I don't wanna withdraw my plea! {louder than last time; basically a shout; he shouts the rest of the time} |
| Judge: | You don't wanna withd/raw your plea?/ |
| Defense lawyer: | /Be quiet/ please. [2 secs.] Your Honor, I would request that you withdraw his plea. If my client doesn't want to, I don't know what I can do about it. |

The ensuing exchange features the defendant continuing to try to describe the conditions under which he has been detained, stressing that he wants some immediate relief from "twenty-four hour lockup . . . in a little cell this big." The judge and attorneys continue to proceed with the dialogue needed to prepare for trial, ignoring this commentary. At one point the judge states that he is ordering a Rule 11 examination, to which the defendant replies:

| Defendant: | I'm not taking no Rule 11. |
| Judge: | Who do you want? |
| Defense lawyer: | Your Honor, Dr. Madigan. |
| Defendant: | Fuck this shit. |

Eventually the defendant tried to hobble out of the courtroom (for a second time).

How do we make sense of the judge's comment "Let the record show that the defendant has withdrawn his plea" immediately following a turn in which the defendant has quite clearly indicated that he does not want to do so? Again we see the primacy of the demands of legally defined dialogic position; regardless of what the defendant wants, the judge (the authoritative voice of the law in this setting) is going to withdraw the plea. He does not hesitate to provide the correct response for this defendant when the defendant refuses to; putting fictional speech into the mouth of one's interlocutor is an important part of discursive practice in some legal settings. The student in the law school exchange is uncooperative in the process, perhaps in part because she is taken aback by this direct a usurpation of her voice, and perhaps because she simply can't divine what the professor is seeking. This creates a problem, however, which the professor eventually solves not by explaining the point he wanted to make, but by speaking for the student. The prisoner also creates a problem when he will not provide the requested locution, will not occupy the position required by the ongoing dialogue; this is not supposed to be quite as easily solved in a criminal law setting. However, the judge and attorneys do override his protests; his own attorney takes his place in the dialogue (despite the defendant's obvious opposition to allowing his voice to be represented in this way). In both cases, the speaking "I" forged by legal discourse for each person is clearly not their own: it is that of a new persona, carved and crafted by the demands of legal discourse.

Notice that, once again, a defining moment in legal discourse and legal legitimacy requires the unmooring of the self from its usual coordinates, a fluidity of voice and footing and position.[50] A deceptive metapragmatic ideology locates justice and even-handedness in this unmooring, in this constructed dialogue that at once anchors and conceals legal hegemony. Layers of intertextual reference provide a new anchoring that furthers this process.[51] As Conley and O'Barr have noted, "the details of legal discourse matter," because it is in and through them that the larger contours of the system of justice are constructed.[52] Conley and O'Barr urge us to bring together a bigger picture generated by sociological analyses of law with the on-the-ground understanding achieved by fine-grained study of legal language. In these chapters, we have seen the importance of such a marriage to grasping the message and import of legal pedagogy as it shapes incipient legal practitioners' worldviews.

Having explored aspects of language structure and ideology that are shared among the classrooms of the study, we now turn to examine differences and variability.

# III

·————·

# DIFFERENCE: SOCIAL STRUCTURE
# IN LEGAL PEDAGOGY

*Through an awareness of intersectionality, we can better ac-*
*knowledge and ground the differences among us and negotiate*
*the means by which these differences will find expression.*[1]

*My difference argument . . . is grounded in empirical realiza-*
*tions, in gendered experiences, and therefore, in women's lives*
*as constructed in society and culture.*[2]

*From here, what we need to do is work, in specific contexts, on*
*the problems of difference.*[3]

A debate has emerged in recent years over the impact of social difference on law
school education. Studies and anecdotal accounts have suggested that women
are disadvantaged in law school classrooms because of differential patterns of participation and inclusion and because of gendered reactions to distinctively legal
discourse styles. Although far less systematic attention has been paid to the effects
of race, class, or school status on students' experience in law schools, there have
been accounts suggesting that students of color also feel excluded in law school
classrooms. In addition, recent work documents negative effects of the law school
milieu for working-class students. In this part of the book, we examine the shape
of the differences and similarities among the classrooms in this study in terms of
race, gender, and school status.

Chapter 7 begins the section with an overview of the different professorial
teaching styles found in the classrooms of the study, analyzed in context. Chapter
8 presents this study's findings on student participation, with particular attention
to race and gender. The chapter analyzes the implications for our understandings
of diversity, both in the law school classroom and beyond it. These chapters sug-

gest that the twin problems of cultural invisibility and dominance, which we have already encountered when scrutinizing the *content* of classroom discourse, are also important issues when analyzing the *structure* of legal teaching. At the same time, in an important check on essentialism, we should note that some students of all races and genders find law school training alienating. In this sense, an improved understanding of the features of this training that impact traditionally marginalized students can benefit other students as well.

# 7

## Professorial Style in Context

In this chapter, we survey the variety of classroom styles found among the professors in the study. It is important to remember that there are continuities to be found across these differences in style, as outlined in Part II. These continuities were not only matters of the content of the lesson conveyed or of common orientations regarding the correct reading of legal texts, the importance of hierarchies of legal authority, and so forth. As we've seen, there were also similarities of discursive form and structure. For example, even teachers who employed a great deal of lecture nonetheless replicated aspects of dialogic form within their own turns, and when they did call on students there were similarities of approach to be found in the questioning. And all of the professors employed exegetical lecturing, sometimes for long periods of time, sometimes interspersed with ongoing questioning of students. At the same time, there was considerable variability among the professors in terms of discourse style. After surveying the variations among classrooms in detail, we return at the end of this chapter to the question of assessing similarities and differences in professorial style, seen now in terms of the contexts provided by social patterning.

## A Diverse Range of Styles

One of the most fascinating aspects of law school classroom discourse uncovered by this study is the combination of underlying structural similarities with, on the surface, a startling array of diverse teaching styles. At one end of the spectrum, we find the most highly stylized Socratic classroom, with heavily structured dialogue dominating (represented here by one of the pilot study classrooms). More common in this study were mixed formats of various kinds. For example, in modified

141

Socratic classrooms, professors loosened the ongoing questioning, provided some answers, and did some lecturing. There were also a number of classrooms in which an almost conversational give-and-take was at times permitted, although question-answer sequences controlled by the professor nonetheless provided a strong structural backbone even in these settings. Finally, one professor relied primarily on a lecture format.

### The Traditional Socratic Teacher: On the Wane?

We have already encountered the most stereotypic Socratic teacher in this research, a professor who taught in one of the classes used for the pilot study. This is the class in which uptake structure mirrored the pragmatic lesson the professor sought to inculcate; for example, in one exchange, he repeated the question "How did this case get to the appellate court?" until he received the desired response ("It was appealed"; Transcript 4.2). It was a class taught in an elite/prestige law school by a white male professor, who himself had been educated in an elite law school. It is interesting that this class was the only one we encountered that maintained the level of strictly stylized questioning typically associated with "pure" Socratic teaching.[1] There have been some indications that the Socratic method is on the wane, at least in certain law schools.[2] Indeed, a recent article describes "The Decline of the Socratic Method at Harvard."[3] The professors included in my actual study used methods ranging from modified Socratic teaching, through use of shorter exchanges and at times almost conversational styles, to a heavy lecture format. This might appear to give some support to those who see a decline in use of strict Socratic teaching.

However, there are some difficulties in assessing either the current general state of Socratic teaching in law schools or the degree to which the current situation represents a marked change from earlier teaching norms. First, most studies have relied on professors' self-reports as to what they are doing, which may not be entirely accurate.[4] For example, one of the professors in my study described his teaching method as a mixture: "I try . . . purposely to get a mix. I don't want to do the same format every day. I want days where I really push them a lot, I want days where I maybe lecture it, there's no sense in falling into a pattern. Patterns create staleness" (Interview 97–I13). This professor spent 91% of class time in monologue or lecture. This does not mean that his assessment was entirely inaccurate, because he did use the remaining 9% of the time to vary the format. However, one would not want to use his self-report as the primary or only source of information about the actual pattern in his classroom. And, indeed, this is not unusual; it is difficult for speakers to keep detailed track of what they are doing.

A second difficulty is that we have no thorough linguistic study of classic Socratic teaching during its heyday. As a result, when discussing the linguistic structure of Socratic teaching, the literature relies on stereotypes and anecdotal descriptions of this teaching method promulgated by either fans or opponents of Socratic teaching. Although there is some agreement on a general definition of the genre—it involves extended questioning of individual students regarding cases assigned for class—from there the details become increasingly difficult to define. For some, it is necessary that the questioning occupy almost all of class time, that it be antagonistic, that no answers or explanations be proffered by the professor, and that the students be called on at random without warning. For others, some subset of these characteristics is all that is necessary. Others rely on a generalized combination of discourse structure and discourse content in defining Socratic teaching: "For many professors, the term 'Socratic' describes a question and answer method in which the professor asks a series of questions of the students, uncovering both preconceptions and cogent legal analysis."[5] We really have no systematic information on the actual distribution of particular characteristics in classrooms considered to be strictly Socratic. It seems possible that even professors considered to be classic Socratic teachers occasionally broke into explanations and lecturing, or that some may have approached the questioning with less ferocity and animosity than one would infer from the stereotype and associated anecdotes. It is unclear under the stereotype how to classify professors who combine classic Socratic questioning with a predictable pattern for calling on students (rather than calling on them with no warning) or with a heavy reliance on volunteers. It is similarly difficult to label a professor who in essence follows the same thread of question-answer sequences that would be found in the typical Socratic classroom (i.e., asking for statements of facts and reasoning, using hypotheticals to test students' understandings) but who does so with a series of students rather than remaining in tight dialogue with just one or two students.

Interestingly, a study published in 1977 by Thomas Shaffer and Robert Redmount seemed to indicate that the Socratic method was on the wane.[6] Their research found that first-year law teaching at Indianapolis, Notre Dame, and Valparaiso (and possibly also UCLA) was heavily oriented toward lecture. Teachers in first-year classes in the Indiana schools spoke "four-fifths of the time," whereas teachers in public-policy-oriented classes spoke "only two-thirds of the time."[7] Shaffer and Redmount seem to define Socratic dialogue in terms of "probing" methods of questioning, which they found to be "not used much at all"; when these methods were used, it was most frequently in the smaller schools and in the generally smaller third-year classes. As I've noted, we don't have quantitative observational data from early Socratic classrooms, and so we don't know to what extent even the most pure examples of Socratic teaching involved a mixture of lecture and questioning. From one perspective, one could look at Shaffer and Redmount's findings as evidence that a nonlecture method of some kind was still very much in use in first-year classrooms: nothing close to 100% or 95% of the time was spent in lecture (by contrast with a straight lecture-style class). This was true in all but one of the classes of this study as well. Friedland's 1994–1995 survey of law professors similarly found that 97% of the respondents reported using Socratic method at least some of the time in first-year classes.[8] In contrast with Shaffer and Redmount's findings, Friedland's respondents recount using Socratic method to a greater degree in first-year classes and lecture method more in upper-level courses.[9]

A third complication lies in the fact that the impact of Socratic teaching may not be attributable in any straightforward way to the amount of floor time it occupies. It may be sufficient that the method is used to some degree in most class hours; this may be enough to convey to students any particular form of reasoning that it embodies, or to intimidate them with the fear of possible public humiliation often mentioned as one of its disciplining functions.

In sum, we do not have enough information to reach a definitive conclusion about the purported decline of Socratic teaching. There is very little empirical information about the actual distribution or shape of Socratic teaching in its reputed heyday to provide a baseline. Furthermore, there is a great deal of variability in the details of how Socratic teaching is defined in the literature, with some writers focusing more on discourse structure and others on a tough or exacting emotional atmosphere. Studies purporting to show the end or decline of Socratic teaching frequently yield substantial evidence of its continuing influence. For example, of the faculty surveyed for an article entitled "The Decline of the Socratic Method at Harvard," the largest group (41.6%) reported using traditional Socratic teaching, and another 25% reported employing a mix of Socratic and other methods.[10] There may indeed be an ongoing influx of alternative teaching methods (and a correlative decline in use of traditional Socratic teaching), but we do not have the evidence at this point to conclude that any of the core features of Socratic teaching have ceased to exert considerable influence in law school training.[11] As we will see, there is considerable methodological difficulty in studying some of the often mentioned features of the Socratic classroom. For example, internal dialogue within a professorial lecture can replicate aspects of the discourse or argument structure, and a professor who calls on multiple students to answer questions (rather than focusing on one or two) can still create an intimidating atmosphere. We turn now to an examination of the more complex, mixed picture of teaching method that emerges from the classrooms of this study.

## The Modified Socratic Teacher

If we rank the classrooms included in our full study in terms of the amount of extended, Socratic-style dialogue (in terms of either amount of time or number of turns), we find that there is a clustering of three classrooms (#1, #4, #5) at the top.[12] The teachers in these classrooms spent between 45% and 60% of the time in extended dialogue, whereas the remaining classes (except for #7, the lecture-dominated class) clustered between 21% and 29%. Similarly, the teachers in classes #1, #4, and #5 spent between 74% and 86% of the turns in extended dialogue with students, whereas teachers in "short-exchange" classes spent 60%, 54%, 40%, and 34%. Note that all of the more Socratic classes in the study had some shorter dialogues, in which multiple students participated for shorter periods of time, as well as some lectures by the professors. For this reason, I characterize them as "modified Socratic" classrooms. This terminology is supported by other deviations from stereotypical Socratic teaching found in these classes, as we will see. We now turn to examine the characteristics of these three modified Socratic classrooms.

Because extended dialogue dominates in these classrooms, we frequently find the class period divided among a small number of students, each of whom participates in a lengthy exchange with the professor. All three professors diverge from dialogue at times, using lecture formats to explicate particular points. In this regard, the teaching varies from standard Socratic format in that some answers are in fact explained and laid out for students, rather than left to emerge in dialogue.

The professors also use humor and other techniques to soften the questioning, again a departure from the stereotypical harshness and humiliation that some deemed to be central to Socratic questioning. If the traditional stereotype portrayed Socratic dialogue as similar to oral argument at the appellate level (where judges sharply question attorneys),[13] the Socratic exchanges in these classrooms seem to more frequently approximate direct examinations, in which the questioner is attempting to elicit and coproduce an integrated narrative. This, of course, does not mean that students do not feel pressure when they are required to sustain lengthy exchanges with their teachers, sometimes under the eyes of more than one hundred classmates. And, unlike a direct examination, the classroom exchange is not rehearsed. The student in a sense occupies a place somewhere in between the witnesses in cross-examinations and direct examinations; although the professor is not the student's attorney, with a strong investment in eliciting a seamless narrative, in these transcripts we find evidence that professors are in fact attempting to ease the dialogic process through a number of devices, such as framing. Professors may not have the complete overlap of interest in production of a smooth narrative found between a client and attorney during a direct examination. However, they do have a strong interest in keeping classroom exchanges going in a coherent and productive fashion. In this sense, there seems to be a difference between the modified Socratic teachers of this study and the opposing counsel bent on breaking down a witness through cross-examination, or even the appellate judge zealously poking holes in an attorney's oral argument.

In this example from Class #4, taught by a white male professor in a relatively highly ranked regional school, we see how the teacher coconstructs a story with his chosen Socratic partner. This student takes up 66% of the student turns on this particular day. The remaining 34% of student turns are taken up by one other student, so that the entire class consists of extended dialogue with two different students. The exchange begins with a fairly typical request for a recitation of the facts to elicit a telling of the underlying story as framed by legal exigencies.

*Transcript 7.1 [4/17/6–7]*

Prof.:    *[turn begins with a summation of a key point regarding the case that he had just finished discussing with another student]* All right. Now let's turn to uh to the *Ricketts* case. *[.30 shuffling noise]*. Uh, let's see, um Ms. B., how are we doing in *Ricketts* and what's going on?

Ms. B.:   Well, there's a conflict between grandfather and granddaughter that um he would give two thousand dollars on demand and 60% interest per annum and said that she didn't have to work. And um, she said that she gave up her work on reliance on this um promise and uh she- () she wants to get the money.

Prof.:    Right, okay. You have the promise of some um money, uh, the granddad to his granddaughter, okay? Um, what we're asking in consideration questions, we always ask about the return promise, right? So, uh, what was the return promise in this case?

Ms. B.:   Well it's not really sure that there was one because she um [[Prof: Right]], she's saying that she um relied on the money and she didn't ()

grandfather really gave her the gift [[Prof.: Okay]] because she does go
back to work, after a year ().

Prof.:     Okay. And when she says "I'd like to collect on, collect on my gift," the
grandfather's estate says what?

Ms. B.:     Lack of consideration.

Prof.:     It was lack of consideration, okay. Back to *Batsakis* again [ . . . ]

By this point, almost halfway though the semester, we see a very smooth coproduction
of the fact narrative. Note the use of "we" inclusive to begin the dialogue, aligning
the professor and student as fellow travelers who are located together within the
bounds of the case narrative, and asking the student to provide some guidance in
explaining "what's going on." The student responds by providing a succinct summary of some of the key details needed for purposes of a legal reading. The professor immediately approves this summary and provides a frame for the student's
ongoing narration; he characterizes the case as a token of the legal-discursive type
"consideration questions," and then indicates that the next step in telling the story
involves discussion of any "return promise" (or absence thereof). The primacy
of legal issues and categories in organizing the narrative is assumed here, and the
particular issue selected for organizing this issue is also mentioned in a casual
manner. As the student proceeds, the professor encourages her with positive
backchanneling ("Right"; "Okay"). Note that through the framing commentary
and questioning, the professor is essentially providing the links needed to move
from one part of the narrative to another.

Thus, following this smooth opening, the professor continues to prompt the
student, using these highly structured question frames, guiding her through a discussion of how legal categories apply to the facts of the case. After eliciting one
side of the argument, he signals a shift to the other side, asking the student to describe "something" that goes in the other "direction": "What's the something?" The
student responds, "Well, that she was able to quit her job, which she did do." The
professor both slightly corrects and builds on this: "Well, let's just say, 'give up job.'
Let's just say, 'give up job.' It's going in this direction. I guess we would have to ask
two questions about that." A great deal of the work of narrative cohesion is done
as the professor takes each response and places it in the larger setting of a legal story,
which is not simply about the conflict at issue but about the process by which a
legal resolution can be reached. Notice also the repetition here as both student and
professor begin turns with "well"; the student's next turn continues this pattern:
"Well, only if he- he sought that term." (We will see more substantial versions of
this cohesion-creating repetition below.)

The basic semantico-referential structure of the dialogue, as it is unfolded
by the professor, proceeds as follows: (a) first, a recitation of relevant facts; (b) a
statement of the grandfather's estate's position; (c) an examination of the argument for the granddaughter, leading to (d) an exchange delving into whether the
granddaughter's actions could constitute "consideration" in this case, with particular attention to the possible application of the categories of "benefit" and "detriment" to the facts; (e) a brief analogy to a previous similar case; (f) a return to the
consideration problem in *this* case, focusing now on whether the granddaughter's

return promise had been "sought"; (g) a discussion of the remedy the granddaughter had requested using an estoppel argument and dissection of the requirements for estoppel. Although the student is clearly an active participant in the dialogue, the professor is in charge, lingering over a point until he is satisfied that discussion has been exhausted, and then moving on. In his turns, the professor frequently provides the necessary legal-discursive framework for the student's responses:

> *Transcript 7.2 [4/17/11, 14]*
>
> Prof.:   *[end of 1.15 turn]* We only have those two questions. Is the thing given as a benefit to the promisor or a detriment to the promisee, and is it given in exchange for the promisor's promise and is the promisor's promise given in exchange for that benefit or detriment, right? We always ask those two questions. Restatement Section 71 puts it in black-and-white, straightforward, nice and simple, all right? Okay. In the actual case, to get back to the actual case, Ms. B., there's no question, I guess, that the promise induced the giving up of job?
>
> Prof.:   *[ . . . later in same class session, end of 1.33 turn . . . ]* but, it also had something to do with the following: "Induce the change of position," this is page ninety-six, "in accordance with a real or apparent intention of the party against ()." "Accordance with a real or apparent intention." What do you make of that?

In each of these two excerpts, the professor reminds the student of the parts of the legal test to be applied, in the first instance putting the parts of the test in the form of questions that the student is to ask herself (see Chapter 4). By doing this, the professor constructs a strong discursive framework that allows the student to simply fill in the blank by applying the legal categories to the facts of the case at hand as she moves through the narrative segments he sets up.

In addition to creating a coherent narrative thread that moves the discussion through relatively clear, semantically delineated segments, the professor's questions also guide the student's responses in terms of form, creating a fairly smooth give-and-take. (This is arguably the point at which the professor-student pair-part structure comes closest to achieving a "monologue in adjacency pair form.") For example, a number of the professor's turns begin with repetition of some part of the student's previous utterance, creating the kinds of discursive links that have been noted in trial talk:[14]

> *Transcript 7.3 [4/17/7–14]:*
>
> | Turn 62/Ms. B.: | Lack of consideration. |
> | T. 63/Prof.: | It was lack of consideration, okay. . . . |
> | | |
> | T. 90/Ms. B.: | I'd say "yes." |
> | T. 92/Prof.: | You'd say "yes." |
> | | |
> | T. 96/Ms. B: | *Hamer.* |
> | T. 97/Prof.: | Looks like *Hamer*, right. |

| T. 98/Ms. B.: | That she has to give up her job in order to get the money. |
| T. 99/Prof.: | She has to give up her job in order to get the money. |

| T. 100/Ms. B.: | Yes. |
| T. 101/Prof.: | Yes, that's right. |

| T. 104/Ms. B.: | Right, that's what the court says. |
| T. 105/Prof.: | That's what the court says, there's no question about that. All right. |

| T. 110/Prof.: | But, what is this that we can't say? |
| T. 111/Ms. B.: | That the return promise was sought for by the granddaughter. |
| T. 112/Prof.: | We can't say that the return promise, "Yes, I'll give up my job," was sought for in exchange for the gift. |

| T. 117/Ms. B.: | What was promised. |
| T. 118/Prof.: | What was promised. |

| T. 121/Ms. B.: | The two thousand dollars. |
| T. 122/Prof.: | The two thousand dollars. |

| T. 127/Ms. B.: | [ . . . ] and that's on the grounds of equitable estoppel- |
| T. 128/Prof.: | Equitable estoppel, uh huh [ . . . ] |

| T. 133/Ms. B.: | [ . . . ] from not fulfilling the promise. |
| T. 134/Prof.: | Estopped from not fulfilling the promise. |

| T. 148/Ms. B.: | No, he didn't even know the situation. |
| T. 149/Prof.: | Right, didn't know the situation, so [ . . . ] |

| T. 152/Ms. B.: | Apparent (intention). |
| T. 153/Prof.: | Or apparent intention. What do you make of that? |

| T. 154/Ms. B.: | Well, then you could- you could argue that the employer had an apparent intention. |
| T. 155/Prof.: | Well, now, why could you argue that? |

The use of parallel repetition in these question-answer sequences builds a sense of semantic cohesion across the two speakers' utterances, contributing to a sense of narrative continuity.[15] It also contributes to a poetic coordination of the participants' speech rhythms just at the point of transition, again promoting a sense of continuity. Scholars studying this kind of patterning have also pointed to its utility in aiding audience comprehension, surely as much an asset with large classes as with juries.[16] (The modified Socratic classrooms ranged from 98 to 115 students.)

The professor at times also induces a similar connective poetic structure between question and answer by using framing tag questions to induce parallel responses (copy) from the student:

Transcript 7.4 [4/17/11]

Prof.:   Yes, in that situation, okay. In the scenario where the grandfather says, "I'll give you money if you stop working." Then it's pretty clear that the stopping of work is given as an inducement for the money, and vice versa, and the money is given as an inducement for the stopping of work. That's that mutual inducement point we're always talking about when we're talking about consideration for bargain () right? We only have those two questions. Is the thing given a benefit to the promisor or detriment to the promisee and the- is it given in exchange for the promisor's promise and is the promisor's promise given in exchange for that benefit or detriment, all right? We always ask those two questions. Restatement Section 72 puts it black-and-white, straightforward, nice and simple, all right? Okay. In the actual case, to get back to the actual case, uh, Ms. B., there's no question, I guess, that the promise induced the giving up of the job.

Ms. B.:   Right, that's what the court says.

Prof.:   That's what the court says, there's no question about that. All right. But, that's only half the story of this bargain, right?

Ms. B.:   Right.

(There are eight instances of this kind of structure in the extended dialogue, which consists of 48 pair-parts.) This excerpt is particularly useful because it also demonstrates several other features worth noting. First, we see the occasional poetic repetition and continuity created by both professor's and student's use of affirmations such as "right" and "yes," which are peppered throughout the transcript.[17] The excerpt also demonstrates one method by which professors who engage in extended dialogue take some of the pressure off students: although the dialogue with this student occupied more than half of the class that day, note that the professor gives her fairly lengthy reprieves while he explicates and fills in blanks. This particular professor speaks for 82% of the time, meaning that although a great deal of the students' class time is spent in extended Socratic dialogues, the students' total time in dialogue (of any kind) with the professor occupies only 18% of class time.[18] In the interstices of the professor's reaction to the student's previous turn and his framing of the subsequent question, as we have seen, we frequently find substantial commentaries that provide crucial narrative and pedagogical links.[19]

If we combine the use of positive affirmations of previous turns, affirmative backchanneling, and repetitive parallelism at the beginning of professor and student turns, we find a very strong supportive frame that provides continuity and cuing, while incorporating student responses into the larger, ongoing pedagogical narrative.[20] In addition, the professor employs an interesting anaphoric structure that in effect supplies the syntactic-grammatical formulae into which student responses will fit. For example:

*Transcript 7.5 [4/17/7, 10]*

Prof.:    Okay. And when she says "I'd like to collect on- collect on my gift,"
          grandfather's estate says what?

Ms. B.:   "Lack of consideration."

Prof.:    [ . . . *end of 2.06 turn* . . . ] Then the case looks more like what, Ms. B.?

Ms. B.:   *Hamer.*

Prof.:    Yes, that's right. So, when we ask question number two here, "was the
          return promise for performance sought in exchange for the promise for
          the money?", [[Ms. B.: Yes]] your answer would be what?

Ms. B.:   "Yes," in that situation.

Prof.:    The court says, what?

Ms. B.:   ("The promise was given without consideration.")

Prof.:    "The promise was given without consideration," and we know, okay?
          that, uh, where there's no consideration, promises aren't enforceable,
          right?

In these examples, the professor in essence provides the first part of a sentence which
the student completes by replacing the anaphoric cue "what" with the specific
content it indicates. In several cases, the content takes the form of reported speech.
Interestingly, toward the end of the class, Ms. B. attempts to fill in a similar blank,
in this case when the professor pauses, creating a potential ellipsis or zero sign:

*Transcript 7.6 [4/17/16]*

Prof.:    Right, the question you would ask yourself of course is, how likely is it
          that somebody would spontaneously quit their job, if there hadn't been
          some-(.)

Ms. B.:   reliance--

Prof.:                --promise, coming the other way. You're saying, "Not very
          likely," right? [ . . . ]

The professor simply continues on through his turn, not pausing to acknowledge
the attempted interjection. But the student's proffered comment reveals the extent to which the professor has succeeded in creating a discursive rhythm in which
the student is literally finishing sentences and thoughts begun in his turns and
questions.

Finally, we can also examine the places in these classroom exchanges where
the generally strong coordination between these particular speakers breaks down.
At one point, for example, the professor asks a question that appears to stump the
student momentarily: "What's estoppel, and who is estopped from doing what, in
the case?" The student responds by saying, "Um . . ." And then the professor moves
into a sequence of cuing and positive commentary designed to facilitate the ongoing discussion: "Two-part question rolled into one." Student: "The grandfather's
estate is getting estopped--" Prof.: "--Yeah, that's- you're on the right track--" Student: "--from not fulfilling the promise." Prof.: "Estopped from not fulfilling the
promise . . ."

At another point, when Ms. B. begins to stumble, the professor again jumps in quite directively: "Okay, hold it right there. We know from the hypothetical that the employer didn't have a real intention, but it says something else, doesn't it?" Student: "(Apparent) intention." Prof.: "Or apparent intention. What do you make of that?" This vigorous approach, which redirects student responses quickly when they begin to stray, is another means by which the professor uses a strongly constraining discursive frame to guide students in coproducing coherent narratives. Similarly, the professor at times uses prosodic features like stress to cue students as to the likely correct response, as in this set of questions: "So, is that all you need to raise this estoppel point? Just a promise?" The student's response ("No") is predictable from a sensitive reading of these cues in the preceding question. At several points in this exchange, the professor also redirects the student by framing a response she has given as correct—but for a different situation. He then emphatically reiterates what the coordinates of *this* situation are (e.g., "Yes, in that situation, okay. . . . In the actual case, to get back to the actual case, Ms. B."; or "Okay, that's really the second question I was going to ask. . . . The first question I was going to ask, though, was . . . "). The professor will also at times forge ahead when the student is floundering and answer his own question. In another turn, the professor supplies dialogue for the student, warning her against a trap that is simultaneously one of thinking and saying:

*Transcript 7.7 [4/17/8]*

Prof.:     All right. So, we would ask the benefit-detriment question. *[writes on board]* Okay? Ask the benefit-detriment question. Benefit in the uncle, well, we might go off on a hair-brained theory about that, but we don't need to, right? Is it a detriment to the promisee, I guess, the answer's pretty obvious, right, Ms. B.? Assuming she really promised that, is it a detriment? Now, don't get caught in this trap, you're gonna say, "Well, not really, because she's going to get this money." Yeah, but that's not the way to think about it. That's not what we mean when we ask if there was a detriment, okay. We don't say, "Gee, is it really worth it for the nephew to give up these three fun things, in exchange for the money? Is it net detriment?" The answer is, "Who cares?" right? You don't look at the detriment () for the thing you promised. You just look at what you were promised. . . . You were gonna say, "Well, maybe not," but now you're gonna definitely say, she said it. [[class laughter]] "Because she's giving up a ten dollars a week, bookkeeping job, no question about it. That's clearly a detriment." Don't get- don't get confused in that net detriment concept. . . . *[continues through 2.23 turn]*

The professor here warns the student of a discursive-cum-thinking trap, holds the dialogue for her, anticipating a possible problem, and in one sense averts a possibly embarrassing (and confusing and time-consuming) tangle. (Although in another sense, he puts words in her mouth that she may never have uttered.) Here, as throughout our modified Socratic classrooms, the professor also employs humor to lighten the tone of the exchange. Thus, in contrast with the stereotypical Socratic exchange, the professor is doing a great deal of work to smooth out bumps in the dialogue, to help and cue the student when she appears to stumble, and to keep a collaborative construction of discourse going. In between, he is also filling in a lot of the legal blanks and questions, stressing certain points or legal tests or specific phrases over and over again, to ensure student comprehension.[21] Indeed, he indulges in a wry metacommentary on this at one point: "Okay, I don't know how to hammer this home anymore, so I'm- [[class laughter]] All right. Let's turn to uh something else."

Throughout many of these exchanges, we have also seen an interesting deployment of "little" discourse markers, such as "well," "all right," "okay," "right," "now," and "wait" on the part of professors. At times, these mark a disagreement and begin an initiated repair, as when the strict Socratic professor in Transcript 4.2 responded, "Well that's a rather general statement. How did this get to the appellate court?", or in Transcript 4.3, where he begins three successive turns (all of which conclude with negative uptake) as follows:

1. "Well, all right now you y- I just wanted you to talk about this one thought (all right) for the moment."
2. "Well now there are two parts [ . . . ] what are the two parts?"
3. "Well n- name the two parts, would you, because people have a lot of trouble with this."

These seemingly small discourse markers can be doing intriguing work, at once quietly redirecting the conversation while also serving a variety of different functions, as we see here. In addition to their marking disagreement or opening the door to repair, Matoesian lists a number of other possible functions for these seemingly minor terms, noting that they can do the work of "instructional markers, as in giving someone instructions for baking a cake" (or, here, parsing a legal text or doctrine), as well as sometimes of epistemic markers, conveying an aura of certainty or authority.[22] This can be particularly powerful when combined with the function of marking transitions in the ongoing exchange, as when we just heard the professor in Class #4 say, "Okay, I don't know how to hammer this home anymore, so I'm- [[class laughter]] All right. Let's turn to uh something else." The "all right" here signals a somewhat emphatic closure to the point he has just finished making, at the same time as he is moving the class along to the next part of the analysis. Although in this case the professor provides explicit metapragmatic signaling of the shift that is occurring, we find a similar structure in many professor utterances without such overt indexing. In these cases, it is the small discourse markers themselves that make the transition. They at times mark the boundaries of portions of the statement of facts or legal test that is being applied, signaling students that it is time to transition from one part of the analysis to another (see Transcripts 7.1, 7.7).[23] If the student has supplied the needed responses, the use of "okay" or "right" is not only serving as an instructional marker, an epistemic marker, and the signal for a transition; it is also ratifying the student's response, reinforcing a desired clarity and decisiveness of thought at a microlinguistic level (see Transcript 7.2).[24] Thus, these subtle discursive markers perform multilayered functions as they contribute to the overall cohesion of the ongoing exchange between professor and student.

We find patterns designed to coach students and to encourage cohesion in the other modified Socratic classrooms as well—of course, in somewhat different combinations and styles. For example, in Class #5, we find the professor using humor in an attempt to pull a student who is having a great deal of difficulty into the dialogue:

*Transcript 7.8 [5/24/3]*

Prof.:    Promises of a limited commitment. What elegant language. What abstract beauty. What could that possibly mean here?

Mr. O.:    To be honest, I only really understood, or I didn't really understand how it fit into the case.

Prof.:    These cases are very, very confusing and perplexing and they make you want to throw the book against the wall. But then most of the cases in this book will do that. Promises of the limited commitment. Try again. What do you suppose that means? Forget about the () case for just a moment. What do you think promises of a limited commitment means?

The ensuing dialogue causes both interlocutors some hard work, as the student struggles with questions he is having difficulty comprehending. The professor neither ridicules the student nor gives up on him (although it seems clear that the student might have wished that the professor did give up at some points!), but continues doggedly to shift the ground of the questions, moving first back to the open-ended prompt, "Tell me more about the () case," then to a question that provides strong structure, "Let's put it this way, what's the contract in that case, if there is one?," and then jumping on the student's first clear response, "That's simple, that's straightforward, and now we're beginning to get somewhere." As the dialogue progresses, the professor uses positive affirmations, repetition, first-person plural-inclusive, structured questions, and reported speech ("as you said before") to provide encouragement and also cohesion with the student's prior responses:

*Transcript 7.9 [5/24/5]*

Prof.:    What are we supposed to have before we have a contract?

Mr. O.:    Consideration?

Prof.:    That's one possibility. Is there consideration here? Is there consideration on both sides of this arrangement? And you're quite right, this section is concerned with consideration. It's one of the things that's going on. Let's try to find some. Is there any obligation on the side of the party ordering the gas?

Mr. O.:    Mmm, I don't think so.

Prof.:    No. Because, as you said before, Mr. O., it was "if" that party decided to order the gas.

In the midst of the dialogue, the professor pauses, as did the professor in Class #4 earlier, to cue the student as to the legal test that is to be applied:

Here we have one of these fancy, very specific oral contracts. Is this barred by the statute of frauds? This isn't a contract involving land, apparently, but there are other problems in the statute of frauds, specifically, the problem of contracts that can't be performed within a year. Is this a contract that can't be performed within a year? It doesn't have any stopping and starting dates in it, does it? So we don't know how long it would take to perform this contract. In your view, is this a contract that cannot be performed in under one year? (5/24/6)

We see again how much more framing and substance is given students here than in the stereotypical Socratic exchange; the different parts of the test are clearly laid out, the part that is applicable in this case is highlighted, and the pertinent facts from the case are even selected for the student, so that he is left with only one out of many calculations to make. At the end of the exchange with this student, the professor implicitly attempts to take responsibility for the discursive trouble in the exchange by saying "I don't know why I'm so inarticulate this morning," and praises the student for "an analytically satisfactory approach to the problem." In attempting to generate interest, this teacher, like the professor in Class #1, also uses a participatory technique to involve the entire class: he periodically asks the class to vote on points that are being raised in the discussion—another departure from the stereotypical format.

Thus, our modified Socratic classrooms retain the intimidating structure requiring one student to remain in extended conversation through large parts of the class time (in some cases, one student would carry the dialogue for an entire class). It is clear from some of the transcripts that this format causes difficulties for some students, regardless of the many discursive features sometimes used to create a smoother and less intimidating environment. There is also some variability in professorial response; as we've seen, not all of the extended dialogues proceed so smoothly, and professors are not uniformly encouraging or gentle. At times the joking responses and other devices used to move the dialogue past problematic moments (talking over, supplying the answer, calling on another student) could certainly leave a bit of a sour taste (as, for example, when in response to a student who says "I would say no, but I'm not sure why," the professor in Class #1 responds, "See, that really takes away from an argument, if you don't know why, you know?" and moves on to another student). On the other hand, the transcripts from these three classrooms contain numerous dialogues in which professors and students produce relatively cohesive and coherent narratives developed through lengthy dialogues. This is in large part due to the ways the professors actually depart from the stereotypical Socratic teaching method, providing a wealth of hints and cues, interstitial explanations, and encouraging metacommentary to facilitate the coproduced dialogue. They also routinely provide answers—that is, they pause for shorter or longer explicit delineations of the doctrines at issue, their application to the facts in particular cases, and the ways analogies can be built between cases. In his interview with me, the professor in Class #4 explains the way he views his method as departing from standard Socratic teaching:

EM:     Would you characterize what you do as Socratic teaching?

Prof.:  I, I- not in a pure sense. Definitely not. Because, the true Socratic method is deeply skeptical. Doesn't provide- never provides an answer. Maybe provides slightly more and less leading questions that leave the impression that the questioner has some point of view. . . . I had people [professors] who talked that way, but I don't do that. You know, I- I think that it's Socratic in the sense that I ask them a lot of questions. And if that's what

Socratic has come to mean, then, okay, it's Socratic. But it's not Socratic in the sense that I won't give answers. It's not Socratic in the sense that I have suspended all judgment. There's no- no question that I'm looking for something in particular nine times out of ten. (.) And I won't leave a case unless I go back to what I consider the key passage, and say, "All right, look at this. It's right here," you know, and hopefully over time, through the process of questioning them on what's important and telling them at the end, they'll start to realize what's important. But I won't leave a subject simply because I haven't gotten the proper answer. I'll fish for it for a while.

This professor goes on to stress that pure Socratic teaching, which avoids giving answers, can also leave students without adequate knowledge of the substance of the area of law being taught (here, contract law): "They really need to know this stuff when they go out and start practicing . . . they're expected to know some of the content of this area of law." Thus, in his view, a teaching method that left the students to glean this content for themselves, concentrating instead solely on a process of reasoning instantiated through endless questions, would fail to achieve an important pedagogical goal in law teaching. Of course, as we have no detailed linguistic study of the older Socratic classes, we cannot know to what extent the features found in our modified Socratic classrooms have always been part of the Socratic teacher's repertoire, the stereotype to the contrary notwithstanding. However, it does appear that to the extent that professors depart from stereotypical Socratic rules, the modified format results in more cohesive, coherent, and probably more pedagogically effective lengthy exchanges. Carrying on these lengthier exchanges, just like extended direct or cross-examination in a courtroom, poses certain discursive challenges and difficulties. In this section we have examined some of the linguistic devices deployed by professors to overcome those problems, to be sure with varying degrees of success.

### The Short-Exchange Teacher: Mixing Dialogue, Lecture, and Conversation

In four of the classes, professors employed less than half of the amount of extended dialogue found in the three modified Socratic classrooms.[25] The structure of exchanges in these classrooms tended to be more free-ranging, with more students chiming in to approximate a give-and-take at times slightly more reminiscent of ordinary conversation (although the constant mediation of professor questions serves as a continual reminder that this is classroom dialogue).[26] All of the classes also included stretches of more typically Socratic extended dialogue, often at the beginning of discussion of a case, when the professor asked a student to state the facts or delineate the key arguments and issues. And, as in all of the other classes, these professors also lectured at times.

*Transcript 7.10 [3/5/8–9]*

*[During the initial exchanges in this class, the professor asks one student to state the facts and lay out the court's decision (turns 1–70), and then engages in shorter*

*exchanges with several other students about the rationale of the case (turns 71–79, 80–86, 87–90, 91–95). Numbers at the left indicate the progression of turns in the class period.]*

96    Prof.:    [ . . . omit first part of 1.33 turn, laying out the "major argument for the plaintiff" in detail . . . ] What's happened to the significance of contract? The enforceability of contracts? Um, let me see, help me out, ah, oh, Mr.- is it- ?

97    Mr. N.:    N. [last name][27]

98    Prof.:    M.?

99    Mr. N.:    N.

100    Prof.:    Oh, N., N., L. [student's first name] N., good-

101    Mr. N.:    The court in answering that would say, I guess [ . . . omitted material (.37 total turn time) . . . ] I think most of the workers working for them are probably on a- when you work you get paid, it's not really a salary per se except probably the owner.

102    Prof.:    Okay, I think you're merging two responses here. One is the response about "What is the expectation?" [writing on blackboard], ah, and your response is "Forget about the workers," uh okay? Or do something else. But the other thing is that I think you're challenging Ms. L.'s claim that the sanctity of contract requires enforcement of the full contract price, and you're saying "no." [ . . . ] It's in recognition that a contract is not an unmediated goal. That there are times when () contract should be modified. (.09 pause) There were some more hands? Any more hands right at this minute, yes, um, Mr. U.?

103    [[class laughter during preceding turn]]

104    Mr. U.:    It just seems that like the uh, the construction- the breach of the construction, is really a victim here of uh, political infighting and as far as the response to the uh comment that he can just go on to other things, if when a contractor plans a job, he plans a job that's going to last three months, ah, that's what he- that's the time set aside for that job. [ . . . omitted material (1.01 total turn time) . . . ] There are a lot of different factors they could have done in expectation of, uh, making a pretty good week's pay which, from the winter, they may not get.

105    Prof.:    Um, yeah. Is that what- [noticing Ms. L.'s hand up] -you're going to respond to him?

106    Ms. L.:    Well, I think I'm on the same line as that where it seems like pretty common sense to say, "Well, they said that they were going to breach on the contract and to stop work right there, but because they didn't know what authority- who had the authority to breach on the contract, that they had delayed." [ . . . omitted material .50 overall turn time . . . ] If they delayed to wait to find out who was right in that part, in that issue, then I think it would have cost them more money than--

107    Prof.:    --so, are you // agreeing with Mr. U.? //

108 Ms. L.:                                        //Yeah, I agree // with him because
they, they (), like you said, to keep these people employed and
everything, but if- if they had paid these people while there was a
delay going on to decide this dispute between the county and- I
think it would have cost them more.

109 Prof.:   Who can say, respond to that on behalf of the county? I mean, what
about the poor workers in this case? The- the workers who heard
from their boss, who got this job with Rockingham County, uh, to
take nine months to fix it, um is it Mr. T.? Yeah?

110 Mr. T.:  () court, the court awarded them any other losses and as far as any
materials [ . . . omit rest of .23 turn . . . ]

111 Prof.:   Uh, the court says that they would be awarded what?

112 Mr. T.:  Uh, //it says, "Any prof- //

113 Prof.:                    //What page// are you on?

114 Mr. T.:  I'm on page 39 [[115 Prof.: Good]], same paragraph. [ . . . omitted
material (.28 overall turn time) . . . ] So, if those were all of the
losses that would have resulted from that, so he could have taken
care of his work; he could have paid the cement trucks, paid
everybody, that's what the court () real well had he stopped at that
time, because he would have got his profit and he could have just
sat back in a rocking chair while the dust settled.

116 Prof.:   Mr. U.?

117 Mr. U.:  But that would have been after the entire litigation process. I mean,
he wouldn't have received that- that- those damages until after the
actual lawsuit went through, ah, the whole litigation process, is that
true?

118 Prof.:   Not necessarily, no. [ . . . omitted material (.36 total turn time) . . . ]
The only issue then is going to be whether uh- compensation, and
how much compensation is owed. Mr.- ?

119 Mr. Q.:  Q [last name]. Q.

120 Prof.:   Q.

121 Mr. Q.:  Yes, he doesn't, according to the law, stated uh, the contractor
should not be paying employees and these other things, he should
be stopping all those kinds of expenses he could control at that
point and then, if that wouldn't be considered part of the damages.

122 Prof.:   Okay, that he could control, all right? [[123 Mr. Q.: Yeah.]] How
can he control his obligation to his laborers?

In this passage, the professor shifts six times between five different speakers, or-
chestrating an exchange that at times is as much among the students as between
professor and student.[28] We see this immediately in turn 102, where the professor invites a connection between this student's comment and a prior answer: "I
think you're challenging Ms. L.'s claim," a very rich metalinguistic move that simultaneously reports and characterizes two different instances of talk (Ms. L.'s
and Mr. N.'s), situating them vis-à-vis one another and animating them as two

sides of a potential debate. The professors in these more "conversational" classes do more frequently encourage the students to occupy different sides of a debate, perhaps those of the parties in the case, or of different policy positions pertinent to the case, and so forth. In this sense, the students are drawn into occupying a role that is generally taken by the professor in the more Socratic classes, in which the teacher frequently winds up taking one position and casting his or her student interlocutor in the other. This does happen in the more conversational short-exchange classes as well, all of which, as noted, contain some more traditional Socratic dialogue. But in moments such as we observed in the previous transcript excerpt, a polyphony of voices joins in exploring and explicating the issues raised by the case under discussion.

In these kinds of moments, as we've seen, the professor operates much like the conductor of an orchestra, drawing out different parts of the argument from the class. This calls on the professor to do more metalinguistic work of a particular kind, recharacterizing and quoting previous utterances to set up the arguments and distinctions that might otherwise simply be stated by the teacher. Thus, we find metalinguistic structuring and restructuring of student utterances by the professor playing a heavy role in creating coherence and continuity in many of these classes. In the previous excerpt, we see the professor first engaging in a meta-pragmatic recasting of Mr. N.'s response as (a) in actuality two responses, which are recharacterized using imputed reported speech ("your response is 'Forget about the workers'" and "you're saying 'no'"), and (b) a "challenge" to Ms. L.'s stated position. Notice, then, the degree to which subsequent professor turns consist of metalinguistic structuring of diverse students' utterances: (a) in turn 102, she concludes by noting that some students were attempting to enter the discourse, and asking, "Any more hands right at this minute?"; (b) in her next turn (105), she begins a response of her own, but interrupts herself to recognize a student interlocutor ("You're going to respond to him?"); (c) her following turn (107) consists entirely of a metalinguistic linking of previous student turns, to clarify their (metapragmatic) relationship with one another ("So, are you agreeing with Mr. U.?"); and the next professor turn (109) is occupied by a request for one of the students to "respond to that on behalf of the county," a request followed by a restatement of the position to which a response is needed (a position, by implication, that was contained in prior student comments); (d) following two turns devoted to clarifying a student response, the professor again in turn 116 returns to her conductor role, calling on Mr. U., who is offering a reply to the previous student's statement; (e) after Mr. U.'s turn, the professor takes time to correct an assumption that Mr. U. made and then moves on to recognize a new speaker, Mr. Q., who chimes in to argue against the side implicitly taken by the previous student speaker.

The work of creating coherence through an exchange such as this involves a careful metalinguistic channeling of ongoing student exchanges, restating comments to make clear (or perhaps at times to create) their connections with one another, parsing student utterances to clarify how they might relate to the overall point of the discussion, correcting or restating aspects of the law or case under discussion in between student turns. Note that discussion of this case began with a fairly standard Socratic exchange between the professor and one student, occupying 70 turns (or 35 question-answer pair-parts) and interrupted only by one "class turn" (in which the entire class responded in unison "The county" to the professor's question "Who breached the contract?"). The first student succinctly summarized the facts in the case, the court's decision, and the rule of the case. The exchange broke down at the point where the professor asked this first student speaker to explain the rationale behind the rule of the case: "There is now an exception to the expectation rule, okay? What I want to know is what's the rationale for that?" At this point a number of students begin to raise their hands and offer their own ideas about the rationale, resulting in a discussion that comes very close to being one among students, with at times only a light degree of moderating from the professor. Most of the turns in these exchanges are volunteered.

For a different way of managing polyphony in a more conversational class, we turn to Class #6, which, like Class #3, was taught by a white female professor in a local law school.[29] Here we see a set of exchanges that at points come even closer to more informal conversation:

*Transcript 7.11 [6/20/7–12]*

| 39 | Prof.: | *[ . . . end of a 7.30 turn summarizing the law of contract formation . . . ]* Give me some idea that you have from reading the cases for today of what constitutes an offer, and what are you trying to set it up against? You're looking to what is an offer and what's not an offer. What are some of the things that are not an offer, and what are some of the features of an offer? (.03 pause) *[ no volunteers, professor calls on student]* Nat? |
|----|--------|----|
| 40 | Nat: | Um an acceptance of an offer is- would kind of be like- it's at the last, the ground where it's the actual- where it actually makes the contract. An offer is distinguished from an invitation of an offer, is when the offeror really wants to have the final power of acceptance. He'd rather have the invitation to offer. That's why the other person has to- the other party has to offer so that they can then accept. |
| 41 | Prof.: | Right. One of the first dichotomies you want to set up when you're asking this question about contract formation- and in an exam, you're always going to anticipate at least in your first-year course that some place there is a question of whether or not something's an offer or something else. *[ . . . omitted material (1.09 total turn time) . . . ]* What is- how would you describe my statement, "I'm going to sell my car for $5,000," if it is not as an offer? Jane? |
| 42 | Jane: | As an expression of your intent to sell your car. |
| 43 | Prof.: | Yeah. An expression of a present intent, but no undertaking of a firm commitment. Ah *[ . . . omitted material, detailing three things that do not count as offers (2.55 total turn time) . . . ]* Okay, Karen, if you open the mail one day and it's a letter from the Acme Flour Company and it says, "I can quote you flour at five dollars a barrel in carload lots." And you just realized you need ten carloads of flour. Could you call up the Acme Flour Company and say, "I accept," and make a binding contract? |

| 44 | Karen: | No, you could call them up and say you've received this offer and // then// |
| 45 | Prof.: | // Well // no, you've got to be very careful. Don't say, "I received this offer in the mail." |
| 46 | Karen: | I received your letter in the mail from your quote? |
| 47 | Prof.: | In the context that I've just described, she's just opening her mail and gets this letter, what would you call this? You would say it's not an offer because why? Tracy? |
| 48 | Tracy: | Is it an advertisement? |
| 49 | Prof.: | It's very likely that it is an advertisement, although I'm not so sure [ . . . ] I think there's something else. In back.*[calling on a student in back who has raised her hand]* |
| 50 | Carrie: | Is it a solicitation? |
| 51 | Prof.: | A solicitation for what, Carrie? |
| 52 | Carrie: | For offers to buy the flour. |
| 53 | Prof.: | Sure, sure. A solicitation for offers, which is another way of saying [ . . . *omitted material (47 sec. total turn time)* . . . ] It's trying to get you to come in and- yeah? |
| 54 | Gwen: | What about, say, in computer magazines where they have like very specific, detailed- or the camera magazines where they have a specific full page with all the prices of every model number, and it's still not an offer? |
| 55 | Prof.: | All right, why not? There's actually quite a good answer to why not [ . . . *omitted material (.30 total turn time)* . . . ] What's the answer to why this is not an offer? |
| 56 | Jane: | Because you only have a limited amount of items that you can sell, and if tons of people respond to your thing saying, "I accept," you only have one car that you can sell. You can't- |
| 57 | Prof.: | All right, you've got the street-level understanding of why the ad is not an offer. Let's put it in terms of offer under contract law. Why is it not an offer under contract law? And think of the reasonable person test. |
| 58 | Nat: | It's also not addressed to anyone specific. |
| 59 | Prof.: | Well, the fact that it's not addressed to a specific person doesn't necessarily mean- I mean one of the things you're bouncing this off is the *Lefkowitz* case, the Minnesota store selling the stole. |
| 60 | Jessica: | The reasonable person wouldn't believe that you were conferring power on them to accept and form a contract. |
| 61 | Prof.: | That's- that's an excellent point. And that is the reason that ads in general are not believed, are not construed as offers, is that no reasonable person reading the ad, no matter how detailed- You're- Gwen's looking at me and she's saying, "Well, *I* would have." |

62    Gwen:    Well, I don't know-

63    Prof.:    Let me finish. Let me finish, then we can discuss it [ . . . *omitted material, finishes point regarding reasonable person (.45 overall turn time); calls on student with hand up . . . ]* Dirk.

64    Dirk:    Uh, an interesting story in the paper today, kind of like () *Lefkowitz* case, Filene's Basement.

65    Prof.:    Yeah, somebody handed it to me. I didn't read it. Tell us.

66    Dirk:    Uh, they said the first one thousand people to show up at seven fifty-five to the *[specifies location]* store could get a thousand dollar shopping spree, all right? So they set the number of people. So then you have to question if it's reasonable then, since they specified the number of people, you know, obviously that's not unlimited. That's specified. But then they said it was actually one thousand people could enter a drawing to get one one thousand dollar shopping // spree //

67    Alicia:                      // yeah// the wording's in there, and it's really confusing, and they say they've done it in Boston and they never had a problem--

68    Dirk:                      --yeah, never had a problem.

69    Prof.:    Never had a problem because who wants to sue? Okay, never- never had a problem because who wants to sue? I'll get the- read quickly and try to find the language. (.11 pause) The ads, which ran in *[omit names of newspapers]*, oh we have Filene's Basement here, now? [[70 class laughter]] And I didn't know it? Where is it? [[71 class laughter]]

72–77    *[omit several turns where students call out the street names, the professor asks for the cross street, students respond, class laughs]*

78    Prof.:    All right, here's what the ad says [ . . . *omitted material, reads ad, (.32 overall turn time) . . . ]* making them eligible for a shopping // spree at each store //

79    Gwen:    // That's bull-//

80    Nat:    // It says "to win." It says "to win." Not "you will get."//

81    Prof.:    "Be one of the first thousand people to win." [ . . . *omitted material, reads terms of settlement with attorney general's office to appease disgruntled customers: a drawing where 60 customers will each get a $1,000 shopping spree . . . ]*

82          [[Class commentary, someone whistles, someone (unidentified) asks, "Each?"]]

83    Prof.:    Each, instead of the thousand. [[84 Class, calling out, one student says, "Instead of one."]] Yeah (). Boy, that's quite the settlement. And that settles (). Anna?

85    Anna:    But, you know, right when I'm really busy, I was at *[grocery store name]* just wanting to buy some stamps at the counter, and there was a woman ahead of me. She had twenty-five coupons for items

|    |    |    | that *[the grocery store]* was out of, and she wanted, what did she call it //rain checks// |
| 86 | Unidentified male student: |    | //rain check// |
| 87 | Gwen: |    | //sure, you can get a rain check //-- |
| (85) | Anna: |    | --for all these twenty-five, and she got rain checks. |
| 88 | Prof.: |    | That's why I waited. Now what is- is this a complaint, or a question, or what now? [[89 class laughter]]. |

Ten different identified students participated in this exchange, along with several unidentified students (and the entire class, at times).[30] As the class moves further into this discussion, we see a breakdown of the strict pair-part structure that generally dominates in these classrooms (including this one); the professor-student pairing of question-answer is interrupted when students respond directly to one another. In turns 67–68, for example, Alicia and Dirk coproduce an account of a story from the newspaper; note the cohesion produced across multiple speakers through parallelism as both students and the professor in three successive turns repeat "never had a problem." After the professor reads the exact wording of the ad, one student begins to express disgust with the story ("that's bull- ") and is interrupted by another student who disagrees, "It says 'to win.' It says 'to win.' Not 'you will get.'" Two students again chime in to help Anna produce her narrative when she has trouble remembering the word for "rain check." In turns 61–63, we see an exchange more typical of informal conversation: the professor pauses in the middle of her comment to respond to an expression on one student's face: "You're- Gwen's looking at me and she's saying, 'Well, I would have.'" This rendition of a perceived response in the form of (fictional) reported speech brings the professor into a less formal discursive space with the student; the student, somewhat startled, responds, "Well, I don't know- ", perhaps a signal that she is reacting to the blurring of genre boundaries. The professor induces laughter from the class a number of times, and the overall informality of the class produces a speech setting that permits the following exchange (toward the end of the class) to seem less harsh than it otherwise might have:

*Transcript 7.12 [6/20/18]*

Prof.:  [ . . . *omit beginning of .27 turn* . . . ] Now I really will dismiss you if you can answer <u>this</u> question. What's the difference between an offer and a promise?

John:  Well, I think (). Your offer gives the offeree the power to accept. You don't have the promise until the offeree has accepted the offer.

Prof.:  Wrong.

John:  Oh.

Prof.:  Close, close.

John:  I spent all night working on that one. [[class laughter]]

Prof.:    Close. He said that you don't have a promise until the offer's accepted. You're wrong by one word. (.05 pause) You see, a promise isn't necessarily a contract. A promise isn't legally enforceable.

John:    Right.

Prof.:    Right. What an offer is [ . . . *omit rest of 1.49 turn explaining definition of* "*offer*" . . . ]

Thus, the overall discursive setting can set the tone for professorial responses, and the student's joking reply carries on the overall tenor of the professor-student responses throughout the class. This was the classroom with the most egalitarian distribution of student speakers in the entire study; it was the class in which 100% of the students spoke during the semester.[31] At one point in the semester, in a move unlike any found in the other classes, the professor put one of the students in the role of judge and two others in the role of attorneys, and had the two students argue to the judge, who took over the professor's role of questioning and moderating the discussion. This was a marked exception to the rule in these classrooms, where student comments are almost never unmediated by professors' turns.[32]

At the same time, we can also note continuities between the methods used to attain continuity and coherence in longer traditional Socratic dialogues and in these more polyphonic exchanges. In the lengthy exchange above (Transcript 7.11), if one ignores the switching of students and imagines only one student respondent instead, there is not all that large a distinction between the earlier portions of this excerpt and many of the Socratic dialogues; the most striking difference is that the professor keeps selecting different students to respond to her ongoing questions. Just as in the extended dialogues, we find many professor turns beginning with positive affirmations such as "right" and "yeah"; we also see repetition of student responses for emphasis and cohesion (turns 42–43, "expression of intent"; turns 50–53, "solicitation for offers"). As did the professors in the more Socratic classrooms, these professors provide significant structuring to the ongoing discussion through mini-lectures and doctrinal exegesis, as well as through the form of their questions. When an answer is not quite on point, we also see instances where the professor recasts that student answer in an encouraging light: "All right, you've got the street-level understanding of why the ad is not an offer. Let's put it in terms of offer under contract law." And where a student is clearly offtrack, the professor also employs interruption and redirection: "Well, no, you've got to be very careful. Don't say 'I received this offer in the mail.'" However, when the student does not come up with a correct answer after one more turn, the professor moves on to another interlocutor, rather than pressing a single speaker to continue. On the one hand, this means that there is less need for coaching and cuing than in the more extended dialogues. One could also say that students are not learning to reason on their feet to the same extent, and that the quick search through the room for a response that will move the conversation along leaves individual contributors little room to recover and develop their arguments. On the other hand, it also relieves individual students of the stress of ongoing dialogue when they are not coming up with the desired responses. In her interview with me, the professor in Class #6 also pointed to the attentional benefits of this approach:

I'll call on a student who I think will give the answer, because it saves a lot of time and I don't think it's any fun to sit there with somebody not knowing the answer and waiting for them to struggle through something. *[ . . . ]* No, I don't try to stay with someone to get to a certain point. I guess I have a low threshold for boredom and I want to keep things interesting and if something gets dull, I switch. (.) And (.) I also think that students have a limited tolerance for staying with the conversation between professor and single student (.) and why waste time? You've got a lot to cover. (Interview 6)

This professor stresses that moving around the class produces a more interesting, quickly flowing discussion, and that this has pedagogical benefits.

We have also seen some variation here; just as with the more Socratic classes, the more conversational, short-exchange classes are not all alike.[33] In the excerpts from Class #3, the professor made heavy use of metalinguistic signaling to draw the comments of diverse students into a coherent, ongoing exchange weighing different sides of the argument. In the excerpts from Class #6, the professor kept an ongoing stream of inquiry going using diverse students, but without similar foregrounding of the speakers. In each case, the professors created coherence and continuity through their questions and exegetical commentary, structuring the topics for student comments down to a limited and more manageable scope. Indeed, both professors begin the discussion with very explicit delineations of the categories and questions on which students should draw in answering questions about the cases assigned for the day.

### The Dialogic Lecturer

Of course, the most explicit linguistic form for "pure" delivery of (semantico-referential) information in these classrooms is the lecture. In one class in the study, Class #7, a lecture structure predominated.[34] The professor talked for 95% of the time in this class, with 4% of the talk in class produced by individual students and 1% produced by the class as a whole. Professor monologue occupied around 91% of class time, with 2% spent in longer focused dialogues, and 8% spent in shorter exchanges.

Despite this apparently quite different discursive structure, it is surprising to find that we could analyze much of the language in this classroom as structured around some kind of dialogic form, despite the fact that in general, lengthy monologues by the professor (ending with questions or prompts) alternate with short student turns. In the excerpt that follows, the professor begins class with a lengthy monologue about the case that was under discussion at the end of the previous class, and then turns to questioning the students:

*Transcript 7.13 [7/10/2–6]*

Prof.:    *[ . . . end of 5.59 turn . . . ]* We haven't gotten very far in contract formation analysis, but we're- we're at the very beginning here, yet. We haven't gotten off the dime yet, so, we're really facing- there are only two choices we've discussed so far, what are they?

Class:    Offer.

Prof.:      Possibility of an offer or--

Student:                              --not an offer--

Prof.:                                        --not an offer, just a third form of
            preliminary negotiations. Which would it be in this case? Mr. C.?

Mr. C.:     Well, I think, this is a- is a more negotiating for responses; we are
            proceeding, it says than more of the way, it gives the fact that it's
            probably an offer rather than a negotiation. So, you would say that since
            the party that responded uh would have had- could reasonably have
            had- could reasonably or should reasonably believe that they have the
            power of acceptance when they're giving an order.

Prof.:      Okay, but, you know, I really- I would caution you a little bit about the
            way in which you articulate it. Now, [paraphrasing student] "The more
            preliminary negotiation, the more likely we've got an offer." We could-
            we could start the process now and negotiate until doomsday, and still
            maybe never find an offer. So, I don't think the- the quantity, per se, or
            the volume of preliminary negotiations is necessarily going to get it.
            What's going to get us into an offer? [ . . . omitted material, reiterating
            and clarifying question (.57 total turn time) . . . ] How do you- how do
            you support that? Ms. H.?

Ms. H.:     Umm, when Glass Works said that they could quote them a price, per
            gross, for immediate acceptance, that would lead defendants to believe
            that they had grounds for an acceptance, these were the grounds that
            they could accept.

Prof.:      Okay. They could also (), according to legal standard, I don't care if it
            was first, I don't care if it was fifty-ninth, in the- in the order of
            correspondence, the first piece of communication, which actually and
            reasonably led the other party to believe the power of acceptance is
            created in the offer. I would certainly agree with you, Ms. H., on an
            empirical basis [ . . . omitted material, elaborating on how to identify an
            offer (2.55 total turn time) . . . ] Okay? Any more questions or observa-
            tions on this? Mm-hmm?

Mr. Y.:     Is there some objective standard by which the court decides whether a
            person has reasonable- reasonably have invested his power of accep-
            tance or is that solely subjective?

Prof.:      Well--

Mr. Y.:         --I'm not clear on what differentiates, say, the first response where
            the () promised them that they will make the shipment. And in the
            second one it says, "Enter our order." I'm not sure as to what (), that
            essential element differentiates, differentiates- (.)

Prof.:      Well, the court, in analyzing the second piece of correspondence, said
            there's clearly an offer on the table, yeah, they received an inquiry to
            what the- what the prices would be. And the court said that what we
            have here is an offer. Now, if the court says that there was an offer,
            hopefully they've got some rationale to establish how that statement, in
            the context of the inquiry that preceded it, will raise actual and
            reasonable belief, on the part of the buyer, that a power of acceptance is
            created in them. Now, the primary focus is- there's nothing in the facts

to suggest any special knowledge that wouldn't otherwise appear to a reasonable person, you're right- the primary focus becomes, what were the reasonable expectations of the prospective buyer? Now, when you asked me if that is a subjective standard or not, the answer has to be, "No, absolutely not," because reasonable is always objective. Reasonable is always measured against this reasonable, objective personality, as distinct from an idiosyncratic, individualized, inside-their-head type of an approach. I think, what you were probably driving at is, is the more basic question, "Is this an individualistic determination on a case-by-case basis?" Absolutely, absolutely. Now, the court said it's an offer. And they give some decent reasons for it. I don't think those reasons are necessarily totally conclusive. You could make a case on the other side. Uh, but, I think they did support it with decent reasoning. They said, "Wait a minute. If this had just been the statement initially, and you start making it look more like the *Kershaw v. Moulton* case, it would- it would particularly fail as an offer then because you would not have a definite quantity. It would be just like *Kershaw v. Moulton* in that sense. They say, 'We offer you these glass jars at the following prices, per gross,' not specifying how many." *[Note elision of voices here, lack of clear demarcation of when court's voice ends.]* And, we're going to see that's the key, that's exactly what you have in *Kershaw v. Moulton*. They offer you barrels of salt at a particular price. No specification of how many barrels. (.) But with no designation of quantity, it's not reasonable to assume that this person would wish to commit himself. (.) So, we would say, the first, basic criterion is going to be an offer. That's going to be the first of the two-part steps necessary. You've got to create that power of acceptance. And it can't happen until you get an offer. Now, we're going to see ways that that offer can die or be killed. *[ . . . omitted material (6.42 total turn time) . . . ]* Any other questions? (.02 pause) Okay, the *Craft* case (.) Now, there is a general rule. A general rule concerning newspaper advertisements. What is the general rule? (.05 pause) Uh, yes, umm, Ms. R.?

Until this final turn, the exchange did not appear to be markedly different from those found in other, more participatory classes. We see an example of the class responding as a whole to one question. When one student gives an unsatisfactory reply, the professor cautions him gently—interestingly, using a metalinguistic correction of how the student "articulates" the point and paraphrasing the student's answer. The ubiquity of forms of reported speech in law professors' talk (see Chapter 6) is evident in this excerpt, as the professor reports first indirectly and then directly what the court said, as well as rephrasing the student's question and answering in a direct quotation ("the answer has to be, 'No, absolutely not'")—an interesting reframing of what is essentially the professor's own speech as the product of an authoritative, almost external voice stating the inevitable. In the professor's direct quotation of the court's speech, there is an intriguing blurring of the boundaries between the court's voice and that of the professor explicating the court's reasoning. From a very clear initial boundary ("The court said, 'Now wait a minute . . . '"), the quotation devolves into murky territory, until at last with the sentence "And, we're going to see . . . ," the professor has clearly moved back into his own voice, as indicated by use of the pedagogical "we." However, as marked in the transcript, it is unclear at what point this shift actually occurred—a by-product of the ubiquitous usurpation of courts' and others' voices in fictional direct quotation forms used so frequently in these classes.

We can discern other similarities between this and other classrooms. Like the professor in Class #6 above, this professor moves around the classroom in search of a correct response and comments approvingly when he receives it. There are very few repeat players in the class as a result of a conscious policy of the professor:

> I try to never have more than- there may be a follow-up question occasionally, but for the most part it's one question per student. I think it's extremely unfair to stay with one student. Not that they shouldn't be prepared to be able to do that, but because, while they're talking they aren't getting any notes. () primary reason to be in class is to get the necessary notes . . . usually what I do is hop around and then the students pay more attention to it. . . . I like students to participate. I want them to participate, it makes it more enjoyable, but I have to admit as a student, I purposefully tried to avoid dialogue because I was there to hone in on what the professor had to say and get it down in my notes. . . . Because the reality is, that I was not going to be ultimately evaluated and graded on my preparation for class. It was going to be my preparation for the exam.

This policy results in a teaching style that is difficult to categorize because despite the heavy preponderance of lecture here, the overall class structure remains somewhat dialogic, although there are far fewer pair-parts than in other classes. One measure of this is the total number of professor turns throughout the semester in this class (586), which is markedly lower than in the other classes. (The next-lowest number, in Class #3, is 1,537, and all of the remaining professors took up more than 3,000 turns, ranging as high as 4,046 turns for the professor in Class #1.)[35] Obviously, particularly in light of the high percentage of class time taken by the professor here, each professor turn would on average be much longer than in other classes.

To generate a skeletal picture of the overall structure in this class, the next text excerpt gives an outline of the remaining turns in the class whose opening was included in Transcript 7.13. This outline includes the time for each turn, along with a sketch of features of the professor's speech that contribute to continuity between turns:

*Transcript 7.14 [7/10/6–17]*

| | |
|---|---|
| Ms. R.: | 13 sec. |
| Prof.: | **1.58 min.**, ending, "why are these advertisements generally considered to be invitations that () preliminary negotiations without binding effect. Mm-hmm, Ms., uh, E." |
| Ms. E.: | 10 sec. |
| Prof.: | "That's right."—**2.06 min.** turn, ending, "Say the advertisement goes beyond that, says, same deal, except first come, first served. Offer or not? (.03 pause) Offer or not? (.04 pause) Mm- hmm." |
| Mr. A.: | 4 sec. |

| Prof.: | 3 sec.—"What's the amount?" |
|---|---|
| Mr. A.: | 4 sec. |
| Prof.: | **4.40 min**, ending, "Does- did the advertisement constitute an offer? Mr. G." |
| Mr. G.: | 16 sec. |
| Prof.: | **9.49 min.**, spelling out facts and issues of next case, ending, "What made this offer extraordinary? What- what took it out of the category of being an ordinary offer? (.03 pause) () if you pick this one up, you're going to be reading all of the materials very, very well. This is a difficult question. Mm-hmm." |
| Mr. B.: | 1 sec. |
| Prof.: | **6 sec.**—"That's not the writ, it's not the writ, the written bid itself, uh, good shot." |
| Mr. B.: | 3 sec. |
| Prof.: | **5 sec.**—"Something, this power of revocation is simply not going to exist on this contract." |
| Mr. D.: | 4 sec. |
| Prof.: | 26 sec.—"Why? [ . . . ] Why did they provide the bond with the bid? (.07 pause)" |
| Ms. F.: | 23 sec. |
| Prof.: | **3.36 min.**, ending, "And you would have to focus on that half of the sentence and then pick up the point that is made in the notes that follow the case. Mm-hmm, Mr. uh, H.?" |
| Mr. H.: | 11 sec. |
| Prof.: | "That's right."—**3.12 min.**, ending, "What does, what does this court, this case tell you that you'll have to do to succeed here? Mr. T.?" |
| Mr. T.: | 9 sec. |
| Prof.: | **12 sec.**—"Well, that was one of six elements in a two-part of the legal standard it focused on. And I want to make sure we get the whole picture. That was one of the elements it focused on. Uh, Ms. N.?" |
| Ms. N.: | 9 sec. |
| Prof.: | **11 sec.**—"Again, you're- you're spelling out a particular element, but, well, what's the broad, what's the broad remedy here? What's the broad option here? Mr. M.?" |
| Mr. M.: | 4 sec. |
| Prof.: | "Okay [ . . . ]"—**7.28 min.** |

In these 26 turns, the professor takes up 23.52 minutes, and the students' total time is 1.51 minutes; he thus occupies more than twelve times the amount of time taken by the students in the dialogue here, although he takes the same number of turns.[36] Notice that if we ignore the amount of time taken by the professor turns, the discursive structure is not unlike that in our short-exchange classes (and, just as in some of those more conversational classes, if we ignore the fact that different student speakers are responding to the questions, we would find some similarities to the more Socratic classes).[37] Thus, we find some striking differences but also con-tinuities in structure among the different classrooms of the study.

## Social Patterns and Teaching Styles

Having identified these differences, we now turn to ask whether there are any ap-parent relationships between professors' teaching styles and social patterns, such as school status. One finding from previous studies points to a difference between elite/prestige law schools and lower-ranked law schools in terms of emphasis on legal theory in teaching; professors in higher-ranked schools reported focusing more on overarching theories behind the law.[38] We find some slight support for that in the transcripts of this study; professors in the higher-ranked schools do explicitly discuss jurisprudential and other theories somewhat more than do the professors in the lower-ranked law schools. One professor who teaches in a regional law school explicitly acknowledges this:

> . . . so I think it's important that they understand the doctrine. And I know, you know, at some of the big-name schools, I think, there's less of that. [ . . . ]Well, you know, if I'm teaching at Harvard I can go in and teach revolutionary theory or [ . . . ] to what extent should we use contract law to advance principles of economic efficiency or redistribution of wealth and so forth. (Interview 7)

This professor goes on to comment that he will at times digress to give his students the bigger picture, but notes that in general, he doesn't think that students are "prepared to say anything intelligent on the entire subject until they first of all know what it is and how it works." On the other hand, though agreeing that there is some-thing of a difference along these lines, another professor, one teaching at a local law school, noted that it was also important to convey some theory to students: "I mean, a certain amount of it *[legal history and theory]* is necessary in order to func-tion well (.) i- if they don't know who the legal realists are they'll be in- they could be embarrassed in a way that would be disempowering [ . . . ]" (Interview 6).

In any case, any differences found among schools of different ranks on this score are dwarfed by an overarching similarity among the classes: in all of these schools, the vast majority of class time in the first semester of first-year Contracts is devoted to learning how to do a legal reading of the cases and to uncovering basic doctrinal principles. All of the professors agree that this is their primary pedagogi-cal task, and they uniformly expressed enthusiasm about performing it. A profes-sor in one of the elite/prestige schools commented that the "first thing" he needed to accomplish, "obviously, is to teach them the core doctrines in contracts." Simi-larly, a professor in one of the local law schools commented that "the law professor's job is to, first of all, familiarize students with the body of information that they're simply going to have to know [ . . . ] and so you go through these ordinary things that virtually every law school class in contracts must go through [ . . . ] on offer, acceptance, consideration, promissory estoppel, etcetera, etcetera. [ . . . ]" The excitement that the professors felt about conveying this kind of knowledge was palpable across the interviews; as one local law school professor explained, "I adore teaching my students [ . . . ] I think the subject is fabulous. I think it's fabulous because [ . . . ] of the significance of contract as, um, one of the basic social structures of everybody's lives [ . . . ]" (Interview 3). This precise sentiment was echoed by one of the elite law school professors in her interview as well. Indeed, in many cases, professors would proceed at points in their interviews to launch enthusiastically into explanations of specific aspects of contract law doctrine pertinent to the discussion. In this sense, the language and logic of the case law assigned to the students, and of contract law in particular, shared center stage for these teachers across all of the schools of the study, both in terms of their own self-representations and in terms of the discussions in their classes.

Another interesting similarity that we have seen among the classes is the presence of a kind of backbone of dialogic structure, even in classes occupied mostly by professor lecture. Whether in this latter case, or in the case of the short-exchange classes, or in the modified Socratic classes, we could outline most of the classes using a pair-part structure, one that only very rarely (predominantly in the more conversational short-exchange classes) gives way to any alternative discursive format. And although this pair-part structure occasionally instantiates something resembling a monologue, we have also seen the ubiquity of multivoiced exchanges in these classrooms—frequently dialogues, often posed as an exchange between opposing voices. We could analyze the metalinguistic ideology conveyed and encoded by the ubiquity of dialogic structure in a number of ways. First, like the semantic content of many class discussions, which is often organized around exploring two opposing arguments, this discursive structure conveys a sense of legal reasoning as fundamentally dialogic: the thought, mirrored precisely in the discourse, emerges from a constant conversation between two distinct positions. Professors convey this even in lectures, as they first pose and then answer questions and as they question the case first from one point of view and then another. In a functionalist mode, one could point to the fit between this and a number of discursive features of legal practice, most notably the question-answer structure used with witnesses in court, by judges in dealing with attorneys both in appellate oral argument and elsewhere, and even by attorneys when dealing with clients. Written legal opinions, which attorneys must be able to parse, generally encompass and discuss two or more differing stances both toward the events in question and the law to be applied, often posing one against the other in the course of explicating the court's decision. In this study, I have also suggested a more profound metalinguistic message conveyed by this focus on textual and linguistic structures: an unmooring of fixed normative stances in favor of this discursively based fluidity, which focuses on linguistic authority and argument.

If the classes shared an emphasis on legal doctrine, with some differentiation around the edges in terms of how much time is spent discussing theoretical issues, then we can ask whether there are any other possible points of differentiation among teachers based on school status. Although the classes all share some kind of backbone of dialogic or at least dialectical structuring, we have also seen that there are some considerable differences among them in terms of overall discourse structure. One possibility is that they differ by school status along lines of discourse style, with perhaps classes in the higher-ranked schools staying closer to the traditional

Socratic style of teaching.[39] Table 7.1 summarizes the discourse profiles. These quantitative profiles include the total percentage of time taken by professor, individual students, and the class as a whole. They also break down the percentage of classroom discussion (in terms of both time and turns) spent in lecture (monologue), more lengthy ("focused") Socratic-style dialogue, and other kinds of interaction.

The classes are ordered in Table 7.1 in terms of their location in the status hierarchy often employed in distinguishing among law schools.[40] Classes #2, #8, and #5 are in law schools ranked in the elite or prestige categories. Classes #4 and #7 are in schools that would be described as regional. And Classes #1, #6, and #3 are in local law schools, including one night school class.

We can see immediately that there is no one-to-one correlation between school status and use of more Socratic styles of teaching; the three most Socratic classrooms (#5, #4, #1) are in an elite/prestige, a regional, and a local law school, respectively, thus, spanning the entire status hierarchy. These three professors do have something in common, however; they are all white male teachers who were trained at elite law schools. They differ in other respects; in terms of teaching experience, one had been teaching 16 to 20 years at the time of the study, another 11 to 15 years, and a third from 1 to 5 years. This last teacher was also younger than the other two (31–35 years old as opposed to 46–50 years old).[41] Thus, the category of modified Socratic teachers includes our youngest and least experienced professor as well as our oldest and most experienced. In the middle range, with 28% and 29% of time spent in extended dialogue, were the two professors of color in the study, who both had been trained at elite/prestige law schools and were teaching in elite/prestige law schools. Included in the lowest Socratic range, using only 21% to 24% of class time for extended dialogue, were two white female professors who had trained in local or regional law schools and were teaching in local law schools. One of these, Class #6, was the most egalitarian classroom in the study in terms of participation patterns. Finally, at the lowest end of the extended-dialogue range was Class #7 (with predominantly lecture); this white male professor had trained at a regional law school and was teaching in a regional law school.

We cannot draw any broad conclusions from so small a sample. But we can pause to note a similarity between the hint of a pattern found among these teachers and that noted by Conley and O'Barr in their (similarly small) sample of small claims court judges.[42] In that study, the authors identified two distinct kinds of "voices," one focused on rules and the other on relationships. These voices were correlated with distinct speech styles ("powerful" versus "powerless") and differing ideological understandings of the law (law as "limitation" versus "enablement"). Interestingly, the judges who most closely followed the rule-based, formalist approaches ("authoritative decisionmakers" and "proceduralists") were all white men with formal legal training. On the other hand, the judges who used the most relational, flexible approaches ("mediators" and "lawmakers") were all women (one African American, the others European American). There was also a category of "strict adherents," who saw the law as beyond their control and simply attempted to apply it strictly (in this category were an African American man and a European American woman). All of the judges who lacked formal legal training fell into the

TABLE 7.1

Classroom Discourse Profiles

| Class | Percentage of Overall Class Time | | | Percentage of Dialogue* (Time) | | | Percentage of Dialogue* (Turns) | | |
|---|---|---|---|---|---|---|---|---|---|
| | Teacher | Student | Class | Monologue | Focused Dialogue | Other | Monologue | Focused Dialogue | Other |
| *Elite/Prestige* | | | | | | | | | |
| 2 | 73 | 25 | 3 | 50 | 28 | 22 | 7 | 54 | 39 |
| 8 | 66 | 32 | 2 | 29 | 29 | 42 | 4 | 40 | 56 |
| 5 | 79 | 21 | 1 | 49 | 45 | 6 | 4 | 81 | 15 |
| *Regional* | | | | | | | | | |
| 4 | 82 | 18 | 0 | 47 | 48 | 5 | 5 | 86 | 10 |
| 7 | 95 | 4 | 1 | 91 | 2 | 8 | 26 | 16 | 58 |
| *Local* | | | | | | | | | |
| 1 | 67 | 31 | 3 | 17 | 60 | 24 | 2 | 74 | 25 |
| 6 | 73 | 25 | 2 | 33 | 21 | 46 | 4 | 34 | 62 |
| 3 | 84 | 15 | 1 | 63 | 24 | 13 | 9 | 60 | 31 |

* Focused dialogue is a series of three of more teacher-student exchanges (i.e., a minimum of six consecutive turns with the same dialogue partners). Please note that, because decimals have been rounded, totals may not equal exactly 100%.

last three categories, whereas, as we've seen, none of the judges in the more rule-based categories lacked legal education. Some of the women in the mediators category had had legal training. Although we obviously do not want to read too essentialist a meaning into these findings, it is interesting that a confluence of gender, race, and status/training appears to correspond roughly with a patterning of discourse in the Conley and O'Barr study, and arguably in my study as well. In both cases, white men with the most elite training are distinguished from the other subjects in the study. Clearly, even if this pattern were to be substantiated in broader studies, we would expect that there would be exceptions; in any case, we need further research to accurately parse the combination of discursive and social/contextual features at work.[43]

I raise this issue simply to point to the as yet largely unstudied differences we may find based on subtle differences among law teachers, individual classes, and law schools. For example, as we've noted, in the 1970s Shaffer and Redmount published a study finding that the discourse in three Indiana law schools was heavily oriented toward lecture. Although again, I would not wish to draw any sweeping conclusions from this coincidence, the class in our study with the heaviest lecture component was a regional law school in the Midwest. I point this out not to suggest any heavy-handed conclusions regarding geography and law school teaching styles, but merely to raise the point that there are many factors to consider in attempting to discern patterning. Along with status of the law school in which the class is taught, we can ask about other aspects of the law school (school culture, location, history, etc.) and about the gender, race, age, background, and other features of the professor and students involved. In addition, the discursive environment in the class itself can obviously have a role to play.

## Summary

In this chapter, we reviewed differences in teaching style across the classrooms in this study, with a focus more on divergences than on similarities. Although some aspects of dialogic structure can be found across all of the classrooms, we have seen some dramatic differences in the degree of professorial control of class discussion. These correspond to divergences in the degree to which professors employ lecture, extended Socratic questioning, and shorter exchanges. We concluded the chapter by asking whether there was any discernable social patterning that might explain the distribution of these divergences in style. We do see some indications that any patterning corresponds more with where professors were trained than where they are currently teaching. Having examined possible connections between discourse and social variation among the professors, we turn now to examine these kinds of patterns in student's classroom discourse.

# 8

·———·

# Student Participation and
# Social Difference: Race, Gender, Status,
# and Context in Law School Classes

Having examined professors' discourse profiles, we turn now to analyze students' participation in the classes of this study. Over the past decade, there has emerged a growing debate over the way students of different races, genders, and backgrounds respond to law school pedagogy. In a study that received much attention, Professor Lani Guinier and her coauthors at the University of Pennsylvania indicted traditional law school teaching for creating a chilling climate that is differentially discouraging to women.[1] Other studies have found a negative response to law schools among students with public interest ambitions, and, because more women and students of color fit this profile, have found that this phenomenon has a differentially negative impact on their experience of law school.[2] In addition, several high-profile legal challenges to affirmative action in law school admissions have brought the question of race in law school to the forefront.[3] In a sense, these cases have highlighted a shocking dearth of empirical research on issues of racial inclusion in law school, despite the arguable centrality of this issue to questions of discrimination and representation in the legal profession. Although there has been a growing literature on the question of gender in law school, the number of empirical studies examining racial dynamics—for example, the effects of legal pedagogy on racial inclusion, and the importance of faculty or student cohort diversity to successful integration—remains much smaller. Indeed, with a few notable exceptions, there has been little systematic empirical attention to the effects of race, class, or school status on students' experiences, although there have been numerous first-person accounts documenting a sense of exclusion among many students of color, as well as among working-class students.[4]

This study tracked both race and gender in law school classrooms, and it is the first to provide systematic observational data on race in these settings. In addition, this is the first observational study of gender in law school classrooms to move beyond counting turns to examine more subtle aspects of interaction. Finally, it is also the first research on law school education that combines detailed observational analysis with a comparison across a diverse range of law schools and professors. This allows us to shed some light on the contours of inclusion and exclusion in law school classrooms through an examination of the discursive environment created for (and, in part, by) students in classroom talk.[5] Although it is unusual for observational work of this depth to include as many different classrooms and schools as we did, it is still important to note that the research is best characterized as a set of comparative case studies, particularly well-suited to giving in-depth pictures of classroom dynamics and to generating hypotheses for further testing in larger samples, rather than to proving statistically validated generalizations. Nonetheless, comparisons among the classrooms of this study can be combined with findings from other observational studies to generate a fuller picture, particularly against the backdrop provided by survey and other quantitative research on law schools. If interpreted with care and in the context of other research, results from in-depth case studies such as those performed for this study can advance our level of understanding and questioning regarding wider patterning, in addition to yielding nuanced qualitative analysis of law school pedagogy. To generate this kind of accumulative matrix for comparison, the following sections summarize not only findings from the eight classrooms of this study, but also some of the results of other relevant studies. Taken together, these combined research findings yield the best picture we can produce at this point of law school classroom dynamics.

A threshold question is that of the effect or importance of student participation profiles in terms of students' overall experience. In other words, what difference does student participation make? On the one hand, the typical first-year law school class is graded almost entirely on the basis of written work; it is unusual to find class participation playing much of a role in professors' grading schemes.[6] On the other hand, researchers in other educational settings have found a link between class participation and students' sense of self-esteem, their overall performance, and their sense of inclusion in the wider communities and professions into which they are supposedly being socialized.[7] One could certainly argue that, apart from whether students' grades are affected, there are potential independent offshoots of low participation rates for certain students: that nonparticipation could nonetheless affect students' morale or their image of which voices are valued in the profession to which they seek entry. As we will see, these arguments find support in research from other educational settings. In addition, law school classrooms in which discourse is largely dominated by white men teach a subtle lesson about the social dimensions of discourse norms in this new arena, about entitlement and whose views matter. At a time when an increasing number of reports are documenting differential inclusion of students of color and women at higher levels of the legal profession, findings on classroom climate may help to elucidate a process that begins in law school but continues on to the highest levels of the profession.[8] In this chapter, we start with an examination of findings on race, then consider gender issues, and conclude with a discussion of the complex matrix created by a study of multiple layers of context, identity, and discourse as they play out in students' talk. One corollary of this is that while some aspects of law school structure may have greater impact on students with traditionally marginalized identities, they may not be helpful for many white male students as well. In this sense, focusing on the experiences of students of color and female students may yield results that are useful for all students.

## Race in Law School Classrooms

Research on the impact of race on school experience in other educational settings has for some time documented the "way in which social inequalities are maintained through the schools."[9] As broad-scale patterns of school failure became apparent through the 1960s in schools serving largely working-class and minority communities (evidenced, for example, by high dropout rates and low success in supporting academic achievement), educational researchers began to perform observational research in classrooms that suggested ways the teaching in these schools might be contributing to the problem.[10] These studies revealed differential treatment ranging from overtly discriminatory practices (e.g., differential allocation of resources, or repeated incredulous questioning of minority children who performed well on tests)[11] to more subtle clashes of language and cultural norms. Erickson and Schultz's and Philips's germinal work demonstrated how differences between mainstream and minority identities, along with affiliated communication styles, could in quiet ways negatively influence the availability of resources to minority students, a result substantiated in another classic study by Cazden and her colleague Michaels.[12] Similarly, James Gee used rhetorical analysis to demonstrate the ways a seven-year-old African American girl's narrative, properly understood, was a tour de force; the child's teacher, however, told her to stop talking and sit down (and eventually had the child sent to the school psychologist on the basis of her "incoherent" storytelling).[13]

This dramatic illustration of the silencing of alternative narrative forms in standard classrooms underscores the point made across numerous studies: that classroom dynamics and misunderstandings can have a strong impact on students' participation and their sense of being valued or heard. Indeed, one study that compared black and white male elementary school students found that "among Black males classroom interaction variables generally had a higher correlation with achievement than was true for the sample of White males," so that black male students' overall success in school seemed to depend even more on the quality of their classroom experience than did the success of white students—a troubling result when taken in combination with findings indicating that they were less likely to have high-quality classroom experiences.[14]

Thus, we see, as Weinstein has eloquently noted, that students learn more than academic lessons in the classroom: "It is a social context in which students also learn social lessons—lessons about appropriate behavior . . . , about one's self as a learner and one's position in a status hierarchy, about relationships with students from other racial and ethnic groups, about the value of competition and cooperation."[15] Interestingly, scholars have been able to trace very specific effects of classroom structure on racial dynamics. Qualitative analysis of classroom interactions has demonstrated the ways that teachers create "communicative status," conferring on favored students a sense that they are "students you can learn from."[16] This status can attach to students regardless of the quality of their answers. Use of recitation (the closest analogue to Socratic dialogue), with its intensely public potential for evaluation of responses (both by teachers and peers), tends to encourage the formation of entrenched, segregated groups.[17] Conversely, classrooms with more "status-leveling factors" and fewer competitive structures encourage the formation of more interracial friendships; at the opposite end of the continuum from recitation are structured programs for cooperative learning, which "were superior in producing positive race relations, pro-social development, and classroom climate for all students."[18] Research results converge on the conclusion that the "formal social interaction of the classroom can influence students' informal interactions" in powerful ways.[19] Hence, even apparently neutral structuring of classroom interaction using particular pedagogical techniques (such as recitation) may contribute to hierarchies that take on a racialized character. This is particularly the case when the indigenous discourse norms of a minority community run counter to the norms embedded (indeed, hidden) in those pedagogical techniques.[20]

There is also a well-established literature documenting differential schooling practices along class lines. Studies in this tradition have located a "hidden curriculum" in the schooling of working-class students: teachers in these classrooms more often train students to submit to authority, to focus on maintaining proper form (rather than developing creative approaches to content), and to tolerate boredom.[21] The more empowered, active attitude toward learning that is encouraged in students from middle- and upper-class backgrounds was vividly demonstrated in a study that involved administering a questionnaire in nine high schools in the Los Angeles area. In response to a forced-choice survey in which one set of answer brackets had been omitted, middle-class students complained about and resisted the forced choice but drew in their own set of answer brackets. Students from lower socioeconomic backgrounds unquestioningly accepted the forced choice but repeatedly asked for permission to draw in the missing answer brackets in order to complete their answer.[22] This vignette demonstrates the telling differentiation that can occur when schooling practices teach only particular students that it is their prerogative to assert themselves, to make decisions independently in their learning process. Thus, work across various kinds of schools points to the importance of a thorough examination of context in understanding classroom dynamics and their impact on students from different backgrounds.

A number of studies have focused on minority students' experiences in college. One observational study found that white students "were asked significantly more complex questions by professors, were pushed more to better their response to professors' questions, and received greater amounts of time during the professors' response to their question than did minority students."[23] Other studies had previously demonstrated that teachers treat students differently depending on their expectations; this subsequent observational study found some of the same differences in treatment between minority and nonminority students as had been found in earlier studies between low- and high-expectation students.[24] Studies of African

American students have shown that they are more likely than their white counterparts to experience largely white college campuses as hostile, alienating, and socially isolating; the stresses of minority status were found to have an effect on their academic achievement that was independent of previous academic preparation.[25] Some studies have shown that the effects are more severe for women of color.[26] And there are indications of a regressive trend at the college level since the early 1980s for non-Asian minority students in general; their attrition rates are rising while their grade point averages have been falling.[27]

Reports from the legal academy on racial inclusion do not add a reassuring note to this generally disheartening picture. Our information on the climate in law school for students of color comes primarily from survey studies and from anecdotal reports. One study, conducted by Taunya Lovell Banks, surveyed students from fourteen private and public law schools across the United States between 1987 and 1989.[28] In addition to findings on gender, this study compared the perceptions and experiences of students of color with those of white male students. It found that students of color were more likely to report that "very few of their professors respect their questions and comments" and that African American students were more likely to "perceive that professors embarrass or put down students, and use offensive humor in class."[29] The study did, however, point to strong positive effects on the class participation of African American students of attending historically African American law schools; in other words, black students talk more freely and contribute more substantially to class discussions when they are not small minorities in the classrooms. Conversely, minority students were less likely to participate proportionate to their numbers in class when the classroom was predominantly white.

Other studies have yielded largely similar results. A 1988 study of law students at the University of California–Berkeley found that white male students reported volunteering in class more frequently than all other students; white men also reported overall more positive feelings of self-esteem and more positive reactions to Socratic teaching.[30] Women of color consistently showed up with the most negative reports regarding participation, self-esteem, and satisfaction with law school teaching. A study of law students at the University of Pennsylvania from 1990 to 1994 found that "race continues to play a strong independent role in predicting law school performance," even with the effects of LSAT and college GPA held constant.[31] Students of color participating in this study also reported use of racially intimidating language in class. A study of nine Ohio law schools turned up similar reports of harassment and silencing that differentially impacted students of color.[32] In both the Berkeley and Ohio studies, students of color were more likely to report that faculty diversity mattered to them than were white students (and white women were more likely to report that it mattered than were white men). Research conducted by the Law School Admission Council found some marked differences between women of color and white women in terms of perceived fairness of the grading process, academic self-concept, experiences of discrimination, and a number of other areas.[33]

A recent study of third-year law students produced interestingly complex results on diversity issues, finding both encouraging evidence of some progress, but also signs of lingering differences in experience for law students of color. Gulati, Sander, and Sockloskie combined their results from a survey of third-year law students at eleven law schools with the findings of two previous studies of law students.[34] On the one hand, they conclude that overall, these law students are satisfied with their law school experiences, and that this is true of students of color and female students as well as white male students at these schools. On the other hand, when they examine the "gloomy" responses to their survey, they find that African American, Asian American, and female students are overrepresented among the most alienated group of third-year law students.[35] This leads them to conclude with a mixed picture: that overall in the schools they examined, race-based differences in satisfaction do not seem widely divergent, but that there are "pockets" of deep dissatisfaction, and that students of color are disproportionately included in these pockets. It would be interesting to learn more about the distribution of these pockets of unhappiness in terms of types of law school contexts, given that there might be systematic problems in some schools but not in others.[36]

### Classroom Patterns: Inclusion and Leading the Class

Against this backdrop, we turn now to examine the findings of this study regarding racial dynamics in law school classrooms. Table 8.1 reports on participation rates in the classrooms of this study in terms of race. One of the most striking patterns is the relatively high level of participation found among students of color in the two classes taught by professors of color (Classes #2 and #8). In terms of turns, students of color participated more (proportionate to their numbers in class) than did white students in both classes (11% more in Class #2; 43% more in Class #8). In terms of time, students of color again participated more (51% more) in Class #8. Interestingly, in the larger of the two classes taught by professors of color (Class #2, which was also the largest class in the study, with 135 students), there is a 15% time disproportion in favor of white students. However, this time disproportion is the smallest of the entire study for classes in which white students took disproportionately more time; in the remaining white-dominated classes, the disproportions ranged from 34% (Class #3) to a whopping 289% (Class #1). Note that if there is a positive effect on student participation from the presence of a professor of color in these classes, it is unlikely to be the product of professorial ideologies regarding race-conscious attempts to remedy any effects of past discrimination, as these two professors differed in their attitudes in that regard. We are left with the interesting question of whether any such positive effect might simply result from the encouraging impact of diversity itself: that the mere presence of professors of color might create an environment that feels less closed or segregated, sending the message that all kinds of people are prototypical and highly competent inhabitants of the legal profession, as well as authorities on legal knowledge. It is also worth noting that both of these classes were taught at elite law schools, so that at least in these cases it does not appear that the elite setting had a dampening effect.

It is also important to note that when we break down further the umbrella category of "students of color," it appears that the 15% disproportion in Class #2 resulted largely from the lack of participation by Asian American students, who

TABLE 8.1

Summaries of Participation Ratios by Race

| Class | Total Time | Total Turns |
|-------|-----------|-------------|
| *Elite/Prestige* | | |
| 2 | 1.15 | .89 |
| 8 | .49 | .57 |
| 5 | 2.04 | 2.00 |
| *Regional* | | |
| 4 | .73 | .87 |
| 7 | 1.34 | 1.06 |
| *Local* | | |
| 1 | 2.89 | 4.44 |
| 6 | .74 | .99 |
| 3 | 1.34 | 1.25 |

Ratios are calculated by dividing the white students' participation rate by that of students of color. 1.0 is the figure that would represent equal participation by students regardless of race. Figures over 1.0 represent an imbalance toward white students' participation; figures under 1.0 represent an imbalance toward participation by students of color.

Participation rates are basically the average number of turns per student. The participation rate for students of color, for example, is the number of turns taken by students of color divided by the number of students of color enrolled in the course. When average participation rates are equal—that is, when the average participation rate for one group divided by the other equals 1.0—each group is participating in proportion to its representation.

had a 220% negative disproportion in terms of time. By contrast, African American students participated proportionately 10% more than did white students in this class, complicating the picture somewhat. Thus, we can see the complexities that are introduced when we examine race using somewhat more fine-grained categories (although even here the categories are crude, obscuring differences within groups such as Asian Americans or Latino/a). There are considerable variations in participation that are obscured by a stark comparison of minority to nonminority students.[37] Interestingly, all the classes with overall ratios favorable to students of color show a negative ratio for one or more groups; in Classes #8 and #4 it is the Latino/a students who are more silent, whereas in Class #6 it is the Asian American students who speak less frequently. As we've seen, use of an overall ratio for students of color in Class #2 obscures the fact that if Asian American students were treated separately, Class #2 would have a relatively egalitarian overall ratio for the remaining students of color. But as we consider differences among subgroups, we have smaller and smaller numbers in each group, limiting considerably any conclusions that can be drawn from the comparisons.

In addition to the two classrooms taught by professors of color, there were two other classes in which students of color achieved positive participation ratios. One of them, Class #6, was taught at a local law school by a white female professor and was overall the most egalitarian class of the study. With 53 students, the class was in the midrange of class sizes and fell into the more conversational end of the pedagogical spectrum. It is the only class in the study in which 100% of the students spoke at least once. It shares with Class #3 the smallest gendered time and turn disparities in the study (in favor of women by small percentages), and with Class #2 the smallest race-based time and turn disparities.[38]

Lest we conclude that the more conversational style of this last class was the key factor in generating more egalitarian participation patterns, we note that the fourth classroom in which students of color participated more than predicted by their numbers is Class #4, taught by one of the more Socratic professors. However, this was the youngest teacher in the study, and although he employed a relatively Socratic format, his classroom style was somewhat relaxed (as we saw in Chapter 6, where he was the leading example of an encouraging modified Socratic teacher). Here we see the complications involved in delineating what aspects of classroom style might be most important in creating an inclusive atmosphere, for we have found positive participation ratios for students of color in both a more conversational and a more Socratic class. A qualitative examination of both classes reveals an underlying similarity that is difficult to quantify: the professors in both classes seemed to adopt less of a distanced position than the prototypical formal law professor, using humor, discourse-cohesive devices, and other signals (including prosody and intonation) to create a somewhat more informal atmosphere than students might expect.

Here it's also intriguing to consider the possibility that these professors are all to some degree operating against a backdrop of the stereotypical law professor created in part by popular culture representations (films such as *The Paper Chase*, books such as *One L*). This is a stereotype that is so austere and intimidating that it is not difficult to appear more humane and informal by comparison. It thus seems possible that—sometimes through indirect commentary, as we've seen, and sometimes without any effort or comment at all—these professors may be invoking a contrast in which they appear relatively benign. Alternatively, of course, the stereotype may at times help cast a long shadow over the classroom, helping to create an intimidating atmosphere that professors would have to actively work against if they wished to create an encouraging atmosphere; so, for example, just the use of the discursive format of Socratic questioning might take on additional significance in light of its representation in popular culture. As we will see, we can find evidence for both positions in the student interviews. In any case, these two professors, neither of whom are in the oldest age group in the study, did seem to create a less formal atmosphere in their classes—although it should be noted that, with its combination of conversational structure and relatively light atmosphere, Class #6 was by far the more informal of the two. This reminds us that even though the effects of a more formal discourse style may be softened by the use of an informal overall tone in particular classrooms, the more formal discourse style can still exert an influence that, in combination with other factors, impacts the overall effect of the teaching (e.g., giving a more relaxed professorial approach a nonetheless somewhat stylized feel).

Another factor worth considering in this regard is the effect of a critical mass of fellow students of color in the class. As can be seen in Table 8.2, there is some variability among the classrooms in terms of the proportions of students of color; minority student cohorts range from 23% in Class #2 to 6.6% in Class #3. The cohorts are largest in the elite and prestige law schools of the study and grow smaller as we move down the status hierarchy. Although the two classes with the largest minority cohorts have positive participation rates for students of color, the class with the third-largest minority cohort (Class #5, with a cohort fairly comparable in size to Class #2's) is one of the worst classrooms in this study in terms of minority participation rates. So it appears that, at least in the classes of this study, a substantial cohort alone, absent other conditions, may not be enough to create an inclusive classroom for students of color. This is underscored by the fact that the two classes with the smallest

TABLE 8.2

Class Size and Cohort Data by Race

| Class | Class Size | Percentage of Students of Color | Participation Ratios: Turns |
|---|---|---|---|
| *Elite/Prestige* | | | |
| 2* | 135 | 23.0 | .89 |
| 8* | 32 | 46.9 | .57 |
| 5 | 98 | 19.3 | 2.00 |
| *Regional* | | | |
| 4 | 106 | 12.3 | .87 |
| 7 | 90 | 7.7 | 1.06 |
| *Local* | | | |
| 1 | 115 | 11.3 | 4.44 |
| 6 | 53 | 11.4 | .99 |
| 3 | 76 | 6.6 | 1.25 |

*Class taught by professor of color.

Ratios are calculated by dividing the white students' participation rate by that of students of color. 1.0 is the figure that would represent equal participation by students regardless of race. Figures over 1.0 represent an imbalance toward white students' participation; figures under 1.0 represent an imbalance toward participation by students of color.

Participation rates are basically the average number of turns per student. The participation rate for students of color, for example, is the number of turns taken by students of color divided by the number of students of color enrolled in the course. When average participation rates are equal—that is, when the average participation rate for one group divided by the other equals 1.0—each group is participating in proportion to its representation.

cohorts of minority students (Classes #7 and #3) had less imbalance in favor of white students than did two of the classes in the middle range in terms of cohorts (Classes #1 and #5). Of course, this does not imply that a substantial minority cohort in a classroom has no positive effects on participation; to the contrary, the two classes with the largest cohorts are two of the three most racially inclusive classrooms. (Note also, however, that these are also classes taught by professors of color, so that there are other potentially encouraging aspects of the settings as well.) But it again suggests that multiple aspects of the context combine to create more or less inclusive environments, so that the positive influence of a minority cohort can sometimes be undermined by other features of the classroom environment. Conversely, the combination of a diverse student body and faculty diversity seem to work well, at least in this study, in creating a learning environment in which students of color are comfortable enough to make their voices heard.

Perhaps the most striking finding on race in the study emerges from an analysis of the dominant speakers in each classroom. It is only in the two classes taught by professors of color that students of color are the dominant speakers. Table 8.3 lists the two students in each class who occupied the most time and turns. We see that students of color become leaders of classroom discussion only in Classes #2 and #8, both of which are taught by professors of color. Interestingly, these two classes occupy opposite ends of the spectrum in terms of size: Class #2 is the largest in the study (135 students) and Class #8 is the smallest (32 students). Thus, we can say that large size alone does not seem to silence minority students, although students of color dominate to the greatest extent in the smaller of these two classes. (Indeed, not only are the first two dominant speakers in that class students of color; the third most talkative student, with 8.68% of the turns in the class, was also a student of color.)

*Summary*

Our findings open up some interesting questions worthy of further exploration. Does the presence of faculty of color create an atmosphere in which students of color feel their own presence to be more legitimate, their contributions more valuable? If this is the case, are there constraints on this effect, situations in which this encouraging aspect of faculty diversity is blunted by other factors worthy of study? For example, this study did not find that the effect of a professor of color on students of color was blunted in elite schools. There might, however, be other aspects of the law school or classroom context that could affect this dynamic. We can also ask: What role does cohort size play? On the one hand, the existence of a sizable cohort of minority students in Class #5 did not lead to favorable participation rates in a class taught by an older white male professor using a relatively formal teaching style in an elite/prestige law school. On the other hand, we did find that both of the two classes with the best participation rates for students of color contained a substantial cohort of students of color, in addition to being taught by professors of color. So it may be that some combination of faculty and student diversity, resulting in both substantial cohorts and available professorial role models, can be important parts of creating more inclusive classrooms and law schools. This would

TABLE 8.3

Race of Dominant Speakers

| | Dominant Speakers by Time | | Dominant Speakers by Turns | |
|---|---|---|---|---|
| Class | Race | % of Total Class Time Taken by Speaker | Race | % of Total Class Time Taken by Speaker |
| *Elite/Prestige* | | | | |
| 2 | 1) White | 1)  3.31 | 1) White | 1)  2.88 |
| | 2) White | 2)  2.64 | 2) African American | 2)  2.66 |
| 8 | 1) African American | 1) 16.65 | 1) African American | 1) 15.94 |
| | 2) Asian American | 2) 14.29 | 2) Asian American | 2) 14.06 |
| 5 | 1) White | 1)  4.55 | 1) White | 1)  4.62 |
| | 2) White | 2)  4.03 | 2) White | 2)  3.41 |
| *Regional* | | | | |
| 4 | 1) White | 1) 3.46 | 1) White | 1) 6.59 |
| | 2) White | 2) 3.16 | 2) White | 2) 5.94 |
| 7 | 1) White | 1) 8.45 | 1) White | 1) 5.57 |
| | 2) White | 2) 7.78 | 2) White | 2) 5.17 |
| *Local* | | | | |
| 6 | 1) White | 1) 9.06 | 1) White | 1) 10.97 |
| | 2) White | 2) 5.97 | 2) White | 2)  7.07 |
| 3 | 1) White | 1) 5.69 | 1) White | 1) 5.45 |
| | 2) White | 2) 5.66 | 2) White | 2) 4.57 |

We were able to reliably track repeat speakers in seven of the eight law schools. We are not able to report statistics for Class #1, one of the local law schools. Because this was the classroom in which the distribution of both time and turns was most heavily skewed toward white students, with a huge disparity, it is unlikely that any students of color occupied a dominant role in the class. This likely scenario is supported by qualitative observation in the classroom tracking the students who emerged as identifiable repeat players.

fit with previous scholarship, discussed earlier, documenting minority students' negative responses to overwhelmingly white schools as well as to the overt and covert forms of racism found in many such settings. It would also fit with findings showing that students of color feel that it makes a difference if they have the experience of being taught by professors of color.[39]

Overall, we found a high degree of variability in terms of minority participation rates, with at times whopping disproportions in favor of white students. (These disproportions were far more marked than were found when analyzing gender.) No clear pattern among the kinds of classes emerged from a comparison across the eight schools of this study, except for the fact that students of color participated more vigorously in classes taught by professors of color in which there were substantial cohorts of minority students—and this was particularly true in terms of dominant speakers. It also is worth exploring whether subtle aspects of classroom discourse can operate to produce a more encouraging atmosphere for learning and participation (possibly for all students, as well as for students of color). Combining our findings with those of existing studies on race, we see that the overall inclusiveness of the classroom and law school as truly egalitarian sites for learning seems to connect with degrees of segregation versus diversity.

## Gender in Law School Classrooms

There has been a continuing line of research for some years documenting gender differences in all kinds of classrooms. At the elementary and high school levels, studies have found that girls are frequently excluded from classroom participation in a number of ways.[40] This exclusion is part of a pattern that is thought to contribute to declining performance throughout female students' years in school.[41] Girls are rewarded for docility, whereas boys are more likely to receive meaningful and extensive instruction when they encounter difficulties and are also more likely to be called on.[42] Teachers tend to insist that boys work through and solve problems, whereas they more frequently hand girls the answers: "A sixth-grade girl is having trouble working out a math problem. The teacher takes the pencil out of her hand and quickly does the problem for her."[43] In a math contest between the boys and girls in a different class, one teacher kept score under the headings "Good Girls" and "Brilliant Boys."[44] Studies indicate that black female students are the most affected by this exclusionary pattern, although there are also encouraging indications of African American girls' psychological resilience in the face of this exclusion.[45]

Studies of college education show a similar pattern and have linked the chilly classroom and campus climate to a gradual process whereby women "revise and scale down their career goals."[46] Again, there are indications that this impacts women of color more than it does white women.[47] A pioneering observational study of 24 teachers at Harvard University found that male students spoke 2.5 times longer overall than women in "the predominant classroom circumstance: i.e., the situation in which the instructor is male and the majority of the students are male."[48] This detailed and nuanced study of classroom language found that in classes taught by women, female students talked almost three times as much as they did when taught by men.[49] In addition to the effects of the teacher's gender, the Harvard study identified a number of differences between men's and women's speech patterns that contributed to inequalities in student participation:

1. In the relatively freewheeling discussion format of these classrooms, women students were more vulnerable to interruption and often did not come back from being interrupted to talk again.
2. Women students tended not to compete with men students for floor time, instead interrupting one another so that they wound up competing for the relatively scarce female-dominated floor time.
3. Women and men tended to speak in clusters or runs, rather than speaking in dispersed patterns; this meant that any existing pattern of domination or underrepresentation would only be heightened.

4. These teachers often let an emphasis on "keeping the flow of discussion going" take priority over encouraging inclusion, permitting those with the quickest response time to dominate classroom discussion; participation then became "based on quick thinking instead of deep or representative thinking" and was biased toward the more verbally assertive (who in this study tended to be white males as opposed to "minorities of either sex" or white females).
5. Because participation earlier in the class session was the best predictor of participation overall, a bias toward volunteers with the quickest response time early in the class contributed to a growing hierarchy in participation overall.[50]

These results suggest that women might be disadvantaged in classrooms where teachers rely heavily on volunteers (a finding that, as we will see, has been replicated in multiple studies and settings).

A number of other observational studies have found similarly high participation rates (especially where students volunteer to speak) and frequent interruptions on the part of male students when compared with females.[51] In survey studies of college teaching, male students report higher rates of talking than do women, and these reported rates of participation and interruption go up in classes taught by women.[52] At the same time, a number of these studies have indicated that classes taught by women might be more egalitarian in gendered dimensions of overall participation than are classes taught by men, because women students report participating a great deal more in classes taught by women as well. In the present study, the classes with the smallest gender disparities (which in these classes favor women, but only slightly)—and therefore the most egalitarian overall distributions by gender—are found in two of the three classes taught by women professors. One survey of 1,059 students in 51 classes in a small midwestern college stressed the effects of peer interaction on gender dynamics, noting that "student gender is a significant component in class participation. Male students are more likely to offer comments or raise questions in their classes. Females respond to the emotional climate of a class more than do males, and most importantly, females' participation is related to their confidence."[53] This is important to keep in mind in assessing the meaning of silence, because it is against the backdrop of existing research on girls' and women's differential silence in educational settings, across many levels, that we must understand the gender patterns found in law school classrooms. In general, studies of gender dynamics in college and graduate-level classrooms have tended not to look systematically at such aspects of context as status and kind of school.[54] But a more general study of graduate and professional training in the United States found that there were higher numbers of women at lower-status schools; it also found that where women were a minority, there were more reports of biased treatment.[55]

There have been far more studies of gender than of race in law school classrooms. The rich literature in this area has focused in part on the distinctive characteristics of law teaching; perhaps the most prominent debate focuses on the use of the Socratic method. With very few exceptions, empirical studies of gender in law teaching have relied either on self-report or on observation by students who were themselves participants in the classes being studied. These studies have generally found differential responses to law teaching by gender. In 1986, Taunya Lovell Banks studied five schools across the country and found a significant difference between men's and women's self-reports regarding voluntary participation in class. Older women students reported more active participation in class than younger women.[56] More women than men reported that their lack of participation was due to feeling insecure or uncertain, although fewer women than men reported that being unprepared was a reason for their failure to participate. Women were more likely to report that the professor's gender affected student participation, and to indicate that women professors encouraged students more than men. Banks followed this initial study with further research in fourteen private and public law schools across the United States from 1987 to 1989, research whose findings largely repeated those of the first with regard to gender.[57]

Subsequent surveys at individual law schools yielded similar results regarding participation in class, with some interesting differences on other issues. A study conducted in 1986 at Stanford Law School found that male students and graduates reported asking questions and volunteering answers in class to a significantly greater degree than did female students and graduates, despite a lack of reported difference between men and women in actual law school performance.[58] A similar study was administered to students at the law school at the University of California–Berkeley (Boalt Hall), examining both gender and race; it also found marked differences between men and women, with white men uniformly more active and positive about their experiences.[59] The Berkeley study also documented a general slide in women's grades relative to men's between 1984 and 1988, based on objective grade data provided by the school. Research conducted by Lani Guinier and her colleagues at the University of Pennsylvania Law School found a similar disproportion in grades; they linked this with a "systematically alienating, three-year educational experience" for women, one key component of which they described as "women's silence in the classroom."[60] More recently, a student group at Harvard Law School collected multiple kinds of data on gender, including information on course grades in required first-year courses between 1996 and 2000.[61] Their results indicated that men were more likely than women to graduate with honors or to earn high first-year grades, and that this trend seems to have increased over the past two years. An accompanying survey of students conducted in 2002–2003 revealed lower levels of confidence and self-assessment for female students at Harvard.[62] A recent survey of Yale law students and accompanying interviews of selected faculty members similarly pointed to perceived differential hesitance among female students regarding class participation, approaching professors after class with questions, and asking for recommendations.[63] On the other hand, faculty members report that in general, the gender balance in classroom discussions at Yale seems to be improving over time.

A study headed by Joan Krauskopf, which examined nine law schools in Ohio, also found gendered differences in classroom experience and in overall responses to law school.[64] In this study, men once again reported asking more questions and volunteering in class more often than did women. Women overall were less likely to respond positively to the Socratic method and were more likely to report a loss of confidence in class, as well as a drop in self-esteem generally. A number of the earlier studies, such as those conducted by Guinier and by Krauskopf, contained accounts of direct harassment based on gender.[65]

In addition, there have been a number of survey studies that did not focus on classroom participation per se, but that tracked attitudes and responses to law schools. Many of these studies found no reported difference in performance (grades, etc.) between men and women; indeed, some found that women and men were equally content. However, other studies found higher rates of distress among women than men even when their actual performance was comparable to the men's.[66] One overall conclusion to be drawn from these studies is that the particular climate and features of a specific law school (and at a specific point in time) may have a strong influence on the degree to which gendered differences in experience emerge. Another lesson is that there are significant aspects of student experience not well mapped by tracking performance alone. Finally, the persistent evidence of women's diminished confidence in law school—and of their lower class participation—seems to indicate problems that continue into postgraduate education.[67] It is against this backdrop that we look to patterns of silence and speech for clues about gender as well as racial integration in law schools.

In addition to survey research, there has been some observational work in law school classrooms. In an early study in 1972, which relied on participant observation as well as interview and survey methods, Alice Jacobs reported, "Although women perform very well academically, it was observed that they consistently interact less frequently than men in the classroom. They volunteer or are chosen to answer questions much less frequently than the men."[68] Similar disparities were found in moot court trials, and Jacobs recounts her impression that women used supplicatory and questioning intonation for oral argument, whereas men used more assertive verbal styles. Despite their generally high level of actual performance, women in this study gave indications of lower self-esteem and career aspirations (although there were obviously multiple factors affecting this pattern at the time). If differential experiences in law school do contribute to lower self-esteem, however, then here is another way these experiences could affect students even if actual law school performance remains unaffected: they could conceivably affect women's sense of their abilities and therefore their career goals and trajectories.

There have been five more recent observational studies of law school classrooms at Yale (2), Harvard (1), and the University of Chicago (2). Four of the five studies were conducted by students who were also taking the classes they were observing. There have been two such efforts at Yale. In the earlier research during the 1980s, students in 19 different classes coded each time a male or female student had a turn.[69] In 15 of the 19 classes, male students spoke more than would be predicted by their proportions in the classes, with ratios ranging up to three times more than the women in the class. Averaging all of the classes, men spoke 63% more frequently than women, proportionate to their numbers in the classes. In the one course in the study that was taught by a woman in this elite law school, men spoke almost twice as much as did women. This is of interest because of questions about the impact of female teachers on women students. One hypothesis is that the presence of female teachers should have an encouraging effect on women students' class participation, and that this effect should be especially strong among the most elite (and presumably empowered) women. On the other hand, some have suggested that working-class women are in fact more likely to buck the system, whereas elite women have gotten where they are in part because they did not challenge the elite men around them.[70] Another hypothesis is that the pressure for conformity to gendered norms around assertive speech becomes greater in elite institutions, affecting both women professors and students.[71] In any case, these findings point us to relatively unexplored questions about the interaction of student and professor gender with institutional status.

A second, more recent student effort during 2001 at the Yale Law School involved classroom monitoring in 23 classrooms, conducted in combination with a survey of law students and interviews with professors.[72] As noted, the survey and interviews revealed that both students and faculty had the impression that female students were more hesitant than male students about speaking in class. These perceptions were given support by the observational findings from classroom monitoring, which showed that in terms of total participation, "men still appear to dominate classroom discussions more than women."[73] This effect was exacerbated when only volunteered turns were examined.[74] On an encouraging note, women's participation did reach equal or greater proportional levels in comparison to men's in a number of larger courses, including first-year courses.[75] Interestingly, women dominated more in courses taught by male professors than they did in those taught by female professors, although we would want to be cautious about drawing too broad a conclusion from this.[76] The Yale report did not find any "distinctive male or female mode of participation."[77]

A student group at Harvard Law School recently undertook a similar investigation, monitoring each of 32 courses for four to seven of the class meetings during the spring semester of 2003 (for a total 190 class meetings monitored, averaging around six class meetings per course).[78] The students adopted a method whereby one male and one female student enrolled in each course both simultaneously coded the same class meetings.[79] They found a significant difference between women and men in participation rates, a difference that they report was largely due to difference in voluntary participation.[80] The "top talkers"—the small group of students who accounted for a high proportion of student turns—were "overwhelmingly male," and this was despite even-handed treatment of speakers by professors. As in the Yale study, crude distinctions in pedagogical style (e.g., between Socratic and non-Socratic teaching) did not seem to generate any clear gender difference in participation.[81] In this study, there was an even more marked pattern of disproportionate male participation in classes taught by female professors: "A male student was 40% more likely than a female to volunteer during a class meeting with a male professor, compared with 106% more likely in courses taught by women."[82] On the other hand, there was variation in women's participation rates among the different classes monitored, with women more likely than men to speak in some of the classes (particularly in response to being called on).[83]

The remaining two observational studies were conducted at the University of Chicago Law School. One, conducted by students, tracked participation for two weeks in nine different courses and included consideration of volunteered versus called-on turns.[84] In 1994–1995, following this initial student effort, Chicago hired outside observers to study classroom interactions. The results of this more disinterested research confirmed the student-run study's finding that male students participated more in class: "The overall probability of a woman student speaking in class was .83 relative to a 1.0 probability of a male student speaking in class."[85] The participation rates for women in classes taught by women was still lower (.79). Similarly, women were less likely to volunteer (.74 as opposed to 1.0) and again had slightly lower rates of volunteering in classes taught by women.

These observational studies documented a pattern in which men speak more than women in most law school classes. It is possible that on an individual level, this difference in participation can have multiple meanings. In other settings, silence has been interpreted in a number of ways, including as a form of resistance. One purpose of this extensive review of relevant literature is to provide a thorough examination of educational settings in the United States so that we can better understand what is known about the meaning of differential female silence in these settings. The link between lowered confidence and differential silence emerges in early education and is found repeatedly in studies ranging from elementary schools through college and into law school. In law schools in particular, I argue, there is an institutional level on which silence has meaning even apart from its interpretation by individual speakers. Law school is, after all, a training in a kind of language. One of the hallmarks of legal training is the instillation of new norms of adversarial speech, and one canonical legal context in which many lawyers will wind up working (the courtroom) requires that attorneys be able to hold up their end of verbal exchanges. Differential silence on the part of women and students of color in law school classrooms therefore takes on institutional meaning along numerous dimensions.[86]

Another issue raised by observational studies is the relationship between gender of professor and student participation. Although surveys had indicated a positive effect of women professors on women students' classroom experience and participation, the observational work raises some questions about possible variations among classes and schools in this regard. Overall, both survey and observational research suggest that students frequently have different responses to law school teaching along lines of gender as well as of race and class. We turn now to the findings from the present study on gender.

### Classroom Patterns: Floor Time and the Socratic Dilemma

Our data tend to confirm the findings of previous studies, which focused only on turns, that male law students generally participate at greater rates than females. In addition to tracking numbers of turns, we also analyzed overall time. In six of the eight classrooms we studied, men spoke more frequently than women and for longer periods of time. These six classrooms included all of the classes taught by men and one of the classes taught by a woman professor (in an elite law school). In these classes, men students had between 10% and 54% more turns than did women (proportionate to their numbers in the class; see Table 8.4). Similarly, men took between 12% and 38% more time in speaking. Notice that the greatest overall gender disparity in participation from the perspective of turns taken (1.54) occurred in

TABLE 8.4

Summaries of Participation Ratios by Gender

| Class | Total Time | Total Turns |
|---|---|---|
| *Elite/Prestige* | | |
| 2 | 1.23 | 1.10 |
| 8 | 1.38 | 1.54 |
| 5 | 1.31 | 1.17 |
| *Regional* | | |
| 4 | 1.23 | 1.17 |
| 7 | 1.38 | 1.17 |
| *Local* | | |
| 1 | 1.12 | 1.15 |
| 6 | .93 | .95 |
| 3 | .93 | .95 |

Ratios are calculated by dividing the men's participation rate by the women's participation rate. 1.0 is the figure that would represent equal participation by women and men. Figures over 1.0 represent an imbalance toward male participation; figures under 1.0 represent an imbalance toward female participation.

Participation rates are basically the average number of turns per student. Women's participation rate, for example, is the number of turns taken by women divided by the number of women enrolled in the course. When average participation rates are equal—that is, when the average participation rate for one group divided by the other equals 1.0—each group is participating in proportion to its representation in class enrollment.

Class #8, a class in an elite law school taught by a woman of color and also the smallest class in the study. In the five classes taught by men, male students spoke from 10% to 17% more frequently than did women. Disparities in terms of time were still sharper (23–38%) in four of these five classes (those taught in the higher-status law schools of that group).

By contrast, women spoke slightly more, proportionately, than did men in the two remaining classes, both taught by women in nonelite schools. These classes were also the most egalitarian in terms of overall distribution of times and turns by gender; they were the only ones with disparities between men and women students under 10%. Thus, even where women's participation exceeds the men's, it does not reach the level of disproportion found in classes where men predominate in classroom discussion.[87] One of these two classes in which women students predominated was also the most egalitarian in terms of the percentage of students who participated, with all students in the class participating at least once during the semester (see Table 8.5). The egalitarian class, taught in a local law school by a

TABLE 8.5

Percentage of Students Who Spoke at
Least Once, by Gender

| Class | Women | Men |
|-------|-------|-----|
| *Elite/Prestige* | | |
| 2 | 96 | 91 |
| 8 | 100 | 86 |
| 5 | 75 | 90 |
| *Regional* | | |
| 4 | 66 | 73 |
| 7 | 90 | 78 |
| *Local* | | |
| 6 | 100 | 100 |
| 3 | 84 | 92 |

We were able to track participation
by individual speakers for seven of the
eight schools.

woman professor, fell at the more conversational end of the spectrum in terms of teaching style. This highlights an interesting issue regarding the effects of less formal style; the class in which women spoke most and the class in which they spoke the least both shared the characteristic of a relatively informal teaching style, and in both cases we had women professors. We see, then, the interestingly divergent possible effects of the same style: it can create a relaxed atmosphere in which women feel freer to speak, but conversely, the lack of formal structure can also make room for societal patterns of gender dominance in discourse to emerge. Note that despite the overall inequality of time and turns in favor of men in Class #8, taught by a woman in an elite law school, more of the women in the class participated than did men (100% of women versus 86% of men), reminding us of the complexities involved in assessing inclusiveness.[88]

Discussions of the effects of pedagogical structure on gender dynamics in law school classrooms have often focused on a particular aspect of formal versus informal teaching: the Socratic method. As noted earlier, some authors have suggested that Socratic structure has a particularly chilling effect on female students' participation. In this study, we coded extended one-on-one exchanges between student and professor as "focused" dialogue (our closest measure for Socratic-type structuring).[89] Chapter 7 outlined the distributions of different kinds of dialogue in the classrooms of the study (see Table 7.1). As we've seen, these figures can be broken down into three categories: the modified Socratic classes, with 45 to 60% of the time (and 74 to 86% of the turns) spent in extended dialogue (Classes #5, #4, #1); the classes characterized by shorter exchanges, with 21 to 29% of the time (and 34 to 60% of the turns) spent in extended dialogue; and the predominantly lecture class, with 2% of time (and 16% of turns) spent in Socratic-style exchanges.

Comparing these results with those reported in Table 8.4, we see that all of the most Socratic classes (#5, #4, #1) have gender imbalances in favor of men. We also see that both of the classes in which there were gender imbalances in favor of women were structured around short exchanges.[89]

If we now ask about the interaction of different forms of dialogue with gender, we find intriguingly mixed results. Table 8.6 summarizes the different gendered distributions of focused and shorter dialogue in the eight classrooms of the study. We can see that women actually participate more in extended dialogues than they do in shorter exchanges in four of the classrooms—and these are the four most elite male-taught classes. In Class #2 (elite school, male teacher) women take 6% more turns than do men in extended dialogues, but 14% fewer turns in shorter exchanges. The same reversal occurs in Class #7, taught by a male teacher in a regional law school. In Class #5, in a prestige law school and taught by a man, we find a dramatic shift: men take 14% more turns in extended dialogue but 75% more in shorter exchanges. A similar, though less dramatic shift occurs in Class #4, taught

TABLE 8.6

Comparison of Extended and Shorter Dialogue Turns, by Gender

| Class | Ratio of Total Focused Dialogue Turns | Ratio of Total Other Dialogue Turns | Shift in Women's Participation from Extended to Shorter Dialogue |
|---|---|---|---|
| *Elite/Prestige* | | | |
| 2 | 0.94 | 1.14 | −.20 |
| 8 | 1.71 | 1.40 | +.31 |
| 5 | 1.14 | 1.75 | −.61 |
| *Regional* | | | |
| 4 | 1.14 | 1.25 | −.11 |
| 7 | 0.68 | 1.21 | −.53 |
| *Local* | | | |
| 1 | 1.15 | 1.04 | +.11 |
| 6 | 1.00 | 0.94 | +.06 |
| 3 | 0.98 | 0.88 | +.10 |
| | Average change in female-taught classes | | +.15 |
| | Average change in male-taught classes | | −.26 |

Ratios are calculated by dividing the men's participation rate by the women's participation rate. 1.0 is the figure that would represent equal participation by women and men. Figures over 1.0 represent an imbalance toward male participation; figures under 1.0 represent an imbalance toward female participation.

Participation rates are basically the average number of turns per student. Women's participation rate, for example, is the number of turns taken by women divided by the number of women enrolled in the course. When average participation rates are equal—that is, when the average participation rate for one group divided by the other equals 1.0—each group is participating in proportion to its representation in class enrollment.

by a male teacher in a regional law school. It is in the classes taught by women, and in the local law school class taught by a man, that women actually improve their participation rates when moving from extended or focused dialogues to less extensive exchanges. This finding is most striking for Classes #6 and #8 because they were the classes with the highest percentage of time spent in shorter exchanges (42% and 46%, as compared with 5–24% in the other classes). Once again, Class #6, taught by a woman in a local law school, has the most egalitarian distribution of discourse by gender, including an absolutely balanced distribution of focused dialogue turns. We are left with two interesting questions about the interaction of gender with teaching style: Why is it that women participate more in extended dialogues than they do in shorter exchanges in the more Socratic classrooms of this study? And how do we understand the difference in women's participation between Classes #6 and #8, both of which are informal conversational classes taught by women?

One possible reason for the distribution we have found around extended dialogues could be that extended, formal (Socratic) exchanges tend to rely less on volunteering and often begin with a teacher calling on a student. If this is the case, higher participation rates for women in extended dialogues could indicate their unwillingness in certain (more Socratic) classes to volunteer answers for shorter exchanges. Conversely, higher participation rates in the shorter exchanges could reflect more willingness to volunteer. A number of the studies noted earlier suggested that women students tend to volunteer less, so that relying on volunteers may help to create gender imbalances in the discussion. Our results give some support to this observation, although again with the caveat that this dynamic changes in different kinds of classrooms. We find that women's participation relative to men's is lower in the category of volunteered turns than in called-on turns in five of the eight classrooms, including all classrooms in elite/prestige law schools.[90] In two of the three more Socratic classrooms, women participate more in called-on as compared with volunteered turns. Indeed, in Class #5, taught by a male professor in an elite/prestige law school, there is a dramatic shift in favor of male participation in the volunteer turns category: a difference of 100%. Overall, women's participation ratio is 32% lower in volunteered than in called-on turns in male-taught classes. Again, there are some interesting complications; in Class #4 (another more Socratic class in which women fare better in extended dialogues), women actually have slightly better ratios in volunteered than in called-on turns. It is likely that some of the more fine-grained aspects of classroom atmosphere in that class, which have already been discussed, may have introduced intervening factors that influenced students' feelings about volunteering. But in two of the three Socratic classrooms, it is plausible that women's reluctance to volunteer contributes to their better participation ratios for Socratic as opposed to shorter exchanges: in these classes, professors generally called on students during Socratic dialogues, so that most voluntary participation occurs in the shorter exchanges (see Table 8.7).[91]

Another interesting finding emerging from analysis of volunteered versus called-on turns sheds some light on the very different features of two classes taught by women, Class #8 (elite school) and Class #6 (local school). Recall that both classes are taught in informal style, but that they are at opposite ends of the scale in terms

TABLE 8.7

Comparison of Called-on and Volunteered Participation Rates, by Gender

| Class | Ratio of Total Called-on Turns | Ratio of Total Volunteered Turns | Shift in Women's Participation from Called-on to Volunteer Turns |
|---|---|---|---|
| *Elite/Prestige* | | | |
| 2 | 0.90 | 1.20 | -.30 |
| 8 | 1.50 | 1.70 | -.20 |
| 5 | 1.30 | 2.30 | -1.00 |
| *Regional* | | | |
| 4 | 1.40 | 1.30 | +.10 |
| 7 | 0.90 | 1.10 | -.30 |
| *Local* | | | |
| 1 | 1.00 | 1.10 | -.10 |
| 6 | 1.10 | 0.80 | +.30 |
| 3 | 1.00 | 1.00 | 0 |
| | Average change in female-taught classes | | +.03 |
| | Average change in male-taught classes | | -.32 |

Ratios are calculated by dividing the men's participation rate by the women's participation rate. 1.0 is the figure that would represent equal participation by women and men. Figures over 1.0 represent an imbalance toward male participation; figures under 1.0 represent an imbalance toward female participation.

of gendered participation, with Class #8 having the highest asymmetry in favor of men, and Class #6 (along with Class #3) having the best for women. As noted earlier, these two classes spend the highest amounts of time in the study using unfocused, shorter dialogues between professor and student (46% and 42%). But when we compare the two classes in terms of voluntary participation, we see that women in Class #8 volunteer 70% *less* than do men, whereas women in Class #6 volunteer 20% *more* than do men. This could have particularly significant impact in light of how much time is spent in shorter, often voluntary exchanges in these classes. Interestingly, during their interviews students from Class #6 commented with approval on the degree to which their professor kept control of the exchanges in the classroom.[92] Thus, although there was an equivalent amount of shorter, voluntered discussion in the two classes, it may be that the degree of professorial control of those exchanges differed.[93] A number of issues for further study are thus suggested by the comparison between these two classes: in asking about possible connections between pedagogical style and gendered participation, we need to investigate the effects of professor gender, particularly in relation to different kinds of law school settings; the distribution of volunteered versus called-on turns; and aspects of professorial control even in relatively informal classrooms. In addition, although we were unable to track students' ages in the study, there is anecdotal information suggesting that the two schools in which women spoke more may have had more older students.[94] Thus, we might also ask about the differences between older and younger women in terms of their assertiveness in less structured dialogues.[95]

## Summary

This study's findings on gender tend to support the picture that has emerged from other research on classroom dynamics, albeit with a few interesting wrinkles suggesting some directions for further study. Overall, women students participated at lower rates than men, a difference that was still worse when we examined only volunteered turns. This fits with previous observational studies of law schools and with many (although not all) of the self-report studies as well. Survey studies such as those conducted at Minnesota and New Mexico did not find the kinds of attitudinal and reported differences between men and women that had been found in much other research. The authors of one of these studies suggested that particular aspects of the law school atmosphere—notably, positive attitudes regarding diversity—might be affecting the result. I have throughout this discussion echoed this focus on context, urging that we examine our results in terms of particular classroom and school contexts.

One such particular context is provided by the status of the school. The three more comprehensive observational studies performed in elite law schools to date (Yale, University of Chicago, Harvard) have not found the kind of positive influence of women professors on women students' participation that has been documented in some other educational settings. In the one class taught by a female professor at an elite/prestige school in this study, women also participated less than did men. On the other hand, in two nonelite law school classes taught by female professors in this study, women participated at nearly equal or slightly higher levels than did men. It is obviously cause for concern if something about the atmosphere or classroom dynamics in our nation's elite and prestige law schools undercuts women law professors as role models or their support for their women students. Of course, we cannot draw any generalized conclusions from this set of case studies, but these findings together certainly suggest that the interaction of school status and gender might bear further examination. This is also particularly interesting in light of the contrary picture that emerged from this study regarding race: two classes taught by professors of color (one of whom was also the woman discussed in this paragraph) at elite schools were characterized by high participation rates on the part of students of color, a result apparently unaffected by status of school.[96]

Another interesting aspect of context is that created by classroom discourse style. Previous studies had indicated a possible negative effect of Socratic teaching on women's participation, as well as of voluntary participation (women being less likely to volunteer or to raise their hands quickly). Again, we found mixed support for this picture, with some new complexities to consider as well. On the one hand, women's overall participation rates in the more elite and more highly Socratic classrooms of this study were lower than men's. On the other hand, if the classroom was more heavily Socratic, women participated at higher levels in longer, Socratic exchanges than in shorter, volunteered colloquies. So we have another interestingly complex result: the most Socratic classrooms are biased overall in favor of male participation, but in those classrooms women participate more in the extended Socratic exchanges. Our findings on volunteered versus called-on turns suggest that in some, but not all, Socratic classes, this dynamic may be fed by women's tendency not to volunteer (which would differentially exclude them from the more voluntary, less formal, shorter exchanges). Thus, if a professor is going to use a more heavily Socratic teaching style, a higher percentage of extended, structured exchanges might produce more egalitarian results than frequent interruptions of those exchanges for shorter interjections, particularly if those interruptions rely primarily on volunteered turns.

Complicating the picture further, we find that the most egalitarian classes in the study in terms of gender, and also the two classes in which women predominated slightly, were taught by women professors at nonelite schools using relatively informal discourse style structured around shorter exchanges. However, there is a slight difference between the two classes: one falls at the lowest end of the informality continuum (with the highest percentages of times and turns spent in shorter exchanges in the study), but the other had significantly fewer shorter exchanges.[97] Thus, categories such as "modified Socratic" and "short exchange" themselves need to be supplemented by examination of other aspects of discourse style and structure. Similarly, the class in which male students predominated to the greatest extent was also taught by a woman professor using a relatively interactive, informal discourse style. So we see that although a less Socratic style may in some circumstances encourage more female participation, this is highly circumscribed by other aspects of the classroom setting. In one case, informality may encourage less aggressive speakers; in another, it may give aggressive speakers freer rein. It seems likely that this might vary in part depending on subtle aspects of professorial control.

These complexities, however, do not obscure an overall pattern in which male students predominate in law school classroom discussions. Although the contours of the patterning differ from those found when we examined race, in both cases we find some indications that, in combination with findings from other studies, point to continued differential effects of gender and race on inclusion in law school classrooms.

## Student Perspectives

In our group interviews with students, a number of interesting themes emerged.[98] In one sense, they point to differences in position and perspective between professors and students, differences that are reflective of the distinct enterprises in which they are engaged. But in many respects, some clear continuities of perspective are already emerging between students and teachers regarding a shared enterprise in the classroom. Here we examine some of these differences and similarities, with an eye to comparing across the different kinds of schools and teachers in the study.

One obvious difference is the degree to which students are concerned with strategies for succeeding and surviving, at both the intellectual and the emotional level. Thus, although they also talk about the content of what they are learning—at times with considerable enthusiasm—they are clearly focused on strategic considerations. They speak of strategies for handling class, homework, and overall balance:

See, I just go for the easy question. *[ . . . ]* in the back, you can tell when no one's going to answer the easy question. (7-15)

I brief every case and leave room on the page for class notes. (5-1)

I- I'm always big on balancing school and job with your life, and I- I made sure that I- I messed around during those couple weeks (exams), I think it's vital to your sanity. (6-2-M)

This focus on strategies leads many of the students to speak with approval of professors who give them overt strategic guidance, as long as the guidance turns out to be useful. For example, students were very pleased with their professor in Class #6 (our most inclusive classroom, taught in a local law school by a female professor), praising her clarity and specific instructions on how to prepare for the exams:

*[The following comments emerge from an informal discussion among four students, who are talking enthusiastically and overlapping their speech.]*

6-1-F:       She definitely gears you towards // the exam- //

6-2-M:                                          // The good // professors can give you signals--

6-3–F:                    --She's the most, and you know she did say that her coll- I remember she told us- ah, the beginning of the semester, that her colleagues have criticized her for being a spoon-feeder.

Interviewer:  Oh really?

6-3-F:       Yeah. But // I-// *[multiple speakers, overlapping speech]*

6-1-F:                    // I // appreciate that so much, the straightforward//ness//

6-3-F:                                                          // Well,//
             I think the- le, y'know, play- I don't see what the point is of playing this hide-the-ball sort of game with students like they do in *The Paper Chase* and that sort of thing, I don't- I don't (serve) what purpose that serves.

On the other hand, there is some dissent from an orientation that focuses to too great a degree on strategy and exams, as with this student from a local law school:

1-F:        But I just feel like that attitude is so pervasive here, everyone is constantly looking towards exams an- and like when the professors say it too, it's like, "Ugh, can't we just learn? Can't anyone just wanna learn?"

1-F:        I don't like that our- that our futures are so dependent on these rankings in the first year, it's so important [Student 3: Right] [Student 2: I do not like that].

Although some studies have stressed the differences between upper- and lower-status law schools in terms of the degree to which professors teach theory as opposed to more practical information, this quote from a student in a local law school foreshadows some convergence among the classes and students of this study.

On the one hand, there are some slight differences in emphasis between some of the more elite classes, favoring theory, and some of the less elite classes. On the other hand, all of the classes in the study retained a heavy focus on case analysis, aimed at elucidating doctrinal issues. This is the backbone of the first-year law school curriculum, and professors across all schools spent much of their time in this kind of endeavor. All of the professors also took care at some points in their teaching to push students into thinking practically about what these legal doctrines would look like in the setting of making arguments or putting together cases in court, and sometimes even in terms of dealing with clients. And there was actually considerable discussion of theory and policy in some of the lower-ranked law school classes, whereas at one of the more highly ranked law schools in the country, students appeared to have less exposure to theory than did some of their counterparts in the study at less prestigious schools. Students in this elite/prestige classroom did complain about the relative dearth of theory, noting that it was not typical of their overall education. But the counterpoint between their complaints and the enthusiastic invocation of theory by students at other, lower-ranked law schools serves as a valuable caution to those who would assume too deterministic an effect of school status:

*[School 2: Elite/Prestige]*

Student 1:  I think I expected to spend more time on the "whys" of law [ . . . ] and that was surprising to me, how much time we actually spent explaining and finding out the details of the doctrine rather than talking about the justifications for the doctrine. [ . . . ] When I was looking into law schools, I specifically wanted to go to a school that would be more theory-oriented and I was told that this school would be one of those schools and just seems to vary from professor to professor.

*[School 7: Regional/State]*

Student 2:  Well, contracts, I mean, [ . . . ] there's a whole- the whole history of capitalism underlying it.

The students in the group from the regional law school went on to discuss in animated fashion the policy and social assumptions behind particular doctrines in contract law and the evolution of contract law from its initial basic assumptions, concluding that "the law kind of reflects how society is." These students certainly seemed no less entranced with (or capable of engaging with) the bigger picture behind doctrine than did their more elite counterparts. It is certainly true that students from less elite schools more frequently praised professors for reminding them of what things would actually look like in practice, and one would not want to deny some average differences among the students in terms of their emphasis on theory versus practice. But these seem to be muted in the first-year curriculum, where even the most elite students have to descend to the level of doctrine when learning how to read cases, and where many professors across all kinds of schools take time here and there to pull in the bigger picture of theory and policy.

As we saw in our initial excerpt, the shadow of popular cultural pictures of law school still looms large in the accounts of first-year law students, with a number of the interviewees making spontaneous comments about the frightening image of Kingsfield or expectations based on *The Paper Chase* or *One L* looming over them. Although the expectations may themselves have created tension for the students in the initial days of class, they generally commented with relief on how unlike this picture their actual law school experience has turned out to be. One group of students remarked with humor on the cooperative stance they feel their professor takes when he senses that he has moved too quickly for them:

[7–11]

Student 1:  Sometimes, I don't know what it is, but like, he'll come in [ . . . ] he'll just go, go, go, go, you know, and then it's all finally over everybody's head; he'll come in the next day and realize that everything went over our heads and he'll go back over it.

Student 2:  See, we sit at the back [ . . . ] we sit in the back and we have a theory that he comes in the next day and everybody's just staring at him and sees all this sea of blank faces and realizes that it's time to slow down and go back over things. [ . . . ]

[omitted material]

Student 1:  () dumb look on their faces () [ . . . ] (like) a cow looking at a train. [[laughter]] You ever see a cow look at a train, they're probably trying to figure out what the hell it is, you know, what is this thing?

Here the image of collaboration between professor and student reaches a very sympathetic level, as the students hypothesize that their teacher can read the sea of blank faces, gazing at him with cow-like expressions, and then adjust his teaching.

Students differentiate between the teaching style of the Socratic method as represented in popular culture (which they report as a relative rarity in their own schools now) and the Socratic teaching they more usually encounter in their classes. On the one hand, some students expressed disapproval of a "hide-the-ball" style of teaching in which professors convey a sense of superiority based on knowing more than the students, in which "you are going to feel stupid as dirt because it's rigged, because the professor taught it ten to twenty years and they know the questions and you don't. [ . . . ] Well, like in *The Paper Chase*. If you have a professor like that which is to humiliate you on purpose" (7–11, 12). However, quite a few felt that there was some value in a modified kind of Socratic teaching that engaged students in extended but not mean-spirited dialogue:

[5-22]

Student 1:  I never raise my hand, but if I'm called on, I don't mind answering. So for me the Socratic method is kind of good, because I never talk if I wasn't called on and I was very intimidated, very uncomfortable about the whole idea and then you realize, it's not that bad. But, so personally, I think it's good because it kind of boosts your self-confidence in your ability to actually say something.

In discussing the professor in this particular classroom, the student notes that he "brings it down a bit more, by the joking or by his style." Note that this student was a woman and provides a good illustration for the quantitative finding above: that in Socratic classrooms, women students speak more when they are called on, perhaps in part because they hesitate to volunteer.[99] For some students, it seems that the most salient distinction is not "Socratic versus non-Socratic" but "unnecessarily mean-spirited versus encouraging." Some allusion to this was found in discussions by students across the various prestige rankings of law schools. At the same time as they appreciated the more encouraging professors, the students also commented with some acerbity on moments when professors did not adequately control the class during Socratic or other discursive exchanges, so that particular students were able to talk for what was viewed as an excessive period of time. When a student who didn't have much to contribute substantively talked for a long time, it could become a confusing distraction. That this can happen in today's modified Socratic classrooms is one sign that many professors have adopted pedagogical models that diverge from the stereotypic Socratic class.[100]

In substantive terms, many students converged on professors' views when discussing their first-year training and their Contracts class in remarks that revealed much insight. Echoing an observation found in many of the professors' interviews about the ubiquity and importance of contract, one student from a local law school explained with energetic passion:

*[6-1]*

Student 1:   Contracts is- it's almost so basic and people sign contracts every day of their lives for whatever reason, whether it's to sign their Visa charge- and there's so much that the general public doesn't understand about where you stand, what your rights are *[ . . . ]* and it's almost like, why isn't Contracts taught your senior year of high school [Student 2: Exactly- like that case about the Carnival Cruise Lines-] *[general comments and exclamations by group, including: Oh my God, that was unbelievable!] [ . . . ]*

*[6–1]*

Student 1:   *[ . . . ]* but Contracts is just so basic, and it's something that everybody- I can't think of how you could live without ever getting through without dealing with a contract; either apartment lease, or your credit cards *[ . . . ]*

Students also commented on the process they were absorbing: of picking up a case and learning to read it, of building analogies, and of parsing language in new ways. Several pointed in particular to the ambiguity of law, a perspective their professors were at pains to get across to students who sought easier answers. Thus, along with some differences in perspective between professors and students, and among students in different kinds of law schools, we find some convergence in perceptions regarding the core task of the first year, which across all of the schools in the study remains centered on learning to read cases and decipher doctrine (with some discussion of policy and theory as part of the picture as well).

## Summary

We find some support for the overall patterning by race and gender that has been documented in other studies. In addition, this study introduces some nuances and complexities that will be important considerations in any thorough examination of these problems. For example, attention to the effects of context emerges as a vital part of understanding these phenomena, from differences among law schools to variations in teaching styles commonly denominated simplistically as Socratic.

One interesting result of comparisons among our classrooms is a more complex definition of inclusiveness; it is clear that inclusiveness is not a uniform characteristic across different dimensions. A classroom can be quite inclusive along lines of gender but not race, and vice versa. For example, Class #8, with among the largest gender disparities against women, is the most inclusive for minority students overall, with a 43% disproportion in favor of students of color in terms of turns and a 51% favorable disproportion in terms of time. This, of course, immediately raises the question of intersectionality, for when we separate out the categories of gender and race in this way, we create ambiguity in one arena even as we gain clarity in another.[101] Another arena worthy of further study is a more fine-grained approach to issues of racial and other social identities; this would call for extensive and systematic interview work in addition to the observational research.

As we add more observations and studies to the foundations already provided, we will be able to point with increasing specificity to the constellations of conditions that create more inclusive, participatory, and effective law school teaching. The complexities involved should not lead us to throw up our hands and settle for comforting oversimplifications. Rather, they provide the more realistic, respectful, and nonessentializing ground from which real understanding continues to emerge.

Behind the nuances and complexities, however, we have also identified some patterning that is consonant with the findings of a number of other studies. This patterning continues to link increased class participation and classroom presence with traditional insiders in the legal profession; that is, white male students tend to predominate. Among the classrooms of this study, male students dominate in the classes taught by white male professors and by a female professor in a higher-ranked school. Women students have more of a voice in classes taught by women in the nonelite classrooms of this study, and students of color are dominant speakers only in the classes taught by professors of color. There are some interesting fluctuations in the patterning, warning us against overly essentialist thinking: students of color also had some positive participation ratios in one regional law school class taught by a white male, as well as in a local law school class taught by a white female. As I've noted, it is important to remember that silence can have many meanings for individual students; we cannot assume that differential silence always proceeds from insecurity or fear. However, differential silence on the part of students of color or white women raises a different, institutional kind of question about cultural invisibility and dominance. We first considered this issue in examining the content of law school pedagogy; now we turn to the question in terms of the structure of law school teaching. If students of color and female students tend to be more silent in law school classrooms, then any differences these students bring with them in terms of experience or background are not given voice in the crucial initial socialization process. To the extent that these differences in experience reflect race, gender, class, or other aspects of social identity, we again see aspects of social structure and difference pushed to the margins of legal discourse.[102] Thus, in addition to this tendency in the content of the message law students are receiving, we find a possible reinforcement of the marginalization in the actual structure of voices in some law school classrooms.

This raises a concern about the overall culture of the classroom, an issue that is independent of concerns about student performance on exams or individual student motivations. Even if there is no connection between class participation and grades, we can still ask what the classroom culture conveys to students about law and its central priorities, particularly during an important initiation into legal thinking. Correlatively, we can also ask what message is conveyed to students regarding which voices can speak in the language of the law. If certain voices, attitudes, and experiences become invisible during lawyers' formative training, this could send a message about what the law values (and about what is deemed unimportant or irrelevant). Of course, we need to proceed with some caution in developing an understanding of how cultural invisibility and dominance become features of training across different law school classrooms. As we have seen, any simplistic or homogeneous model of this process is likely to be inaccurate. However, to the degree that we find an erasure of the voices and experiences of traditionally marginalized people, we uncover important clues to the underlying worldview that, consciously or not, is conveyed to law students. We also gain a better understanding of features of the law school experience that may contribute to differential alienation and marginalization on the part of students of color and women.

# IV

•———•

# CONCLUSION: READING, TALKING, AND THINKING LIKE A LAWYER

*The first-year curriculum persists as it does because any other one would mean that law teachers could no longer engage in normative legal thought and might actually have to know something about the world and how it works. We might have to know why cross default clauses appear routinely in loans. We might have to know why the Supreme Court routinely accepts some circuit conflicts and ignores the rest. We might even have to know why the going rate for drunken assault is greater in Buffalo than in Tallahassee.*

*That would be inconvenient. When it comes to normative legal thought, law teachers have a real comparative advantage in the academy. Almost no one else does it, and one needs to know relatively little detail about how the world works in order to engage in the practice. . . . In contrast, when it comes to knowing about cross default clauses, circuit conflicts, and drunks in Tallahassee, law professors clearly lack comparative advantage as against both practitioners and other, more formally trained empiricists like historians or sociologists.[1]*

Throughout this volume, we have followed the very particular shape of lawyers' training in the normative, mediated through attitudes toward text, authority, and language. In subtle but powerful ways, the specific technical requirements of a legal reading guide students away from a more accustomed form of moral reasoning, anchored more closely to social context. Instead, law students begin to accept a form of moral reasoning in which context and normativity are read only through the exigencies of legal tests and texts. Social context is unmoored and thinned, rendered in almost commodified form: as the bits and pieces of information needed to create analogies in legal-textual frameworks. In the process, legal reasoning gains an appearance of ubiquitous, indeed, promiscuous engagement with social particulars, while building a core that is virtually impervious to grounded social analysis. As Schlegel points out, this creates an uneasy paradox in which courts must all the time make decisions about issues that they are incapable of thoroughly grasping. Worse, it is possible that the system of legal language hides from them even the truth of their own limitations. At the same time, traditional outsider students continue to be differentially silenced in the prototypical law school classroom, blocking one of many potential routes by which alternative understandings of social contexts and norms could enter the mainstream legal conversation. As such routes are closed in the course of legal education, nascent lawyers learn an increasingly closed discourse, widening the gap between themselves and their future clients.

# 9

·———·

# Legal Language and American Law: Authority, Morality, and Linguistic Ideology

We return now to the themes with which the book began, with the added vantage given by our in-depth examination of similarities and differences across the classrooms of this study. First, we have seen that context matters to the understanding of law school training in a number of ways. In the classroom, aspects of the immediate context are crucial in the dynamics that create more and less inclusive discussions. These include, but are certainly not limited to, the demographic backgrounds of students and professors, the size and linguistic structuring of the class itself, and the status, history, location, and culture of the law school. Contextual cues in class also point the way to the shared epistemology that is conveyed in all of these classrooms, despite surface differences in discourse style. Finally, some kinds of context are ignored or omitted, creating a blind spot in the understanding of social conflict taught to law students.

This brings us to a second important finding: the way legal language in this society shares with capitalist epistemology more generally a kind of double edge. In the second section of the chapter, I discuss this phenomenon, which carries with it both a powerful potential and a potential danger. However, as the third section of this conclusion argues, in the legal arena we see the primacy of language and linguistic ideology in mediating this double edge. It is in and through the inculcation of approaches to text, reading, and language that the legal version of commodification—of a social structural sleight of hand—takes place. On the one hand, this means that legal language is deeply imbricated with social power in multiple ways. On the other hand, the independent importance of this linguistic level means that the process of legal training in particular, and of legal translation in general, cannot be analyzed as a mere reflex of power dynamics. Certainly social power has an impact at the many levels delineated here. But we can also see that

207

there are irreducible and contingent aspects of the interactions, identities, and cultural understandings revealed and forged in the languages of law and of law school classrooms.

Finally, we consider the broader implications of this study's findings for policy decisions about legal training and the legal system itself. If the law in a democratic state aspires to apply to all citizens fairly, then the hidden exclusions that are created by subtle cultural invisibility and cultural dominance in legal training and language need to be addressed. Although there are no simple answers, one obvious starting point involves increased diversity and inclusion in the legal academy, among law students, and in the legal profession more generally. This conclusion is supported by both the quantitative and qualitative findings of the study. But increased diversity will make little difference if any divergences in vision are stifled through the process by which students are socialized (as they must be) to the canons of a distinctively legal reading. Thus, another important step would be taken if law schools were to achieve and teach a more self-conscious understanding of the limitations of legal language for apprehending social phenomena, training students to be wary of the hubris that inheres in law's aspiration of universal translation across so many diverse social realms.

## The Importance of Context

The debate over inclusion and diversity in law school training (and in society more generally) sometimes proceeds in terms of either/or choices, as if social differences such as race and gender were either all-determining or nonexistent. This study suggests an alternative vision, one that is more complicated and perhaps less satisfying to those who like their pictures of social reality painted in stark all-or-nothing terms. This more complex view is compatible with recent, more contextualist approaches to the issue of social difference that have been proposed by scholars studying race and gender, both in and outside the legal academy.[1]

### Lesson One: Be Cautious When (as You Must) You Essentialize Context

In a sense, this study's results demonstrate the very practical utility of these contextualist approaches in making sense of empirically observable patterns. For example, some research on gender in college classrooms has assumed that results from studies conducted in different schools addressed the same phenomenon. In one case, for instance, a study that did not find significant gender effects at a "large northwestern university" represented its result as contradicting earlier studies in other schools that did find gender effects.[2] There are several difficulties with this approach, and each involves an essentializing step.

First, in assuming that findings in any given school or classroom can, in transparent fashion, be used to talk about *the* college (or law school) classroom, this kind of approach takes a particular school or classroom as an "essential" or typical class. The authors of the "large northwestern university" study proclaimed, "Our data suggest there are not major sex-related behavior differences in the college class-room."[3] But what they in fact found was that there were no major sex-related be-havior differences in a set of classrooms in one university. It seems obvious that this does not mean that previous authors who found sex-related differences in other settings were wrong. In many of these studies we have no detailed information about key aspects of the schools' contexts: their histories, status, or general cultures, for example. In a refreshing, if unusual, attempt to acknowledge the potential impact of such factors, a later study that did not find gender differences raised the possi-bility that the school's particular history and situation might be affecting its find-ings: the school was Vassar, a longtime women's college that had only recently begun admitting men.[4] Similarly, in my discussion of the findings of the present study, I have identified aspects such as school status, class size, and professorial style and identity as potentially important factors.

There are additional difficulties with viewing studies conducted in different schools as contradictory if they reach differing results on gender or race. Gender or race may mean something different in different class settings, depending on the particular configuration of the school and classroom settings; perhaps gen-der may be salient in one arena but not in another. Indeed, even the same con-textual features—small class size, for example, or a Socratic style of teaching—can take on different meanings depending on nuances of context. Of course, some form of essentializing of context is necessary in order to compare across class-rooms, but the point here is that we must work toward more sensitive and fine-grained understandings, while not abandoning the effort to step back and see larger patterns.

Thus, the first lesson about context to be drawn from this research is that careful delineation of the fine-grained aspects of context—school, class, teacher, students, discourse style—is necessary if we are to understand what combinations of con-textual factors help to produce more inclusive classrooms. We have seen that smaller, more informal classrooms do not necessarily produce gender equality, and that there are nuanced differences among Socratic teachers that can contribute to quite different senses of context for students. In the move to a more complex view, we can draw on the work of scholars who have written on race and identity, such as María Lugones and Kimberlé Crenshaw. These writers have argued that the experience of people at the margins of society can contribute to our understand-ing of human experience in general, because certain aspects of the formation of identity that are problematic for everyone are brought into still sharper relief in the experience of those who must negotiate across more boundaries in our soci-ety. If all of us possess a multiple sense of identity, if all of us must at times trans-late across different worlds, then perhaps those for whom these processes are a continuing, urgent necessity can be our best teachers about the way context and identity shape human interactions. One lesson we can learn from these experts is to listen more carefully for everyday forms of multilingualism, becoming more aware that the same person can and often does speak differently in different con-texts. Thus, if we observe an individual in only one context and imagine that we have a complete picture, we will be mistaken. Again, there is a direct contribution to fairly mundane empirical problems here, for this means that it is possible for two people to become fluent in the language of the law while feeling quite different senses of comfort or ownership.

Some scholarship has indicated that there are differences among law schools in terms of typical pedagogical style, overall goals of legal training, and law school cultures. A study of students and professors at 22 law schools by Alfred Smith found "significant differences in cognitive styles among law schools."[5] Teaching at elite schools was not as rigidly focused on rules, but "aim[ed] to cope with legal ambiguities and alternatives," whereas lower-status schools tended to be "oriented to law practice and black letter law."[6] Zemans and Rosenblum similarly noted that graduates of elite schools were more likely to "emphasize analytical thinking and the theoretical basis of the law" than those of "non-national" law schools.[7] Robert Granfield makes a similar point in his comparison of Harvard and Northeastern law schools, as does Christa McGill in her contrast of three law schools that differ in status.[8] Although my study does provide some support for this view, finding somewhat more emphasis on theory in the more elite classrooms (with some exceptions, however), it also provides some important cautionary notes.

First, law professors in all of the first-year classrooms of this study are heavily focused on teaching a legal reading of cases, which is a genre unlike any students had likely encountered before law school. During this initial exposure to law in the first semester of law school, we see some striking similarities in overall emphasis in these classrooms. Although it is important to notice status-based differences, a full picture must also take account of these empirically observable similarities in first-year classroom discussions across diverse law schools. It seems likely that differences among the schools will become more marked during subsequent semesters, after students have assimilated the rudiments of the new genre, and will also be more noticeable in the overall curricula of the schools. But the initial task facing law students during their first semester is the same across law schools of different statuses, and this is reflected in the classroom discussions when carefully analyzed.

Second, there are differences among schools of similar rankings. A local law school in a city may be quite different from one located in a rural area, as might be a large state university (i.e., regional) law school located in the farm belt from a smaller, regional law school in an urban center. Thus, generalizations about institutions based only on status rankings may elide other distinctions that are also having an impact on schools' priorities and cultures.

Third, there are individual differences among professors that do not map neatly onto traditional status hierarchy divisions. Several of the professors in this study who taught in local or regional law schools had a keen interest in aspects of legal theory, which they conveyed to their students, whereas one of the professors in a very elite law school downplayed theoretical discussions. As we have seen, professors teaching at lower-status institutions who were trained at elite law schools may turn out to share some aspects of pedagogical style regardless of where they are teaching. In addition, professors as individuals do not always remain in one kind of law school throughout their careers. Indeed, one of the professors in this study who taught at a local/regional school subsequently moved into teaching at an elite/prestige law school. Thus, it would not be surprising to find some differentiation among professors based on their career aspirations. It seems important, then, to give full weight to differences among law schools by status while also acknowledging the complexities that do not permit us to paint a completely deterministic picture of their impact. This picture would contain a balanced view of similarities and differences in pedagogy across different kinds of law schools, rather than erasing one part of the picture in favor of the other.

This study, then, demonstrates that school status, race, gender, and other aspects of social context all matter, but they have their effects in complex interactions that require careful contextual analysis. The social differences among students and classrooms affect the interactions and learning that occur in law school in ways that can be characterized as "underdeterminate";[9] that is, race and gender are important, in some ways formative, but not completely determining aspects of classroom exchanges. Students of different race or class backgrounds, of different genders or sexual preferences or ages can be simultaneously "different" and the "same": they may respond similarly to some aspects of context but differently to others. Professors of different backgrounds or generations may approach teaching differently even within the same institution. As we struggle with this more complicated picture, we have to use more particular and careful questions, asking how the mixture of school profile, discourse style, teacher profile, class composition, student profile, interactive dynamics, and the content of discussion may have combined to create more or less egalitarian sites for learning and discussion.[10]

### Lesson Two: The Role of Contextual Cues in Signaling Cultural-Linguistic Epistemologies

A second lesson about context to be drawn from this study is the role of contextual cues in conveying a shared underlying epistemology. Thus, we have seen that subtle aspects of the pragmatic structure of classroom discourse shift students' attention away from accustomed social contextual anchors and toward new legal-contextual frameworks. Even professors with apparently different discourse styles may reproduce similar dialogic formats—one in dialogue with a student, the other using an apparently dialogic form with himself during a monologue—but each conveying a sense of the importance of argument and a certain form of dialogic questioning to the new legal persona inculcated during legal training. Through this dialogic format, old identities are unmoored and a new, discursively anchored identity emerges, one whose primary navigation points emerge from a parsing of written texts and legal authority.

### Lesson Three: Legal Erasures of Context through Discourse Structure

This brings us to the third lesson about context found in this study: the way prototypical legal discourse tends to erase particular aspects of social context. As Regina Austin explains:

Generally insensitive to context, legal analysis as it is reflected in judicial opinions can leave out much that seems relevant to an assessment of whether justice has been done. I cannot count the number of times that I have come to the end of an opinion and been perplexed and dismayed because some essential fact or element seemed to be missing. The opinion could not possibly contain the whole story. There had to be something else about the particular circumstances or the larger setting, which frames it, that would have made the parties' actions explicable or the courts' rulings more intelligible.[11]

Auerbach comments that "relentless doctrinal analysis [has] . . . severely restricted the range and depth of inquiry."[12]

Although the legal profession has typically sought to understand this restriction as serving the ends of objectivity, the omission of some aspects of context and not others has never occurred without subjective and socially shaped input. Elkins notes:

A lawyer's world view acts as a perceptual screen for incoming sensory data. Language concepts [i.e., linguistic categories] screen and structure one's perception and allow one to organize information and experiences. . . . At the most rudimentary level of perception, then, what the lawyer characterizes as "out there" is not a true picture of an objective event or scene but a personal and social assessment. This subjectivity of factual data has significance for both the postulates of the legal system and for practical lawyering. The legal persona, with its particular world view, excludes a vast body of information from its awareness.[13]

This study provides empirical evidence supporting Austin's and Elkins's assessments. We have excavated with some precision the ways morality and social context are pushed to the margins of discourse, not only in the language of law school classrooms, but also in the legal discourse that is taught to students. In this reformulation, law students learn to perform surface readings that in a sense gobble up social context while preventing this kind of context from entering the core of a legal approach to text.

## The Genius and Danger of the Common Law: A Language of Abstract/Concrete Reasoning

In Chapter 6, we briefly considered the relationship between this core legal approach to text and aspects of capitalist epistemology. Social theorist Moishe Postone has pointed out that there is a "double character" peculiar to capital, time, and labor in capitalist societies: they exist as at once abstract and concrete categories.[14] The "impersonal, abstract, and objective" mediation of the abstract level conceals the way people are disadvantaged, their concrete labor alienated or taken from them. There is an appearance of freedom in that individuals are at "liberty" to sell their labor power on the impersonal market, but in fact there are strong constraints limiting individual freedom and bargaining power. As Postone notes, the move to an abstract level in capitalist societies does actually open up some new, potentially liberating possibilities, freeing workers from the more direct compulsion and force used to extract labor in feudal societies. At the same time, there is more risk that the indirect form of compulsion will be concealed, leaving a false illusion of freedom to lull those in its sway.

Although the parallel is not exact, the legal epistemology discernable in law school pedagogy also has an interestingly double quality, sweeping myriad concrete details into constantly developing abstract categories. The legal system appears to provide an "impersonal, abstract, and objective" mediation of social conflict, leading ordinary citizens to expect fairness and freedom to pursue justice through the courts.[15] Yet, as we have seen, this abstract level of legal discourse can also conceal the injustices and power inequalities that continue to be enacted through the legal system. Indeed, the move to abstract legal categories itself omits some kinds of context while including others—thus actually perpetuating forms of cultural dominance and invisibility while appearing neutral.

Thus, there is a danger that lies right beside a certain genius in the common law system. On the one hand, it contains a potentially liberating movement between abstract categories and concrete social detail that can erase some forms of prejudice, insisting that people who are similarly situated with regard to doctrinal categories be treated in similar ways. This opening has permitted people with less social power than their adversaries to win some victories in court, appealing to abstract legal doctrines surrounding concepts such as rights, with their at least aspirational correlate of equal application. As Patricia Williams explains in her well-known essay:

> Rights are to law what conscious commitments are to the psyche. This country's worst historical moments have not been attributable to rights *assertion* but to a failure of rights commitment. . . . To say that blacks never fully believed in rights is true. Yet it is also true that blacks believed in them so much and so hard that we gave them life where there was none before; we held onto them, put the hope of them into our wombs, mothered them and not the notion of them. . . . "Rights" feel new in the mouths of most black people. It its still deliciously empowering to say. . . . The concept of rights, both positive and negative, is the marker of our citizenship.[16]

Even where rights are spelled out in constitutions or legislation, it is the application of this legal language in particular cases, performed in the United States in part through the mechanism of case law references and readings, that gives it life. And that process, like the concept itself, relies partially on the ongoing delineation, through doctrinal development, of abstract categories that guide the analogies by which one particular situation may be rendered similar to another.

At the same time, we have also seen that the very move away from context into abstract categories that permits this kind of promise for the disempowered in legal arenas also contains a dangerous erasure. Some aspects of morality and context that disappear in the common law sleight of hand actually hold keys to deciphering the social meaning of the conflict at hand, as Regina Austin notes. And the apparent neutrality of this process conceals the overall truth that in the U.S. legal system, despite some important victories for the disempowered, it is disproportionately the "haves" who come out ahead—just as, in the analogical process by which common law jurists make one concrete situation equivalent to another, the move between abstract and concrete also contains hidden cultural assumptions.[17] We have traced in some detail the way this process works in the law school class-room, shifting students' attention away from social contextual cues and norma-tive assessment toward layers of legal-textual authority.

Baker perceptively summarizes the multiple effects of the classroom shift docu-mented in my study.[18] In addition to erasing socially relevant aspects of context that are not important to legal doctrine, legal reasoning "reformulates relatively concrete facts at higher levels of abstraction," losing the "detailed particulars of a socially situated narrative" in its quest for commensurability.[19] It also "disrupts what small amount of phenomenological narrative coherence remains in a case" as it prioritizes analogical comparison.[20] Finally, students are unmoored from ethical and social identities, attached to new legal roles as adversarial speakers on either side of an argument. This substitutes an amoral attachment to legal form for a situated sense of loyalty to substantive ends and values.[21] Hirsch notes that in this setting dominant cultural forms are "highly visible," from the ready control of discourse exercised disproportionately by white male students through the pre-dominance of decontextualized language that "tends toward disconnection from moral entailments."[22] Although this patterning is indeed quite visible from the outside, it is also true that metalinguistic speech and ideology in law school class-rooms naturalize the dominance of one cultural form over others.[23] Thus, some-thing that is actually culturally shaped takes on the appearance of being neutral or natural. Winter makes a similar point about the tacit power of seemingly uncontroversial categorization processes, which smuggle normative content into legal decision making: "Law is always ideological in the sense that it enforces (and reinforces) the dominant normative views of the culture."[24] This study adds the insight that an inevitably social dimension of law is also "imported," as Jonathan Yovel would say, through pragmatics and metapragmatics.[25] Yovel's theory of "nor-mative importation" carefully delineates the mechanisms by which language in general (and legal language in particular) is always quietly drawing on and inter-nalizing social norms. The tacit character of this linguistic structuring makes its effects difficult to discern.

## Language, Linguistic Ideology, and Legal Epistemology: Within and beyond Social Power

As we have examined the process by which law students are initiated into an ab-stract-yet-concrete approach to human conflict, we have continually observed the central mediating role of language and linguistic ideology. Susan Philips's pioneer-ing sociolinguistic article on legal education described the process as, at core, lin-guistic, as "learning the cant."[26] In an early article on the topic, James Elkins also pointed out the central role of *talking* like a lawyer to the construction of the legal persona and its characteristic mode of thought.[27] I have built on their observations here to delineate the way this language-learning process relies on an ideology of text and language—a linguistic ideology. Focusing on ideology, according to

Woolard and others, "makes a promising bridge between linguistic and social theory."[28] As have linguistic anthropologists working in other settings, I, too, have found that linguistic ideology forms a crucial organizing backbone for ongoing linguistic interaction and socialization. Michael Silverstein notes that

> any indexical process, wherein signs point to a presupposed context in which they occur (i.e., have occurred) or to an entailed potential context in which they occur (i.e., will have occurred), depends on some metapragmatic function to achieve a measure of determinacy or textual coherence. . . . It turns out that the crucial position of ideologies of semiosis is in constituting such a "default" mediating metapragmatics. . . . In short, ideology construes indexicality by constituting its metapragmatics. . . . Ideologies present invokable schemata in which to explain/interpret the meaningful flow of indexicals.[29]

In socializing law students to a new ideology of language and text, law professors accomplish a profound reorientation in the initiates' very processing of the "flow of indexicals" that is the foundation of communication. Thus, the role of language ideology as a backbone is particularly highlighted in this setting by the specific role that language plays in legal epistemology.

As we have seen, there is an unusually central role for linguistic ideology in law school socialization, because it is in and through manipulations of language that nascent attorneys learn to wield the special power of their profession. Proper application of the legal tests and categories, gleaned from a proper legal reading of written legal texts, is the foundation on which legally trained professionals draw in claiming authority. Thus, the linguistic ideology that undergirds legal training orients students' attention to layers of legal-textual authority. There is no need to claim that we will generate factual accuracy (in the usual sense) from such a reading, for the core compass orienting the reader remains "what the court, or legislature, said"—and then, in turn, what the position of that court or legislature was in the hierarchy of legal text generators. What we accept as true for the purposes of making a legal decision may not conform accurately to what happened, but that is rarely a matter of concern; once a court has met certain threshold requirements (it has jurisdiction to decide the matter, its decision was not clearly erroneous, etc.), it has the performative power to *find* facts. Thus, the legal reader's task is not to uncover what actually happened (more usually the mandate of the social scientist), but to correctly discern the facts as found by the authoritative court. These facts, read through a filter of doctrinal language also extracted from written legal texts, must then be sorted out in a way that permits the building of analogies.

To accomplish this requires a reading focused on layers of authoritative language and oriented by linguistic ideology. This linguistic ideology equates the proper alignment of language with authoritative legal knowledge, and thus also with proper application of the law. Legal epistemology rests on linguistic processes: expert deciphering of written legal texts, appropriate use of analogies and concomitant legal-linguistic frames, making arguments within these frames, ability to speak in the various voices and from the various stances required to argue effectively (sometimes to anticipate your opponent's argument, sometimes to make an argument for your client, or, if you are a judge, to weave between alternative positions in coming to a decision, which may in turn instantiate yet another point of view). In other words, in legal language, we know this fact because it was found and written down (entextualized) by an authoritative court, operating under correct metalinguistic rules and with the proper authority. One of the miracles of this system is its ability to combine certainty with such a flexible—indeed, at times deliberately agnostic—approach to social reality. The legal epistemology taught in the prototypical first-year U.S. law classroom, embodied in the practice of learning to read cases, employs a set of linguistic procedures to generate knowledge that is at once flexible enough to encompass almost any conceivable context, while still generating certainty (defined within linguistic parameters) and rules with knowable parameters (again linguistic), that nevertheless change as they are applied.

From a world in which normative judgment is circumscribed by a rich sense of social context—who someone was, the full depth of feelings and motives that inspired certain actions, the circumstances that conspired to push events in one way or another, personal histories, social inequalities, and more—law students are moved into a new world, in which legal judgment is circumscribed by linguistic norms, texts and the arguments they permit, and layers of authoritative language. The orienting compass that guides them is metalinguistic in the strongest sense: an ideology of language that circumscribes social reality completely. Justice is done if the proper linguistic protocols are observed, if the opposition of voices is literally represented in apparently dialogic form in court and in written opinions—as it is also in law school classrooms. Gal and Irvine would call this "iconicity": linguistic ideology reading language form as a mirror of social phenomena.[30] (It is also an example of "erasure," because a focus on procedure renders invisible the ways some oppositional voices and viewpoints are not making it into the discussion at all.) As Morris explains, a core aim of legal reasoning is "to rupture linguistic forms, polite forms, non-lawyerly forms, and to introduce a necessary pugilism" as it imposes "a limiting order, an institutionalized order, a boundarying of rationality."[31] As I've demonstrated, this reorientation in epistemology is accomplished in large part through a shift in linguistic practices, effectuated in and through a shift in linguistic ideologies.

The intimate relationship between linguistic ideology and legal epistemology has been noted by a number of language-and-law scholars in recent years. Susan Hirsch has carefully dissected the role of linguistic ideology in Kenyan courts, demonstrating that conceptions about words and their proper deployment in courtroom storytelling effectively frame and limit what can be said and known about social conflict.[32] Greg Matoesian takes this insight into U.S. courtrooms, using a detailed analysis of speech to show "how linguistic ideologies interface in a reflexive moment with male hegemony and structures of language use to form an epistemological strategy. . . . What counts as knowledge, as a fact, and how do we know?"[33] And in her volume on changes of plea in Arizona courts, Susan Philips traces how judges appeal to a monolithic "legal interpretive framework" that undergirds "the claims of lawyers to a universalistic scientific and moral epistemology and to direct apprehension of this epistemology by an individual mind rather than a sociocultural mind."[34] Her analysis demonstrates that metalinguistic ideology regarding the relationship of written text to spoken practice operates to conceal the politically laden, structured diversity found in judges' actual use of language, despite judges' own metalinguistic assertions to the contrary. In this study, we have examined in detail the core tenets of this U.S. legal interpretive framework and have reconfirmed the central role of linguistic ideology to legal epistemology.

The introduction of metalinguistic mediation into our model of law brings with it an interesting paradox. On the one hand, I have outlined the way linguistic filtering conceals the impact of social power, in the process contributing to the perpetuation of social inequalities through law. Future lawyers and judges are trained in a metalinguistic structure that directs attention away from some aspects of social norms and contexts, permitting the professionals charged with performing legal analysis to ignore systematic inequities in society and in the administration of the legal system itself. At the same time, this metalinguistic level is not simply a reflex of power dynamics, transparently converting the interests of the powerful into legal results. As Patricia Williams and others have pointed out, relatively powerless members of society have occasionally prevailed in legal settings.[35] And not every problem addressed by the legal system is reducible to a straightforward calculus in which the contesting parties stand for power interests in the wider society; nor do the people involved in legal cases uniformly understand themselves or their choices in these terms. Of course, where law intercedes, issues of power are never very far away.[36] But it is important to recognize as well how linguistic mediation introduces an irreducible dynamic of its own, imbued with cultural creativity and responsive to particular contexts and people. In this sense, I take seriously Constable's admonition against reducing our understanding of law and justice to a monolithic focus on power.[37]

In demonstrating that language and culture together bring dynamics of their own to bear on legal processes, findings from linguistic anthropology can be said to partially parallel insights drawn from the cognitive sciences. For example, Winter has argued that regularities in the structuring of "cognitive and cultural infrastructures" explain core aspects of legal reasoning.[38] He contrasts this view with the assumptions of a standard or narrow "rationalist" model, which understands reason as "linear, hierarchical, propositional, and definitional."[39] The process of analogical reason that is fundamental to law can seem arbitrary when judged by this rationalist model, but when analyzed in terms of embodied cognitive categories and structures (metaphors, for example, or image schemas), legal reasoning seems far more principled.[40] The cognitive approach described by Winter is in some ways complementary to the linguistic anthropological analysis undertaken in this book, while also differing in some important respects. For example, the two approaches both look to aspects of pragmatism and social context in parsing legal epistemology, although their emphasis in this regard is quite different. Similarly, both forms of analysis insist that there are regularities, anchored to context and culture, that are often ignored by dominant paradigms focusing on propositionality. In this sense, both perspectives push us to look past an either/or mentality which insists that either legal reasoning is entirely governed by a narrow, positivist rationality, or it is not ordered at all. On the one hand, attempts to generate static, propositional rules that can predict legal decision making fail, because they are too sterile to capture the ongoing social-contextual creativity of actual legal problems and decisions. On the other hand, the nihilist despair into which disappointed skeptics then fall, concluding that legal results reflect "what the judge ate for breakfast" or naked economic interests, underestimates the powerful regularities of pragmatics in cultural process.[41]

Here, however, cognitivists and anthropological linguists part company, for whereas cognitivists look to the contextual and grounded character of human categorization for pragmatic regularities, linguists examine the actual process by which these categories (and other, messier regularities in human communication) are given life in speech. Although cognitive analysis focuses extensively on the language of metaphor, metonymy, and cultural categorization, it does not examine language as a system in use. Because of its central concern with the way individuals internalize cognitive maps, the school of cognitive theory on which Winter relies tends to brush quickly by issues of social and group processes, where anthropological linguistics and sociolinguists explicitly examine structures of social interaction and cultural exchange. Depending on what (metaphorical!) perspective we adopt, we can see this either as a conflict (with each side holding warring visions of how pragmatics order social and legal knowledge) or a happy division of labor (with each school attending to important and complementary issues).[42] Whatever one's vantage, it is striking to note that both approaches urge us to abandon a polarized logic, in which the language of law is (or should be) either entirely determinative of outcomes or a transparent reflection of social context. Similarly, I would urge that we abandon a dichotomy that views linguistic exchange as either entirely devoid of power dimensions or as completely determined by social power.[43]

From the perspective of law and literature, James Boyd White has similarly appealed for us to take seriously the particular combined linguistic-cultural-ethical orientation that characterizes law as a field. He grants that law should not be taught "without economics, or politics, or psychology, or history" (and I would add sociology and anthropology, at the very least!), but White also insists that none of these should be permitted to completely displace the study of law

> as a distinctive activity of mind and imagination. . . . It is, and should be taught as, a discipline of thought and argument with its own structure, its own elements, at the center of which is the activity of claiming meaning for human experience, individually and collectively, and doing so in a language that is at once a source of authority and itself subject to perpetual revision.[44]

This leads White to advocate a "revived case method" as the ideal format for law teaching, one in which a law student will approach cases as practice for the real world, learning to think and live

> at once with the materials of law, its language and institutions, and with the realities of the world: the needs of her client, the demands of the other lawyer, the character of the judge and jury. And this offers [the law student] a life in which . . . she is called upon to have and recognize real commitments.[45]

In many ways, White is calling for an approach that linguistic anthropologists would endorse: one that takes seriously the indigenous language and culture of the legal field, while also opening the door to interdisciplinary studies of law as it interacts with society, economics, politics, psychology, and so forth. However, the question of how we are to balance these two ways of understanding law is a difficult one, and White tends to take a very optimistic view of the possibilities for "intellectual integration" among diverse disciplines.[46]

By contrast, Dorf (like Schlegel, with whom we opened this section) presents a pessimistic view of the likelihood that those trained in law can or will obtain the expertise necessary to translate empirical research:

> Legal questions almost invariably call for some mixture of normative and empirical analysis. Although the Socratic method can be used to lay bare the empirical assumptions associated with various normative claims, it provides no tools for testing those assumptions. . . . Despite legal realism's successful critique . . . , to a significant degree American legal education and American legal reasoning continue to proceed from Langdell's premise that the answers to difficult legal questions are to be found in the reports of judicial decisions.[47]

We have seen empirical support for Dorf's characterization in the transcripts of this study: when it is time to discuss the assumptions about society and people that underlie the judicial decisions students read, law professors routinely invite speculation and anecdote. When law professors stray into the realms addressed by the social sciences, there is no attempt to achieve the kind of "internal" interdisciplinary understanding of other fields urged by White. (Nor is there any reason, given what we now know about law school training, to expect that they would have been given the tools to do so.) By contrast, students are faced with systematic demands for proof and evidence when they are discussing legal texts and tests. White would doubtless respond that his optimism about the possibilities of genuine interdisciplinary integration is more a hope for the future than a description of the current state of our academic discourse. But one concern that lingers after a close examination of current law teaching is the closed nature of the linguistic system taught to first-year law students. Without some countervailing instruction, this system can easily lend itself to a form of methodological arrogance, in which its practitioners feel themselves able to master any material with which they are presented by running it through a legal reading. This kind of reading has its strengths, but it also has its blind spots, and unlike many social science fields (although certainly not all), law's metalinguistic structure does not have a mechanism by which its own basic orientations and structure of authority can be opened to question.[48] To the contrary, it inculcates a sense of rampant capacity to translate all kinds of events and situations without regard to the possibility that the translation may miss the mark in important ways, or that it needs to be open to alternative sources of authority and epistemologies.

Silverstein warns of the kind of "misfire" that can occur when would-be "translators" imagine that they can transparently move between different culturally embedded systems of meaning, denying the inevitable "transformation" that must occur in this situation.[49] The further we move into the kind of meaning that relies on context and pragmatics, the less likely the possibility of transparency becomes, and, to the degree that the translator is unaware of this problem, the more likely it is that he will have a mistaken conception of what it is he is actually accomplishing. This is the foundation for Silverstein's insistence that cultures as we usually conceive them cannot actually be translated in the usual sense of the word, because any attempt to explain the meaning of one cultural system in the language of another involves an inevitable transformation. This is also true of attempts to communicate between disciplines that have very different starting premises. The more we assume transparency in this situation, the less accurate our understanding will become. If this is the case, then there is reason to fear much inaccuracy in legal attempts at translation, because the gap between legal and other possible frames is not adequately problematized or theorized in standard legal approaches. To be fair, it's important to note that social scientists sometimes also proceed as if it were possible to understand law from the inside, or to communicate with legal professionals, without any real effort at translation—an equally mistaken approach (although probably without the same social ramifications, given the very different institutional positions and functions of legal and social science discourse).

## Cultural Invisibility/Dominance and "Neutral" Legal Language: Law School and Legal Categories in a Democratic State

At a very broad level, this study has outlined a tension between abstract categories and conceptions of justice, on the one hand, and, on the other hand, the democratic ideals of inclusion that require social, contextual, and grounded moral reasoning. When considered in terms of this tension, the problem of cultural invisibility/ dominance in legal training emerges as a profound challenge. There is without question a certain genius to a linguistic-legal framework that treats all individuals the same, in safely abstract layers of legal categories and authorities, regardless of social identity or context. And the framework is still more powerful because of its ability to gobble up contextual details from each particular case, run them through a purportedly neutralizing filter of analogy and doctrine, and reach results that are at once guided by rules and yet that also are always changing those rules through a shifting ground of constructed facts. At the same time, this process conceals the ways legal results are often quite reflective of existing power dynamics, while simultaneously pulling lawyers away from grounded moral judgment and fully contextualized consideration of human conflict. This can produce an ongoing alienation: of legal decision making from ethics and of lawyers from socially shared values. The legal system itself, while purporting to serve all citizens equally, can hide behind the screen provided by its legal-linguistic filter, concealing even from itself the way that inequities are integral to its structure. There is no easy or quick fix to solve this dilemma; professors cannot cease teaching their students the epistemological-linguistic frame they will need to use in practice. Clearly, however, to confront the problem we need the kind of understanding that research such as that presented in this book can provide.[50] And, as Burns has eloquently argued, there is ground for hope that some counterbalance can be achieved through other kinds of legal discourses: the blend, for example, that is found in the trial, or in the more clinically based education that attempts to prepare students for trials, mediations, and client interviews.[51] However, as even the most ardent advocates of alternative approaches to legal training admit, the linguistic system that I have outlined in this book remains the lingua franca through which all attorneys must at some point operate, and so cannot be easily dismissed or ignored.[52]

The great question here, as in so many other domains of this society, remains whether it is possible to keep the powerful positive aspects of one side of this double edge without having also to accept the deleterious aspects of the other side. This is a question that has obvious global dimensions, as the hegemony of Western approaches to law, justice, and social context undergoes ever more rapid expansion internationally.[53] Of course, its impact in each part of the world will work through particular mediations dictated in part by local circumstances, and the hegemonic vision will itself shift and be partially reconstructed in this process.[54] But as we see the inexorable march of social change that spreads the "rule of law" but also carries with it deepening class disparities, widespread dissolution of older forms of social cohesion and accompanying normative grounding, and in some cases increased criminal violence, the task of analyzing this particular aspect of a hegemonic ideology takes on added urgency.[55] The double edge of legal reasoning uncovered in U.S. law school classroom discourse offers the possibilities but also the dangers that come with this move to a particular form of abstraction, which can erase those aspects of social context that lead to bias, but can also obliterate aspects of the social surround that permit an in-depth understanding of social inequalities. Facing this dilemma is a crucial task for any legal system with democratic ideals, and it is a core challenge confronting those using the legal language through which such a system operates. Whether through direct export of American legalism, or through its indirect effect on U.S. legal-political attitudes and policies, this challenge is rapidly reaching far beyond the geographic borders of the United States.

What, then, are we to make of this powerful, linguistically circumscribed system of legal knowledge? Through linguistic analysis we can see the centrality of discursive patterning and ideologies of language to wider social processes. In some cases, as we have noted, the web of language surrounding legal decision making can be viewed as a protection for those with less power. On the other hand, there is cause for concern regarding systematic exclusion or marginalization of the very aspects of social context that might matter most to the powerless. If those wielding the analogies and formulating the linguistic ideologies tend to be relatively homogeneous in terms of race, gender, class, and other socially situated features of identity, then there is less chance that alternative views and approaches will be heard. (This directs our attention to the elites in the legal profession as particularly important sources of decisions about the construction of legal frames.) The very construction of fact from complex contexts, as well as the selection of salient facts for analogical reasoning, tacitly draws on deeply cultural assumptions (although the process represents itself as natural and neutral).[56] It seems unlikely that we will be able to achieve a truly democratic legal system with a homogeneous judiciary guiding this process, or with homogeneous legal education setting the scene for what transpires as law students enter the profession.

Furthermore, the law school classroom is itself arguably the site of more than lessons about technical law. As Weinstein notes, educational research has demonstrated that how we structure classroom interactions affects how we "create settings in which students can learn lessons of caring, justice, and self-worth."[57] Studies from educational settings where teachers and researchers have sought new solutions, rather than giving up on students of color, have shown us that changes in pedagogical structure and philosophy can make an enormous difference.[58] The benefits from successful racial integration in classrooms extend to white students as well as students of color, and they also extend beyond more narrowly conceived educational advantages (which have indeed been demonstrated), to wider social benefits. The synergy between the educational and social advantages is only heightened in law school settings, where part of what nascent attorneys must learn is the wider perspective needed to write, administer, and enforce laws in a diverse, democratic society. A study of Harvard and University of Michigan law students has documented that the students themselves feel diversity in law school to be a vital component of their legal education; as one student said, "I cannot see how law can be properly learned without diverse perspectives and opinions."[59] Another student in the study noted that "cultural and ethnic diversity is more important in law school than many other studies," and this perspective was broadly shared by the majority of the students surveyed in both schools.[60]

Diversity in the classroom, then, is beneficial to white students, to the overall project of legal education in our society, and to those students of color who succeed. Ironically, a recent study has raised the difficult question of whether it is beneficial to those students of color who do not succeed.[61] The ensuing debate over affirmative action in law school has raised a number of important issues that beg for further study. One thing seems clear: the law school experience itself still seems to be differentially damaging to some students of color. There is a fierce debate over why. A question that has emerged from this debate is whether it would be better for African American students overall if law schools were to abolish affirmative action.[62] There appears to be agreement that doing so would diminish the numbers of African American students in elite law schools, a prospect that has raised some understandable worries about the potential impact on the (already slow) process of integration at the highest levels of our nation's legal and political systems.[63] In this regard, an important concern raised by the present study is the possibility that lowering the size of the minority cohorts at elite schools would have a cascading effect on even the students of color who are successful under the current system, now left without the support of a cohort (and likely with diminishing numbers of role models on the faculty and in the higher echelons of the profession).[64] Certainly, before giving up on real integration and facing major losses to so many of their students and educational goals, law schools should consider the paths that have been successfully followed in other educational settings, where pedagogical innovation has benefited not only students of color, but all students involved.[65] In this way, law schools could better serve all of their students, while also providing an educational experience that best prepares all future lawyers for the practice of law in a democratic state and diverse world.[66]

One part of this step would involve more sophisticated and careful attention to details of law school and classroom culture and context.[67] Another important step would be taken if those trained in law could be made more aware of the limitations tacitly built into the very framework of the language in which they work. As we have seen, an empirically informed perspective helps to problematize the process of legal translation itself, challenging complacent presumptions regarding the transparent character of legal language. Like all human language, legal language is embedded in a particular setting, shaped by the social context and institution surrounding it. Systematic study of this contextual molding provides an important antidote to the hubris that inheres in standard legal metalinguistic assumptions and pushes legal professionals to remember the limits of their knowledge. Excellent translation, whether across disciplines or among people, begins with epistemological modesty; it is only when we recognize that there are other possible perspectives and frameworks that we can start to comprehend them.[68] The arrogance that accompanies a closed linguistic system can contribute to the alienation of lawyers and the legal system from the people they are supposed to serve, because it can prevent those speaking the language of law from truly hearing alternative perspectives.[69] This study has laid out some of the basic metalinguistic structures that render legal language at once powerful and problematic. Understanding the problems alongside the power might help law students balance the intoxicating appeal of their new language with a realistic reminder of its limitations.

# Notes

## Part I

1. Langdell, preface, vi.
2. Heath, *Ways with Words*, 367–368.

## Chapter 1

1. Zemans and Rosenblum, *Public Profession.*
2. The impetus for much of this research developed from Michael Silverstein's seminal work on metapragmatics, linguistic ideology, and the place of pragmatics in the social realization of language structure. See Silverstein, "Shifters," 11–55; Silverstein, "Language Structure," 193–247; see also the set of essays on this subject in Schieffelin et al., *Language Ideologies.*
3. To avoid excessive use of so-called scare quotation marks, I have generally limited their use to the first introduction of phrases, such as "think like a lawyer." When used in this way, the quotation marks indicate one of several ideas that I hope readers will keep in mind during subsequent uses of such phrases. First, these initial scare quotes will frequently be used to indicate folk terminology: that is, phrases or words used within the culture I am studying (here, the U.S. legal profession and academy). Words like "think" in this context are to be read as an indigenous category that we are unpacking through linguistic and cultural analysis, rather than terms to be taken at face value. I want the reader to understand that I maintain a similar analytic distance regarding the legal academy's indigenous caste system that divides law schools into "elite," "local," and so forth—as well as toward terms such as "other" or "minority," terms that have long been problematized within fields like anthropology. Second, quotation marks may index the first use of a term that has a particular, more technical meaning in this book than in common usage (for example, "double edge"). Quotes may also signal terms used figuratively or metaphorically, or terms directly quoted from the writings or speech of others (or both, as for example when I say that scholars have written of law "on the books" and law "in action").

Another metapragmatic note: throughout the book, I would advise readers who are interested in some of the more technical points to focus on the notes. In the interests of creating a more accessible text, I have relegated many of the more technical points to the endnotes.

4. This combination has produced a data set that is quite rich, which I will continue to mine in future work on the intersection of language, socialization, and institutional practices.

5. As will be explained later in the book, I take the notion of a "double edge" from the work of Moishe Postone, which carries forward the Frankfurt School tradition. At the same time, I think somewhat similar notions can be found in the work of both Weber and Durkheim (see below).

6. I am indebted in particular on this point to Susan Hirsch, a leading anthropologist of language and law whose work on Kenyan courts has served as a model for our field. Hirsch's research carefully delineates how the language of law can simultaneously perpetuate domination and yet also open possibilities for resistance, because "there are always gaps to be exploited by those who seek a hearing for their experiences." Hirsch, *Pronouncing and Persevering*, 246. I have also been influenced more directly by Hirsch's insightful comments on my work, nudging me to think more thoroughly about the "cultural dominance" half of this dichotomy. Hirsch, "Making Culture Visible," 127. Discussions with Leti Volpp, as well as my reading of her work, also helped to underscore this point for me. Volpp, "(Mis)Identifying Culture."

7. See discussion in Chapter 2; also see, for example, work by the Scollons linking discourse and worldviews. Scollon and Scollon, *Intercultural Communication*. As noted in the text, at the level of linguistic analysis, this study offers insights into the very subtle ways metalinguistic filtering can operate to convey or alter worldviews and norms, particularly in settings of initiation or socialization into new identities.

8. Levi, *Introduction*.

9. This sketch is obviously designed to highlight some of the more dramatic examples of the overall process described in this book; as we will see, the day-to-day reorientation of students is generally more mundane and subtle. This "ideal typical" vignette merely helps to crystallize some of the patterns documented in less crude form throughout the rest of the book. On the merits of ideal types, see Weber, *Economy and Society*. However, note that the dialogue and examples in this vignette are taken from actual transcripts and reported real-life instances.

10. These exchanges are taken from Transcript 4/1/1–7.

11. Transcript 6/2/1.

12. Transcript 1/7/9.

13. Williams, *Alchemy*, 85.

14. Id., 84.

15. See Stover, *Making It and Breaking It*; Erlanger et al., "Law Student Idealism"; Erlanger and Klegon, "Socialization Effects," for discussions of declining student concern with altruism and public interest during law school.

16. There is a debate in the literature over the causes of the documented shift away from public interest work during law school; some attribute this to diminishing interest from law students as they become more indoctrinated by law school training (and as they eye the pay differential between public interest and more lucrative jobs); others attribute it to a diminishing supply of public interest jobs. (See note 15 above.) This book points to aspects of legal training and epistemology that in themselves might contribute to a shift away from public interest ambitions.

## Chapter 2

1. For just a few examples of debates and commentaries on this issue, see the classic discussions by Bohannan, Beidelman, and Gluckman: Bohannan, *Justice and Judgment* and "Ethnography and Comparison"; Gluckman, *Ideas in Barotse Jurisprudence*; Beidelman, "Swazi Royal Ritual"; as well as more recent writings. See also John Comaroff and Roberts, *Rules and Processes*; Lazarus-Black and Hirsch, *Contested States*.

2. Anthropologists and sociolegal scholars have for many years provided trenchant attacks on singular notions of the law in particular societies, pointing out that there are usually multiple visions in any given society of what the law is and how it operates. Thus, how law is conceived may in part depend on to whom you are speaking. See, for example, Greenhouse et al., *Law and Community*; Lazarus-Black and Hirsch, *Contested States*; Starr and Collier, *History and Power*.

3. On the issue of divergences between lay and expert conceptualizations of the law, see, e.g., Bumiller, *Civil Rights Society*; Sarat and Felstiner, *Divorce Lawyers*; Sarat and Kearns, *Law in Everyday Life*. On divergences among experts in approaches to law, see, e.g., Conley and O'Barr's discussion of the way judges differ in their approach to decision making. Conley and O'Barr, *Rules versus Relationships*. On differences among laypeople in their views of law, see, e.g., Greenhouse, *Praying for Justice*; Williams, *Alchemy*. And for a nice blurring of any sharp division between lay and expert understandings, see Yngvesson, *Virtuous Citizens*.

4. Early legal realism cast doubt on the conventional legal conception that "a decision of any lawsuit results from the application of a legal rule or rules to the facts of the suit." Frank, *Law and the Modern Mind*, xii. Realists were also concerned about the way law worked in people's lives apart from formal court decisions. See, e.g., U. Moore and Callahan, "Law and Learning Theory." The social scientists who took up the challenge left by the legal realists in the past two decades formed the field of law-and-society scholarship, which brings together many different disciplines in the study of the real-world effects of law. See, e.g., Abel, *Law & Society Reader*; Lempert and Sanders, *Invitation*; Macaulay et al., *Law & Society*.

5. See Pound, "Law in Books and Law in Action"; see also Llewellyn's famous list of "common points of departure" for "real realists," which includes a "distrust of traditional legal rules and concepts in so far as they purport to *describe* what either courts or people are actually doing" and "a distrust of the theory that traditional prescriptive rule-formulations are *the* heavily operative factor in producing court decisions." Llewellyn, "Some Realism about Realism," 1222. This distinction in legal discussions has interesting parallels with a wider cultural distinction between "book" learning and "practical" learning, which might be fruitfully explored.

6. This is an insight that is by no means original to me; the legal realists themselves and many scholars following in their footsteps since have taken formal legal doctrine seriously, of course without assuming that the formal framework in any way captures the full picture of what happens in the translation of formal doctrine to practice. See, e.g., Llewellyn, "On Warranty of Quality"; Scheppele, *Legal Secrets*. Law-and–social science scholars have also taken quite seriously the study of legal experts and have looked carefully at how their experience shapes the practice of law. See, e.g., Abel, *American Lawyers*; Abel and Lewis, *Lawyers in Society* I, II, III; Nelson et al., *Lawyers' Ideals*; Sarat and Felstiner, *Divorce Lawyers*. For an examination of the gendered dimensions of legal epistemology in action among practicing attorneys, paralegals, and legal secretaries, see Pierce, *Gender Trials*.

A similar debate about the place of expert knowledge in the understanding of social institutions can be found among scholars (especially anthropologists) studying religion.

Although anthropologists are predictably concerned about the way people on the street understand their religion (see, e.g., Jean Comaroff, *Body of Power*), they also have traditionally devoted some time to understanding how religious experts interpret and understand religious symbolism. See, e.g., Reichel-Dolmatoff, *Amazonian Cosmos*. Silverstein notes that "institutions with procedural formalism, e.g., religion, law, etc., are particularly prone to 'expert/lay' divergences" in perspective between those controlling the institutions and those otherwise inhabiting them. Silverstein, personal communication, 10/11/05.

7. Ronald Dworkin makes a similar point when he urges that we pay attention to professional ideologies, which he terms the "internal, participants' point of view," in understanding law, pointing to law as an "argumentative" practice. Dworkin, *Law's Empire* 13–14.

8. Sociolegal scholars studying legal practitioners have turned up many examples of informal ideologies and views of the legal profession. See, e.g., Conley and O'Barr, *Rules versus Relationships* (views of small claims court judges); Pierce, *Gender Trials* (views of attorneys and paralegals); Sarat and Felstiner, *Divorce Lawyers* (views of divorce attorneys about law and the legal system); Sarat, *When the State Kills* (views of death penalty defense attorneys).

9. Scholars in sociolegal studies have for some time been demonstrating that law in the United States is anything but a level playing field. Galanter, "Why the 'Haves' Come Out Ahead." In the legal academy, other successors to the legal realist movement from the fields of critical legal studies, feminist jurisprudence, and critical race theory, along with other critical scholars, have added strong critiques pointing out the ways that apparently neutral aspects of law are in fact heavily value-laden. See, e.g., Bartlett and Kennedy, *Feminist Legal Theory*; Cover, *Justice Accused*; Crenshaw et al., *Critical Race Theory*; Fineman, *Illusion of Equality*; Kelman, *Guide to Critical Legal Studies*; *Critical Legal Studies* special issue;[1] Williams, *Alchemy*. There have been allied critiques of the methods and content of American legal education. See, e.g., Bell, "Black Students in White Law Schools"; Hantzis, "Kingsfield and Kennedy"; Kalman, "To Hell with Langdell!"; D. Kennedy, *Legal Education and the Reproduction of Hierarchy*; Menkel-Meadow, "Portia in a Different Voice"; Romero et al., "The Legal Education of Chicago Students."

10. See, e.g., MacKinnon, *Feminism Unmodified*; Althouse, "The Lying Woman"; Ansley, "Race and the Core Curriculum in Legal Education"; Frug, "Re-Reading Contracts"; Lawrence, "The Id, the Ego, and Equal Protection"; Matsuda, "When the First Quail Calls."

There are actually three issues here: (1) the "on the ground" administration of justice in multiple legal and quasi-legal settings; (2) the implicit skewing hidden within formal legal categories, epistemology, and forms of discourse; and (3) the differential inclusion of "outsider" students and perspectives from law school classroom discussions. Interestingly, the second issue, which is the discourse structure of legal language, mediates the other two; it is one of the most obvious bridges connecting the two quite different social settings (law in practice, law school training). I would argue that the invisibilities and silences that emerge during the inculcation of legal language in law school classrooms become hardened and habitual through multiple means in the administration of justice (linguistic and nonlinguistic, to be sure, but at least one of the linguistic means is the core of formal metalinguistic structuring outlined in this volume). In the process, it becomes less relevant what a student's background is, for once someone has thoroughly internalized the metalinguistic system of legal reasoning, she or he will begin to habitually marginalize some aspects of social context and morally grounded reasoning. (This does not mean that he or she will inevitably turn away from alterative languages and points of view—even within the rich realm of diverse legal professional "dialects"—but it does mean that a new kind of "bilingualism" will be necessary, and it will take some additional effort to maintain these multiple perspectives.)

11. After feminist scholars called attention to this particular doctrinal problem, there was a move away from a "reasonable man" and toward a "reasonable person" standard. However, a mere lexical substitution may not do the trick if the unmarked category "person" still tends (as unmarked categories often do) to indicate the assumptions associated with the hegemonic stereotype of a typical "person," that is, a male. On marked and unmarked categories, see Silverstein, "Language and the Culture of Gender"; Mertz, "Beyond Symbolic Anthropology." On the issue of how these unconscious assumptions infiltrate the notion of the reasonable man or person, see, e.g., De Cosse, "Simply Unbelievable: Reasonable Women"; Nourse, "Passion's Progress."

12. Some anthropologists and others may doubtless insist that what I describe as "gender" here should properly be denominated "sex." I have chosen to follow the dominant convention used in the legal literature, from formal doctrines regarding gender discrimination through the scholarly literature on gender in law and law schools, partially with an eye to rendering the text more accessible. On issues of essentialism, see, e.g., Spelman, *Inessential Woman*; Harris, "Race and Essentialism in Feminist Legal Theory"; Obiora, "Neither Here nor There." For a summary of this problem as it affects debates over international human rights, see Higgins, "Anti-Essentialism, Relativism, and Human Rights."

13. As Fineman explains, her conception of a gendered life

> begins with the observation that women's existences are constituted by a variety of experiences—material, psychological, physical, social, and cultural—some of which may be described as biologically based while others seem more rooted in culture and custom. . . . My difference argument . . . is grounded in empirical realizations, in gendered experiences, and therefore, in women's lives as constructed in society and culture. (Fineman, *The Neutered Mother*, 48)

14. Fineman underscores the difficulties that inhere in struggles to encompass some aspects of gendered experience under equality models: "What are we feminists to do with motherhood, both as a practice and an ideological structure? . . . There is no autonomy to be found in motherhood. Motherhood is mired in dependency—the dependency of the child, in the first instance, and the dependency of that person assigned responsibility for caretaking, in the second instance." Fineman, *The Autonomy Myth*, 169. Here, as Fineman so sharply delineates for us, the supposedly clear lines between biological and social roles blur, posing a difficult theoretical dilemma. The combination of women's biological role in human reproduction and of standard sociocultural allocations of caretaking roles in many societies does create a pattern in which those who are biologically women wind up differentially responsible at the social level for caretaking. Men, of course, can wind up being allocated caregiving responsibility as well, hence Fineman's provocative metaphorical move to denominate men who are primary caretakers "mothers," extending to them the same protections and supports as would be extended to female mothers. Fineman, *The Neutered Mother*, 234–235. Her insistence on looking at social context to provide meaning for arguments over sameness and difference is echoed in my work by a focus on the complex and varied strands of linguistic patterning that overlap but also diverge, depending on context. I take seriously Calhoun's injunction that it is in the tension between sameness and difference that we find one of the core issues facing this generation of social theorists. Calhoun, *Critical Social Theory*. Feminist theorists like Fineman, along with critical race theorists, have taken us a long way in rethinking this conceptual puzzle.

15. In this conception of a double edge, I draw on Moishe Postone's interpretation of Marx. Postone, *Time, Labor, and Social Domination*. This issue is discussed in more detail at the end of Chapter 6. There I discuss a parallel between the "double character" that

Postone locates in aspects of capitalist society and epistemology, and the form of abstract-concrete reasoning used in U.S. law. Like Postone, I point to a potentially liberating aspect of this double edge, one that exists side by side with a dangerous possibility of abstraction away from attention to injustice and inequality. For an argument with affinities to this, see Yngvesson, *Virtuous Citizens*, 119–127: "The 'double reality" of these [legal] processes is that they are both about domination and refusal, about complicity with power and struggles against relations of power."

16. Jane Larson, personal communication.

17. Or, to make patent a fairly obvious connection with some central issues in jurisprudence, in interpreting orders from the sovereign, not to mention in many other more complexly posed issues surrounding law and interpretation.

18. See Whorf, *Language, Thought and Reality*; Sapir, *Selected Writings*.

19. This determinist reading was already part of the Herderian tradition's cultural understanding of language.

20. See Lucy, *Grammatical Categories* and "Whorf's View of the Linguistic Mediation of Thought"; Silverstein, "Language Structure and Linguistic Ideology" and "Whorfianism."

21. Whorf, *Language, Thought and Reality*, 139–140. Thus, Whorf compared English and Hopi as a way of illustrating how differences between language can affect the background assumptions with which speakers habitually approach the world:

> Such terms as 'summer, winter, September, morning, noon, sunset' are with us a nouns, and have little formal linguistic difference from other nouns. They can be subjects or objects, and we say 'at sunset' or 'in winter' just as we say 'at the corner' or 'in an orchard.' . . .
>
> In Hopi however all phase terms, like 'summer, morning,' etc. are not nouns but a kind of adverb, to use the nearest SAE [Standard Average European language] analogy. They are a formal part of speech by themselves, distinct from nouns, verbs, and even other Hopi "adverbs." . . . These 'temporals' are not used as subjects or objects, or at all like nouns. . . .
>
> Our own "time" differs markedly from Hopi "duration." It is conceived as like a space of strictly limited dimensions, or sometimes as like motion upon such space. . . . Hopi "duration" seems to be inconceivable in terms of space or motion, being the mode in which life differs from form. (Whorf, *Language, Thought and Reality*, 142, 143, 158)

We see here the contrasting ontologies implicit in the structuring of grammatical categories.

22. See Silverstein, "Language Structure" and "Metapragmatic Discourse." Anthropological linguist Michael Silverstein and literary theorist Jacques Derrida have both pointed, from somewhat different perspectives, to a focus on words as a form of objectification. See Chandler, "The Problem of Purity," for an exposition of the continuities between these two traditions.

23. See Silverstein, "Shifters," "Language and the Culture of Gender," and "Metapragmatic Discourse"; see also Hanks, *Referential Practice*. For relevant background, see Garvin, *A Prague School Reader*; Peirce, *Collected Papers*, vol. 2; Sapir, *Selected Writings*; Saussure, *Course in General Linguistics*; Whorf, *Language, Thought and Reality*; Jakobson, "Closing Statement," "Shifters, Verbal Categories and the Russian Verb," and *On Language*. For an overview and introduction, see Mertz, "Beyond Symbolic Anthropology."

24. For the uninitiated, let me briefly introduce some key concepts. These concepts emerge not only from linguistics but also from the broader field known as "semiotics,"

the study of signs. When focusing on "signs," scholars are able to study all varieties of communicative signaling, including but not confined to linguistic communication. See generally Mertz and Parmentier, *Semiotic Mediation*. A common analytic division distinguishes several ways that language (or signs generally) carries meaning: (1) semantics: the decontextual meaning that is given by conventional "definition"; for example, when I say "rose," you can interpret what I am saying in part because you know that the word "rose" generally indicates flowers of a certain kind; (2) pragmatics: the meaning that develops from contexts of speaking; for example, it is pretty difficult to understand the actual meaning or referent of a phrase such as "this rose" without knowing about the context in which it was spoken (because the word "this" generally indicates things that are close by in such a context of communication)—thus part of the meaning of that phrase when it is used (the pragmatic part) comes from its context, for example, from the existence of a flower that is situated close to the speaker of the utterance; (3) syntax: the meaning that relies on the groupings of words into phrases, one with another, in utterances; for example, our deciphering of the phrase "this rose" also depends in part on the relationship of the two words to one another and our understandings of what it means to string these two particular words together in this way (a word of the syntactic Determinant category followed by one of the Noun category, making up a regular phrase type).

25. See Silverstein, "Shifters" and "Metapragmatic Discourse." For work that similarly focuses on the social context of discourse and language socialization, see Bakhtin, *The Dialogic Imagination*; Vygotsky, *Collected Works*, vol. 1; Wertsch, *Vygotsky and the Social Formation of Mind*.

26. For early scholarship pointing the way on this issue, see Kurylowicz, "Deictic Elements"; Prague School, *Melanges Linguistiques*.

27. Contrast this view with the attempts of self-appointed language "purists" to keep language static (e.g., the efforts of pundits such as William Safire to chastise people for "incorrect" and otherwise shocking shifts in language use), and you will understand why anthropological linguists take particular pleasure in poking fun at those who would attempt to police and stop grammatical variation or change. See Silverstein, "Monoglot 'Standard,'" 15. Scholars focusing on how social power issues emerge around fights over language would add that "correct" usage almost always reflects which speakers in a society have greater or less power, status, and/or prestige.

28. When we refer to previous contexts of speaking, linguists would say that we are speaking "interdiscursively."

29. Gumperz, *Discourse Strategies*; Duranti and Goodwin, *Rethinking Context*; Duranti, *Linguistic Anthropology*. Brenneis has consistently drawn our attention to the role of coproducers of narrative as well as to the role of the audience in structuring speech, particularly in legal and political discourse. Brenneis, "Grog and Gossip" and "Performing Passions"; see also Duranti and Brenneis, *The Audience as Co-Author*.

30. See Silverstein, "Limits of Awareness." Creative acts of language use, playing against past routinized usages, enter the shared reservoirs of grammar and discourse structures to change them. Thus, a new form of poetry at once draws on existing understandings of what poetry is and has been, plays against those previous understandings, and alters future understandings. This kind of process is at work all over in the law, in politics, and in society generally. For example, Victor Turner tells us that Beckett changed the notion of the martyr in deploying commonly shared symbols to creative new use. See Turner, *Dramas, Fields, and Metaphors*.

31. See (Ochs-)Keenan, "Sliding Sense of Obligatoriness"; Parmentier, "The Political Function of Reported Speech"; Silverstein,"Metaforces of Power in Traditional Oratory." This relationship, which is at once iconic (mirroring) and indexical (relying on

context for meaning), means that the discursive structure is an "indexical icon" of the social or political model it reinforces and instantiates.

32. Silverstein, "Poetics of Politics"; see also Mertz and Weissbourd, "Legal Ideology."

33. The distinction between "model of" and "model for" was introduced by anthropologist Clifford Geertz, *Interpretation of Cultures*.

34. This propensity for dismissing usage and pragmatics as chaotic finds its mirror image in a monolithic focus on decontextual and referential aspects of language as the primary source of linguistic order. In 1979, Silverstein first traced a cross-cultural pattern in which there is "a tendency to rationalize the pragmatic system of a language, in native understanding, with an ideology of language that centers on reference-and-predication." Silverstein, "Language Structure," 208. If this is true, we would expect native speakers (and sometimes "expert scholars" as well) to focus more on referential units like words and on semantic or grammatical structuring, rather than on contextual, pragmatic, or creative structuring in language use. Mertz and Weissbourd suggest that if there is such an underlying tendency in our conscious reflection on language, it must be refracted differentially through the lens of each particular social time and place. Mertz and Weissbourd, "Legal Ideology and Linguistic Theory," 282 n. 14. They find examples of a particular form of this "preference for reference" in Western linguistic and jurisprudential thought, which (like language ideology more generally) has frequently focused systematic analysis on semantico-referential, presupposable meaning, while viewing linguistic creativity, contextual aspects of language, and pragmatics as unsystematic and chaotic. Id.

35. See, e.g., Bauman, *Story, Performance, and Event*; Brenneis and Myers, *Dangerous Words*; Briggs, *Competence in Performance*; Duranti and Goodwin, *Rethinking Context*; Gumperz, *Discourse Strategies*; Hill and Irvine, *Responsibility and Evidence in Oral Discourse*.

36. This difficulty exists even, or especially, with the speech act theorists. See, e.g., Searle, *Speech Acts*. For an in-depth discussion of the general division between presupposing and creative (or entailing) aspects of language use, see Silverstein, "Language Structure." See also Yovel, "The Language beyond Law," on speech act theory and legal language.

37. Woolard and Schieffelin, "Language Ideology," 57 (citing Silverstein, Heath, and Irvine). Woolard and Schieffelin provide a very useful overview of this field of study. See also Silverstein's pioneering 1979 article on linguistic ideology, "Language Structure and Linguistic Ideology," and the articles in Scheiffelin et al., *Language Ideologies*.

38. Gal and Irvine, "Boundaries of Languages." Gal and Irvine's concept of "iconicity" applies when speakers perceive there to be a common "essence" that is shared by the linguistic form and aspects of the social identity that this form indexes.

39. See Silverstein, "Metapragmatic Discourse." In this and more recent work, Silverstein has carefully delineated the crucial role of indexical structuring in mediating the "real-time" unfolding of social meaning. Silverstein, "Indexical Order."

40. See, e.g., Schieffelin, *Give and Take of Everyday Life*; Schieffelin and Ochs, *Language Socialization across Cultures*; Kulick and Scheiffelin, "Language Socialization"; Foley, *Anthropological Linguistics*, 345–358. See also Gergen, *Cultural Psychology*; Shweder and Levine, *Culture Theory*; Watson-Gegeo and Nielsen, "Language Socialization in SLA."

41. Ochs, *Culture and Language Development*, 145, 163–165.

42. These linguistic routines index, or point to, the social values that they seek to inculcate. This is the kind of connection between the external social world and the internal developing understanding of the child that Vygotskian scholars have sought, including their search to "specif[y] the mechanisms that connect early linguistic activity that is inextricably tied to the concrete extralinguistic environment and later linguistic activity involving abstract definitions." Wertsch, introduction, in *Culture, Communication and Cognition*, 16.

43. See Duff et al., "Learning Language for Work and Life"; Jacobs-Huey, *Becoming Cosmetologists*; Philips, "The Language Socialization of Lawyers"; see generally Berger and Luckmann, *Social Construction of Reality.* Here Silverstein would speak of second-order indexicalities of identity. Silverstein, "Indexical Order."

44. Finkelstein, "Studies in the Anatomy Laboratory," 23.

45. See Turner, *Dramas, Fields, and Metaphors*; Van Gennep, *Rites of Passage*; see also Goffman, *The Presentation of Self.*

46. Turner, *Dramas, Fields, and Metaphors*, 259.

47. Id., 195–198. Note that while neophytes are in a liminal state, separated from society, they would technically be referred to as "initiands"; on their return to society, they would gain the status of "initates." Through much of the text of this book, I eschew the more technical vocabulary in discussing law students as initiates, but it should be recalled that while they are in law school (and particularly in their first year), the correct technical term would be initiand.

48. Van Gennep, *Rites of Passage*, 11.

49. P. Garrett and Baquedano-Lopez, "Language Socialization"; see also Brenneis and Macaulay, "Learning Language." In addition to issues of morality and personhood, P. Garrett and Baquedano-Lopez point to both narrative and linguistic ideology as important foci for ongoing research on linguistic socialization. As we will see, new forms of narrative and mediating linguistic ideology are indeed important parts of the linguistic socialization process in law schools.

50. Bourdieu and Passeron, *Reproduction.*

51. See, e.g., Anyon, "Social Class and School Knowledge"; Collins, "Socialization to Text" and "Differential Treatment and Reading Instruction"; J. Gee, "Narrativization of Experience"; Heath, *Ways with Words* and "Toward an Ethnohistory of Writing"; Mehan, *Learning Lessons*; Michaels, "Narrative Presentations"; Philips, "Participant Structures and Communicative Competence"; Wortham and Rymes, *Linguistic Anthropology of Education.* Wortham points to several basic tenets that have anchored the linguistic anthropology of education: connection of micro- and macrolevel processes, examining linguistic patterns in use, and a focus on the speaker's point of view. Wortham, "Introduction." In addition, he would add four more central foci that he sees as promising avenues for moving the field forward: creativity, indexicality, regimentation, and poetic structure. These concepts obviously fit within the Silversteinian framework outlined earlier.

52. See, e.g., Goody and Watt, "Consequences of Literacy"; Olson, "Utterance to Text."

53. See, e.g., Gough, "Implications of Literacy"; Scinto, "Text, Schooling, and the Growth of Mind"; Scribner and Cole, "Literacy without Schooling"; Street, *Literacy in Theory and Practice.*

54. Scribner and Cole, "Literacy without Schooling."

55. Street, *Literacy in Theory and Practice*; see also Baton, "Literacy in Everyday Contexts."

56. Collins, "Literacy and Literacies," 75–76 (emphasis added).

57. In a similar vein, work following in the tradition of L. S. Vygotsky focusing on linguistic mediation in children's development has demonstrated that the same task, using the same combination of writing and speech, may be absorbed differently depending on the culturally constructed perceptions and approaches people bring to it. See Saxe et al., "The Social Organization of Early Number Development;" Wertsch, *Vygotsky and the Social Foundation of Mind* and *Culture, Communication, and Cognition.*

58. Collins and Blot, *Literacy and Literacies*, xviii; Heath, *Ways with Words.*

59. See, e.g., Cazden, *Classroom Discourse*; Cook-Gumperz, "Schooling and Literacy"; J. Gee, "The Narrativization of Experience in the Oral Style"; Mehan, *Learning Lessons*;

Michaels, "Narrative Presentations"; Philips, "Participant Structures and Communicative Competence." Philips's early study underlined the crucial role of language in education; she demonstrated the serious misunderstandings that followed when Anglo teachers failed to understand Native American children's norms for talk. Philips, *The Invisible Culture*.

60. See Anyon, "Social Class and School Knowledge"; J. Gee, "The Narrativization of Experience in the Oral Style"; Michaels, "Sharing Time"; and sources cited in notes 55 and 61–63.

61. James Gee concludes that the student's narrative makes sense of her world:

She works out the problems in a quite sophisticated way, in terms of a conflict of natures (the Greeks, an oral society that ultimately gave birth to Western literacy, would have understood this perfectly). She carries it out with a full utilization of prosody, time and sequence markers, an intricate aspect system (actional, habitual, iterative), and parallelism and repetition, and as suspenseful thematic development. (J. Gee, "The Narrativization of Experience in the Oral Style," 24)

62. See Collins, "Language and Class in Minority Education"; Collins and Michaels, "Speaking and Writing"; Heath, *Ways with Words*; Labov, "The Logic of Nonstandard English"; Mehan, *Learning Lessons*.

63. See Collins and Blot, *Literacy and Literacies*; Calhoun and Ianni, *The Anthropological Study of Education*; Roberts and Akinsanya, *Schooling in the Cultural Context*.

64. See Bernstein, *Class, Codes, and Control*; Bourdieu and Passeron, *Reproduction*; Bowles and Gintis, *Schooling in Capitalist America*; Eggleston and Gleason, "Curriculum Innovation and the Context of the School."

65. See, e.g., Parsons, "The School Class as a Social System."

66. See, e.g., Bowles and Gintis, *Schooling in Capitalist America*.

67. Apple, *Ideology and Curriculum* and *Teachers and Texts*; Giroux, "Theories of Reproduction and Resistance in the New Sociology of Education."

68. Apple explicitly builds on Gramscian theory, which imputed importance to the role of culture and insisted on attention to the ways that people resist dominant cultures. See Apple, *Ideology and Curriculum*. A similar argument is currently being made about politics and law generally. See discussion in Mertz, "Legal Loci and Places in the Heart," 973; key current works on resistance include Comaroff and Comaroff, *Of Revelation and Revolution*, vols. 1 and 2; Lazarus-Black and Hirsch, *Contested States*; Scott, *Weapons of the Weak* and *Domination and the Arts of Resistance*.

69. Carnoy and Levin, *Schooling and Work*. Some might argue that there is not necessarily an inherent antagonism between these two functions, because the individualist "rights" orientation in U.S. society can arguably be understood as serving and resonating with a liberal conception of the autonomous, isolated citizen-subject. On the limitations of rights models, see Bumiller, *The Civil Rights Society*; but see Williams, *Alchemy*, on the power of a concept of rights for the subordinated.

70. See Leacock, "Education in Africa: Myths of 'Modernization.'"

71. See Bourdieu and Passeron, *Reproduction*; see also Bourdieu, *Distinction* and *Homo Academicus*.

72. That is to say, schooling contributes to reproduction of social structure both through recruitment and through the messages that are inculcated during the process of education. Bourdieu, "Cultural Capital and Pedagogic Communication."

73. Collins, "Literacy and Literacies."

74. Yon, "Highlights and Overview," 423.

75. Id.

76. Wortham, "Linguistic Anthropology of Education"; see also Collins and Slembrouck, "Reading Shop Windows," 21, who build on Silverstein's framework to demonstrate how "particular 'micro' contextual meanings are always construed in terms of a potentially open and sequentially-enacted series of higher-order 'macro' contextual assumptions."

77. John Austin, *Province of Jurisprudence*; Dworkin, *Law's Empire*; on H. L. A. Hart and others, see also Mertz and Weissbourd, "Legal Ideology and Linguistic Theory"; Weissbourd and Mertz, "Rule-Centrism versus Legal Creativity."

78. See, e.g., Levi, *Introduction*; Minow, *Making All the Difference*; Solan, *Language of Judges*; Williams, *Alchemy*; Winter, *Clearing in the Forest*; D. Kennedy, "Form and Substance in Private Law Adjudication"; see generally Bishin and Stone, *Law, Language and Ethics*. Elkins notes the close relationship between "thinking like a lawyer" and "speaking like a lawyer." Elkins, "The Legal Persona," 741–742.

79. Levi, *Introduction*; G. Edward White and Jason Freitag also make similar arguments. G. E. White, *The Marshall Court* (attributing power to shifting cultural ideas and intellectual history in the development of doctrine); Freitag, "Translating" (tracks the linguistic genealogy of the phrase "due process" through multiple historical periods). See G. E. White, "The Marshall Court," for an interesting account of the evolution of doctrine in piracy cases.

80. J. B. White, *Justice as Translation*.

81. See D. Kennedy, *Legal Education and the Reproduction of Hierarchy*; Williams, *Alchemy*. There is also a growing literature on the language used in particular legal settings, from courtrooms to law offices of various kinds. See, e.g., Conley and O'Barr, *Just Words*; Danet, "Language in the Legal Process"; Frohmann, "Discrediting Victims' Allegations"; Hirsch, *Pronouncing and Persevering*; Lazarus-Black, "Rites of Domination"; Maynard, *Inside Plea Bargaining*; Matoesian, *Reproducing Rape* and *Law and the Language of Identity*; Philips, *Ideology*; Sarat and Felstiner, *Divorce Lawyers*.

82. Areeda, "The Socratic Method"; Condlin, "Socrates' New Clothes"; Groves, "Toward a More Effective Program"; Heffernan, "Not Socrates, but Protagoras"; D. Kennedy, *Legal Education and the Reproduction of Hierarchy*; Landman, "Anent the Case Method"; Vitiello, "Professor Kingsfield." There have also been a number of histories and social science studies of law school education. See, e.g., Stevens, *Law School*; Stover, *Making It and Breaking It*; and relevant discussion in Friedman, *A History of American Law*; see also the early major review of the literature in this area by Maru, *Research on the Legal Profession*.

83. Thus, for example, commentators have had to distinguish among various kinds of Socratic teaching, at times lumping somewhat different teaching styles under the same label. See Cramton, "Current State of the Law School Curriculum"; Morgan, "The Case Method." As Vitiello notes, a "readily accepted definition" of the Socratic method isn't easy to find. Vitiello, "Professor Kingsfield," 961.

84. See ABA, *Report and Recommendations: The Role of Law Schools*, 13; Rhode, *In the Interests of Justice*; Teich, "Research on American Law Teaching," 170. Hawkins-León states that "the two primary methods of law teaching today are the Socratic Method and the Problem Method," with Socratic teaching dominating. Hawkins-León, "The Socratic Method," 1. Some scholars, however, claim that the Socratic method is on the wane. Shaffer and Redmount, *Lawyers, Law Students, and People*; Kerr, "Decline." As we will see in Chapter 7, the results of these studies still leave us somewhat unclear as to the actual trajectory of law school teaching, in part because of the lack of a uniform definition of "Socratic method," in part because they rely on self-report rather than observational data, and in part because we have no comparable data from earlier periods of time against which to assess their claims.

Whatever the overall trajectory, Socratic method teaching remains a hot topic for law professors and students, as evidenced by ongoing discussions in professional publications, in materials for law students, on law school web sites, and in law professor blogs. See, e.g., Leiter, "The 'Socratic Method' "; Beldar, "Method to the Socratic Madness."

85. See Teich, "Research on American Law Teaching," 170. For some, it is important that the professor call on students selected for Socratic exchanges without warning. Vitiello, "Professor Kingsfield," 965. Definitions vary widely (see discussion in Chapter 7).

86. See Dickinson, "Legal Rules"; see also Arnold, *Symbols of Government*; Robinson, *Law and the Lawyers*; Frank, "Why Not a Clinical Lawyer-School?"; Frank, "A Plea for Lawyer Schools" and "A Disturbing Look at the Law Schools"; Pound, "The Scope and Purpose of Sociological Jurisprudence."

87. Under the aegis of "critical" scholarship, I include critical race theory, critical legal studies, feminist legal theory, and some extensions of poststructuralist and queer theory to legal arenas. See, e.g., Crenshaw, "Foreword"; Hantzis, "Kingsfield and Kennedy"; D. Kennedy, *Legal Education and the Reproduction of Hierarchy*; Menkel-Meadow, "Feminist Legal Theory"; Ramachandran, "Re-Reading Difference"; Rhode, "Missing Questions"; Unger, *Law in Modern Society*.

88. See Friedland, "How We Teach," 28; Johnson, *Schooled Lawyers*, 179; Menkel-Meadow, "What's Missing," 600; Stevens, *Law School*, 156–158; but see Shaffer and Redmount, *Lawyers, Law Students, and People*, 168. As Menkel-Meadow points out, law teachers today use Socratic method teaching for quite different substantive ends than originally envisioned by Langdell, "some pointing to the political underpinnings of the rules, others to the efficiencies of the rules, others to the competing arguments that can be made 'on either side' of the rule, anticipating its change in other factual circumstances." Menkel-Meadow, "What's Missing," 600. This observation is supported by the findings of our study, which track Socratic-type structures through quite diverse topics and even discourse formats.

89. Johnson, *Schooled Lawyers*, xvii.

90. Zemans and Rosenblum, *Making of a Public Profession*, 204–206. This observation finds support in a number of studies documenting a move away from idealism and moral concerns during law school. See, e.g., Erlanger et al., "Law Student Idealism"; Stover, *Making It and Breaking It*. Janoff found that in one law school, female law students begin to suppress a relational orientation after the first year, moving more to impersonal and abstract rights approaches. Janoff, "The Influence of Legal Education."

91. D. Kennedy, *Legal Education and the Reproduction of Hierarchy*, 17–20; see also Shaffer, "Moral Implications," 190.

92. J. B. White, "Doctrine in a Vacuum," 35. In his recent book, *From Expectation to Experience*, 1–7, 14–15, J. B. White maintains this fundamental perspective but also paints a somewhat more complex view of the situation: no class ever lives up to our highest expectations, and in reality law school teaching does not map neatly onto a stereotype of "doctrine in a vacuum," although the image does capture some important "forces" at work in legal education.

93. This is a theme echoed throughout much of the literature criticizing Socratic method teaching. See, e.g., Bryden, "What Do Law Students Learn?"; Landman, "Anent the Case Method"; Llewellyn, "The Current Crisis in Legal Education"; Patterson, "The Case Method."

94. See Chester and Alumbaugh, "Functionalizing First-Year Legal Education"; Dallimore, "The Socratic Method"; Frank, "Why Not a Clinical Lawyer-School?"; Vukowich, "The Lack of Practical Training in Law Schools."

95. See Cutler, "Inadequate Law School Training"; David, "The Clinical Lawyer-School"; Devitt, "Why Don't Law Schools Teach Law Students How to Try Lawsuits?"

96. See, e.g., Baker, "Transcending the Legacies of Literacy"; Burton, "Cultivating Ethical"; Calleros, "Training a Diverse Student Body"; Cunningham, "Lawyer as Translator"; Stanchi, "Resistance Is Futile." In recent years, there have been interesting attempts to bridge divisions among traditional law teaching, clinical approaches, and social science as part of a movement toward a "new legal realism." See Conley, "How Bad Is It"; Trubek, "Crossing Boundaries."

97. Stone, "Legal Education on the Couch."

98. Id., 412–428. On law student distress and alienation, see,.e.g., Carrington and Conley, "The Alienation of Law Students"; Benjamin et al., "The Role of Legal Education"; Glenn, "Some Thoughts." J. M. Mitchell, taking a different approach, drew on cognitive and developmental theories of expert and novice thinking to develop a list of suggested improvements on the traditional teaching methodology. J. Mitchell, "Current Theories on Expert and Novice Thinking." For one updated resource on alternative teaching methods in law, see Torres and Lundwall, "Moving beyond Langdell II." As noted earlier, the current literature is replete with suggested innovations and novel applications of psychology or sociology to legal education, particularly in the areas of clinical teaching and legal writing. Unfortunately, a status gap between these fields and that of other law professors means that the latter are unlikely to value or read (and thus learn from) their colleagues' often better informed understandings of pedagogical innovations.

99. See, e.g., Boyle, "Employing Active-Learning Techniques"; Jacobson, "A Primer on Learning Styles"; Richmond, "Teaching Law to Passive Learners"; Randall, "The Myers-Briggs Type Indicator"; Ripps, "A Curriculum Course."

100. See Daicoff, "Lawyer Know Thyself," for a comprehensive review of the literature dealing with the lawyer and law student personality and other attributes. Daicoff draws on empirical research to document an overall shift during law school away from interest in people, emotions, interpersonal matters, and altruism, and a concomitant shift toward emphasis on logic, rationality, rights, rules, authoritarianism, achievement, competitiveness, and aggression. In this original article, Daicoff suggests that some of these aspects of law school training might actually fit well with the overall professional profile found in successful lawyers, and thus might serve a useful purpose despite appearances to the contrary. In her recent book on the same issue, Daicoff adds a new, more hopeful perspective, arguing that although some of the less attractive aspects of legal education might serve professional ends, it is important to counterbalance these with training that takes account of skills and traits often neglected or disfavored in legal education—as a way to mitigate the negative effects of lawyers' prototypical approach on public confidence in the profession, on professional ethics, and on lawyer satisfaction. Daicoff, *Lawyer, Know Thyself.* For contrary results on lawyer satisfaction, indicating relatively positive satisfaction levels among lawyers in Toronto, Chicago, and Minnesota, see Hagan and Kay, *Gender in Practice*; Heinz et al., "Lawyers"; Mattessich and Heilman, "The Career Paths."

101. Banks, "Gender Bias in the Classroom" and "Gender Bias in the Classroom (2)"; Guinier et al., *Becoming Gentlemen.*

102. See, e.g, Areeda, "The Socratic Method"; Harno, *Legal Education*; Konop, "The Case System"; Louiseaux, "The Newcomer"; Morgan, "The Case Method"; Vitiello, "Professor Kingsfield."

103. E. Garrett, "Becoming Lawyers."

104. Id.; see also Stropus, "Mend It."

105. Vitiello, "Professor Kingsfield," 989.

106. Actually, to put it in more technical terms, the argument is that there is an "iconic" or mirroring "fit" between the two. And because the discursive form of the Socratic method uses contextual (metapragmatic) structuring to create this fit, there is also an "indexical" link. In Chapter 4, I explain how classroom discourse is an "indexical icon" of the legal discourse to which it trains students; at the same time, there is a kind of "iconic indexical" character to the classroom metapragmatics.

107. See Smith, *Cognitive Styles*; Zemans and Rosenblum, *Making of a Public Profession*, 57.

108. E. G. Gee and Jackson, "Current Studies."

109. Zemans and Rosenblum, *Making of a Public Profession*, 136. A number of studies found that lawyers viewed general and practical skills as most essential in practice; these were the very skills that they felt were most lacking in their law school education.

110. Garth and Martin, "Law Schools"; see also Martin and Garth, "Clinical Education as a Bridge."

111. Garth and Martin, "Law Schools," 508.

112. See Kimball and Farmer, "Comparative Results"; Lorenson, "Concentrating on a Single Jurisdiction"; see also studies cited in Teich, "Research on American Law Teaching."

113. Bryden, "What Do Law Students Learn?"

114. Philips, "The Language Socialization of Lawyers."

115. Conley and O'Barr, *Just Words*; Hirsch, *Pronouncing and Persevering*; Matoesian, *Reproducing Rape*; Philips, *Ideology*. See Brenneis, "Language and Disputing"; Mertz, "Legal Language" and "Language, Law, and Social Meanings" for overviews of this area of research.

116. For example, although Matoesian documents the ways legal discourse reinforces patriarchal norms, he also demonstrates how rape victims can fight back within the framework of legal language. Matoesian, *Law and the Language of Identity*. Conley and O'Barr painstakingly trace the linguistic features that render language relatively more "powerful" or "powerless" and connect this with larger patterns in which litigants use more "rules-oriented" versus "relational" discourse. Conley and O'Barr, *Rules versus Relationships*. Although they do empirically demonstrate the preference for rules in legal discourse, they also provide a nuanced picture of how this varies among judges, so that language remains a partially independent level requiring separate analysis. See also Briggs, *Disorderly Discourse*. In this regard, scholars of language and law fit into a long line of scholarship in legal anthropology, which has for some time painted a rich picture of the role of law in societies. Jane Collier's early ethnographic work, for example, traced how legal categories used by the Zinacantecos had a logic of their own but also were affected by wider Mexican state institutions. Collier, *Law and Social Change*. Sally Falk Moore famously characterized this kind of social field, in which we can find both autonomous and nonautonomous dimensions, a "semi-autonomous" social field. S. F. Moore, "Law and Social Change." Moore's later work on "customary law" on Kilimanjaro provided an exemplary ethnographic account of this kind of mixed dynamic as it transmutes through historical change. S. F. Moore, *Social Facts and Fabrications*.

117. See Briggs, "Notes on a Confession." Here we can again point to a long tradition in anthropology of research on the imposition of hegemony through law, from Laura Nader's germinal work through that of scholars such as Jean and John Comaroff. Nader, *No Access to Law* and *The Life of the Law*; Comaroff and Comaroff, *Of Revelation and Revolution*, vols. 1 and 2; see also Coombe, *The Cultural Life of Intellectual Properties*; for overviews, see S. F. Moore, *Law and Anthropology*; Goodale and Mertz, "Anthropology of Law."

118. Hirsch, *Pronouncing and Persevering*, 90; Philips, "Local Legal Hegemony"; see also Briggs, "Notes on a Confession."

119. Merry, *Getting Justice and Getting Even.*

120. Sarat and Felstiner, *Divorce Lawyers*; Merry, *Colonizing Hawai'i*, 262. On how a metalinguistic filter can operate to translate social and economic changes into issues of language and identity, see Mertz, "Sociolinguistic Creativity."

121. Greenhouse, *Praying for Justice*; see also Greenhouse et al., *Law and Community*; Mertz, "Legal Loci and Places in the Heart." The work of Lazarus-Black carries this analysis of law at the edges of identity and community through time in a number of different Caribbean communities, tracking as well the global dimensions involved. Lazarus-Black, *The Vanishing Complainant.* Gooding provides a poignant and precise analysis of how the mediation of legal language and epistemology erases core aspects of Native American identity. Gooding, "Place, Race, and Names"; see also Mertz, "The Uses of History."

122. For examples of analyses that locate legal and political language in a social context while not reducing it to being a reflex of that context, see Brenneis, "Performing Passions" and "Telling Theories." See also Mertz, "Consensus and Dissent." Anthropologists have also pointed to how law embodies the cultural logics of the societies they serve; see Rosen, *The Anthropology of Justice*; Geertz, *Local Knowledge*; Domínguez, *White by Definition.*

123. Part II provides a detailed sociolinguistic study of law school teaching; Part III explores at length issues of diversity and law school training. No study to date has used tape and transcript analysis of law school classes along the lines of sociolinguistic studies of other classroom settings. However, there has been some close attention to law school training. Although Stone's study does not use direct transcripts of classsroom speech, he employs a psychoanalytic framework to analyze observed interactions. Stone, "Legal Education on the Couch." Shaffer and Redmount use transcript material to illustrate their finding of "erosion" in the traditional Socratic style and to demonstrate the advantages of more "low-pressure" teaching styles. Shaffer and Redmount, *Lawyers, Law Students, and People.* Both Stover and Philips use material from their own experience as social scientists going to law school. Stover, *Making It and Breaking It*; Philips, "The Language Socialization of Lawyers." And Granfield uses some direct quotation of classroom exchanges to illustrate aspects of law school training. Granfield, *Making Elite Lawyers.*

## Chapter 3

1. See, e.g., Spradley, *Participant Observation*, 3–16 and passim; Geertz, *Interpretation of Cultures*, 3–30; Greenhouse et al., *Law and Community*, 7–21.

2. See, e.g., Mehan, *Learning Lessons*; Cazden, *Classroom Discourse*; Heath, *Ways with Words.*

3. Cazden, *Classroom Discourse*, 3–4.

4. For a study of differential treatment of students in high- and low-ability reading groups, see Collins, "Socialization to Text"; for a study of schools in two neighboring rural communities, see Heath, *Ways with Words*; for a comparison across classrooms with students from differing cultural and social class backgrounds, see Cazden, *Classroom Discourse.*

5. Conley and O'Barr, *Rules versus Relationships*, 125, 172–177.

6. Sarat and Felstiner, *Divorce Lawyers.*

7. Conley and O'Barr, *Rules versus Relationships*, 165, 173.

8. Matoesian, *Reproducing Rape* (tracing gendered patterns in talk about rape in the courtroom); Merry, *Getting Justice and Getting Even* (tracing differences across class in discourse and orientation toward law); Frohmann, "Discrediting Victims' Allegations."

9. If a student's identity was not clear from the tape and was missing from the in-class coder's sheet, we coded it as "unknown."

10. Interestingly, students in several of the schools actually approached our coder before the coder had invited students to these small group interviews; they wanted to be sure their perspectives would be included in the study. As noted, I also performed on-site intercoder reliability checks. In addition to passing review by the Human Subjects Committee of the American Bar Foundation, we underwent additional IRB review as requested by individual schools.

11. Thus, for example, a "focused" dialogue was one in which the professor interacted with one student for more than two exchanges (four turns); a "nonfocused" dialogue involved the professor engaging several different speakers for no more than one consecutive turn each.

12. In several cases where coders left the project before completing an entire semester of tapes, another coder checked each turn that had already been coded, in effect recoding, and then finished the remaining classes. We were fortunate to have one stalwart coder who single-handedly coded many of the schools, thus ensuring quite high consistency even between schools. She also served as a standard when other coders encountered difficult coding decisions. We also conducted formal intercoder checks.

13. Nancy Matthews and Susan Gooding, the two project managers, were each meticulous in their concern for detail, often personally checking turn-by-turn through the schools to ensure consistency in coding.

14. In addition, we developed overviews of the semester for each classroom, both through overarching school ethnographies and through tracking sheets that charted how doctrines and legal issues were presented through the semester, and kept track of how social context, role-playing, and metalevel discussions were handled in each class.

15. A classic discussion can be found in Sacks et al., "A Simplest Systematics," 7; see also Atkinson and Drew, Order in Court; Matoesian, Reproducing Rape.

16. Transcription conventions are outlined at the front of the book. In adopting them, I have been responsive to Conley and O'Barr's admonition: "Those of us who do law and language research must . . . rethink our transcription conventions. . . . [Some] transcripts are extremely difficult for nonspecialists to work with." Conley and O'Barr, Just Words, 139.

17. For purposes of much of the quantitative analysis reported here, we removed backchannel and background comments. However, we retained the coding for future analysis, which can compare and contrast different kinds of classrooms and speech styles along these dimensions as well.

18. As noted, conversation analysts have developed a useful analytic framework for studying conversation. An adjacency pair is a unit of conversation consisting of two turns, in which one speaker takes the first turn (the first "pair-part") and another speaker takes the second (the second pair-part). Generally, the first pair-part provides a frame for the second; so, for example, if I greet you ("Hi"), my first turn places some pressure on you to greet me back. Or, more to the point here, if I ask you a "question," there is a strong conversational framing favoring a second pair-part "answer" to that question. See Levinson, Pragmatics, 303–304, for an introduction to these concepts.

19. The silent turn here functions in the same way that a spoken response might if the student had said "I don't know" or "Could you give me some help?" In this sense, it could be interpreted as a "zero sign," indicating, perhaps, that the speaker is having difficulty answering.

20. The term "minority" has rightfully been critiqued as Eurocentric; worldwide, it is clearly the case that the many groups lumped together under that aegis are the majority. Because I am synthesizing work from numerous studies (focusing on the United

States, where whites have traditionally formed the majority of the population), I use various terminologies; when the word "minority" is used, it is to be read as having a bracketed meaning.

## Part II

1. Levi, *Introduction*, 3–4.
2. Williams, *Alchemy*, 164.

## Chapter 4

1. Turow, *One L*, 47–49.
2. Angel, "What It's Like," 809–813.
3. In similar fashion, one might begin the study of a particular religious ritual by examining a canonical version from which specific performances of the ritual in different times and places is likely to vary. Of course, this gives rise to a number of interesting debates and issues; for example, are individual performances simply renditions or "versions" of the canonical form, or is the relationship more complex? Barbara Hernnstein Smith has argued compellingly against an approach that deems many renditions of folk tales to be mere versions of some underlying, canonical story (the "Cinderella" story, perhaps). Hernnstein Smith, "Narrative Versions."

Another set of concerns: Does it matter that the priest or shaman works from a rich and complex symbolic understanding of what is happening if that model is not shared by the bulk of the people participating in the ritual? What is the relationship between expert knowledge and folk knowledge in such matters? One tradition in anthropological studies of religion has focused on expert knowledge, as if religious experts were the key source of cultural understandings of religious practices. Indeed, anthropological work focusing on expert religious understandings at times relied on single members of a society to translate the "religious system" of an entire group. See, e.g., Reichel-Dolmatoff, *Amazonian Cosmos*. This can be problematic for those who approach the religious system as something that is shared and social and differentially understood. Thus, some anthropologists have insisted on understanding the way religion is translated by the people on the street, examining the refraction of religious lore and canon through the practices of these people. See, e.g., Jean Comaroff, *Body of Power*.

In this case, we deal with a genre (Socratic method law school teaching) as it is performed in practice, and so we are observing an intersection of the expert knowledge of the "high priest" (in this case, forgive the metaphor, the professor) and the lay understanding of the congregation (the students) as they come together in a jointly produced performance. Although some of the classrooms in this study approximate the standard Socratic style, even in these classes we find some variation from the canonical approach (hence my use of the label "modified Socratic" to describe them). One of the classes in the original pilot study for this project did come very close to the prototypical Socratic style, and so I use transcripts from that classroom to illustrate the prototype in action. (Because we did not tape an entire semester for the pilot classrooms, we cannot determine to what degree even the teaching in this class might have begun to diverge from the standard image over time, just as we cannot really be sure that any actual class ever completely conformed to the legend, as we'll see in Chapter 7.)

4. Bauman and Briggs, "Poetics and Performance," 67.
5. Id., 68.

6. Id., 72–74.

7. Or, in some cases, a text-artifact can be the physical rendition of the text in speech and/or action.

8. Silverstein, "Secret Lives of Texts," 81 and passim; see also Silverstein and Urban, "Natural History." Thus, if I read you a story about the history of a clan, or the legal profession, we could distinguish (1) a text-artifact (the written story); (2) a number of possible denotational texts, centered on the content of the story (the meaning each teller and listener takes from the story; think, perhaps, of asking multiple listeners to retell the story after I've read it, and then analyzing how the various "Rorschachs" we generate from this exercise do and don't overlap); and (3) a number of possible "interactional" texts, centered on what I am doing when I read the story (e.g., initiating you into the clan or the legal profession, warning you about the dangers of the past so that you will behave differently now). Note, then, that as in so many instances of linguistically generated meaning, there is a metalevel structuring that forms the backbone of how we create and understand "texts."

I have chosen not to use the more technical vocabulary throughout this volume but, as noted, have generally indicated the distinction between text-artifact and other kinds of text by speaking of the written texts found in legal opinions and casebooks when talking about legal text-artifacts. It is also interesting to note that, again on a more technical level, the method used here does not allow me to generate an account of group interactions such as classes in terms of the individual participants' denotational or interactional texts. (Indeed, it is difficult to imagine doing this in any fine-grained, ongoing way, for any substantial group of people.) The interviews whose results are reported in Chapter 7 do give us some sense of possible points of differentiation along these dimensions. But my primary emphasis here is on the institutional level and the ways patterned institutional discourse styles reregiment participants' orientations to the reading of text-artifacts more superficially, and, further, to the entextualization, recontextualization, and interpretation of conflict stories or texts and other legally relevant social narratives.

9. The authority of previously written legal cases also depends on the status of the court from which the opinion was issued. In the federal court system, for example, an opinion of the U.S. Supreme Court would have more authority as precedent than an opinion of one of the intermediate federal appellate courts (e.g., the First or Second, etc., Circuit Courts of Appeal).

10. When I speak of the precedential "text," I want to point to the conflation in native ideology of what Silverstein would call text-artifact with the texts that are in play in the process of making precedents. This conflation is encouraged by the fact that there is frequently a heavy focus on a precise word or phrase from the original text-artifact, so that a linguistic formula such as "inherently dangerous" is literally repeated in the new text-artifact. This reification of and focus on "surface segmental" aspects of the language, where written tokens of the type are taken as iconic with (indeed identical with, unmediated by text) each other, is an instance of the ideological predisposition for reference discussed in Chapter 2, note 34.

11. A more precise articulation of the way the legal "classification changes as the classification is made," as Levi puts it, is more readily achieved by using the analytic framework provided by linguistic anthropology than by using the "indigenous" legal theoretic approach, even of the more sophisticated variety. As noted previously, legal scholars and practitioners seem to have difficulty holding onto both aspects of the process at once, thus sliding alternatively into naïve referential reification and skeptical nihilism. See Mertz and Weissbourd, "Rule-Centrism versus Legal Creativity"; Winter, "A Clearing in the Forest," 11. Nor does legal theory provide a clear framework for sorting out how legal language operates in the process of entextualization and recontextualization.

12. Bauman and Briggs, "Poetics and Performance," 76–78. This is one example of how the "metapragmatic" level plays an important role in structuring communication.

13. As Silverstein notes, reading a written text is "a socioculturally contextualized practice of entextualization, which demands its own ethnographic account." Silverstein, "Secret Life of Texts," 81. To be interpreted by readers, the written text-artifact

> stimulates an entextualization in an appropriate context; it is the mediating instrumentality of a communicative process for its perceiver, for example, a reader of an alphanumeric printed page such as the one before you. To confuse the mediating artifact and its mode of production ("inscription") for a text and the sociosemiotic processes that produce it perpetuates a particular fetishized substitution. (Silverstein and Urban, "Natural History," 2 n. 1)

One reason this confusion is not useful is that it obscures the necessary processes of contextualization that occur every time anyone encounters and seeks to make sense of a written text. Instead, this conflation encourages a naïve "referentialist" ideology that views writings as self-contained, as self-interpreting apart from human agency. Any resulting analysis will lack precision in tracing the role of written texts in semiotic mediation—in creating relationships among the human beings who are communicating with one another by means of those writings. It will similarly elide distinctions among the varying kinds of entextualizations that can emerge from the same written text, thereby losing the analytical capacity for sorting out how, when, where, and why these variations occur.

14. In other words, what we would call "pragmatic" aspects of meaning. Note that performance is only one modality through which written texts can be entextualized and contextualized; they can obviously be rendered or interpreted in other formats as well. (And I use "contextualized" here as a shorthand way of communicating the more involved process through which "chunks" of discourse are created as texts ["entextualization"], removed from one context ["decontextualized"] and used in another context ["recontextualized"].)

15. And of course, the teacher will not have the original written text-artifact in front of him or her, nor will the students be referring to it; they will likely have a printed rendition of this classic written text (or an excerpt thereof) in their textbooks. In this narrow technical sense, almost no one is reading the "identical" written text, unless they have borrowed the same book from another interpreter.

16. By "index," we mean that it carries significance because it points to its meaning in context. See Peirce, *Collected Papers.*

17. Bauman and Briggs, "Poetics and Performance," 32.

18. Collins, "Socialization to Text," 203; see also de Castelle and Luke, "Defining 'Literacy' "; Olson, "From Utterance to Text."

19. Collins, "Socialization to Text," 204–206; see also Cook-Gumperz, "Schooling and Literacy," 16.

20. For an in-depth exposition of this dynamic generally, see Bauman and Briggs, "Poetics and Performance," 34–38.

21. Collins, "Socialization to Text," 224.

22. As noted in Chapter 2, the Socratic method has been the subject of controversy from its inception. It emerged as part of a larger theory of the law that was introduced at the Harvard Law School in 1870 by Christopher Columbus Langdell. (The story is replete with symbols significant in the American cultural tradition.) Langdell's method was modeled on an ideal type of the question-and-answer style of Socratic dialogue, using casebook readings from appellate cases as the foundation for discussion. After overcoming some vociferous early opposition, this teaching method soon became the dominant mode of teaching in American law schools. Stevens, *Law School,* 59–64. Langdell connected his

pedagogical innovation with his more general quest to establish the study of law as a true science:

> Law, considered as a science, consists of certain principles or doctrines. To have such a mastery of these as to be able to apply them with constant facility and certainty to the ever-tangled skein of human affairs, is what constitutes a true lawyer; and hence to acquire that mastery should be the business of every earnest student of law. (Langdell, preface, vi–vii)

In this view, the data of legal science were to be found, for the most part, in legal opinions, which were to be studied in the way that zoologists and botanists study animals and plants so that the data can be properly classified. Langdell viewed his brand of Socratic method teaching as a superior way of teaching students this classification process. Ironically, although his substantive vision of legal science has long since been discredited, Landgell's closely allied innovation in legal pedagogy has remained the signal method for law teaching through current times. The debate in the legal academy, reviewed in Chapter 2, continues to rage. Popular representations of law school in the United States, in books and film, have made a harsh variety of Socratic method teaching synonymous with law school pedagogy in the public eye. See, e.g., *The Paper Chase*; Turow, *One L*.

23.  Transcript 4.1 presents a curious combination of messages. On the surface, the professor invokes Kingsfield (an intimidating professor on whose class the film *The Paper Chase* focused) to reassure this year's class that he has no desire to intimidate them. On the other hand, his use of directly reported speech to stand in Kingsfield's shoes (or speak in his voice), even if only humorously and for a moment, reminds them vividly of the authoritative position he occupies while also indexing (if in caricature) an image of the distinctive, combative legal discourse they are about to enter.

24.  Bourdieu and Passeron, *Reproduction*, 109.

25.  D. Kennedy, *Legal Education*, 3.

26.  J. Gee, "The Narrativization of Experience," 24; see discussion in Chapter 2.

27.  Data for this discussion were drawn from one of the two classrooms used in the pilot study that I performed prior to conducting the full-blown study, because it is the class that conforms most closely to the canonical Socratic style. The class was held in a law school that would be categorized as an elite/prestige law school, by a quite senior white male professor, himself trained at an elite law school.

28.  See discussion of Van Gennep and Turner in Chapter 2.

29.  See Mertz, "Consensus and Dissent," for a more in-depth discussion.

30.  Note in Transcript 4.2 the use of "Well" by the professor to mark disagreement and to signal his ensuing cue to the student that she needs to try again. This gives her an opportunity to repair her previous, off-the-mark response, and also provides a brief delay in which she can rethink her reply. When the student mimics the professor with her own "Well," we can understand it as also marking a brief delay, at the same time as it provides a form of coherence with the professor's previous utterance. In Chapter 7, we track issues of coherence, repair, reframing, and discourse markers in more detail; in Chapters 6 and 7 we examine further the dialogic form found in law school classrooms. As we will see, small words like "well," "now," "all right," and "wait" are frequently carrying heavy discursive loads in these classrooms.

31.  Compare this excerpt with Transcript 4.7, in which a professor similarly interrupts a student who attempts to begin her retelling of the conflict story in this case—fairly predictably, given more usual storytelling norms—by introducing one of the main characters. Again the student is refocused on legal frames for her narrative.

32. Of course, in pragmatic terms, the repeat itself indexes an unsuccessful answer, and this structural pragmatic message is often reinforced through pitch and intonation. Thus, although there is nonuptake in a referential sense, there is some pragmatic response in the subsequent question to the previous answer, the response being a negative indication about the answer that preceded it. Conversation analysts would approach this as a form of repair, in which the professor is attempting to prompt the student to correct her previous utterance.

33. Collins, "Socialization to Text"; see also Anyon, "Social Class and School Knowledge"; Leacock, "Education in Africa." On uptake generally, see Collins, "Using Cohesion Analysis."

34. This opens up some interesting comparisons between professorial modes of discursive control in law classrooms and judges' approaches to maintaining courtroom control. See Philips, *Ideology*. An obvious parallel is the constant control of turns and therefore shaping of ongoing discourse by attorneys and judges. Id.; see also Atkinson and Drew, *Order in Court*.

35. There are actually a variety of possible procedural wrinkles; for example, the case may have been shaped by the procedures of the administrative agency whose decision is under review. For ease of reference I use the trial court as a model here.

36. Levi, *Introduction*.

37. Toulmin, *The Uses of Argument*, 98–99.

38. As noted in Chapter 2, anthropological linguists would speak of this as an indexical and iconic relationship, drawing from the work of Charles Sanders Peirce. By "index," we mean that it carries significance because it points to its meaning in context. Interestingly, in this case, the language used is also an icon of its meaning; that is, it carries meaning by virtue of a similarity in shape or form (just as, for example, a triangle can represent a pyramid by virtue of a shared form). See Peirce, *Collected Papers*; see also Mertz, "Beyond Symbolic Anthropology." When these two functions combine to create an indexical icon—that is, signs carrying meaning both by pointing to context and by echoing the form of that which they represent—they become particularly potent vehicles for cultural meanings. See Silverstein, "Metaforces of Power"; Mertz, "Recontextualization as Socialization." Silverstein and Parmentier have demonstrated how political oratory can operate as an indexical icon of the social structure it reinforces. Silverstein, "Metaforces of Power"; Parmentier, "The Political Function of Reported Speech." One interesting implication of this sort of analysis is that the pragmatic structure of language may, in certain crucial institutionalized situations, work at a level of which speakers are unaware to make some social outcomes seem natural or inevitable. This subliminal aspect of the pragmatic structure of major cultural discourse forms would seem to be of particular interest in situations where language is used for socialization and the creation of new social identities.

As we have seen, the structure of classic Socratic classroom discourse mirrors the ideology it seeks to impart at the same time as it points to aspects of text that are ideologically significant. If we were to look for the legal equivalent of the "model of the polity" that is sometimes mirrored and indexed in political rhetoric, the parallel here would be the core legal model of argumentative discourse as a source of truth. As we will see, this fundamental trope lies at the heart of the model of justice that is conveyed to law students, providing epistemological anchoring and normative orientation. In Peircean terms, then, Socratic classroom discourse is an indexical icon of the worldview it attempts to convey, and thus can arguably pack a powerful subliminal punch in reorienting students to a new legal reading of texts.

At the same time, we've seen that there is a more subtle way in which the very structure of Socratic questioning is reflexive, using pragmatic structure in the classroom to impart a new, heavily indexical orientation to the reading of conflict stories. Here we might talk of a slightly different dynamic, in which the classroom discourse's indexical structure teaches through a reflexive mirroring (as opposed, for example, to teaching through a more semantico-referential "explanation" of what it seeks to convey). At this more local level, then, we might talk of a kind of *iconic indexical* structure to classroom discourse, just in the sense that it reorients students through a mirroring indexical calibration of classroom discourse to the metapragmatics of a new textual ideology. Arguably, then, there is a double indexical mirroring of legal-discursive structures occurring through Socratic method teaching. This would only further reinforce a sense of fit between the classic pedagogy and what it seeks to impart, regardless of its actual efficacy.

39. There is, however, an interesting commonality between Collins's lowest status group and the law school class analyzed in this section; in both, there is arguably a break with the "liberal" notion that semantic meaning is what a text is all about. Instead, the meaning of texts lies in the pragmatic orientation that teachers impart through regimenting classroom speech. At the same time, there is an obvious difference between highest and lowest status classrooms. The low-ability students are taught to submit to the text—to pronounce it and nothing else—whereas the law student's pragmatic discipline is aimed at mastery and manipulation. In exploring contrasts among such differing social settings and approaches to text, we can begin to see the relation between social power and the regimentation of text, enacted in the critical process of socialization to text through the de- and recentering of written texts in classroom speech. We can also see that it would be a mistake to read transparently from discourse form to social function.

40. Although the parallel is striking, I do not mean to imply here any transparent continuity between the discourse style of the classroom and the discourses used in legal practice of various kinds. Rather, the classroom discourse is a semiotic disciplining to a new form of reading and discursively organizing written texts, and this form of reading will of course be multiply recontextualized in the various speech settings of legal practice.

41. See Chapter 6. In *Divorce Lawyers and Their Clients*, Sarat and Felstiner demonstrate that divorce lawyers commonly urge their clients to separate off parts of themselves, distancing from emotion in order to concentrate on forming a self that thinks effectively in legal terms. As we will see, law professors urge a similar separation on their students, pushing them toward a self defined in terms of legal-discursive positioning. See Mehan, "The Construction of an LD Student," 274, for discussion of a broadly defined distinction between the removed stance of professionals and the more local, contextual construction of self found in everyday discourse. I locate the abstract self of law school and legal discourse within this broad professional category, but I also point to distinctive features of the abstract individual who emerges in and through legal language.

42. Footing will be discussed in more detail in Chapter 6. The concept is adapted from the work of Erving Goffman, who distinguished different possible kinds of positions people could hold in producing speech. For example, the person who speaks an utterance is the "animator," while someone who composed the words spoken is the "author." Silverstein would characterize the original Socratic dialogues as in fact a form of "dialectic monologue" in which a single voice in the Bakhtinian sense is presented through the literary device of adjacency-pair structures, $(A_1;B_1);(A_2;B_2); \ldots$ for speakers A and B (personal communication, 9/23/05). We see the closest approximations to this in the more canonical Socratic classrooms of this study, but only when things are going relatively smoothly. (See Transcripts 4.2 and 4.3, for some rather mixed examples from one of the pilot study classes, which used the most strictly Socratic style, and Transcripts 7.1, 7.3, 7.4,

and 7.5, analyzing a single class in which professor and student in a modified Socratic class-room coproduced a very smooth case narrative.) Of course, even in the more Socratic class-rooms, there are many instances where students do not take their cues, and their voices then emerge quite clearly as distinct from that of the professor. Alternatively, the goal of a Socratic exchange might be to in fact draw forth several different voices, as when the pro-fessor argues one position (say, the plaintiff's) while asking the student to argue another (perhaps the defendant's). (Or different students may occupy these positions.) And then there are the classrooms characterized more by shorter exchanges, in which a merry po-lyphony of voices can sometimes be heard. (See Transcripts 7.8, 7.10, 7.11, and 7.12 for examples of nonmonologic exchanges.) Interestingly, though, one could analyze some segments of the more diffuse exchanges, involving multiple students, as coproduced mono-logue—as when the professor provides a frame punctuated by questions that individual students (or even the class as a whole) chime in to answer correctly in simple words or phrases.

43. Although there is some discussion of statutes (i.e., legislation passed by legisla-tures such as Congress), regulations, and other legal genres, reading cases overwhelmingly dominates the first-year classes of this study. We therefore primarily focus on the struc-ture of the case law genre and core features of a legal reading thereof. Where relevant, I also point out aspects of other genres, demonstrating that they indeed only accentuate further the aspects of a legal reading outlined in our discussion of reading cases. On the case law genre generally, see Mertz, "'Realist' Models," "The Uses of History," and "Con-sensus and Dissent"; J. B. White, *The Legal Imagination* and *When Words Lose Their Mean-ing*. In first-year Contracts classes, the Uniform Commercial Code is a common subject for this kind of discussion, although professors vary considerably in the degree to which they focus on the UCC. More advanced skills needed for reading the genre of statutes or uniform laws (such as parsing legislative history) are generally reserved for upper-level courses.

44. J. L. Austin, *How to Do Things with Words*. See Yovel, "Language beyond Law" and "What Is Contract Law 'About'?" for important discussions of performativity in legal language.

45. This discussion of legal texts and readings relies on the linguistic data collected for this study and presents structural features of the discursive logic of case law that are commonly highlighted by professors. Thus, the organization of this part of the chapter reflects the categories that emerge from linguistic analysis of the data, rather than the ca-nonical order of the dissection of cases as it occurs in classes. As we will see, that ordering is somewhat different, typically beginning with a recitation of the facts or procedural his-tory, and then moving on to the legal issue and holding.

46. Black, *Law Dictionary*, 731.

47. Note that this is a form of "intertexuality."

48. In Silverstein's terms, the procedural history provides one kind of "interactional text" for the reading of cases. Silverstein "Metapragmatic Discourse," 36. Note that pro-cedural history is only one variety of the interactional texts that can be found in legal opin-ions. Insiders can read certain appellate opinions as expressions of power struggles among competing judges or justices, as the products of negotiations among judges and clerks (who write substantial portions of many decisions), as attempts to mediate political or social struggles of various sorts, and so forth.

49. On the concept of a metalinguistic filter that interprets social change and sub-tly impacts people's worldviews, see Mertz, "No Burden to Carry" and "Sociolinguistic Creativity."

50. Levi, *Introduction*, 3–4.

51. J. B. White, *When Words Lose Their Meaning*, 268.

52. See Mertz, "Consensus and Dissent."

53. Levi, *Introduction*, 18.

54. Id.

55. See, e.g., Matoesian, *Law and the Language of Identity*; Pomerantz, "Attributions of Responsibility."

56. Appellate courts generally refuse to second-guess trial courts on factual issues, in part out of deference to the firsthand opportunity that the trier of fact (the jury or, in a bench trial, the judge) had to observe and assess witnesses in person (an aspect of evidence known as "demeanor evidence"). Only in exceptional instances, where a trial court has made a "clearly erroneous" decision, will an appellate court intervene over issues of fact; these kinds of cases are not typically included in casebooks because they don't help in elucidating doctrine.

57. Again, note the use of seemingly little words like "wait" in this transcript to mark pedagogical transitions; here it signals an interruptive repair in which the professor seeks clarification. See also Transcript 4.18, in which the professor uses "Wait now" for similar purposes; later in the transcript she uses "Well, now wait a second" to interrupt the student's narrative and initiate an instructional repair in which she explains how the legally structured narrative should be ordered, and then gives the student an opportunity to try again.

58. Here we see the use of "okay" and "all right" as emphatic markers serving multiple discursive purposes; Chapter 7 discusses this phenomenon in depth.

59. This is obviously not true in the Civil Procedure classes taught to first-year students, and it is likely that there is also variation regarding discussions of procedure in some other classes, such as Legal Writing.

60. Note that, as Levi's analysis demonstrates, the courts themselves may not be able to clearly articulate the principle behind their decisions to view some analogies as apt and others not. Rather, there may be an amorphous, culturally based sense that one set of events ought to be remediated by law and others not—and some decisions may lack even that sense of coherence. Over time, a doctrinal principle gains coherence as courts and commentators perceive a guiding principle behind the evolving decision. The genius of this is that shared cultural understandings can slowly enter the law as principles through a gradual process wherein courts express a general, emergent social consensus (much in the way Robert Burns has argued juries do; see Burns, *A Theory of the Trial*). The danger, of course, is that there may be a variety of opinions as to how certain situations should be dealt with across various strata of a society, and that the courts have much better access to elite than nonelite points of view (clearly problematic in a purportedly democratic state).

61. This is something of a simplification, as the class discussion had evolved into a more complex discussion of the issues surrounding unilateral contract formation, as when an offeror invites acceptance through performance. But understanding of these complexities is not necessary to the central point I'm making here.

62. One could think of this as reading for varying "interactional texts." The recourse to "unregulated" storytelling in law school classrooms finds an interesting parallel in the jury room, where jury members during deliberations often tell stories that are not part of the formal evidence (and therefore have not been subjected to the usual legal procedural safeguards, such as cross-examination). Bennett and Feldman, *Reconstructing Reality*.

63. Sarat and Felstiner, *Divorce Lawyers*, document the way that divorce attorneys use this kind of narrative to lower their clients' expectations of the legal process while also increasing their dependence on the attorney's networks and expertise.

64. This is an example of how political and legal texts can serve as indexical icons of political and social structures, as discussed earlier.

## Chapter 5

1. In this classroom, unlike most of the others in the study, the professor called on students by their first names. In accordance with our human subjects protocol, I have changed the names of the students so as not to provide identifying information, but I am using first names in the text to convey the informal character of the discourse.

2. Note that the first "I'm sorry?" here initiates an abortive comprehension check; the professor didn't initially understand the student. The "Oh" signifies her quick comprehension of the student's comment, followed by an apology.

3. See Yovel on the related concept of "normative importation" and in the context of contract law. Yovel, "The Language beyond Law" and "What Is Contract Law 'About'?"

4. Of course, because no exacting linguistic study of the Socratic method in its heyday exists, we cannot be sure to what extent the stereotype captured actual practice. It could be that even the classic Socratic teachers paused here and there for mini-lectures or gave students answers to a greater degree than is admitted by the standard stereotype. See Chapter 7.

5. Transcript 4.16, in which a modified Socratic teacher briefly digresses to discuss the possible influence of race on a case under discussion, illustrates the fact that there is overlap among the different teaching styles I've identified. In this case, the professor gives a brief lecture that is bracketed on each side (and in the middle) by question-answer format.

6. See also Chapter 4, note 42.

7. Technically, the UCC is a proposed uniform law that must be separately adopted in each state if it is to have effect there, and the states are free to refuse entirely or to adopt with alterations. It is quite common, however, for first-year Contracts classes to use the UCC itself rather than any particular state statute.

8. It is also the case that both of the professors of color in the study (one woman, one man) are included in this group of teachers who rely more on shorter exchanges. It is obviously inadvisable to generalize from these findings, however, partly because this study does not involve a large random sample that would permit such a generalization, and partly because that sort of approach would invite an essentializing of race and discourse that is unsupported by any solid research. (By contrast, there are some indications in the social science literature of possible gendered differences in approaches to discourse, although the area is predictably rife with debate, and again it would be important to give careful consideration to the nuances and variations found across contexts.)

9. Note, however, that 47% of class time is spent in dialogue of some sort, as opposed to 10% in the predominantly lecture class, a marked difference.

10. Transcript 4.15, also from a short-exchange classroom, shows the open texture of policy discussions in such classes, with two students speaking one after the other, unmediated by the professor (a very rare occurrence in the law school classrooms of this study, found for the most part in the short-exchange classrooms). Yet in Transcript 4.18, at the end of the chapter, we see once again the versatility of discussion in these classrooms, as the professor uses a more typical Socratic form to invite a statement of facts from the student, and then repeatedly interrupts to be sure the student properly separates legal conclusion from initial fact construction.

11. See Chapter 4, note 48.

12. In one sense, it will not be surprising to hear that teachers can use vastly different styles to convey the same ideas. But there is a particular question about this in law,

where the teachers are attempting to shift students' approach to discursive style itself, along with accompanying ideologies of text and language. The mystique surrounding Socratic training in law schools has survived generations of assaults by now; this study suggests some reasons why that might be. At the same time, it demonstrates the multitude of ways professors can convey the same message through a variety of discursive forms.

13. Philips, *Ideology*, 28.

14. Id., 85.

## Chapter 6

1. I except scholars who have examined the law school process critically and/or from an empirical point of view—for example, Robert Granfield, whose sociological study of law school education takes a somewhat similar approach to the question. Granfield, *Making Elite Lawyers*.

2. See, e.g., Kahlenberg, *Broken Contract*; Kerlow, *Poisoned Ivy*; Granfield, *Making Elite Lawyers*.

3. This is by no means unique to legal education. For example, the Gaelic speakers I studied during my doctoral dissertation research had a phrase, "no burden to carry," that distilled an older linguistic ideology regarding their language. See Mertz, "Language and Mind" and "No Burden to Carry."

4. See, e.g., Erlanger and Klegon, "Socialization Effects"; Granfield, *Making Elite Lawyers*; D. Kennedy, *Legal Education*.

5. Granfield, *Making Elite Lawyers*, 52.

6. Id., 59, 98.

7. For a discussion of the way language and language ideologies can act as filters for social experience and the formulation of social identity, see Mertz, "Pragmatic and Semantic Change" and "Sociolinguistic Creativity."

8. On conceptualizing language as more than a transparent filter for legal interaction, see Mertz, "Language, Law, and Social Meanings."

9. See Sarat and Felstiner, *Divorce Lawyers*.

10. See Bakhtin, *The Dialogic Imagination*.

11. See Briggs, *Disorderly Discourse*; Matoesian, *Law and the Language of Identity*; Parmentier, "The Political Function of Reported Speech"; Tannen, "Waiting for the Mouse."

12. Matoesian, *Law and the Language of Identity*, 111.

13. Goffman, *Forms of Talk*.

14. Id., 128.

15. See Hanks, *Referential Practice*.

16. Of course, this use of imagined direct quotation is not unique to law teaching; it is also found in everyday conversation, as well as in other kinds of teaching. On the one hand, it may have one kind of shared impact across many contexts; that is, it makes the point more vividly, in essence dramatizing it. On the other hand, it is necessary to examine each context carefully to understand the social, institutional, and normative functions of proceeding in this more dramatic or vivid way. In this case, we are examining the metapragmatic meaning of a move into direct quotation in the particular context of legal discourse and pedagogy.

17. Matoesian, *Law and the Language of Identity*, 105, 155–159.

18. See Bennett and Feldman, *Reconstructing Reality in the Courtroom*; Pennington and Hastie, "A Cognitive Theory of Juror Decisionmaking."

19. Matoesian, *Law and the Language of Identity*, 107.

20. There is an interesting shift in speech styles when the professor begins to quote the Indiana company: "Listen, we got this law in Indiana . . . " This shift does arguably serve a pedagogical function: to keep students engaged through a more vivid rendition of the hypothetical exchange. But it also seems to signal a change from "professor speak" to the language of the "man on the street," conveying a sense that we are moving out of a classroom and listening in on "real" talk. As we move further into the turn, the professor slides back into a more formal legal-pedagogical register, using phrases like "common-wealth of Indiana" and "can be made subject to Indiana's law." Interestingly, when we begin to hear the defendant company's voice, there is once more a shift to a more informal style: "Forget that, I don't do business here."

21. The student actually employs an interesting hybrid quotation form to re-present the response of the plaintiff. He begins with the form usually associated with indirect quota-tion ("the seller [con]tends that"). Use of "that" (a syntactic subordinator) is generally ac-companied by subordination of the remaining part of the quotation to the quoting frame, with predictable shifts in deictics. Instead, the student then produces a quotation that is at first ambiguous, but proceeds into a directive that is clearly in direct quotation form ("allow the personal jurisdiction"). The resulting quotation contains an intriguing combination of analytic remove—making us aware of the student's voice—and immediacy (albeit an im-mediacy that would not work well in actual dialogue with the court, as it employs a style gen-erally used by higher status interlocutors to lower status ones). By the end of the turn, the student has shifted to indirect quotation to represent the language of the contractual clause in question, permitting a nested hierarchy of quotation styles within the short turn that marks off *quoted speech within quoted speech*: the student quoting the plaintiff quoting the contract.

22. Silverstein, personal communication, 9/23/05.

23. Id.

24. See discussion in Chapter 4, note 42. Interestingly, it seems that the most coop-erative turn-taking in the modified Socratic classrooms approaches this ideal more closely than does the more antagonistic discussion found in prototypical Socratic pedagogy. Breaks in the monologic voice are more common when professors do not work as hard to coproduce a smooth narrative. Minimally, continued negative uptake (such as that seen in Transcripts 4.2 and 4.3) indexes a discordant voice that does not fit into the planned narrative stream. When students cannot produce the desired responses, their voices quickly emerge as distinct from that of the (sometimes increasingly overtly frustrated) professor. Even in the smoothest of coproduced Socratic narratives, one can generally discern a mini-mal distinction between the voices that emerge from the interplay of "teacher who is ex-perienced in using this discourse" and "student who is awkwardly attempting to enter a new discourse," often evidenced through quite subtle linguistic features. (And, minimally, through pronominal shifts, as in "What would you argue . . . ?" and "I would argue that. . . . ") Furthermore, as noted, the professors sometimes introduced distinct voices and accompanying shifts in footing into the smoothly coordinated exchanges during role-plays and hypotheticals. Thus the overall picture is quite complex.

25. Again, even in the most seamless of direct examinations we generally find the residual difference in footing indicated by the deictic difference inherent in basic pronomi-nal usage (Attorney: "Did you . . . ?"; Witness: "I did . . . "; etc.), which identify one voice as the "author-ized" source of key information, and the other as the conductor in charge of the flow of talk. And there are often more marked shifts, as when an attorney comments from his or her distinctive perspective on the narrative emerging from the client during direct examination.

26. See Ochs and Schieffelin, "Language Socialization and Acquisition"; Ochs, intro-duction; Schieffelin, *The Give and Take of Everyday Life.*

27. Matoesian, *Law and the Language of Identity*, 107.

28. Here we also see an example of the quick distillation of complex positioning into an easily recontextualized label; this process is ubiquitous in case analysis, and indeed is arguably one of the key semiotic processes through which previous texts are put into action in quick-moving legal discourse, especially as precedents. Of course, in this process, much is simplified, elided, or lost (with complex aspects of social context as a particularly likely casualty).

29. This would likely be different in classes where professors teach the "relational contracts" model, using more sociologically oriented casebooks such as Ian Macneil's original work in the area, or the more recent Wisconsin Contracts materials. See Macneil, *Contracts*; Macaulay et al., *Contracts*. Relational contract approaches do generalize across contexts when developing categories for classifying the relationships with which contract law must deal. In this sense, they move away from socially specific analysis. However, relational contract theory moves decisively into social context in its attention to the relationships that surround formal contracts and, in this sense, takes an important step in the direction of incorporating contextual considerations into legal analysis.

30. There are a few interesting exceptions, for example, cases involving family members.

31. In a sense, this may be even more alienating for students concerned with problems of social inequality, because they will have to restrain strong feelings to perform this act of stepping back. Because the focus of this study was on Contracts classes, it is beyond my scope to discuss further this interesting question: How do students respond to courses in which the very subject matter that law turns into doctrine is social identity?

32. On relational contract from a pedagogical perspective, see Macneil, *Contracts*; Macaulay et al., *Contracts*.

33. Ochs, introduction, 5; see also Schieffelin and Ochs, *Language Socialization*.

34. Schieffelin, *The Give and Take of Everyday Life*, 75–80.

35. Initiated repairs of various kinds have been observed in numerous other linguistic settings, including, notably, courtrooms. In her study of change of plea in Arizona courts, Philips notes in particular a technique she calls "nailing it down," in which judges "simply ask question after question" until they overcome any resistance or denial on the part of defendants and manage to elicit testimony in the desired form. Philips, *Ideology*, 95. The professor in this excerpt arguably takes the process still further, literally directing the student to repeat the exact word needed for him to proceed further in the exchange. But certainly the overall form of law school dialogue, with professors' persistent and sometimes repetitive questioning, can be viewed as having some affinities to this kind of demand for repair on the part of judges (and attorneys), who are similarly reliant on question-answer adjacency pairs in achieving some quite specific, legally constrained, discursive goals.

36. A few of the professors occasionally reminded the students of the historical era in which the case took place; one professor in particular did this far more than the others. However, in the overall sample, invocation of history was unusual.

37. See Nourse, "Passion's Progress," for an astute analysis of how such doctrinal analysis can conceal and naturalize a culturally based and biased calculus.

38. As we have seen, this attempt to reach the street level is at times indexed by shifts in speech style, which are essentially a form of breakthrough to performance.

39. Bernard Weissbourd has similarly described law as a kind of semiotic nexus. Weissbourd, personal communication.

40. A study of attorneys by Garth and Martin revealed that although attorneys can be quite critical of the efficacy of some aspects of legal education, they tend to agree that teaching this background grammar of legal reasoning is one important function that law schools do well. Garth and Martin, "Law Schools."

41. Postone, *Time, Labor, and Social Domination*, 159.

42. Id., 144–148.

43. Id., 158–159.

44. Id., 160.

45. Matoesian, *Law and the Language of Identity*, 37–68.

46. Philips, *Ideology*, 122.

47. Id., 87.

48. Philips discusses this when dealing with the intertextual relationship between written and spoken legal genres. Id., 27–47.

49. Id., 90–91.

50. Elkins notes that lawyers "might reasonably be compared to the 'shape-shifting' figure of Greek mythology—Proteus," constantly shifting between roles and perspectives. Elkins, "The Legal Persona," 750. See also Noonan, *Persons and Masks of the Law*, 19, 167, for a warning that law in its heavy use of roles and masks risks "classifying individual human beings so that their humanity is hidden and disavowed," urging instead that "the community of rational discourse is rooted in the history of human beings. Persons speak to persons, heart unmasked to heart."

51. See Bauman and Briggs, "Poetics and Performance"; Hirsch, *Pronouncing and Persevering*.

52. Conley and O'Barr, *Just Words*, 129.

## Part III

1. Crenshaw, "Mapping the Margins," 1241.

2. Fineman, *The Neutered Mother*, 48. This conception of the construction of gendered lives is the basis of Fineman's conclusion that "women can and should converge to organize around overlapping experiences." Id., 54.

3. Minow, *Making All the Difference*, 390.

## Chapter 7

1. Because this classroom was part of the pilot study, we do not have a semester-long set of transcripts available for the classrooms in the full study. Thus, we cannot provide the thorough, statistically informed picture of the overall distribution of turns that is available for the classrooms in the final study. It is important to have the fuller picture given by a full semester's worth of taping, we have found, because there can be considerable variation among classes in such characteristics as the length of student-professor exchanges, even in the same classroom.

2. See, e.g., Shaffer and Redmount, *Lawyers, Law Students, and People*.

3. Kerr, "Decline."

4. See, e.g., Friedland, "How We Teach," 27–31. Friedland circulated questionnaires to 2,000 law professors and received 574 responses; he notes that "no claims are made for the survey's scientific validity," but argues that the survey nevertheless provides some insight into law professors' practices. Id., 3. (It's unclear on what principle the professors and schools were selected, but the process does not appear to have been strictly random.)

He did find that 97% of the respondents reported using Socratic method teaching "at least some of the time in first year classes." Id., 28. There is no attempt to define Socratic teaching in the survey. The law professors who responded to this survey also reported using a variety of other teaching techniques, particularly in upper-level classes.

5. Id., 28 n. 77; see also Kerr as an example of someone who includes more specific constraints in his definition:

> I consider "traditional" Socratic method to be a teaching style in which the professor selects a single student without warning and questions the student about a particular judicial opinion that has been assigned for class. Often the professor begins by asking the student to state the facts of the case and then asks the student to explain how the court reasoned to an answer. The professor might then test the student's understanding of the case by posing a series of hypotheticals and asking the student to apply the reasoning of the case to the new fact patterns. The purpose of this questioning is to explore the strengths and weaknesses of various legal arguments that might be marshaled to support or attach a given rule of decision. To that end, the professor's inquiries are often designed to expose the weaknesses in the student's responses. (Kerr, "Decline," 113 n. 3)

6. See Shaffer and Redmount, *Lawyers, Law Students, and People*, 166.

7. Id.

8. Friedland, "How We Teach," 28.

9. Id., 28–29.

10. Kerr, "Decline," 122–123.

11. For example, one alternative teaching method mentioned by Friedland is role-playing. "How We Teach," 30. As we will see, however, depending on one's definition of role-playing, it is possible that some kinds of role-play are viewed by many professors as inherent to Socratic teaching. Again, sorting this out and determining with any accuracy just how much change has occurred is close to impossible in the absence of detailed observational data from earlier eras.

12. The three classrooms are in law schools that range from the second largest to the smallest schools in our study (ranging from more than 1,500 students to under 800). Class #1 is the classroom where our research began, and Class #8 was the last to be studied.

Class #1 had 115 students and was a standard, large, first-year Contracts class in an urban local law school in the northeastern United States. The teacher was a European American male in his late forties, a graduate of an elite law school with more than ten years of teaching experience at the time we taped his class. He conducted the class in a format that conformed relatively closely to the stereotype of Socratic law school teaching, calling on students using formal address (Ms. or Mr. + surname), and then asking them to describe and discuss assigned cases. The overall tone in the classroom was noticeably humorous, with repeated laughter by the students and joking by the instructor. With 11.3% students of color, the class was less diverse than the national average (see Table 3.1) and fell into the middle range of the classrooms in the study in terms of diversity. Asian Americans constituted the largest minority group (7.0%) and African Americans the smallest (4.3%). There were no Latino students in the class. In terms of gender, this classroom was again in the middle range relative to other classes in this study and had a slightly higher percentage of women (43.5) than the national average.

Please note that the total percentages given for students of color in each class may include students who were not African American, Asian American, Latino, or Latina, but who also would not be identified as white or Caucasian. We recognize that the kind of classification necessary for quantitative studies of this kind is necessarily crude and lacks the subtlety or precision that more fine-grained qualitative work on race would permit.

Class #4 was another of the larger and more Socratic classrooms in the study. This class of 106 students was taught by a European American man in his early thirties, in a law school that was toward the top of the regional tier of law schools. Trained at an elite law school, this teacher was the least experienced in the study, with fewer than five years in law teaching. Using formal address and a seating chart, he regularly called on students to discuss the day's cases for extended periods. With 12.3% students of color, this class came right after the classes in elite/prestige schools (which were the three most diverse classes in the study) in terms of diversity; however, unlike those classes, this class was considerably less diverse than the national average. This can be seen in every category: 5.7% African American students, 3.8% Asian American students, and 2.8% Latino/a students. The class was third-highest in the study in its percentage of women (44.3).

Class #5 was one of the five large (90+) classes in the study. It had 98 students and was taught by a European American male in an elite/prestige law school. It was one of the most traditional Socratic classrooms in the study in terms of tone and style. The teacher, a man in his midforties who was trained at an elite law school, was one of the most experienced in the study (with more than fifteen years' experience). The class was the third most diverse in the study, with 21.4% students of color: 10.2% African American, 6.1% Asian American, but only 2.0% Latino/a. There was also one Native American student in this class. With 40.8% women, the class fell into the lower-middle range of classes in this study in terms of gender diversity.

13. At oral argument, judges on an appeals court question the attorneys about the case, pointing out deficiencies and pushing them to clarify their arguments. Notice that professors in a classroom of first-year students face a more daunting task, in that they have to keep some kind of discussion going in order to do their job, and they are working with novices not yet fully trained to keep up their part of a difficult exchange. One has to wonder, then, if even the toughest Socratic teachers haven't always employed some of the devices found in our modified Socratic classrooms, just as a matter of pedagogical (and discursive) necessity.

14. Matoesian, *Law and the Language of Identity*, 54–55; see also Atkinson, *Our Masters' Voices*; Tannen, "Repetition in Conversation."

15. There are 14 examples of this in a set of 48 pair-parts (thus constituting more than a quarter of the total pair-parts in the extended dialogue).

16. Atkinson and Drew, *Order in Court*; Tannen, "Repetition in Conversation."

17. The professor begins his turn with positive affirmations of the student's previous turn, such as "right," "yeah," or "okay" in 19 of his 48 turns. He also backchannels the student's ongoing turns using "right" and "okay" at several points.

18. In one of the other modified Socratic classrooms, we find a similar pattern, with the professor talking 79% of the time and clearly giving the students significant breaks. The third modified Socratic classroom has a somewhat less marked distribution in favor of the professor, but he nonetheless occupies almost 70% of class time (67%), leaving the students to hold the floor for only 31% (the remaining percentage is attributed to the whole class, as when the entire class responds to a question).

19. This is one reason that uptake analysis proves to be less fruitful in the modified Socratic classroom; the impact of a student response on the subsequent professor question is significantly attenuated by these intervening discursive segues. A better measure of how the student response is received is frequently found at the beginning of the professor turns in these classes, rather than in the question with which the professor turn ends.

20. To add them up precisely: 19 instances of professor-initial affirmations, 8 of student-initial iconic repetitions/parallelism, 14 instances of professor-initial repetitive parallelism, 2 instances of supportive professor backchannels, totaling 43 instances of cohesive-supportive discursive devices in a sequence of 48 pair-parts. (Note that, of course, some of the devices overlap within a single pair-part.)

21. This also occurs frequently within turns, as when the professor repeats a phrase that a student has produced that is particularly apt ("He's awarding them their expectations, okay, he's awarding them their expectations"), or repeats a phrase he himself has introduced (" 'in accordance with a real or apparent intention of the party against ().' 'Accordance with a real or apparent intention' ").

There is an interesting similarity between law professors' efforts to provide a framework for students' legal narratives in these classrooms and the way that teachers in earlier educational settings build a scaffolding so that students can learn and produce appropriate narratives. Michaels, "Narrative Presentations." The parallels we have found between linguistic routines used here and those used in early education or language socialization suggest that there are some powerful discursive tools in use to help reorient students' linguistic practices.

22. Matoesian, personal communication, 11/21/05.

23. Transcript 7.7 provides some very nice examples of this: the professor begins with an "all right" that marks off the doctrinal question that students are supposed to ask themselves. Note that the segment that is marked off here is simultaneously a chunk of discourse (question-answer pair-part), a projected mental process (approaching the problem as chunks of doctrine to be analyzed in Q/A form), and a section of the applicable legal doctrine ("benefit-detriment question").

In his ensuing commentary, the professor urges the student (and the rest of the class along with her) to quickly reach (epistemic and discursive) certainty by asking (and answering at the same time) the question "right?" three times in succession. (This obviously also contributes to poetic structure as well.) In each case, the student is urged to consider and quickly reject tempting but legally incorrect lines of thought, and this small discourse marker is urging agreement at the same time as it serves multiple other discursive and pedagogical functions.

24. Matoesian suggests that these be thought of as epistemic stance instructions, "bounding each instruction in a sequence but also conveying an aura of epistemic certainty or authority to the proposition." Matoesian, personal communication, 11/21/05. He notes that to the degree that these function iconically with "an epistemologically and ontologically privileged form of knowledge," imparted through the professor's legally framed discourse, there is a subtle mirroring of linguistic and legal authority. Id. It would be interesting to compare the patterning found in law school training with that in other forms of pedagogy to discern more clearly the line separating authoritative features of professors' discourse generally from the features that might be more distinctive to legal training.

25. There is a marked disparity between the amounts of shorter dialogue found in these classes and that found in two of the three modified Socratic classrooms (5% and 6% in these two modified Socratic classes as compared with 13%, 22%, 42%, and 46% in the short-exchange classes). The third modified Socratic classroom (Class #1) provides an interesting exception: there 60% of the time was spent in focused dialogue, but 24% of the time was spent in shorter exchanges. We classified it as a modified Socratic classroom because the overall structure of individual classes in Class #1 was similar to that found in the other modified Socratic classes, with only a few students serving as the key interlocutors on any given day. However, the professor routinely paused to take questions from numerous students at the end of the lengthy Socratic discussions. This contributed to a

higher percentage of shorter exchanges in that classroom than was found in the other, more Socratic classrooms.

26. There is also some variation among the short-exchange classes, with Classes #2 and #3 (interestingly, at opposite ends of the law school status hierarchy) actually having more time spent in extended exchanges than in shorter ones, despite the fact that in each category their relative percentages placed them as considerably less Socratic than the more Socratic classrooms, and as having percentages of shorter discourse most similar to the more conversational classes. The difference in each case is taken up by professor mono- logue, which in Class #2 occupied 50% of the time and in Class #3 occupied 63% of the time. Thus, we could understand these classes as falling closer on the continuum to the lecture-style class than did the two other short-exchange classes (which had 29 and 33% monologue, respectively) and as having a fairly eclectic mix of discourse styles overall.

27. To protect the identities of informants, I have identified students only by an initial (Ms. L., Mr. U., etc.), and these are not the actual initials of their last names. In classes where professors called on students by their first names, I have substituted alter- native first names to convey the overall informal character of the discourse while still preserving anonymity.

28. This night school Contracts class, taught in a local law school, was the third- smallest in the study, with 76 students. The teacher, a European American woman trained at a regional law school, was in her late forties. One of the more experienced teachers in the study, she had been teaching more than ten years. The class was one of the more infor- mal classes in the study, although the teacher did engage in some focused Socratic-style exchanges and extended lecturing. This was the least diverse classroom of the study, with only 6.6% students of color and 32.9% women. There were no Asian American students and only 1.3% African American students. Interestingly, however, the percentage of Latino/ a students was above the national average (5.3).

29. With only 53 students, this Contracts class in a local, midwestern law school was the second-smallest in the study. It was taught by a European American woman in her early forties, trained at a local law school. She was an experienced teacher (more than ten years of teaching). A highly informal classroom characterized by the use of first names and many student-initiated turns, this was also the most egalitarian classroom in the study in terms of gender participation rates. The class far exceeded the national average at the time in percentage of women (54.7); along with Class #8, it had the highest percentage of women in the study. But the class was at the low end in terms of racial diversity, with only 11.3% students of color. In a profile quite similar to that of Class #1 (also taught at a local law school in an urban setting), Class #6 had a high representation of Asian American students (5.7%) and relatively low percentages of African American and Latino/a students (fewer than 2% each). This class, obviously, had "other" minority students as well.

30. As noted in the text, it's a bit difficult to delineate the pair-part structure here at times, but we can count roughly 20 professor turns here mixed in with the turns of the 10 identified and several unidentified students.

31. To be sure, it was also one of the smaller classes, with 53 students. But two of the classes with still smaller numbers of students did not have 100% participation rates, so the difference cannot be attributed solely to the class size.

32. Although, as noted in Chapter 2, there are indications (particularly from the writings of clinical and legal writing professors) that this kind of more active role-play- ing exercise may be growing in popularity along with other nontraditional pedagogical techniques.

33. The remaining short-exchange classrooms were Class #2 and Class #8. Class #2, the largest in the study (135 students), was taught in an elite/prestige law school by a

man of color. The teacher, himself trained in an elite school, was in his midthirties and had been teaching for more than five years. Like the other short-exchange classes, this class did include traditional Socratic features, including some use of the traditional method of calling on students (using formal address) to discuss the day's assigned cases. However, there was also fairly regular rupturing of this formality, with students breaking in to ask questions. This was one of the two most racially diverse classrooms in the study, with 24.0% students of color: 8.1% Asian American and 10.5% African American students. The percentage of Latino students (4.4) was slightly below the national average. In terms of gender, the class was slightly below the national average, with 40.7% women (placing it at the low end of the middle range in terms of classrooms included in this study).

Class #8, also in an elite/prestige law school, was the smallest in the study, with only 32 students. The teacher, a woman of color, was in her early forties and had been teaching more than ten years. A highly informal class, it was also by far the most diverse in the study, with 46.9% students of color: 12.5% African American and 21.9% Asian American students. But the percentage of Latino/a students (3.1) was actually below the national average. The class also had the highest percentage of women in the study (56.2).

34. This Contracts class was taught in a midwestern regional law school; it had 90 students. The professor was a European American male in his late forties who had been trained at a regional law school and was among our more experienced teachers (more than fifteen years). Along with Class #3, this class was at the low end of the study both in terms of racial diversity and gender balance. It had only 7.7% students of color: 3.3% African American, 3.3% Asian American, and 1.1% Latino/a. The class was 33.3% female.

35. Another measure of the degree of ongoing dialogue is the percentage of continuing student turns found in each class (as opposed to first turns). Only 28% of student turns in Class #7 are continuing turns, as opposed to 45 to 90% in the other classes.

36. This is a striking example of why counting turns alone fails to give an adequate picture of overall classroom dynamics.

37. An enduring difference, noted earlier, is the greater number of professor questions devoted to drawing out the desired responses in Socratic classes. However, even in the less focused exchanges we see that although the professors are switching speakers more frequently, they still have to at times fish for promising responses, dropping hints and cues and encouraging comments such as "If you pick this one up, you're going to be reading all of the materials very, very well. This is a difficult question."

38. See Zemans and Rosenblum, *Making of a Public Profession.*

39. It is not uncommon in hierarchical systems to find stricter adherence to certain rhetorical forms in the higher categories. See, e.g., Bright and Ramanujan, "Sociolinguistic Variation," 157, 158–159; Errington, "On the Nature of the Sociolinguistic Sign," 287, 289, 296–303. Garth and Martin have noted that the position of elite law schools in the competitive hierarchy depends in part on the mobilization of similar kinds of symbolic capital. Garth and Martin, "Law Schools and the Construction of Competence," 469, 504–505.

40. In using these categories, I am not endorsing them as measures of merit. Indeed, several classes in schools ranked lower in the status hierarchy do a better job of creating inclusive atmospheres for all of their students, while conveying the legal reasoning skills common to all of the classrooms with arguably as great or more efficacy than some more highly ranked classrooms and schools. However, as anthropologists have always been quick to point out, the indigenous culture's own status hierarchy is an important piece of any adequate sociocultural analysis. It is in that sense that I deploy these categories here, in the same spirit as a social scientist studying a caste system would provide information on the relevant hierarchies without endorsing them.

41. Note that age and years of teaching experience are given in terms of ranges in part to ensure protection of confidentiality.

42. Conley and O'Barr, *Rules versus Relationships*, 58–81.

43. Another factor well worth considering in the future is differences among successive generations of law students; there are at least some indications in recent reports from some of the most elite law schools, from which Socratic teaching can be said to have originally emanated, that at this point in time professors are experimenting with varied and combinations of different teaching formats. See Kerr, "Decline"; Neufeld, "Costs of an Outdated Pedagogy?"; Yale Law Women, *Yale Law School*; Rakoff, "The Harvard First-Year Experiment."

## Chapter 8

1. Guinier et al., *Becoming Gentlemen*.

2. See, e.g., Granfield, *Making Elite Lawyers*.

3. *Grutter v. Bollinger*; *Hopwood v. Texas*; see also Lempert et al., "Michigan's Minority Graduates."

4. For some notable exceptions, see the discussion that follows.

5. For a more detailed account, which includes more complete sets of tables and quantitative results, see Mertz et al., "What Difference Does Difference Make?" (with Wamucii Njogu and Susan Gooding). This report of our research contains more in-depth descriptions of the nuances of classroom discourse patterning in terms of race and gender.

6. This was true of the professors in this study and is reported ubiquitously in the literature on first-year law school teaching as well.

7. See, e.g., Finn, *School Engagement and Students at Risk*; Bossert, *Tasks and Social Relations*; Weinstein, "The Classroom as a Social Context."

8. See, e.g., ABA, *MacCrate Report*; Curran, *Women in the Law*, 18–32, 39–40; Hocker and Foster, "The African-American Lawyer," 20; Wilkins and Gulati, "Why Are There So Few Black Lawyers"; Multicultural Women Attorneys Network, *The Burdens of Both*, 19–27; Eaves et al., "Gender, Ethnicity, and Grades"; Merritt and Reskin, "The Double Minority."

9. Weis, introduction, 1; see also Rist, "Student Social Class and Teacher Expectations."

10. See Weis, introduction, 3–5, 11–15, passim; Kozol, *Savage Inequalities*, 3–6, passim. As Sarah Michaels and James Collins noted:

> It is widely publicized that many children are not acquiring literacy skills to a level that meets official notions of minimum adult competency and that a disproportionate number of these children are from ethnically and linguistically diverse backgrounds. For these reasons, it is important to investigate (a) those classroom activities that encourage the development of literacy skills, (b) the interaction between reader and child during these activities that either provides or denies access to instruction and practice, and (c) the relationship between community-based oral discourse style and the acquisition of literacy. (Michaels and Collins, "Oral Discourse Styles," 219–220)

11. For example, a study of "Hispanic" children in school noted:

> If the class happens to be short a textbook, a puzzle, a desk, or something else, the child to be left out will be Hispanic. The teacher somehow does not "see" the child and everyone else gets materials. This Hispanic child will, then, share a textbook or whatever with someone else, preferably another Hispanic. The teacher explains that Hispanics are more cooperative than the other children, so it's all right. (Ortiz, "Hispanic-American Children's Experiences in Classrooms," 78)

12. Erickson and Shultz, *The Counsellor as Gatekeeper*; Philips, *The Invisible Culture*; Cazden, *Classroom Discourse*.

13. J. Gee, "Narrativization of Experience in the Oral Style," 24; see also Cazden, *Classroom Discourse*.

14. E. Kennedy, "A Multilevel Study of Elementary Male Black Students and White Students," 107. Black male students were also more responsive to school size and the overall socioeconomic status (SES) level at schools, so that smaller schools with lower overall SES composition increased their comfort in participating in class. Id., 109. There is some controversy around the concept of culturally different learning styles and needs. See J. Mitchell, "Black Children after the Eighties." The dangers of crude or essentializing approaches obviously loom large in this area. But carefully contextualized work has actually demonstrated that improved learning resulted for some minority children from application of difference-oriented pedagogical techniques. See, for example, Hue-Pei and Mason, "Social Organizational Factors in Learning to Read"; Barnhardt, "Tuning In"; Tharp, "Psychocultural Variables."

15. Weinstein, "The Classroom as a Social Context," 525.

16. Morine-Dershimer, "Instructional Strategy."

17. Bossert, *Tasks and Social Relations*.

18. Weinstein, "The Classroom as a Social Context," 505, 514.

19. Id., 519.

20. See, e.g., Philips, "Participant Structures and Communicative Competence" and *The Invisible Culture*.

21. See Anyon, "Social Class and the Hidden Curriculum"; Lubeck, "Kinship and Classrooms"; Wilcox, "Differential Socialization in the Classroom."

22. Mickelson, "The Case of the Missing Brackets," 80–82.

23. Trujillo, "A Comparative Examination of Classroom Interactions," 639.

24. Id., 639–640; this differential treatment did not appear to extend to graduate students, of whom professors seemed to have similar expectations regardless of race.

25. Smedley et al., "Minority-Status Stresses." For a general review, see Sedlacek, "Black Students on White Campuses."

26. See, e.g., Fox, "Women and Higher Education," 241, 244, 249. But also note that there are indications that some black women receive strong support from their families in their college ambitions: "There is evidence . . . that black parental attitudes have traditionally been relatively more favorable to college education for daughters than for sons." Carnegie Commission on Higher Education, *Opportunities for Women in Higher Education*, 41.

27. Smedley et al., "Minority-Status Stresses," 434.

28. Banks, "Gender Bias in the Classroom."

29. Id., 535–536.

30. Homer and Schwartz, "Admitted but Not Accepted."

31. Guinier et al., *Becoming Gentlemen*, 27 n. 74, 46, n. 117; for reports on other law schools, see Dowd, "Diversity Matters" (University of Florida Law School); L. Wilson and Taylor, "Surveying Gender Bias" (Northern Illinois University College of Law).

32. Krauskopf, "Touching the Elephant," 324.

33. Wightman, *Women in Legal Education*.

34. Gulati et al., "The Happy Charade." The authors note potential skewing in their results regarding third-year students, as it is the more motivated students who show up for class at this point in law school. (In fairness, it should be noted that a number of previous studies in this area faced difficulties—difficulties that Gulati and his coauthors did not—with response rates, so that there are relatively few existing studies without

some kind of methodological problem limiting our reading of their results. Because my study relies on observational research, I use summaries of other kinds of research simply to provide a broad backdrop for this study, focusing more intensively only on other observational studies.)

35. Id. "Gloomy" responses included students indicating that they were pessimistic about their future career opportunities and dissatisfied with their law school experiences; in addition, they felt that law school was unnecessarily competitive, and they did not agree that faculty treated students respectfully.

36. See discussion of context in Chapter 9.

37. See Mertz et al., "What Difference Does Difference Make?," 63–64.

38. Note that two of the three classes with the smallest racial disparities had disparities in favor of students of color.

39. See also findings from Yale Law Women, *Yale Law School*, 22, 70–71, 81–82, that students of color feel more comfortable seeking out professors of color for mentoring and career help, and that they feel that the presence of professors of color on the faculty provides important role models.

40. Forms of exclusion include calling primarily on boys; giving boys more specific feedback and praise focusing on their work but praising girls for their appearance or neatness; allowing little time for reflection when calling on students, which differentially selected for more aggressive (disproportionately male) speakers; sex segregation outside the classroom, with boys more often involved in active pursuits; and textbooks that feature male achievements, largely leaving female contributions invisible. M. Sadker and Sadker, *Failing at Fairness*; see also Good and Sikes, "Effects of Teacher Sex and Student Sex on Classroom Interaction."

41. AAUW, *Shortchanging Girls, Shortchanging America*, 8–11; M. Sadker and Sadker, *Failing at Fairness*, 77–98; Gilligan et al., *Making Connections* 10, 24–27.

42. M. Sadker and Sadker, *Failing at Fairness*, 79–83; see also D. Sadker and Sadker, "Sexism in American Education," 57; Serbin and O'Leary, "How Nursery Schools Teach Girls to Shut Up."

43. M. Sadker and Sadker, *Failing at Fairness*, 80–81.

44. Id., 64. The authors of this study also point to the effects of pervasive and frequently denigrating sex segregation in schools, as in the following example:

TEACHER: You have written wonderful stories. I want each and every one of you to get a chance to read them out loud. All the girls should go to [the student teacher]. If you talk very softly and don't bother anyone, you can read your stories in the hall. The boys will stay in the classroom with me. (Id., 74–75, 58–63)

45. Jordan, "Teacher-Student Interactions"; M. Sadker and Sadker, *Failing at Fairness*, 50. The AAUW study showed African American girls maintaining their self-esteem better than their white counterparts: where the percentage of white girls expressing positive self-esteem moved from 55% in elementary school to 22% in high school, black girls began higher (65%) and dropped only 7 points (to 58%). AAUW, *Shortchanging Girls, Shortchanging America*, 9. (Of course, this does not mean that self-esteem and support from family can compensate for pervasive subtle institutional discrimination.) "Hispanic" girls were reported as beginning at the highest levels of all in elementary school (68%) but showed the most dramatic drop (to 30%, a drop of 38 percentage points). Even with this dramatic drop, however, Latina girls were expressing higher self-esteem in high school than white girls. Id. Because the study showed that a feeling of importance in the family was crucial to these self-esteem measures, these findings would seem to indicate that African American and Latino families are providing better support to their adolescent females than are white families. (For

similar findings, see Brutsaert, "Changing Sources of Self-Esteem among Girls and Boys in Secondary Schools," 436–437.) This hypothesis is bolstered by the observation that in the other main determinant of self-esteem, academic confidence (to which schools would obviously be an important contributor), African American girls experienced a significant drop. Id.; see also Drury, "Black Self-Esteem and Desegregated Schools," 100.

46. See Feldman, *Escape from the Doll's House*, 21–36; M. Sadker and Sadker, *Failing at Fairness*, 166–167, 168–177, 186; see also Holland and Eisenhart, *Educated in Romance*; Hall and Sandler, *The Classroom Climate*.

47. Fleming, *Blacks in College*, 138–149; Fox, "Women and Higher Education," 241, 244, 249. But note that here, as we observed earlier with regard to some girls of color, there are also indications that some black women receive strong support from their families in their college ambitions. Carnegie Commission on Higher Education, *Opportunities for Women in Higher Education*, 41.

48. Krupnick, "Women and Men in the Classroom," 18. In recent years, the gender gap among undergraduates has narrowed; it will be interesting to examine what, if any, effect this has had on classroom dynamics.

49. Id., 19. Interestingly, our findings lend only partial support to a similar picture in our law schools, for although the two classes in which women had positive participation rates were taught by women, one of the most gender-imbalanced classes of the study was also taught by a woman. This was a class with a more informal, voluntary participation structure, fitting with other findings of the Krupnick study.

50. Id., 19–24.

51. See Brooks, "Sex Difference in Student Dominance Behavior"; Karp and Yoels, "The College Classroom"; Sternglaz and Lyberger-Ficek, "Sex Differences in Student-Teacher Interactions in the College Classroom"; see also Constantinople et al., "The Chilly Climate"; Cornelius et al., "Student-Faculty Interaction in the College Classroom." But see Heller et al., "Assessment of the Chilly College Climate for Women." As we suggest regarding studies of law students' experiences, it seems valuable in this area for researchers to take context into account to a greater degree; as things stand, we cannot tell whether differences among schools might explain some variations in the findings of these studies.

52. Crawford and MacLeod, "Gender in the College Classroom"; O'Keefe and Faupel, "The Other Face of the Classroom"; Wingate, "Sexism in the Classroom," 105.

53. Fassinger, "Understanding Classroom Interaction," 94. Interestingly, a study of undergraduates found that men's self-esteem was less linked to their relational surround than was women's: women's self-esteem was more linked to processes of attachment to others, whereas men's was more connected with "an individuation process in which [their] personal distinguishing achievements [were] emphasized." Josephs et al., "Gender and Self-Esteem," 399–400.

54. They have, however, looked at effects of disciplines or divisions within schools.

55. Feldman, *Escape from the Doll's House*, 15–16, 71; see also Carnegie Commission on Higher Education, *Opportunities for Women in Higher Education*, 53.

56. Of the women students who were under thirty years old, 26.5 to 27.7% reported weekly participation; 44.6% of the women over thirty reported participating on a weekly basis. Banks, "Gender Bias," 141 n. 19. Similarly, younger women were far more likely to report infrequently or never participating. Id.

57. Banks, "Gender Bias (2)," 530–535.

58. Taber et al., "Gender, Legal Education, and the Legal Profession," 1239. Note that one study that compared students' self-reports with their actual scores and grades found a high correlation between self-reports and the actual data, although of course this doesn't

erase the need for caution in this regard. Tucker et al., "Whatever Happened to the Class of 1983?," 156.

59. Homer and Schwartz, "Admitted but Not Accepted," 50. Of the white men, only 36% said that they never asked questions in class, whereas more than half of all other groups responded that they never asked questions (52% men of color, 53% white women, 61% women of color). Id. There were similar results when students were asked whether they volunteered answers in class, but the picture reverses for frequent participation (with higher percentages of white males reporting that they volunteered answers in class and lower percentages of the other students). White males also had a distinctly more positive response to Socratic teaching as well as to law school generally and had overall higher self-esteem; they were the least likely to report that racial or gender diversity in the faculty mattered. See Mertz et al., "What Difference Does Difference Make?" for an in-depth discussion of the Homer and Schwartz results, as well as of other studies summarized in this chapter.

60. Guinier et al., *Becoming Gentlemen.* The survey portion of the University of Pennsylvania study indicated that women reported a participation rate almost half that of men, with first-year females far more likely to say that "men are called on more often than women and receive more time and more follow-up in class, that the sex of students affects class experience, and that sexist comments are permitted" in class.

61. Neufeld, "Costs of an Outdated Pedagogy?," 540.

62. Id., 540–541, 548–550. The results regarding grades rely on percentages of women and men garnering honors or higher grades; they do not control for entering credentials. The survey sample of more than 1,000 responses represents a better response rate than has been the case in some survey studies of individual law schools, with 52% and 50% of the first-year class responding to fall and spring surveys, as well as 40% of the second-year and 33% of the third-year students returning responses for the spring survey.

63. Yale Law Women, *Yale Law School*, 13–19, 29–33, 81. Like the Harvard study, the Yale study had a somewhat better than average response rate (44%) compared to some other surveys that have been conducted in individual law schools, with a decline by year of law school roughly comparable to that in the Harvard study. To the authors' credit, they note that there were substantially more responses from women than men to this survey. (Although my core focus here is on observational studies, I pause here to stress that it is important in survey research to give overt consideration to methodological issues such as response rates, confidence intervals, and potential skewing. An insufficient response can necessitate abandoning a survey if it isn't possible to take adequate account of resulting deficiencies; in any case, a properly limited interpretation of results in light of methodological limitations is important in all kinds of research. In Chapter 9, I discuss the possible tensions between this kind of cautious approach, or humility, and some of the tendencies of legal training and legal discourse.)

64. Krauskopf, "Touching the Elephant"; 30% of men but only 15% of women reported asking questions frequently in class; 46% of men but 54% of women reported that they "never/seldom volunteer in class" Id., 314, 325–326.

65. See also reports on difficulties faced by women in legal education issued by the ABA Commision on Women, *Elusive Equality*, and the Chicago Bar Association. McNamee, "Alliance for Women."

66. A two-phase study at a large state university law school, published in 1978, found substantial differences between men and women, with women less likely to rate themselves as approximating the traits of an "ideal" lawyer and more likely to report dissatisfaction with their classroom and overall law school experiences. Robert and Winter, "Sex-Role and Success in Law School." Women performed as well as men in terms of grades, but far

more women than men who were successful still disliked law school. A study by Garrison et al. (Brooklyn Law School) found overall similarities between women and men with regard to many aspects of law school experience, including grades and honors and sense of comfort regarding interactions outside of class; however, female students did report lower class participation and more overall distress than did male students. Garrison et al., "Succeeding in Law School," 520, 525; see also Ogloff et al., "More Than 'Learning to Think,' " 195. Fortunately, research has found indications of diminution in student distress, at least at some law schools, by the third year. See Gulati et al., "The Happy Charade." On the other hand, several psychological studies have shown differential continuing distress among female law students. McCleary and Zucker, "Higher Trait- and State-Anxiety"; McIntosh et al., "Stress and Health."

In a 1987 survey of Harvard law school graduates, Granfield found differences both between women and men and also among women who differed by race, class, and occupational goals. Granfield, *Making Elite Lawyers*, 103–106. For example, women who entered law school with altruistic motives were more likely to be unhappy than those with more careerist motives. Over half of the women surveyed said they believed that the faculty was biased against women. A study conducted by the Law School Admission Council found some gender-based differences between men's and women's experiences of law school, including academic self-concept, experiences of discrimination, and perceived fairness. Wightman, *Women in Legal Education*. There have also been indications of gender differences in recent reports from individual law schools. Schwab, "A Shifting Gender Divide" (Columbia); Bowers, "Women at the University of Texas Law School."

On the other hand, an early survey of students in two national law schools during 1974–1975 found women students actually reporting a more positive response to Socratic teaching than was found in men. Schwartz, "Law, Lawyers and Law School," 448–451; see also Schwab, "A Shifting Gender Divide," 324–325. Two studies conducted in state law schools (New Mexico and Minnesota) in the 1970s and 1980s found little difference between men and women. Teitelbaum et al., "Gender, Legal Education, and Legal Careers"; Mattessich and Heilman, "The Career Paths of Minnesota Law Graduates: Does Gender Make a Difference?"; see also Garrison et al., "Succeeding in Law School" (finding no gendered differences in grades or honors at Brooklyn Law School). The authors of the New Mexico study concluded that contextual factors such as class size and degree of faculty diversity might affect students' reactions to law teaching. Ogloff et al., "More Than 'Learning to Think,' " make essentially the same point, noting that we cannot generalize from individual schools to all law schools.

67. See, e.g., Guinier, *Becoming Gentlemen*; Granfield, *Making Elite Lawyers*; Homer and Schwartz, "Admitted but Not Accepted"; Krauskopf, "Touching the Elephant"; McCleary and Zucker, "Higher Trait- and State-Anxiety"; McIntosh et al., "Stress and Health"; Ogloff et al., "More Than 'Learning to Think' "; Wightman, *Women in Legal Education*.

68. Jacobs, "Women in Law School," 470.

69. Weiss and Melling, "The Legal Education of Twenty Women." In 5 of the 19 courses, fewer than a third of classes were coded; in the remaining courses, over two-thirds of the classes were coded. Id., 1363–1365.

70. Guinier and her coauthors suggest that

working-class women had grown accustomed to challenging societally prescribed roles during their struggle to gain admission to law school. Once they were in law school, they were not about to give up. In other words, these women had socialized themselves to be successful, active participants who took charge of their education as they had taken charge of the course of their lives and careers. (Guinier et al., *Becoming Gentlemen*, 33 n. 86)

71. This institutional hypothesis does a somewhat better job of explaining differences found among different kinds of law schools, because there are women from a variety of backgrounds in many law schools (although admittedly, the distribution may vary). Pressure for conformity can obviously be exerted in multiple ways, including through the responses of students to one another and to the professor in the classroom, in addition to the more obvious top-down channels. Female professors can themselves be subject to institutional pressures, which may vary systematically in ways we have yet to uncover.

72. Yale Law Women, *Yale Law School*. Students in these classes monitored between 2 and 7 class meetings in each course (averaging around 4 meetings), tracking aspects of student turns. This study introduced some new approaches not found in the earlier Yale observational effort: here volunteered turns were distinguished from called-on turns, and responses were characterized as "response," "question," or "comment." Student monitors also noted the attendance for each class session coded and calculated participation as a ratio of students actually present each day, where possible. (There are arguments for and against using overall class enrollment rather than daily attendance for ratios, but certainly the approach adopted required additional work and showed a very thoughtful effort. It also has the benefit of yielding data on gendered patterns of attendance for the classes that were monitored.)

73. Id., 36. If a strict rule for delineating female- versus male-dominated participation is used, categorizing even classes in which one group exceeds the other by a ratio of only 1.007, for example, then the distribution of gender domination looks fairly even (with 12 classes dominated by men and 11 dominated by women.) However, if we remove classes in which the ratio of male-female total turns is essentially even (any classes in which the ratio ranges from .97 to 1.03), then the distribution shifts considerably, because all of those classes are ones in which women's relative participation exceeds men's by a very small margin. With this alteration, we arrive at a distribution in which 12 classes are dominated by men, 6 by women, and 5 are essentially even. As noted in the report, imbalances in favor of men tend to exceed those in favor of women.

74. Id.

75. Id., 97.

76. Id. Of the 6 classes in which female students clearly dominated, only 1 was taught by a female professor. (Women dominated in 5 of the 18 classes taught by male professors and 1 of the 5 classes taught by female professors. Male students dominated in 2 of the remaining classes taught by women, and participation was roughly even in the other 2 female-taught classes. This leaves a distribution in which 2 of 5 classes taught by women and 3 of 18 classes taught by men had roughly even participation in terms of gender.) The report commendably called for further research, pointing to areas that need further examination based on this initial investigation.

77. Id., 37. Monitors kept track of whether classes were "strict Socratic," which was defined as involving no notice to students who were called on; Socratic method with "on-call" notice to participants in advance; volunteers called on when hands were raised; and "free-form discussion, no one is called on." Id., 98.

78. Neufeld, "Costs of an Outdated Pedagogy?," 522. As noted earlier, the students also conducted a set of surveys and collected data on grade and honors distributions by gender. In addition, they collected information on extracurricular activities, use of available mental health care, and employment, as well as conducting eight single-sex focus groups to aid in formulating and supplementing the survey results.

79. There were no statistically significant differences between the male and female coders. Id. The class monitors tracked turns in terms of gender of speakers, class attendance, whether the turn was volunteered or not, and the individual identities of speakers (which allowed for a variety of calculations regarding repeat speakers).

80. Id., 531.

81. Id., 533.

82. Id. The Harvard report suggests that some of this disparity may be attributable to the fact that there tends to be higher overall participation in classes taught by women.

83. Id., 533. This finding fits well with others pointing to men's greater propensity to volunteer. It also suggests that women may fare better in classes where they are called on.

84. K. Wilson and Levin, "The Sex-Based Disparity in Class Participation." This was the first student-run observational effort to consider the issue of volunteered turns. As an anthropologist who is also participating in the research in this area, I have watched with great interest a process by which student-run observational work appears to have built on itself over the years, with each new study incorporating and improving on innovations from prior efforts (as well as from other sources). At a time when there is a great deal of discussion of how best to encourage empirical work in the legal academy, I think we should take note of this kind of process; it is tempting for trained social scientists to express only skepticism about efforts by legal professionals in this regard, but absent formal graduate social science training for everyone involved, it might be important to view the public discussion itself as a forum for genuine interdisciplinary communication and advancement. On concerns over empirical work published in law reviews, some quite understandable, see Epstein and King, "The Rules of Inference"; on attempts to build productive interdisciplinary discussion about the intersection of social science and law, see Erlanger et al., "Foreword"; Macaulay, "The New versus the Old Legal Realism"; and other articles in the *Wisconsin Law Review* "New Legal Realism" Symposium (vol. 2005, no. 2).

85. Becker, "How to Do a Gender Study at Your Law School," n.p.

86. Certainly, as social psychologists relying on power-dependence theory might assert, a more talkative speaker may in fact be dependent on the less talkative speaker, and withholding speech can be an expression of power. And, in individual instances, student silence can of course perform this function. Mertz, "Silence and the Speakable." But the fact that student silences may have multiple meanings interpretable at the individual level does not obviate the wider structural and institutional significance of those silences. This is particularly the case in light of the patterns documented from childhood through law school of both differential silencing and lowered confidence among some students, as well as in light of the institutionalized meaning of assertive speech in legal education and institutions more generally.

87. This would help to quiet any concerns about "reverse discrimination."

88. In what could be considered the reverse situation, scholars have had to mull over this kind of complexity in unraveling the "Queen Bee" problem, where one or two dominant female speakers might skew the numbers so that women's situation looks better than it actually is. We did not find evidence for this effect in the classrooms of this study. However, the general point about complex gender dynamics is reinforced by an analysis of the statistics on mean numbers of individual student turns and minutes by gender among the classes of this study. See Mertz et al., "What Difference Does Difference Make?," 47–48. On the one hand, the gender inequities in Class #8 persist in these statistics, with female students having a mean number per speaker of 17.7 minutes as compared with men, who had 28.3 minutes. At the same time, women students' mean number per speaker in most of the other classes fell between 3.8 and 4.7 minutes. Thus, women students who did speak

in Class #8 spoke over four times longer than in most other classes. The classroom with the next highest mean minutes per female student speaker was our most egalitarian class (#6), in which women students who spoke had means of 8.7 minutes, less than half the time of the women in Class #8. This is for the most part reflective of a class structure in Class #8 that allowed the students who did participate to take much longer than average time on the floor.

89. It is, of course, important to remember that we are here measuring participation in extended dialogues. This is only a rough proxy for Socratic exchanges; we have noted some of the complexities involved in attempting to determine what makes a dialogue Socratic, and then in trying to ascertain the effects of Socratic dialogue on participants. Quantitative measures of participation obviously do not capture how participants feel about their experiences; it would be quite possible for two students who spoke for similar amounts of time in extended dialogues to feel quite differently, one feeling exhilarated and the other alienated and angry. As noted in my previous descriptions of the individual classes, the classes that I have characterized as modified Socratic did conform to the prototypical Socratic model along a number of qualitative dimensions as well, although they were all characterized by more humor and less harshness than would be expected under the stereotype.

90. Remember, however, that one of the most gender-imbalanced classes in favor of men was also a short-exchange class, so that we cannot read in any simplistic way from class format to gender dynamics without looking at other aspects of classroom discourse as well.

91. The observational studies at Yale, Chicago, and Harvard all had similar findings regarding women's lower rate of participation in volunteered turns (see text). Note that in my study, the skewing toward men in elite/prestige, and regional law schools was exacerbated when we calculated overall time as opposed to merely counting turns. Hence, it is possible that the disparities revealed in other observational studies, which counted turns, may actually be slighter than the actual disparities in time between male and female students.

92. Research in elementary school settings has already stressed the importance of this aspect of smaller, informal classrooms: "Small group experiences may actually reinforce rather than counteract gender stereotypes" unless there is a conscious effort made to counteract this tendency. Weinstein, "The Classroom as a Social Context," 511. Well-structured cooperative teaching methods were found to be superior for all students, in addition to working better in creating more successfully integrated and egalitarian classrooms. Interestingly, the most recent student-run Yale observational research concluded that "students prefer and find more equitable a managed classroom discussion which allows a range of voices to be heard." Yale Law Women, *Yale Law School*, 14. One-third of the respondents preferred "panels or on-call" systems to other systems for managing classroom discussion, including the more classic "cold-call" approach, in which students are called on without warning.

93. To complete the picture, we should mention that Class #3 had equal participation ratios for men and women in both volunteered and called-on categories, meaning that the distinction between volunteering and being called on does not seem to have gendered dimensions in this class.

94. Students from Class #6 mentioned the unusually high number of older students in the class—merely a reported perception on their part, but perhaps worth noting in passing here. Class #3 was a night school class in a local law school and thus also a potential candidate for having a higher than usual number of older students.

95. Class #8 was also quite small, 32 students, as opposed to the 53 students in Class #6; so again, we might want to ask about variations in control and relative structuring of

turns in classes of various sizes. And there is also the issue of whether we would find variation across different law school subjects, a question we cannot address because we held this particular factor constant in this study.

96. Note that these classes also contained substantial cohorts of students of color. The fact that the same professor, who is a woman of color, might lead a class that has an underrepresentation of women but an overrepresentation of students of color raises the important point that we must also focus on the intersections of kinds of identity in understanding classroom dynamics. See Mertz et al., "What Difference Does Difference Make?," 75–80.

97. Class #6 was high in this regard (46% time, 62% turns in shorter exchanges), and Class #3 was lower (13% time and 31% turns in shorter exchanges). Thus, although the two classes are roughly comparable in terms of the amount of time spent in Socratic exchanges (21 and 24%), it would be fair to characterize Class #3 as more Socratic or formal because of the lower amount of informal exchange. (The difference is accounted for by the amount of time spent by the professor in lecture, or monologue: 63%).

98. Student interviews were not part of our original project design, but we began these interviews during the first phase of data collection in response to a request from students in one of the elite/prestige classes. Having undertaken this step, we proceeded to offer students in the remaining schools an opportunity to participate in interviews where possible. The resulting focus groups should not be viewed as representative of the average student; certainly, in the first case, where the students themselves initiated the focus groups, these were the students with more than average interest in having a voice in the ultimate study results and with the time and energy to participate. On the other hand, once the decision to offer focus groups to the students was made, we did make an effort to encourage all students to participate, and so the groups were not entirely self-initiated. We were able to obtain student interviews in one elite, one prestige, one regional, and one local law school, giving us a nice array across the status hierarchy. Three of the professors teaching these classes were male and one was female; one was a professor of color, and the remaining three were European American. (As noted earlier, we obtained professor interviews in six of the eight classrooms, again spanning the status hierarchy and including professors of both genders and diverse races.) Thus, the resulting data cannot be treated as evidence of "typical" students' opinions but can be used as qualitative information to supplement the picture obtained from observing them in class and speaking with their professors.

99. Students in Class #7 specifically commented that any gender or race differences in participation were more likely the product of women's differential hesitation about volunteering rather than any bias on the part of the professor; this was a class that relied heavily on volunteered turns.

100. The idea that some aspects of traditional Socratic teaching could be retained while shifting many other characteristics of law school training has been part of the ongoing discussion of pedagogical reform for some time. See, e.g., Garner, "Socratic Misogyny?" The present study, along with recent observational studies from Yale and Harvard, suggests that this has already happened in some so-called Socratic classrooms and that some law professors are experimenting with mixed approaches to teaching.

101. My coauthors and I have elsewhere discussed the difficulties of coding for race, given that any attempt to pin people down into simpler, more essentializing categories of necessity obliterates important aspects of their identity. Mertz et al., "What Difference Does Difference Make?," 78–80. For the purposes of providing some empirical information on race, particularly in light of the dearth of such studies, our team proceeded using the typical, more simplistic categories in tracking participation rates, but not without considerable, ongoing struggle over the process. My decision to proceed in this way was heavily

influenced by the thought that were we to permit the dilemmas involved in coding race to dissuade us from going forward, yet another study would emerge with information only on gender, leaving a continuing silence on racial dynamics in the law school classroom.

102. I have mentioned age as another possible consideration. I also would add sexual preference, an identity about which we were unable to collect any systematic information in this study.

## Part IV

1. Schlegel, "Walt Was Right," 604.

## Chapter 9

1. See, e.g., Frug, *Postmodern Legal Feminism*; Abrams, "Title VII and the Complex Female Subject"; Coombe, "Contesting the Self"; Larson, "Imagine Her Satisfaction."

2. Even the title of an article reporting findings from the study makes this generalizing premise evident: see Boersma et al., "Sex Differences in College Student-Teacher Interactions: Fact or Fantasy?" This title presupposes that the results of a single study can definitively answer the question whether or how gender works in all classrooms.

3. Id., 783.

4. Constantinople et al., "The Chilly Climate," 549.

5. Smith, *Cognitive Styles*, 131.

6. Id.

7. Zemans and Rosenblum, *The Making of a Public Profession*, 57.

8. Granfield, *Making Elite Lawyers*; McGill, "Producing Lawyers."

9. See Mertz, "A New Social Constructionism for Sociolegal Studies," 1246–1248.

10. Catherine Krupnick has urged a similarly complex and contextual approach to creating more egalitarian sites for learning. Krupnick, "Women and Men in the Classroom," 25.

11. R. Austin, "Bad for Business."

12. Auerbach, *Unequal Justice*, 276.

13. Elkins, "The Legal Persona," 742–743. Note the covert nature of this semiotic mediation, which characterizes a very social categorization process as above subjectivity, thereby concealing its own social origins. Elkins draws on Scheingold's observation that the legal worldview is "more deluding than some other[s]" in that it perpetuates a myth that "thinking like a lawyer" is actually the equivalent of performing objective analysis that "strip[s] a problem, any problem, down to its essentials." Scheingold, *Politics of Rights*, 161, cited in Elkins, "The Legal Persona," 740–741. Ironically, subscribing to this myth means that those trained to "think like a lawyer" have no training that would allow them to "critically analyz[e] and assess[] the assumptions underlying the lawyer's peculiar view of the world." Id.

14. Postone, *Time, Labor, and Social Domination*, 144–160.

15. Merry, *Getting Justice and Getting Even*.

16. Williams, *Alchemy*, 163–164.

17. Galanter, "Why the 'Haves' Come Out Ahead"; R. Austin, "Bad for Business"; Winter, *A Clearing in the Forest*. Fish describes law as "at once thoroughly rhetorical and engaged in effacing its own rhetoricity." Fish, "The Law Wishes," 195.

18. Baker, "Language Acculturation Practices," 134–135.

19. Id., 134.

20. Id.

21. Id. In his helpful comments on this study, Baker also suggested how the structure of law school language as described in this research might reinforce the marginalization of traditional outsiders, while also leaving them with a sense of internal conflict and alienation. Id., 137–140. He counsels against despair, however, pointing out that outside of the first-year classroom there are numerous other possible sites in law schools for resistance to the dominant vision conveyed in formal training.

22. Hirsch, "Making Culture Visible," 127–128. Hirsch contrasts the core pedagogy of anthropology, which pushes students to problematize their own cultural assumptions, with that of law.

23. I include both students from traditionally excluded groups and scholars from other disciplines in my category of "outsider" here.

24. Winter, *A Clearing in the Forest*, 331. In an insightful passage, Winter takes critical legal theorist Duncan Kennedy to task for ceding the ground of unconscious cultural categorization by concentrating too much on judges' overtly political motivations: "The truly radical insight is that judges are ideological precisely when they are not acting in an overtly political way. The insight that categorization is socially motivated means that categorization . . . is always a normatively loaded process." Id., 331. Susan Philips has demonstrated that this tacit ideological loading goes beyond processes of categorization to the structuring of language in use. Philips, *Ideology*. Thus, from multiple directions, there is support for the idea that the apparently abstract process of legal reasoning is actually deeply imbricated in social context and change. Here I would agree with Winter's critique of attempts by legal theorists such as Sunstein to delineate an abstract structure of legal reasoning without adequately theorizing a social dimension; in this respect, Edward Levi did indeed do a better job than many of his successors (although I would also agree with Winter when he dissents from Levi's "uncritical celebration of analogical reasoning in law"; just because this reasoning process does incorporate changing social norms over time does not mean that it does so fairly; Winter, *A Clearing in the Forest*, 257–258).

25. For further discussion of "normative importation" in law, see Yovel, "The Language beyond Law," "What Is Contract Law 'About'?," and "Rights and Rites."

26. Philips, "The Language Socialization of Lawyers."

27. Elkins, "The Legal Persona."

28. Woolard, "Language Ideology," 27.

29. Silverstein, "The Uses and Utility of Ideology," 128–129.

30. Gal and Irvine, "The Boundaries of Languages and Disciplines."

31. Morris, "Not Thinking Like a Non-Lawyer." Morris shares my view that there is a distinctive linguistic approach associated with law, which lawyers generally attempt to summarize in the somewhat misleading phrase "thinking like a lawyer." (Note the interesting folk-Whorfian theory iconically associating language and thought; for more commentary on this issue, see Mertz, "Language and Mind.") As Morris notes, lawyers have no corner on the market of rigorous thought, but like all professionals they have a specialized professional discourse; they "think like lawyers" when they employ this discourse just as doctors "think like doctors" when they use the discourse and accompanying orientation to which they are professionally trained.

32. Hirsch, *Pronouncing and Persevering*, 234–235.

33. Matoesian, "Law and the Language of Identity," 41.

34. Philips, *Ideology*, 82.

35. Williams, *Alchemy*.

36. This is the case because use of law by definition invokes the power of the state to resolve actual or potential disputes, allocate benefits, exact punishment, and so forth. See

Merry, *Getting Justice*, for an incisive description of the paradoxical dilemma that this creates for litigants. There does exist a substantial ethnographic, psychological, and clinical literature now demonstrating that people come to the law with a variety of expectations and desires, and that in many cases, litigants want above all to have their stories heard or to be treated fairly. Cunningham, "Lawyer as Translator"; Lind and Tyler, *The Social Psychology of Procedural Justice.*

37. Constable, *Just Silences.* Constable and I do still seem to differ in our understanding of the social, and we also diverge because I continue to feel that it is important to include issues of power in the analysis of law, though without permitting them to erase all other considerations. However, I am persuaded by Constable's warning about the reductive dangers of an analytic stance that translates everything legal into matters of "power." Woolard expressed a similar concern in her 1998 article, when she mentioned that members of a discussion group to which she belonged

> were struck by the apparent absurdity of nineteenth-century philology's relentless reading of spiritual qualities from linguistic structures. We wondered if the single-minded reading of power into and out of communicative practices that has characterized our own late-twentieth-century sociolinguistics will look as ludicrously obsessive in another century's retrospective and whether we should not attend to some of these other dimensions of social subjectivity [eg., identity or affiliation]. (Woolard, "Language Ideology," 28 n. 8)

Of course, Woolard here is speaking of communicative practices generally, not legal language in particular, which I take to be one kind of communicative practice in which power dimensions become more clearly ubiquitous. However, in talking about a partially independent metalinguistic level, my work (like that of a number of other anthropological linguists) reaches beyond analysis of power to talk about epistemology, which, as we have seen, intersects with questions of identity and personhood, of narrative and agency, of morality and context, and a number of other dimensions that cannot be understood in terms of power dynamics alone.

38. Winter, *A Clearing in the Forest*, 11.

39. Id., xiv.

40. As Brenneis notes, "This is clearly not just a matter of cognition; it rather draws upon the whole gambit of cultural views of personhood, intention, and action, drawing its strength from specific shared understandings of the complex relationships among truth, desire, excitement, and aesthetics." Brenneis, "Telling Theories," 7. And all of this just begins the story, for having considered the level of culture, we also have to take into account the patterning that anthropologists and sociologists have at times distinguished as "social structure" as well: asking how kinship, economy, politics, religion, education, law, and other institutions structure our relationships and inscribe the possibilities for action.

41. See Mertz and Weissbourd, "Legal Ideology and Linguistic Theory," for an analysis of this issue in both legal and linguistic theory.

42. Given the highly favored status in legal circles of the metaphor RATIONAL ARGUMENT IS WAR, cognitivists might warn us that this is an uneven choice! One strength of Winter's cognitivist analysis is that it moves analysis of analogy beyond the myth of an even playing field, opening the door to a more socially grounded examination of why certain analogies and metaphors might be likely to prevail in certain circumstances. On the other hand, the individual-cognition-focused method of much of the work in the field limits a fuller examination of the broader social and linguistic dynamics at work in particular cases. The power of one metaphor over another is not merely a matter of its fit with some

universal human embodied sense, but is also a function of the social and discursive settings in which they are deployed.

An even stronger constraint of this kind exists in linguistic analysis drawing on the principles of generative grammar derived from the highly influential work of Noam Chomsky. In a sophisticated invocation of this approach to study the language of judges, for example, Solan convincingly critiques judges' use of linguistic justifications for their decisions. Solan, *The Language of Judges*. Solan draws on the asocial analytic tools of generative grammar to show us that language structure cannot possibly provide the predictable, determinative results sought by judges. Thus, judges wind up reaching into linguistic justifications selectively, as is convenient for the results they wish to achieve: "Judges do not make good linguists because they are using linguistic principles to accomplish an agenda distinct from the principles about which they write." Id., 62. But, as I have demonstrated, judges' agendas are nonetheless heavily linguistic in a different sense, organized around metalinguistic principles that are analyzable using a different, more socially grounded branch of linguistics.

We do not have to end our understanding of legal language when we have specified a set of available metaphors (without attempting a *socio*linguistic analysis of the circumstances under which they are used by different people, and to what ends). And we can move beyond a (well-grounded) critique of judges' failure to be consistent in their invocation of acontextual grammatical principles to a substantive linguistic analysis of what they *are* doing with language. But (in an attempt to impose some of my own metapragmatic structuring here!), let me say that these quibbles with fellow analysts of language-and-law should not be taken to indicate disrespect for their rigorous and thought-provoking entries into the discussion. In each case, there are areas of substantial agreement among the conclusions reached by different forms of linguistic analysis, despite some of our marked differences in approach.

43. It is for this reason that I am not drawn to the agenda proposed by some (not all) conversation analysts, those who seem bent on posing a stark choice: we can either analyze all spoken exchanges (including legal ones) as instantiating certain rules for conversation, devoid of any wider social or institutional contexts or power dimensions, or we can analytically reduce all spoken exchanges to mere reflexes of wider social power, without any sensitivity to individual differences (or, indeed, to the data at all!). Travers, "Understanding Talk." Although adherents to this view pose the choice as one between relatively pure descriptivism and imperialist theorizing, of course even the "descriptive" accounts of conversation analysts are shaped by tacit theoretical agendas, so that the event is not described exactly as it would be understood by the participants themselves. (And one could certainly argue that unanalyzed theoretical agendas pose more of a hazard to scientific analysis than do clearly acknowledged ones.) But in either case, it seems needlessly combative and reductive to pose a choice between attentiveness to the particularities of different speech situations and analysis of wider social and institutional inputs when both are necessary and important to a full understanding of the dynamics at work in language use. See Conley, "Power Is as Power Does." This more comprehensive view has been in evidence for some time among some scholars of law and language, whose varied approaches to the question range from Hirsch's ethnographic work based on lengthy fieldwork in Kenya, through the courtroom ethnographies of Philips and O'Barr and Conley, to Matoesian's analyses based on videotapes and transcripts. These scholars also bring a multitude of disciplinary and theoretical perspectives to their work, from anthropological linguistics to conversation analysis, and from a neo-Marxist-inspired focus on hegemony to analyses of culture and metalinguistics whose roots can be traced as much to Durkheim, Weber, Geertz, Sapir, Whorf, Jakobson, and Silverstein as to any

other school of thought. Thus, any attempt to lump this group together and characterize them all as adherents of a nonexistent, monolithic "language and power" school is indicative of a superficial understanding of the scholarship, and therefore unlikely to be particularly useful.

44. J. B. White, *From Expectation to Experience*, 178.

45. Id., 179.

46. J. B. White, *Justice as Translation*, 3–21. J. B. White's ambitious conception of interdisciplinary translation would require those bridging the boundaries between disciplines to put themselves in the shoes of practitioners of each field: to hold in mind the actual discourses and ways of approaching the world that characterize each discipline. This requires a far more profound understanding than can be provided by a quick reading of the results of someone's paper or book, or even the adoption of a method from another field. Providing a somewhat less optimistic view, Wayne Booth cedes this kind of "internal" understanding to the experts in a field (he calls this "Rhetoric 1") but hopes that we can nonetheless communicate across disciplines in a more indirect fashion, through a sense that there are colleagues whose expertise we trust though we don't completely understand it ("Rhetoric 2") and through sharing a general framework for assessing scholarship that allows us to judge others' arguments as apparently coherent, as reflecting intellectual engagement, and so forth. Booth, *The Vocation of a Teacher*, 311–327.

47. Dorf, "Foreword," 38.

48. For a striking contrast, see Hirsch's description of her approach to initiating undergraduate students into the perspectives and language of anthropology. Hirsch, "Making Culture Visible."

49. Silverstein, "Translation, Transduction, Transformation," 91–95. Silverstein would reserve the word "translation" for the most transparent end of the spectrum, where language most closely approximates "European ideological construals of it" as primarily denotational. Id., 75. Once we move into the realm of indexical meaning, Silverstein would either talk about "transduction" (in which we attempt to "find a way to index something comparable" in one language using another) or "transformation" (where we shift "source material contextualized in specific ways into configurations of cultural semiosis of a sort substantially or completely different from those one has started with"). Id., 88, 91. In other words, Silverstein would not use the word "translation" at any point in this volume to describe the processes I am discussing. Because I am concerned with actually communicating ("transducing"?) the insights of linguistic anthropology (including Silverstein's) in a way that is comprehensible to legal and other scholars, I am in the ironic position of declining to use Silverstein's proposed terminology in an effort to better convey some of the basic insights of his field. For those familiar with his terminology, however, let me just add here that I am in effect attempting to urge those using legal language to become aware of the inevitable transformation involved in the imposition of legal frames across diverse social arenas, and to encourage something that more closely resembles transduction when legal scholars and social scientists enter into conversation with one another.

50. I have elsewhere noted the possibility that legal discourse can begin to shift to a more complex, contextual approach through attention to its own margins; in the legal academy, this would include legal writing classes and clinical instruction. Mertz, "Teaching Lawyers the Language of Law." Rakoff suggests another possible route, using the categories of "embedded" and "nonembedded" perspectives to suggest that legal thinking can both be embedded in a rich consideration of "cases, statutes, and the like" yet also be "theoretically rich and, still further, sophisticated in its use of the methods of other disciplines." Rakoff, "Law, Knowledge," 1281.

51. Burns, *Theory of the Trial*; for examples of creative, alternative approaches to teach-ing and studying legal discourse, see Amsterdam and Bruner, *Minding the Law*; Cunningham, "Lawyer as Translator"; Davis, "Law and Lawyering" and "Contextual Legal Criticism." These kinds of approaches open the door to one way that legal pedagogy could help transform the profession, perhaps incrementally, from within; students would still learn the core "grammar" of legal discourse, but would also receive extensive education on diverse ways of deploying it in practice.

52. As Baker, who is quite critical of some aspects of legal pedagogy and discourse, notes:

> Although it is certainly possible, indeed likely, that rule-based reasoning . . . provides an impoverished account of moral decision-making, it is difficult to imagine legal de-cision-making that does not rely on some degree of abstraction. . . . Legal analogies may debilitate and deform the more original and authentic accounts of the underly-ing human conflict, but it is hard to see why legal analysts would not want to be guided, at least in part, by the prior deliberations and vicarious exemplars of other legal pro-fessionals. (Baker, "Language Acculturation Practices," 145–146)

He goes on to add that an ability to conceive and articulate the arguments on each side of a combative argument is a necessary skill for attorneys, and so must be taught in some form or other (although he urges that professors become more thoughtful about this). In other words, some of these features of legal discourse are indeed part of the core language taught to all initiates.

53. Garth and Dezalay, *The Internationalization of Palace Wars*; Goodale, "The Glo-balization of Sympathetic Law"; Nader, *The Life of the Law*; Santos and Rodriguez-Garavito, *Law and Globalization from Below*; Riles, *The Network Inside Out*.

54. Lazarus-Black, *The Vanishing Complainant*; Merry, *Human Rights and Gender Violence*.

55. See Greenhouse et al., *Ethnography in Unstable Places*; Nader, *The Life of the Law*.

56. See Winter, *A Clearing in the Forest*, 331. One of the most interesting features of legal language is its use of some very common linguistic features: analogy, for example, and "reasoning through cases." These features are found in other fields, including psycho-analysis, medicine, and anthropology. Brenneis, "Telling Theories"; Forrester, "If *p*, Then What?" Yet the same forms lead to quite different overall discursive practices and results, as can be seen if we contrast Hirsch's description of education in anthropology with the description here of legal education. Hirsch, "Making Culture Visible." In anthropology, analogy and serial case discussions are used to open a field for exploration, unsettling taken-for-granted cultural canons and prejudices. Though there are certainly anthropology-internal hierarchies and canons, there is no organized adjudication of the analogies used by professors and students, nor is a particular sequence of cases inevitably prescribed as the only possible official precedential genealogy. (Perhaps the closest parallel is the sequence by which histories of the field and subfields are taught and described in scholarly writing, proceeding inevitably through certain figures—Malinowski, say, or Boas. But if a profes-sor chooses to skip them and start the history elsewhere, the class or text will not be in-validated by a higher authority.)

Colleagues who study comparative professions have commented to me that they see no difference in kind between legal and other professional discourses, pointing to some basic structures of reasoning or closed expert terminologies that law shares with other fields. I would not deny this, and there are some interesting insights to be gleaned by observing these similarities. But it is also important to acknowledge some crucial contextual differ-ences among the professions as well, so that, for example, in law the use of analogy and cases occurs in a quite singular linguistic-institutional context, which I have endeavored to convey in this volume. There are certainly levels of authorizing hierarchy in most fields, but the role of the state in monitoring and ratifying interpretive sequences in law, in combination with the particular canons used for contextualizing written texts, give to legal language a flavor all its own. (French and Italian, for example, share many features, and it is important to take note of them. However, speaking French is not the same thing as speaking Italian. See Morris, "Not Thinking Like a Non-Lawyer," for a similar argument.) This is not to exalt the form of legal reasoning as superior (in fact, I have indicated ways that it closes and limits possibilities as compared with other, arguably similar discourses). But it is to argue that one must not transpose an apparently similar semiotic form (analogy) from one discourse to another, assuming transparency, without a careful look at the institutional and metalinguistic contexts that give it meaning in each. I should add, lest the reader think that I have singled out legal discourse for criticism, that social scientists who attempt to study law without attempting to grasp the internal mandates of legal discourse can be no less guilty of fundamental misreadings. It is, in fact, ironically possible that the very fact of an open-textured semiotic style in fields like anthropology can blind its practitioners to the strictures of a field like law when they attempt to make their own analogies in efforts to analyze and understand legal practices.

57. Weinstein, "The Classroom as a Social Context."

58. Id.; Gurin et al., "Diversity and Higher Education"; see also Hue-Pei and Mason, "Social Organizational Factors in Learning to Read"; Barnhardt, "Tuning In"; Tharp, "Psychocultural Variables."

59. Orfield and Whitla, "Diversity and Legal Education," 164. This study, which achieved an 81% response rate, essentially replicated findings of an earlier study by the authors that had a much lower response rate but also looked at more schools. The Michigan and Harvard students in the later study agreed in substantial numbers that their legal education had benefited in important ways from racial diversity in classrooms—and this included white students as well as students of color. The students felt that diversity had enhanced understanding of the kinds of legal or community issues they would encounter as professionals, of rights, of criminal justice, and of conditions in various social and economic institutions pertinent to the legal issues they studied. Diversity in the classroom was found to enhance how topics were addressed in a majority of their law school classes. In addition, they reported an enhanced ability to work and get along with members of other races and agreed that conflicts over race ultimately had positive or neutral effects on their learning experiences. The idea that racial diversity and any hypothesized accompanying need for "political correctness" on the part of white students stifled class discussion found little support in this study, where no more than 9% of students in either school agreed that classroom diversity had any kind of negative effect on class discussion.

60. One student commented that "cultural and ethnic diversity is more important in law school than many other studies." Id., 167. On the strength of numerous studies as well as other arguments pointing to the beneficial role of diversity in education, the Supreme Court recognized the importance of diversity to education in general and law school in particular in the *Grutter* case. The majority opinion took notice of

> numerous expert studies and reports showing that . . . diversity promotes learning outcomes and better prepares students for an increasingly diverse workforce, for society, and for the legal profession. Major American businesses have made clear that the skills needed in today's increasingly global marketplace can only be developed through exposure to widely diverse people, cultures, ideas, and viewpoints.

High-ranking retired officers and civilian military leaders assert that a highly quali-fied, racially diverse officer corps is essential to national security. (*Grutter*, 3–4)

61. Sander, "Systematic Analysis." Sander finds that only some of the difference be-tween how white students and students of color fare can be attributed to divergences in entering credentials. He attributes most of the remaining difference to the results of affir-mative action, that is, that students of color are not well-matched with the law schools they attend.

62. Id.; a number of the critiques of Sander's study, his statistics, and the issue he raises regarding affirmative action were published in the *Stanford Law Review* in 2005; see, e.g., Dauber, "The Big Muddy." In addition to disputing his quantitative methods and specific results, critics have also argued against the potential policy implications Sander draws regarding affirmative action. Sander himself characterized the question of "the con-sequences of eliminating racial preferences on the production of black lawyers" as a "side issue" in his original article, and at times seems to take seriously the fact that there is much that needs to be researched and considered before coming to any firm conclusion as to the best policy response to his findings. Sander, "Reply," 1996, 2003, 2013.

63. Wilkins, "A Systematic Response"; Chambers et al., "The Real Impact"; see also Sander, "Reply," 2003: "It is of course true that ending racial preferences in law admis-sions would substantially reduce black enrollments at elite law schools. This is a real and valid concern, as I noted . . . , and it would clearly be a central concern in actual discus-sions aimed at addressing the mismatch effect."

64. If it is clear that abolishing affirmative action would roll back any progress that has been made to date at desegregation of the elite law schools, then it seems likely that a diminished supply of black graduates from the elite schools might translate to an even smaller supply of potential black law professors than currently exists. (There is apparently some debate over the effect on upper echelons of the profession, but certainly one point of view states that the most elite law firms tend to draw from the most elite law schools, including when hiring black students.) Sander dismisses Ayres and Brooks's suggestion that stereotype threat might affect black students' performance, but it is possible that ste-reotype threat is just one example of a wider set of cultural problems that remains largely unexamined and unstudied in law schools. Sander, "Reply," 1963; see Ayres and Brooks, "Affirmative Action." From an anthropological vantage, the many reports of discomfort and alienation from law students of color open the possibility of a different kind of "mis-match," one created by divergent understandings and communications, by unconscious or implicit bias, by social gaps that result from a legacy of discrimination and segregation. Sander himself, in earlier work with Gulati, helped to reveal differential "pockets" of alien-ation among law students of color. Gulati et al., "The Happy Charade" (although this would of course be only one piece of a larger picture). Orfield and Whitla have documented the differentially segregated experience of white students at Michigan and Harvard, many more of whom had lived and gone to school in exclusively same-race settings than had students of color. On the other side, this study has uncovered stark discursive disparities in class-room discussions for students of color, a pattern not found in the classes taught by pro-fessors of color where there are significant cohorts of students of color. Some aspects of discourse patterning may also play a role in racial dynamics in class. We earlier reviewed the evidence and arguments that classroom discourse, culture, and overall climate can have effects on student confidence and self-concept that are independent of grades. Along similar lines, a recent investigation by Yale law students revealed differential discomfort on the part of students of color (and female students) regarding seeking out law professors for counsel on everything from schoolwork to jobs. These kinds of social and cultural gaps have yet to be well studied or accounted for; indeed, it is difficult to imagine them being

adequately encompassed using quantitative models (although I'm always open to being convinced to the contrary!).

65. See discussion above, and in Chapter 8. As this book went to press, I had the exciting opportunity to read a draft of the forthcoming Carnegie Foundation book reporting the findings of its own recent study of legal education, entitled "Educating Lawyers." The Carnegie Foundation research's conclusions dovetail with my study's findings in many respects and also incorporate current perspectives from educational research to suggest possible shifts in legal pedagogy and assessment. It will undoubtedly serve as an important source for law teachers who seek new ideas for improving legal pedagogy.

66. If law schools were to take this direction, then the jolt that they have received as a result of the Sander study could be turned to positive effect. The extreme path of eliminating affirmative action could in a sense be understood as giving up on real integration of law schools, a patently undesirable and undemocratic result in a racially diverse society largely run by lawyers. But Sander is correct that an alternative strategy of integration without appropriate concern for the students of color who might fall by the wayside is also unacceptable. All the demonstrated benefits of diversity to law schools and white law students, as well as to successful law students of color, do not obviate the imperative to consider the needs of the overall population of law students of color. One obvious step to prevent a Scylla-and-Charybdis choice—between resegregation of the most powerful, elite sector of the profession, and sacrifice of too many black law students along the road to integration—is for law schools to pay more attention to the strategies that have worked in other educational settings and to be more willing to develop innovative pedagogy that will benefit not only students of color but all students.

67. As Davidson notes, this more contextual approach to understanding educational settings also permits a more sophisticated understanding of race itself: as "scholars increasingly recognize previously unpredicted manifestations of race," a careful analysis of school- and classroom-level contextual factors can help us to "incorporate the more fluid, situational conceptions of social categories" and thereby to achieve more accurate analysis of "the reproduction of social inequality" in educational settings. Davidson, *Making and Molding Identity*, 17–18.

68. Here again, in Silversteinian terminology, I am arguing not for "translation" but for even just a very rudimentary attempt at laying the groundwork for "transduction." For an economist's call for more humility in the interpretation and use of social science by those in legal arenas, see Donahue, "The Case for More and Better Empirical Research."

69. For a discussion of the empirical evidence revealing growing alienation and corresponding differences in orientations between attorneys and laypeople, see Daicoff, *Lawyer, Know Thyself*. Elkins's early article pointed out the problematic character of the lawyer's persona: "The lawyer considers himself a neutral, rational, and objective problem solver . . . representing certain events in the world . . . [by] structuring all possible human relations into the form of claims and counterclaims." Elkins, "The Legal Persona," 739. Unfortunately, as Elkins points out, the "myth of rationality in the legal profession is founded on a model of human behavior" that omits unconscious and nonrational motivation and behavior: "Like classical economic theory, it views man as totally rational and influenced in his decisionmaking only by external objective factors," whereas both lawyers and their clients operate in the world using a combination of internal and external, rational and other guideposts. Id. See also Menkel-Meadow, "What's Missing," on the importance of the "human arts" of lawyering, and Noonan, *Persons and Masks of the Law*, on the importance of viewing rationality in the context of larger humanity. This may have contributed to the ironic situation that current legal thinking has moved closer to that of economics at the price of more realistic understanding of (and communication with) law's intended subjects, who, as Daicoff points out, tend to differ considerably in their orientation.

# Bibliography

Abel, Richard. *American Lawyers.* New York: Oxford University Press, 1989.

———, ed. *The Law & Society Reader.* New York: New York University Press, 1995.

Abel, Richard, and Philip Lewis, eds. *Lawyers in Society.* Vols. 1, 2, and 3. Berkeley: University of California Press, 1988–1989.

Abrams, Kathryn. "Title VII and the Complex Female Subject." *Michigan Law Review* 92 (1994): 2479–2540.

Althouse, Ann. "The Lying Woman, the Devious Prostitute, and Other Stories from the Evidence Casebook." *Northwestern University Law Review* 88 (1994): 914–994.

American Association of University Women [AAUW] and Greenberg-Lake Analysis Group. *Shortchanging Girls, Shortchanging America: A Call to Action.* Washington, DC: American Association of University Women, 1991.

American Bar Association [ABA]. *Unfinished Business.* Chicago: American Bar Association, 1995.

American Bar Association Commission on Women in the Profession. *Elusive Equality: The Experiences of Women in Legal Education.* Chicago: American Bar Association, 1998.

American Bar Association Section on Legal Education and Admissions to the Bar. *Report and Recommendations: The Role of Law Schools.* Chicago: American Bar Association, 1979.

———. *A Review of Legal Education in the United States.* Chicago: American Bar Association, 1994.

———. Task Force on Law Schools and the Profession. *Narrowing the Gap: Legal Education and Professional Development—An Educational Continuum* [*MacCrate Report*]. Chicago: American Bar Association, 1992.

Amsterdam, Anthony, and Jerome Bruner. *Minding the Law.* Cambridge, MA: Harvard University Press, 2000.

Angel, Marina. "What It's Like to Be Part of a Perpetual First Wave or the Case of the Disappearing Woman." *Temple Law Review* 61 (1988): 799–846.

Ansley, Frances Lee. "Race and the Core Curriculum in Legal Education." *California Law Review* 79 (1991): 1511–1597.

Anyon, Jean. "Social Class and School Knowledge." *Curriculum Inquiry* 11 (1981): 3–42.

———. "Social Class and the Hidden Curriculum of Work." *Journal of Education* 165 (1980): 67–92

Apple, Michael. *Ideology and Curriculum.* Boston: Routledge and Kegan Paul, 1979.

———. *Teachers and Texts.* Boston: Routledge and Kegan Paul, 1986.

Areeda, Phillip. "The Socratic Method." *Harvard Law Review* 109 (1996): 911–922.

Arnold, Thurmond. *The Symbols of Government.* New Haven: Yale University Press, 1935.

Atkinson, John. *Our Masters' Voices: The Language and Body Language of Politics.* London: Methuen, 1984.

Atkinson, John, and Paul Drew. *Order in Court: The Organization of Verbal Interaction in Judicial Settings.* Atlantic Highlands, NJ: Humanities Press, 1979.

Auerbach, Jerold. *Unequal Justice.* New York: Oxford University Press, 1976.

Austin, J. L. *How to Do Things with Words.* New York: Oxford University Press, 1962.

Austin, John. *The Province of Jurisprudence Determined.* London: Weidenfeld and Nicolson, 1954.

Austin, Regina. " 'Bad for Business': Contextual Analysis, Race Discrimination, and Fast Food." *John Marshall Law Review* 34 (2000): 207–243.

Ayres, Ian, and Richard Brooks. "Does Affirmative Action Reduce the Number of Black Lawyers?" *Stanford Law Review* 57 (2005): 1807–1853.

Baker, Brook. "Language Acculturation Practices and Resistance to In'doctrine'ation in the Legal Skills Curriculum and Beyond: A Commentary on Mertz's Critical Anthropology of the Socratic, Doctrinal Classroom." *John Marshall Law Review* 34 (2000): 131–161.

———. "Transcending the Legacies of Literacy and Transforming the Traditional Repertoire: Critical Discourse Strategies for Practice." *William Mitchell Law Review* 23 (1997): 491–563.

Bakhtin, Mikhail M. *The Dialogic Imagination.* Trans. Caryl Emerson and Michael Holquist. Austin: University of Texas Press, 1981.

Banks, Taunya Lovell. "Gender Bias in the Classroom." *Journal of Legal Education* 38 (1988): 137–146.

———. "Gender Bias in the Classroom (2)." *Southern Illinois Law Journal* 14 (1990): 527–599.

Barnhardt, Carol. "Tuning In: Athabaskan Teachers and Athabaskan Students." In *Cross-Cultural Studies in Alaskan Education*, vol. 2, ed. Ray Barnhardt, 144–164. Fairbanks, AK: Center for Cross-Cultural Studies, 1982.

Bartlett, Katharine, and Rosanne Kennedy, eds. *Feminist Legal Theory: Readings in Law and Gender.* Boulder, CO: Westview Press, 1991.

Baton, David. "Literacy in Everyday Contexts." In *Literacy and Motivation: Reading Engagement in Individuals and Groups*, ed. Ludo Verhoeven and Catherine Snow, 23–38. London: Lawrence Erlbaum, 2001.

Bauman, Richard. *Story, Performance, and Event: Contextual Studies of Oral Narrative.* New York: Cambridge University Press, 1986.

Bauman, Richard, and Charles Briggs. "Poetics and Performance as Critical Perspectives on Language and Social Life." *Annual Review of Anthropology* 19 (1990): 59–88.

Becker, Mary. "How to Do a Gender Study at Your Law School." Ms. 1999.

Beidelman, T. "Swazi Royal Ritual." *Africa* 36 (1966): 373–405.

Beldar. "Method to the Socratic Madness of Law Schools?" BeldarBlog, Oct. 24, 2003, http://beldar.blogs.com/beldarblog/2003/10/method_to_the_s.html.

Bell, Derrick A., Jr. "Black Students in White Law Schools: The Ordeal and the Opportunity." *Toledo Law Review* 1970 (1970): 539–558.

Benjamin, G. Andrew H., Alfred Kazniak, Bruce Sales, and Stephen Shanfield. "The Role of Legal Education in Producing Psychological Distress among Law Students." *American Bar Foundation Research Journal* 11 (1986): 225–252.

Bennett, Lance, and Martha Feldman. *Reconstructing Reality in the Courtroom.* London: Tavistock, 1981.

Berger, Peter, and Thomas Luckmann. *The Social Construction of Reality.* Garden City, NY: Doubleday, 1966.

Bernstein, Basil. *Class, Codes, and Control.* London: Routledge, 1975.

Bishin, William, and Christopher Stone. *Law, Language, and Ethics.* Mineola, NY: Foundation Press, 1972.

Black. *Law Dictionary.* St. Paul, MN: West, 1983.

Boersma, P. Dee, Debora Gay, Ruth Jones, Lynn Morrison, and Helen Remick. "Sex Differences in College Student-Teacher Interactions: Fact or Fantasy?" *Sex Roles* 7 (1982): 775–784.

Bohannon, Paul. "Ethnography and Comparison in Legal Anthropology." In *Law in Culture and Society*, ed. Laura Nader, 401–418. Chicago: Adline, 1969.

———. *Justice and Judgment among the Tiv.* London: Oxford University Press, 1957.

Booth, Wayne. *The Vocation of a Teacher: Rhetorical Occasions 1967–1988.* Chicago: University of Chicago Press, 1991.

Bossert, Steven. *Tasks and Social Relations in Classrooms: A Study of Instructional Organization and Its Consequences.* Cambridge, UK: Cambridge University Press, 1979.

Bourdieu, Pierre. "Cultural Capital and Pedagogic Communication." In *Reproduction in Education, Society and Culture*, ed. Pierre Bourdieu and Jean-Claude Passeron, 71–107. London: Sage, 1977.

———. *Distinction.* Cambridge, UK: Cambridge University Press, 1984.

———. *Homo Academicus.* Stanford: Stanford University Press, 1988.

Bourdieu, Pierre, and Jean-Claude Passeron, eds. *Reproduction in Education, Society and Culture.* London: Sage, 1977.

Bowers, Allison. "Women at the University of Texas Law School: A Call for Action." *Texas Journal of Women & Law* 9 (2000): 117–165.

Bowles, Samuel, and Herbert Gintis. *Schooling in Capitalist America.* London: Routledge and Kegan Paul, 1976.

Boyle, Robin. "Employing Active-Learning Techniques and Metacognition in Law School: Shifting Energy from Professor to Student." *University of Detroit Mercy Law Review* 81 (2003): 1–31.

Brenneis, Donald. "Grog and Gossip in Bhatgaon: Style and Substance in Fiji Indian Conversation." *American Ethnologist* 11 (1984): 487–506.

———. "Language and Disputing." *Annual Review of Anthropology* 17 (1988): 221–237.

———. "Performing Passions: Aesthetics and Politics in an Occasionally Egalitarian Community." *American Ethnologist* 14 (1987): 236–250.

———. "Telling Theories." Ms. 2005.

Brenneis, Donald, and Ronald Macaulay. "Learning Language, Learning Culture." In *The Matrix of Culture: Contemporary Linguistic Anthropology*, ed. Donald Brenneis and Ronald Macaulay, 7–11. Boulder, CO: Westview, 1996.

Brenneis, Donald, and Fred Myers, eds. *Dangerous Words: Language and Politics in the Pacific.* New York: New York University Press, 1984.

Briggs, Charles. *Competence in Performance: The Creativity of Tradition in Mexicano Verbal Art*. Philadelphia: University of Pennsylvania Press, 1988.

————, ed. *Disorderly Discourse: Narrative, Conflict, and the Social Construction of Inequality*. New York: Oxford University Press, 1996.

————. Introduction. In *Disorderly Discourse*, ed. Charles Briggs, 3–40. New York: Oxford University Press, 1996.

————. "Notes on a Confession: On the Construction of Gender, Sexuality, and Violence in an Infanticide Case." *Pragmatics* 7 (1997): 519–546.

Bright, William, and Attipat Ramanujan. "Sociolinguistic Variation and Language Change." In *Sociolinguistics*, ed. J. B. Pride and Janet Holmes, 157–166. The Hague: Mouton, 1972.

Brooks, Virginia. "Sex Difference in Student Dominance Behavior in Female and Male Professors' Classrooms." *Sex Roles* 8 (1982): 683–690.

Brutsaert, Herman. "Changing Sources of Self-Esteem among Girls and Boys in Secondary Schools." *Urban Education* 24 (1990): 432–439.

Bryden, David. "What Do Law Students Learn? A Pilot Study." *Journal of Legal Education* 34 (1984): 479–506.

Bumiller, Kristin. *The Civil Rights Society: The Social Construction of Victims*. Baltimore: Johns Hopkins University Press, 1988.

Burns, Robert. *A Theory of the Trial*. Princeton, NJ: Princeton University Press, 2001.

Burton, Angela Olivia. "Cultivating Ethical, Socially Responsible Lawyer Judgment: Introducing the Multiple Lawyering Intelligences Paradigm into the Clinical Setting." *Clinical Law Review* 11 (2004): 15–47.

Calhoun, Craig. *Critical Social Theory*. Cambridge, UK: Blackwell, 1995.

Calhoun, Craig, and Francis Ianni, eds. *The Anthropological Study of Education*. The Hague: Mouton, 1976.

Calleros, Charles. "Training a Diverse Student Body for a Multicultural Society." *La Raza Law Journal* 8 (1995): 140–165.

Carnegie Commission on Higher Education. *Opportunities for Women in Higher Education: Their Current Participation, Prospects for the Future, and Recommendations for Action*. New York: McGraw Hill, 1973.

Carnegie Foundation for the Advancement of Teaching. *Educating Lawyers*. San Francisco: Jossey-Bass, in press.

Carnoy, Martin, and Henry Levin. *Schooling and Work in the Democratic State*. Stanford: Stanford University Press, 1985.

Carrington, Paul, and James Conley. "The Alienation of Law Students." *Michigan Law Review* 75 (1977): 887–899.

Cazden, Courtney. *Classroom Discourse: The Language of Teaching and Learning*. Portsmouth, NH: Heineman, 1988.

Chambers, David, Timothy Clydesdale, William Kidder, and Richard Lempert. "The Real Impact of Eliminating Affirmative Action in American Law Schools: An Empirical Critique of Richard Sander's Study." *Stanford Law Review* 57 (2005): 1855–1898.

Chandler, Nahum. "The Problem of Purity: A Study in the Early Thought of W. E. B. DuBois." Ph.D. diss., University of Chicago, 1997.

Chester, Ronald, and Scott Alumbaugh. "Functionalizing First-Year Legal Education: Toward a New Pedagogical Jurisprudence." *University of California at Davis Law Review* 25 (1991): 21–84.

Collier, Jane. *Law and Social Change in Zinacantan*. Stanford: Stanford University Press, 1973.

Collins, James. "Differential Treatment and Reading Instruction." In *The Social Construc-*

*tion of Literacy*, ed. Jenny Cook-Gumperz, 117–137. New York: Cambridge University Press, 1986.

———. "Language and Class in Minority Education." *Anthropology & Education Quarterly* 14 (1988): 299–326.

———. "Literacy and Literacies." *Annual Review of Anthropology* 24 (1995): 75–93.

———. "Socialization to Text: Structure and Contradiction in Schooled Literacy." In *Natural Histories of Discourse*, ed. Michael Silverstein and Greg Urban, 203–228. Chicago: University of Chicago Press, 1996.

———. "Using Cohesion Analysis to Understand Access to Knowledge." In *Literacy and Schooling*, ed. D. Bloome, 67–97. Norwood, NJ: Ablex, 1987.

Collins, James, and Richard Blot. *Literacy and Literacies: Texts, Power, and Identity.* Cambridge, UK: Cambridge University Press, 2003.

Collins, James, and Sarah Michaels. "Speaking and Writing: Discourse Strategies and the Acquisition of Literacy." In *The Social Construction of Literacy*, ed. Jenny Cook-Gumperz, 207–222. New York: Cambridge University Press, 1986.

Collins, James, and Stef Slembrouck. "Reading Shop Windows in Globalized Neighborhoods: Multilingual Literacy Practices and Indexicality." *Working Papers on Language, Power & Identity* 21 (2004).

Comaroff, Jean. *Body of Power, Spirit of Resistance: The Culture and History of a South African People.* Chicago: University of Chicago Press, 1985.

Comaroff, Jean, and John Comaroff. *Of Revelation and Revolution: Christianity, Colonialism, and Consciousness in South Africa.* Vol. 1. Chicago: University of Chicago Press, 1991.

Comaroff, John, and Jean Comaroff. *Of Revelation and Revolution: The Dialectics of Modernity on a South African Frontier.* Vol. 2. Chicago: University of Chicago Press, 1997.

Comaroff, John, and Simon Roberts. *Rules and Processes: The Cultural Logic of Dispute in an African Context.* Chicago: University of Chicago Press, 1981.

Condlin, Robert. "Socrates' New Clothes: Substituting Persuasion for Learning in Clinical Practice Instruction." *Maryland Law Review* 40 (1981): 223–283.

Conley, John. " 'How Bad Is It Out There?' Teaching and Learning about the State of North Carolina's Legal Profession." *North Carolina Law Review* 82 (2004): 1943–2016.

———. "Power Is as Power Does: A Reply to Travers." *Law & Social Inquiry* (forthcoming).

Conley, John, and William O'Barr. *Just Words: Law, Language, and Power.* Chicago: University of Chicago Press, 1998.

———. *Rules versus Relationships: The Ethnography of Legal Discourse.* Chicago: University of Chicago Press, 1990.

Constable, Marianne. *Just Silences: The Limits and Possibilities of Modern Law.* Princeton, NJ: Princeton University Press, forthcoming.

Constantinople, Anne, Randolph Cornelius, and Janet Gray. "The Chilly Climate: Fact or Artifact?" *Journal of Higher Education* 59 (1988): 527–550.

Cook-Gumperz, Jenny. "Schooling and Literacy: An Unchanging Equation?" In *The Social Construction of Literacy*, ed. Jenny Cook-Gumperz, 16–44. New York: Cambridge University Press, 1986.

Coombe, Rosemary J. "Contesting the Self: Negotiating Subjectivities in Nineteenth-Century Ontario Defamation Trials." *Studies in Law, Policy & Society* 11 (1991): 3–40.

———. *The Cultural Life of Intellectual Properties.* Durham, NC: Duke University Press, 1998.

Cornelius, Randolph, Janet Gray, and Anne Constantinople. "Student-Faculty Interaction in the College Classroom." *Journal of Research & Development in Education* 23 (1990): 189–197.

Cover, Robert. *Justice Accused.* New Haven: Yale University Press, 1992.

Cramton, Roger. "The Current State of the Law School Curriculum." *Journal of Legal Education* 32 (1982): 321–329.

Crawford, Mary, and Margo MacLeod. "Gender in the College Classroom: An Assessment of the 'Chilly Climate' for Women." *Sex Roles* 23 (1990): 101–122.

Crenshaw, Kimberlé. "Foreword: Toward a Race-Conscious Pedagogy in Legal Education." *National Black Law Journal* 11 (1989): 1–14.

———. "Mapping the Margins: Intersectionality, Identity Politics, and Violence against Women of Color." *Stanford Law Review* 43 (1991): 1241–1299.

Crenshaw, Kimberlé, Neil Gotanda, and Gary Peller. *Critical Race Theory: The Key Writings That Formed the Movement.* New York: New Press, 1995.

Critical Legal Studies Special Issue. *Stanford Law Review* 36 (1984): 1–674.

Cunningham, Clark. "Lawyer as Translator, Representation as Text: Towards an Ethnography of Legal Discourse." *Cornell Law Review* 77 (1992): 1298–1387.

Curran, Barbara. *Women in the Law: A Look at the Numbers.* Chicago: American Bar Foundation, 1995.

Cutler, A. S. "Inadequate Law School Training: A Plan to Give Students Actual Practice." *American Bar Association Journal* 37 (1951): 203.

Daicoff, Susan. *Lawyer, Know Thyself: A Psychological Analysis of Personality Strengths and Weaknesses.* Washington, DC: American Psychological Association, 2004.

———. "Lawyer, Know Thyself: A Review of Empirical Research on Attorney Attributes Bearing on Professionalism." *American University Law Review* 46 (1997): 1337–1427.

Dallimore, Suzanne. "The Socratic Method: More Harm Than Good?" *Journal of Contemporary Law* 3 (1977): 177.

Danet, Brenda. "Language in the Legal Process." *Law & Society Review* 14 (1980): 445–564.

Dauber, Michele Landis. "The Big Muddy." *Stanford Law Review* 57 (2005): 1899–1914.

David, Leon Thomas. "The Clinical Lawyer-School: The Clinic." *University of Pennsylvania Law Review* 83 (1934): 1–22.

Davidson, Ann L. *Making and Molding Identity in Schools: Student Narratives on Race, Gender, and Academic Engagement.* Albany: State University of New York Press, 1996.

Davis, Peggy Cooper. "Contextual Legal Criticism: A Demonstration Exploring Hierarchy." *New York University Law Review* 66 (1991): 1635–1681.

———. "Law and Lawyering: Legal Studies with an Interdisciplinary Focus." *New York Law School Law Review* 37 (1992): 185–207.

de Castelle, Suzanne, and Allan Luke. "Defining 'Literacy' in North American Schools." *Journal of Curriculum Studies* 15 (1983): 373–389.

De Cosse, Sarah A. "Simply Unbelievable: Reasonable Women and Hostile Environment Sexual Harassment." *Law & Inequality* 10 (1992): 285.

Devitt, Edward. "Why Don't Law Schools Teach Law Students How to Try Lawsuits?" *Cleveland State Law Review* 29 (1980): 631–640.

Dickinson, John. "Legal Rules: Their Function in the Process of Decision." *University of Pennsylvania Law Review* 79 (1931): 833–868.

Domínguez, Virginia. *White by Definition: Social Classification in Creole Louisiana.* New Brunswick, NJ: Rutgers University Press, 1986.

Donahue, John, III. "The Case for More and Better Empirical Research in Law Schools." Paper presented in plenary session at the Association of American Law Schools Meetings, Washington, DC, 2006.

Dorf, Michael. "Foreword: The Limits of Socratic Deliberation." *Harvard Law Review* 112 (1998): 4–83.

Dowd, Nancy. "Diversity Matters: Race, Gender, and Ethnicity in Legal Education." *Florida Journal of Law and Public Policy* 15 (2003): 11–56.

Drury, Darrel W. "Black Self-Esteem and Desegregated Schools." *Sociology of Education* 53 (1980): 88–103.

Duff, Patricia, Ping Wong, and Margaret Early. "Learning Language for Work and Life: The Linguistic Socialization of Immigrant Canadians Seeking Careers in Healthcare." *Modern Language Journal* 68 (2002): 189–222.

Duranti, Alessandro. *Linguistic Anthropology.* New York: Cambridge University Press, 1997.

Duranti, Alessandro, and Donald Brenneis, eds. *The Audience as Co-Author.* Special issue of *Text* 6 (1986).

Duranti, Alessandro, and Charles Goodwin, eds. *Rethinking Context: Language as an Interactive Phenomenon.* Cambridge, UK: Cambridge University Press, 1992.

Dworkin, Ronald. *Law's Empire.* Cambridge, MA: Harvard University Press, 1986.

Eaves, David, et al. "Gender, Ethnicity, and Grades: Evidence of Discrimination in Law Firm Interviews." *Law & Inequality* 7 (1989): 189.

Eggleston, John, and Denis Gleeson. "Curriculum Innovation and the Context of the School." In *Identity and Structure*, ed. D. Gleeson, 15–27. Driffield, UK: Nafferton Studies in Education, 1977.

Elkins, James. "The Legal Persona: An Essay on the Professional Mask." *Virginia Law Review* 64 (1978): 735–766.

Epstein, Lee, and Gary King. "The Rules of Inference." *University of Chicago Law Review* 69 (2002): 1–133.

Erickson, Fred, and Jeffrey Shultz. *The Counselor as Gatekeeper: Social Interaction in Interviews.* New York: Academic Press, 1982.

Erlanger, Howard, Charles Epp, Mia Cahill, and Kathleen Haines. "Law Student Idealism and Job Choice: Some New Data on an Old Question." *Law & Society Review* 30 (1996): 851–864.

Erlanger, Howard, Bryant Garth, Jane Larson, Elizabeth Mertz, Victoria Nourse, and David Wilkins. "Foreword: Is It Time for a New Legal Realism?" *Wisconsin Law Review* 2005 (2005): 335–363.

Erlanger, Howard, and Douglas Klegon. "Socialization Effects of Professional School: The Law School Experience and Students' Orientation to School Reform." *Law & Society Review* (1978): 11–35.

Errington, J. Joseph. "On the Nature of the Sociolinguistic Sign: Describing the Javanese Speech Levels." In *Semiotic Mediation: Sociocultural and Psychological Perspectives*, ed. Elizabeth Mertz and Richard Parmentier, 287–310. New York: Academic Press, 1985.

Fassinger, Polly A. "Understanding Classroom Interaction: Students' and Professors' Contributions to Students' Silence." *Journal of Higher Education* 66 (1995): 82–96.

Feldman, Saul D. *Escape from the Doll's House.* New York: McGraw Hill, 1974.

Fineman, Martha Albertson. *The Autonomy Myth: A Theory of Dependency.* New York: New Press, 2004.

———. *The Illusion of Equality: The Rhetoric and Reality of Divorce Reform.* Chicago: University of Chicago Press, 1991.

———. *The Neutered Mother, the Sexual Family, and Other Twentieth Century Tragedies.* New York: Routledge, 1995.

Finkelstein, Peter. "Studies in the Anatomy Laboratory: A Portrait of Individual and Collective Defense." In *Inside Doctoring*, ed. Robert Coombs, Scott May, and Gary Small, 22–42. New York: Greenwood Press, 1986.

Finn, Jeremy. *School Engagement and Students at Risk.* Washington, DC: U.S. Department of Education, National Center for Educational Statistics, 1993.

Fish, Stanley. "The Law Wishes to Have a Formal Existence." In *The Fate of Law*, ed. Austin Sarat and Thomas Kearns, 159–208. Ann Arbor: University of Michigan Press, 1991.

Fleming, Jacqueline. *Blacks in College*. San Francisco: Jossey-Bass, 1984.

Foley, William. *Anthropological Linguistics: An Introduction*. Oxford: Basil Blackwell, 1997.

Forrester, John. "If *p*, Then What? Thinking in Cases." *History of the Human Sciences* 9 (1996): 1–25.

Fox, Mary Frank. "Women and Higher Education: Sex Differentials in the Status of Students and Scholars." In *Women: A Feminist Perspective*, 3d ed., ed. Jo Freeman, 238–255. Palo Alto, CA: Mayfield, 1984.

Frank, Jerome. "A Disturbing Look at the Law Schools." *Journal of Legal Education* 2 (1949): 189–192.

———. *Law and the Modern Mind*. New York: Anchor Books, 1963.

———. "A Plea for Lawyer Schools." *Yale Law Journal* 56 (1947): 1303–1344.

———. "Why Not a Clinical Lawyer-School?" *University of Pennsylvania Law Review* 81 (1933): 907–923.

Freitag, Jason. "Translating *Nisi Per Legem Terrae*: The Semiotics of Due Process." LLM thesis, Northwestern University, 1995.

Friedland, Steven. "How We Teach: A Survey of Teaching Techniques in American Law Schools." *Seattle University Law Review* 20 (1996): 1–44.

Friedman, Lawrence. *A History of American Law*. New York: Simon and Schuster, 1973.

Frohmann, Lisa. "Discrediting Victims' Allegations of Sexual Assault." *Social Problems* 38 (1991): 213–226.

Frug, Mary Joe. *Postmodern Legal Feminism*. New York: Routledge, 1992.

———. "Re-Reading Contracts: A Feminist Analysis of a Contracts Casebook." *American University Law Review* 34 (1985): 1065–1140.

Gal, Susan, and Judith T. Irvine. "The Boundaries of Languages and Disciplines: How Ideologies Construct Difference." *Social Research* 62 (1995): 967–1001.

Galanter, Marc. "Why the 'Haves' Come Out Ahead: Speculations on the Limits of Legal Change." *Law & Society Review* 9 (1974): 95–160.

Garner, David. "Socratic Misogyny? Analyzing Feminist Criticisms of Socratic Teaching in Legal Education." *Brigham Young University Law Review* 2000 (2000): 1597–1649.

Garrett, Elizabeth. "Becoming Lawyers: The Role of the Socratic Method in Modern Law Schools." *Green Bag 2d* 1 (1998): 199–208.

Garrett, Paul, and Patricial Baquedano-Lopez. "Language Socialization: Reproduction and Continuity, Transformation and Change." *Annual Review of Anthropology* 31 (2002): 339–361.

Garrison, Marsha, Brian Tomko, and Ivan Yip. "Succeeding in Law School: A Comparison of Women's Experiences at Brooklyn Law School and the University of Pennsylvania." *Michigan Journal of Gender and Law* 3 (1996): 515–550.

Garth, Bryant, and Yves Dezalay. *The Internationalization of Palace Wars: Lawyers, Economists, and the Contest to Transform Latin American States*. Chicago: University of Chicago Press, 2002.

Garth, Bryant, and Joanne Martin. "Law Schools and the Construction of Competence." *Journal of Legal Education* 43 (1993): 469–510.

Garvin, P. J. *A Prague School Reader on Esthetics, Literary Structure, and Style*. Georgetown, DC: Georgetown University School of Language, 1964.

Gee, E. G., and Donald Jackson. "Current Studies of Legal Education: Findings and Recommendations." *Journal of Legal Education* 32 (1982): 471–505.

Gee, James. "The Narrativization of Experience in the Oral Style." *Journal of Education* 167 (1985): 9–35.

Geertz, Clifford. *The Interpretation of Cultures.* New York: Basic Books, 1973.

———. *Local Knowledge: Further Essays in Interpretive Anthropology.* New York: Basic Books, 1983.

Gergen, Kenneth. "Social Understanding and the Insciption of Self." In *Cultural Psychology: Essays on Comparative Human Development,* ed. James Stigler, Richard Shweder, and Gilbert Herdt, 596–606. Cambridge, UK: Cambridge University Press, 1990.

Gilligan, Carol, Nona Lyons, and Trudy Hanmer, eds. *Making Connections: The Relational Worlds of Adolescent Girls at Emma Willard School.* Cambridge, MA: Harvard University Press, 1980.

Giroux, Henry. "Theories of Reproduction and Resistance in the New Sociology of Education." *Harvard Educational Review* 53 (1983): 257–293.

Glenn, Peter. "Some Thoughts about Developing Constructive Approaches to Lawyer and Law Student Distress." *Journal of Law and Health* 10 (1995–1996): 69–77.

Gluckman, Max. *The Ideas in Barotse Jurisprudence.* New Haven, CT: Yale University Press, 1965.

Goffman, Erving. *Forms of Talk.* Philadelphia: University of Pennsylvania Press, 1981.

———. *The Presentation of Self in Everyday Life.* New York: Anchor Books, 1959.

Good, Thomas, and Neville Sikes. "Effects of Teacher Sex and Student Sex on Classroom Interaction." 65 *Journal of Educational Psychology* 65 (1973): 74–87.

Goodale, Mark. "The Globalization of Sympathetic Law and Its Consequences." *Law & Social Inquiry* 27 (2002): 401–415.

Goodale, Mark, and Elizabeth Mertz. "Anthropology of Law." In *Encyclopedia of Law and Society: American and Global Perspectives,* ed. David Clark. London: Sage, in press.

Gooding, Susan Staiger. "Place, Race, and Names: Layered Identities in United States v. Oregon, Confederated Tribes of the Colville Reservation, Plaintiff-Intervenor." *Law & Society Review* 28 (1994): 1181–1229.

Goody, Jack, and L. P. Watt. "The Consequences of Literacy." In *Literacy in Traditional Societies,* ed. Jack Goody, 27–68. Cambridge, UK: Cambridge University Press, 1968.

Gough, Kathleen. "Implications of Literacy in Traditional India and China." In *Literacy in Traditional Society,* ed. Jack Goody, 69–84. New York: Cambridge University Press, 1968.

Granfield, Robert. *Making Elite Lawyers: Visions of Law at Harvard and Beyond.* New York: Routledge, 1992.

Greenhouse, Carol. *Praying for Justice: Faith, Order, and Community in an American Town.* Ithaca, NY: Cornell University Press, 1986.

Greenhouse, Carol, Elizabeth Mertz, and Kay Warren. *Ethnography in Unstable Places: Everyday Lives in Contexts of Dramatic Political Change.* Durham, NC: Duke University Press, 2002.

Greenhouse, Carol, Barbara Yngvesson, and David Engel. *Law and Community in Three American Towns.* Ithaca, NY: Cornell University Press, 1994.

Groves, Harry. "Toward a More Effective Program in the Small Law School." *Journal of Legal Education* 12 (1959): 52–66.

*Grutter v. Bollinger,* 539 U.S. 306 (2003).

Guinier, Lani, Michelle Fine, and Jane Balin. *Becoming Gentlemen: Women, Law School, and Institutional Change.* Boston: Beacon Press, 1997.

Gulati, Mitu, Richard Sander, and Robert Sockloskie. "The Happy Charade: An Empirical Examination of the Third Year of Law School." *Journal of Legal Education* 51 (2001): 235–235.

Gumperz, John. *Discourse Strategies*. New York: Cambridge University Press, 1982.

Gurin, Patricia, E. Dey, S. Hurtado, and G. Gurin. "Diversity and Higher Education: Theory and Impact on Educational Outcomes." *Harvard Educational Review* 72 (2002): 330–366.

Hagan, John, and Fiona Kay. *Gender in Practice: Lawyers' Lives in Transition*. New York: Oxford University Press, 1997.

Hall, Roberta, and Bernice Sandler. *The Classroom Climate: A Chilly One for Women?* Washington, DC: Association of American Colleges, Project on the Status and Education of Women, 1982.

Hanks, William. *Referential Practice: Language and Lived Space among the Maya*. Chicago: University of Chicago Press, 1990.

Hantzis, Catherine. "Kingsfield and Kennedy: Reappraising the Male Model of Law School Teaching." *Journal of Legal Education* 38 (1988): 155–164.

Harno, Albert. *Legal Education in the United States*. San Francisco: Bancroft-Whitney, 1953.

Harris, Angela. "Race and Essentialism in Feminist Legal Theory." *Stanford Law Review* 42 (1990): 581–616.

Hawkins-León, Cynthia. "The Socratic Method–Problem Method Dichotomy: The Debate over Teaching Method Continues." *Brigham Young University Education & Law Journal* 1998 (1998): 1–18.

Heath, Shirley Brice. "Toward an Ethnohistory of Writing in American Education." In *Writing: The Nature, Development, and Teaching of Written Communication*, ed. Marcia F. Whiteman, 25–46. Hillsdale, NJ: Lawrence Erlbaum, 1982.

———. *Ways with Words: Language, Life, and Work in Communities and Classrooms*. Cambridge, UK: Cambridge University Press, 1983.

Heffernan, William. "Not Socrates, but Protagoras: The Sophistic Basis of Legal Education." *Buffalo Law Review* 29 (1980): 399–423.

Heinz, John, Kathleen Hull, and Ava Harter. "Lawyers and Their Discontents: Findings from a Survey of the Chicago Bar." *Indiana Law Journal* 74 (1999): 735–758.

Heller, Jack F., C. Richard Puff, and Carol J. Mills. "Assessment of the Chilly College Climate for Women." *Journal of Higher Education* 56 (1985): 446–461.

Herrnstein Smith, Barbara. "Narrative Versions, Narrative Theories." *Critical Inquiry* 7 (1980): 213–236.

Higgins, Tracy. "Anti-Essentialism, Relativism, and Human Rights." *Harvard Women's Law Journal* 19 (1996): 89–126.

Hill, Jane, and Judith Irvine, eds. *Responsibility and Evidence in Oral Discourse*. Cambridge, UK: Cambridge University Press, 1992.

Hirsch, Susan. "Making Culture Visible: Comments on Elizabeth Mertz's 'Teaching Lawyers the Language of Law: Legal and Anthropological Translations.' " *John Marshall Law Review* 34 (2000): 119–129.

———. *Pronouncing and Persevering: Gender and the Discourses of Disputing in an African Islamic Court*. Chicago: University of Chicago Press, 1998.

Hocker, William Cliff, and Maurice Foster. "The African-American Lawyer: A Demographic Profile." *National Bar Association Magazine* 5 (April 1991): 20.

Holland, Dorothy C., and Margaret A. Eisenhart. *Educated in Romance: Women, Achievement, and College Culture*. Chicago: University of Chicago Press, 1990.

Homer, Suzanne, and Lois Schwartz. "Admitted but Not Accepted: Outsiders Take an Inside Look at Law School." *Berkeley Women's Law Journal* 5 (1990): 1–74.

*Hopwood v. Texas*, 78 F.3d 932 (5th Circuit 1996).

Hue-Pei Au, Kathryn, and Jana M. Mason. "Social Organizational Factors in Learning to Read: The Balance of Rights Hypothesis." *Reading Research Quarterly* 17 (1981): 115–152.

Jacobs, Alice. "Women in Law School: Structural Constraint and Personal Choice in the Formation of Personal Identity." *Journal of Legal Education* 24 (1972): 462–473.

Jacobs-Huey, Lanita. *Becoming Cosmetologists: Language Socialization and Identity in an African-American Beauty College*. PhD diss., University of California, Los Angeles, 1999.

Jacobson, M. H. Sam. "A Primer on Learning Styles: Reaching Every Student." *Seattle University Law Review* 25 (2001): 139–177.

Jakobson, Roman. "Closing Statement: Linguistics and Poetics." In *Style in Language*, ed. Thomas Sebeok, 350–377. Cambridge, MA: MIT Press, 1960.

———. *On Language*. Ed. Linda Waugh and Monique Monville-Burston. Cambridge, MA: Harvard University Press, 1995.

———. "Shifters, Verbal Categories and the Russian Verb." In *Selected Writings*, Vol. 2, 130–147. The Hague: Mouton, 1971.

Janoff, Sandra. "The Influence of Legal Education on Moral Reasoning." *Minnesota Law Review* 76 (1991): 193–238.

Johnson, William. *Schooled Lawyers: A Study in the Clash of Professional Cultures*. New York: New York University Press, 1978.

Jordan, Jacqueline. "Teacher-Student Interactions: Effects of Student Race, Sex, and Grade Level." *Journal of Educational Psychology* 78 (1986): 14–21.

Josephs, Robert, Hazel Markus, and Romin Tafarodi. "Gender and Self-Esteem." *Journal of Personality & Social Psychology* 63 (1992): 391–402.

Kahlenberg, Richard. *Broken Contract: A Memoir of Harvard Law School*. Boston: Faber & Faber, 1992.

Kalman, Laura. "To Hell with Langdell!" *Law & Social Inquiry* 20 (1995): 771–773.

Karp, David A., and William C. Yoels. "The College Classroom: Some Observations on the Meanings of Student Participation." *Sociology & Social Research* 60 (1976): 421–439.

Kelman, Mark. *A Guide to Critical Legal Studies*. Cambridge, MA: Harvard University Press, 1987.

Kennedy, Duncan. "Form and Substance in Private Law Adjudication." *Harvard Law Review* 89 (1976): 1685–1778.

———. *Legal Education and the Reproduction of Hierarchy*. New York: New York University Press, 1983.

Kennedy, Eugene. "A Multilevel Study of Elementary Male Black Students and White Students." *Journal of Educational Research* 86 (1992): 105–110.

Kerlow, Eleanor. *Poisoned Ivy: How Egos, Ideology, and Power Politics Almost Ruined Harvard Law School*. New York: St. Martin's Press, 1994.

Kerr, Orin. "The Decline of the Socratic Method at Harvard." *Nebraska Law Review* 78 (1999): 113–134.

Kimball, Edward, and Larry Farmer. "Comparative Results of Teaching Evidence Three Ways." *Journal of Legal Education* 30 (1979): 196–212.

Konop, Thomas. "The Case System: A Defense." *Notre Dame Law Review* 6 (1931): 275–283.

Kozol, Jonathan. *Savage Inequalities: Children in America's Schools*. New York: Crown, 1991.

Krauskopf, Joan. "Touching the Elephant: Perceptions of Gender Issues in Nine Law Schools." *Journal of Legal Education* 44 (1994) 311–340.

Krupnick, Catherine. "Women and Men in the Classroom: Inequality and Its Remedies." *On Teaching and Learning: Journal of the Harvard-Danforth Center* 1 (1985): 18–25.

Kulick, Don, and Bambi Schieffelin. "Language Socialization." In *A Companion to Linguistic Anthropology*, ed. Alessandro Duranti, 349–368. Malden, MA: Basil Blackwell, 2004.

Kurylowicz, J. "The Role of Deictic Elements in Linguistic Evolution." *Semiotica* 5 (1972): 174–183.

Labov, William. *Sociolinguistic Patterns*. Philadelphia: University of Pennsylvania Press, 1972.

Landman, Jacob. "Anent the Case Method of Studying Law." *New York University Law Review* 4 (1927): 139–160.

Langdell, Christopher Columbus. Preface. In *Cases on the Law of Contracts*. Boston: Little, Brown, 1871.

Larson, Jane. " 'Imagine Her Satisfaction': The Transformative Task of Feminist Tort Work." *Washburn Law Journal* 33 (1993): 56–75.

Lawrence, Charles, III. "The Id, the Ego, and Equal Protection: Reckoning with Unconscious Racism." *Stanford Law Review* 39 (1987): 317–388.

Lazarus-Black, Mindie. "The Rites of Domination: Practice, Process, and Structure in Lower Courts." *American Ethnologist* 24 (1997): 628–651.

———. *The Vanishing Complainant*. Champaign: University of Illinois Press, 2006.

Lazarus-Black, Mindie, and Susan Hirsch, eds. *Contested States: Law, Hegemony and Resistance* New York: Routledge, 1994.

Leacock, Eleanor. "Education in Africa: Myths of 'Modernization.'" In *The Anthropological Study of Education*, ed. Craig Calhoun and Francis Ianni, 239–250. Chicago: Mouton, 1976.

Leiter, Brian. "The 'Socratic Method': The Scandal of American Education." *The Leiter Reports*, Oct. 20, 2004, http://webapp.utexas.edu/blogs/archives/bleiter/000294.html.

Lempert, Richard, David Chambers, and Terry Adams. "Michigan's Minority Graduates in Practice: The River Runs through Law School." *Law & Social Inquiry* 25 (2000): 395–505.

Lempert, Richard, and Joseph Sanders. *An Invitation to Law and Social Science*. New York: Longman, 1986.

Levi, Edward. *An Introduction to Legal Reasoning*. Chicago: University of Chicago Press, 1949.

Levinson, Stephen. *Pragmatics*. Cambridge, MA: Cambridge University Press, 1983.

Lind, E. Allan, and Tom Tyler. *The Social Psychology of Procedural Justice*. New York: Plenum, 1988.

Llewellyn, Karl. "The Current Crisis in Legal Education." *Journal of Legal Education* 1 (1948): 211–220.

———. "On Warranty of Quality, and Society." *Columbia Law Review* 36 (1936): 699–744.

———. "Some Realism about Realism: Responding to Dean Pound." *Harvard Law Review* 44 (1931): 1222–1264.

Lorenson, Willard. "Concentrating on a Single Jurisdiction to Teach Criminal Law: An Experiment." *Journal of Legal Education* 20 (1968): 361–365.

Louiseaux, Pierre. "The Newcomer and the Case Method." *Journal of Legal Education* 7 (1954): 244–251.

Lubeck, Sally. "Kinship and Classrooms: An Ethnographic Perspective on Education as Cultural Transmission." *Sociology of Education* 57 (1984): 219–232.

Lucy, John. *Grammatical Categories and Cognition: A Case Study of the Linguistic Relativity Hypothesis*. Cambridge, UK: Cambridge University Press, 2003.

———. "Whorf's View of the Linguistic Mediation of Thought." In *Semiotic Mediation: Sociocultural and Psychological Perspectives*, ed. Elizabeth Mertz and Richard Parmentier, 73–97. New York: Academic Press, 1985.

Macaulay, Stewart. "The New versus the Old Legal Realism: 'Things Ain't What They Used to Be.' " *Wisconsin Law Review* 2005 (2005): 365–403.

Macaulay, Stewart, Lawrence Friedman, and John Stookey. *Law & Society: Readings on the Social Study of Law.* New York: W. W. Norton, 1995.

Macaulay, Stewart, John Kidwell, and William Whitford. *Contracts: Law in Action.* 2d ed. Philadelphia: Matthew Bender, 2003.

MacKinnon, Catherine. *Feminism Unmodified: Discourses on Life and Law.* Cambridge, MA: Harvard University Press, 1987.

Macneil, Ian. *Contracts: Exchange Transactions and Relations.* Mineola, NY: Foundation Press, 1978.

Mattessich, Paul, and Cherlyle Heilman. "The Career Paths of Minnesota Law School Graduates: Does Gender Make a Difference?" *Law and Inequality Journal* 9 (1990): 67–73.

Martin, Joanne, and Bryant Garth. "Clinical Education as a Bridge between Law School and Practice: Mitigating the Misery." *Clinical Law Review* 1 (1994): 443–456.

Maru, Olavi. *Research on the Legal Profession.* Chicago: American Bar Foundation, 1986.

Matoesian, Gregory. *Law and the Language of Identity: Discourse in the William Kennedy Smith Rape Trial.* Oxford: Oxford University Press, 2001.

———. *Reproducing Rape: Domination through Talk in the Courtroom.* Chicago: University of Chicago Press, 1993.

Matsuda, Mari. "When the First Quail Calls: Multiple Consciousness as Jurisprudential Method." *Women's Rights Law Reporter* 11 (1989): 7–10.

Mattessich, Paul, and Cheryl Heilman. "The Career Paths of Minnesota Law Graduates: Does Gender Make a Difference?" *Law & Inequality* 9 (1990): 67–73.

Maynard, Douglas. *Inside Plea Bargaining: The Language of Negotiation.* New York: Plenum Press, 1984.

McCleary, Roseanna, and Evan Zucker. "Higher Trait- and State-Anxiety in Female Law Students." *Psychological Reports* 68 (1991): 1075–1078.

McGill, Christa. "Producing Lawyers: Institutional Hierarchy and the Social Structure of Law Schools." PhD diss., Duke University, 2002.

McIntosh, Daniel, Julie Keywell, Alan Reifman, and Phoebe Ellsworth. "Stress and Health in First-Year Law Students: Women Fare Worse." *Journal of Applied Social Psychology* 24 (1994): 1474–1499.

McNamee, Gwen. "Alliance for Women Battles Law School Gender Bias." *Chicago Bar Association Record* 9 (May 4, 1995): 38.

Mehan, Hugh. "The Construction of an LD Student: A Case Study in the Politics of Representation." In *Natural Histories of Discourse,* ed. Michael Silverstein and Greg Urban, 253–276. Chicago: University of Chicago Press, 1996.

———. *Learning Lessons: Social Organization in the Classroom.* Cambridge, MA: Harvard University Press, 1979.

Menkel-Meadow, Carrie. "Feminist Legal Theory, Critical Legal Studies, and Legal Education or 'The Fem-Crits Go to Law School.' " *Journal of Legal Education* 38 (1988): 61–85.

———. "Portia in a Different Voice: Speculations on a Women's Lawyering Process." *Berkeley Women's Law Journal* 1 (1985): 39–63.

———. "What's Missing from the MacCrate Report: Of Skills, Legal Science, and Being a Human Being." *Washington Law Review* 69 (1994): 593–624.

Merritt, Deborah, and Barbara Reskin. "The Double Minority: Empirical Evidence of a Double Standard in Law School Hiring of Minority Women." *Southern California Law Review* 65 (1992): 2299–2359.

Merry, Sally. *Colonizing Hawai'i: The Cultural Power of Law.* Princeton, NJ: Princeton University Press, 2000.

————. *Getting Justice and Getting Even: Legal Consciousness among Working-Class Americans.* Chicago: University of Chicago Press, 1990.

————. *Human Rights and Gender Violence: Translating International Law into Local Justice.* Chicago: University of Chicago Press, 2005.

Mertz, Elizabeth. "Beyond Symbolic Anthropology: Introducing Semiotic Mediation." In *Semiotic Mediation: Sociocultural and Psychological Perspectives*, ed. Elizabeth Mertz and Richard Parmentier, 1–19. New York: Academic Press, 1985.

————. "Consensus and Dissent in U.S. Legal Opinions: Narrative Control and Social Voices." In *Disorderly Discourse: Narrative, Conflict, and the Social Construction of Inequality*, ed. Charles Briggs, 135–157. Oxford: Oxford University Press, 1996.

————. "Language and Mind: A Whorfian Theory in U.S. Language Law." *Working Papers in Sociolinguistics*, 93. Austin, TX: Southwest Educational Laboratory, 1982.

————. "Language, Law, and Social Meanings: Linguistics/Anthropological Contributions to the Study of Law." *Law & Society Review* 26 (1992): 601–633.

————. "Legal Language: Pragmatics, Poetics, and Social Power." *Annual Review of Anthropology* 23 (1994): 435–455.

————. "Legal Loci and Places in the Heart." *Law & Society Review* 28 (1994): 971– 973.

————. "A New Social Constructionism for Sociolegal Studies." *Law & Society Review* 28 (1994): 1243–1265.

————. " 'No Burden to Carry': Cape Breton Pragmatics and Metapragmatics." PhD diss., Duke University, 1982.

————. "Pragmatic and Semantic Change: A Cape Breton System of Personal Names." *Semiotica* 44 (1983): 55–74.

————. " 'Realist' Models of Judicial Decision-Making." *Working Papers and Proceedings of the Center for Psychosocial Studies*, 15. Chicago: Center for Psychosocial Studies, 1987.

————. "Recontextualization as Socialization: Text and Pragmatics in the Law School Classroom." In *Natural Histories of Discourse*, ed. Michael Silverstein and Greg Urban, 229–249. Chicago: University of Chicago Press, 1996.

————. "Silence and the Speakable in U.S. Law School Classrooms." Paper presented at the Law & Society Association meetings, Chicago, 1993.

————. "Sociolinguistic Creativity: Cape Breton Gaelic's Linguistic Tip." In *Investigating Obsolescence*, ed. Nancy Dorian, 103–116. Cambridge, UK: Cambridge University Press, 1989.

————. "Teaching Lawyers the Language of Law: Legal and Anthropological Translations." *John Marshall Law Review* 34 (2000): 91–117.

————. "The Uses of History: Language, Ideology, and Law in the United States and South Africa." *Law & Society Review* 22 (1988): 661–685.

Mertz, Elizabeth, Wamucii Njogu, and Susan Gooding. "What Difference Does Difference Make? The Challenge for Legal Education." *Journal of Legal Education* 48 (1998): 1–87.

Mertz, Elizabeth, and Richard Parmentier, eds. *Semiotic Mediation: Sociocultural and Psychological Perspectives.* New York: Academic Press, 1985.

Mertz, Elizabeth, and Bernard Weissbourd. "Legal Ideology and Linguistic Theory: Variability and Its Limits." In *Semiotic Mediation: Sociocultural and Psychological Perspectives*, ed. Elizabeth Mertz and Richard Parmentier, 261–285. New York: Academic Press, 1985.

Michaels, Sarah. "Narrative Presentations: An Oral Preparation for Literacy with First Graders." In *The Social Construction of Literacy*, ed. Jenny Cook-Gumperz, 94–116. Cambridge, UK: Cambridge University Press, 1986.

———. "Sharing Time: Children's Narrative Styles and Differential Access to Literacy." *Language in Society* 10 (1981): 423–442.

Michaels, Sarah, and James Collins. "Oral Discourse Styles: Classroom Interaction and the Acquisition of Literacy." In *Coherence in Written and Spoken Discourse*, ed. Deborah Tannen, 219–244. Norwood, NJ: Ablex, 1984.

Mickelson, Roslyn. "The Case of the Missing Brackets: Teachers and Social Reproduction." *Journal of Education* 169 (1987): 78–88.

Minow, Martha. *Making All the Difference.* Ithaca, NY: Cornell University Press, 1990.

Mitchell, Jacquelyn. "Black Children after the Eighties: Surviving the New Technology?" *Harvard Educational Review* 55 (1985): 354.

Mitchell, John. "Current Theories on Expert and Novice Thinking: A Full Faculty Considers the Implications for Legal Education." *Journal of Legal Education* 39 (1989): 275–297.

Moore, Sally Falk, ed. *Law and Anthropology: A Reader.* Oxford: Blackwell, 2005.

———. "Law and Social Change: The Semi-Autonomous Field as an Appropriate Subject of Study." *Law & Society Review* 7 (1973): 719–746.

———. *Social Facts and Fabrications: Customary Law on Kilimanjaro, 1880–1980.* Cambridge, UK: Cambridge University Press, 1986.

Moore, Underhill, and Charles Callahan. "Law and Learning Theory: A Study in Legal Control." *Yale Law Journal* 53 (1943): 1–136.

Morgan, Edmund. "The Case Method." *Journal of Legal Education* 4 (1952): 379–391.

Morine-Dershimer, Greta. "Instructional Strategy and the 'Creation' of Classroom Status." *American Educational Research Journal* 20 (1983): 645–661.

Morris, Robert. "Not Thinking Like a Non-Lawyer: Implications of 'Recognization' for Legal Education and Intellectual Due Process." Paper presented at Knowledge & Discourse: Speculating on Disciplinary Futures, 2nd International Conference, Hong Kong, June 2002. *Web Proceedings*, ed. C. Barron, P. Benson, and N. Bruce, July 2003, available at http://ec.hku.hk/kd2proc/default.asp.

Multicultural Women Attorneys Network. *The Burdens of Both, the Privileges of Neither.* Chicago: American Bar Association, 1994.

Nader, Laura, ed. *The Life of the Law: Anthropological Projects.* Berkeley: University of California Press, 2002.

———. *No Access to Law: Alternatives to the American Judicial System.* New York: Academic Press, 1980.

Nelson, Robert, David Trubek, and Rayman Solomon, eds. *Lawyers' Ideals, Lawyers' Practices: Transformations in the American Legal Profession.* Ithaca, NY: Cornell University Press, 1992.

Neufeld, Adam. "Costs of an Outdated Pedagogy? Study on Gender at Harvard Law School." *American University Journal of Gender, Social Policy & Law* 13 (2005): 511–594.

Noonan, John T., Jr. *Persons and Masks of the Law.* Berkeley: University of California Press, 1976.

Nourse, Victoria. "Passion's Progress: Modern Law Reform and the Provocation Defense." *Yale Law Journal* 106 (1997): 1331–1448.

Obiora, Leslye. "Neither Here nor There: Of the Female in American Legal Education." *Law & Social Inquiry* (1996): 355–432.

(Ochs-)Keenan, Elinor. "A Sliding Sense of Obligatoriness." In *Political Language and Oratory in Traditional Societies*, ed. M. Block, 93–112. London: Academic Press, 1975.

Ochs, Elinor. *Culture and Language Development.* Cambridge, UK: Cambridge University Press, 1988.

———. Introduction. In *Language Socialization across Cultures*, ed. Bambi Schieffelin and Elinor Ochs, 1–13. Cambridge, UK: Cambridge University Press, 1986.

Ochs, Elinor, and Bambi Schieffelin. "Language Acquisition and Socialization: Three Developmental Stories and Their Implications." In *Language, Culture, and Society*, ed. Ben Blount, 470–512. Prospect Heights, IL: Waveland, 1994.

Ogloff, James, David Lyon, Kevin Douglas, and V. Gordon Rose. "More Than 'Learning to Think Like a Lawyer': The Empirical Research on Legal Education." *Creighton Law Review* 34 (2000): 73–212.

O'Keefe, Tim, and Charles Faupel. "The Other Face of the Classroom: A Student Ethnography." *Social Spectrum* 7 (1987): 141–155.

Olson, D. R. "From Utterance to Text: The Bias of Language in Speech and Writing." *Harvard Educational Review* 47 (1977): 257–281.

Orfield, Gary, and Dean Whitla. "Diversity and Legal Eduation: Student Experiences in Leading Law Schools." In *Diversity Challenged: Evidence on the Impact of Affirmative Action*, ed. Gary Orfield and Michal Kurlaender, 143–174. Cambridge, MA: Harvard Educational Publishing Group and The Civil Rights Project, 2001.

Ortiz, Flora Ida. "Hispanic-American Children's Experiences in Classrooms: A Comparison between Hispanic and Non-Hispanic Children." In *Class, Race, and Gender in American Education*, ed. Lois Weis, 63–86. Albany: State University of New York Press, 1988.

*The Paper Chase*. Film. Directed by James Bridges; based on the novel by John Jay Osborn Jr. 1973.

Parmentier, Richard. "The Political Function of Reported Speech: A Belauan Example." In *Reflexive Language*, ed. John Lucy, 70–97. Cambridge, UK: Cambridge University Press, 1993.

Parsons, Talcott. "The School Class as a Social System: Some of Its Functions in American Society." *Harvard Educational Review* 29 (1959): 297–318.

Patterson, Edwin. "The Case Method in American Legal Education." *Journal of Legal Education* 4 (1951): 1–24.

Peirce, Charles S. *Collected Papers of Charles Sanders Peirce*. Vol. 2. Ed. C. Hartshorne and P. Weiss. Cambridge, MA: Harvard University Press, 1974.

Pennington, Nancy, and Reid Hastie. "A Cognitive Theory of Juror Decisionmaking: The Story Model." *Cardozo Law Review* 13 (1991): 519–557.

Philips, Susan. *Ideology in the Language of Judges: How Judges Practice Law, Politics, and Courtroom Control*. New York: Oxford University Press, 1998.

———. *The Invisible Culture: Communication in Classroom and Community on the Warm Springs Indian Reservation*. New York: Longman, 1982.

———. "The Language Socialization of Lawyers: Acquiring the 'Cant.' " In *Doing the Ethnography of Schooling: Educational Anthropology in Action*, ed. George Spindler, 176–209. Prospect Heights, IL: Waveland, 1988.

———. "Local Legal Hegemony in the Tongan Magistrate's Courts: How Sisters Fared Better Than Wives." In *Contested States: Law, Hegemony, and Resistance*, ed. Mindie Lazarus-Black and Susan Hirsch, 59–88. New York: Routledge, 1994.

———. "Participant Structures and Communicative Competence." In *Functions of Language in the Classroom*, ed. Courney Cazden, Vera John, and Dell Hymes, 370–394. New York: Teacher's College Press, 1972.

Pierce, Jennifer. *Gender Trials*. Berkeley: University of California Press, 1995.

Pomerantz, Anita. "Attributions of Responsibility: Blamings." *Sociology* 12 (1978): 115–121.

Postone, Moishe. *Time, Labor, and Social Domination: A Reinterpretation of Marx's Critical Theory*. Cambridge, UK: Cambridge University Press, 1993.

Pound, Roscoe. "Law in Books and Law in Action." *American Law Review* 44 (1910): 12–34.

———. "The Scope and Purpose of Sociological Jurisprudence." *Harvard Law Review* 25 (1912): 489–516.

[Prague School.] "Mélanges Linguistiques dédiés au Premier Congrès des Philologues Slaves." *Travaux du cercle Linguistiques de Prague* 1 (1929): 7–29.

Rakoff, Todd. "Law, Knowledge, and the Academy: An Introduction." *Harvard Law Review* 115 (2002): 1278–1287.

———. "The Harvard First-Year Experiment." *Journal of Legal Education* 39 (1989): 491–499.

Ramachandran, Banu. "Re-Reading Difference: Feminist Critiques of the Law School Classroom and the Problem with Speaking from Experience." *Columbia Law Review* 98 (1998): 1757–1794.

Randall, Vernellia R. "The Myers-Briggs Type Indicator, First Year Law Students, and Performance." *Cumberland Law Review* 26 (1995): 63–101.

Reichel-Dolmatoff, Gerardo. *Amazonian Cosmos: The Sexual and Religious Symbolism of the Tukano Indians.* Chicago: University of Chicago Press, 1974.

Rhode, Deborah. *In the Interests of Justice: Reforming the Legal Profession.* Oxford: Oxford University Press, 2005.

———. "Missing Questions: Feminist Perspectives on Legal Education." *Stanford Law Review* 45 (1993): 1547–1566.

Richmond, Michael. "Teaching Law to Passive Learners: The Contemporary Dilemma of Legal Education." *Cumberland Law Review* 26 (1995–1996): 943–959.

Riles, Annelise. *The Network Inside Out.* Ann Arbor: University of Michigan Press, 2000.

Ripps, Stephen. "A Curriculum Course Designed for Lowering the Attrition Rate for the Disadvantaged Student." *Howard Law Journal* 29 (1986): 457–480.

Rist, Ray C. "Student Social Class and Teacher Expectations: The Self-Fulfilling Prophecy in Ghetto Education." *Harvard Educational Review* 40 (1970): 411–451.

Robert, E. R., and M. F. Winter. "Sex-Role and Success in Law School." *Journal of Legal Education* 29 (1978): 449–458.

Roberts, Joan, and Sherrie Akinsanya. *Schooling in the Cultural Context.* New York: D. McKay, 1976.

Robinson, E. *Law and the Lawyers.* New York: Macmillan, 1935.

Romero, Leo, Richard Delgado, and Cruz Reynoso. "The Legal Education of Chicano Students: Mutual Accommodation and Cultural Conflict." *New Mexico Law Review* 5 (1975): 177–231.

Rosen, Lawrence. *The Anthropology of Justice: Law as Culture in Islamic Society.* Cambridge, UK: Cambridge University Press, 1989.

Sacks, Harvey, Emanuel Schegloff, and Gail Jefferson. "A Simplest Systematics for the Organization of Turn-Taking for Conversation." In *Studies in the Organization of Conversational Interaction,* ed. J. Schenkein, 7–55. New York: Academic Press, 1978.

Sadker, David, and Myra Sadker. "Sexism in American Education: The Hidden Curriculum." In *Women, Work, and School: Occupational Segregation and the Role of Education,* ed. Ielie R. Wolfe, 57. Boulder, CO: Westview Press, 1991.

Sadker, Myra, and David Sadker. *Failing at Fairness: How Our Schools Cheat Girls.* New York: Macmillan, 1994.

Sander, Richard. "A Reply to Critics." *Stanford Law Review* 57 (2005): 1964–2016.

———. "A Systematic Analysis of Affirmative Action in American Law Schools." *Stanford Law Review* 57 (2004): 367–483.

Santos, Boaventura de Sousa Santos, and Cesar Rodriguez-Garavito. *Law and Globalization from Below: Towards a Cosmopolitan Legality.* Cambridge, UK: Cambridge University Press, 2005.

Sapir, Edward. *Selected Writings of Edward Sapir: Language, Culture, and Personality.* Ed. David Mandelbaum. Berkeley: University of California Press, 1970.

Sarat, Austin. *When the State Kills: Capital Punishment and the American Condition.* Princeton, NJ: Princeton University Press, 2001.

Sarat, Austin, and William Felstiner. *Divorce Lawyers and Their Clients: Power and Meaning in the Legal Process.* Oxford: Oxford University Press, 1995.

Sarat, Austin, and Thomas Kearns, eds. *Law in Everyday Life.* Ann Arbor: University of Michigan Press, 1993.

Saussure, Ferdinand de. *Course in General Linguistics.* Ed. C. Bailey and A. Sechehaye. London: Duckworth, 1983.

Saxe, G., M. Gearheart, and S. Guberman. "The Social Organization of Early Number Development." *New Directions for Child Development* 23 (1984): 19–30.

Scheingold, Stuart. *The Politics of Rights: Lawyers, Public Policy, and Political Change.* New Haven: Yale University Press, 1974.

Scheppele, Kim Lane. *Legal Secrets: Equality and Efficiency in the Common Law.* Chicago: University of Chicago Press, 1988.

Schieffelin, Bambi. *The Give and Take of Everyday Life: Language Socialization of Kaluli Children.* New York: Cambridge University Press, 1990.

Schieffelin, Bambi, and Elinor Ochs, eds. *Language Socialization across Cultures.* Cambridge, UK: Cambridge University Press, 1986.

Schieffelin, Bambi, Kathryn Woolard, and Paul Kroskrity, eds. *Language Ideologies: Practice and Theory.* Oxford: Oxford University Press, 1998.

Schlegel, John Henry. "Walt Was Right." *Journal of Legal Education* 51 (2001): 599–609.

Schwab, Claire. "A Shifting Gender Divide: The Impact of Gender on Education at Columbia Law School in the New Millenium." *Columbia Journal of Law & Social Problems* 36 (2003): 299–337.

Schwartz, Audrey James. "Law, Lawyers and Law School: Perspectives from the First-Year Class." *Journal of Legal Education* 30 (1980): 437–469.

Scinto, Leonard. "Text, Schooling, and the Growth of Mind." In *Semiotic Mediation: Sociocultural and Psychological Perspectives,* ed. Elizabeth Mertz and Richard Parmentier, 203–218. New York: Academic Press, 1985.

Scollon, Ronald, and Suzanne Scollon. *Intercultural Communication.* New York: Blackwell, 1995.

Scott, James. *Domination and the Arts of Resistance: Hidden Transcripts.* New Haven: Yale University Press, 1990.

———. *Weapons of the Weak: Everyday Forms of Peasant Resistance.* New Haven: Yale University Press, 1985.

Scribner, Sylvia, and Michael Cole. "Literacy without Schooling: Testing for Intellectual Effects." *Harvard Educational Review* 48 (1978): 448–461.

Searle, John. *Speech Acts: An Essay in the Philosophy of Language.* Cambridge, UK: Cambridge University Press, 1969.

Sedlacek, William E. "Black Students on White Campuses: 20 Years of Research." *Journal of College Student Personnel* 28 (1987): 484–495.

Serbin, Lisa, and Daniel O'Leary. "How Nursery Schools Teach Girls to Shut Up." *Psychology Today* (July 1975): 56–58.

Shaffer, Thomas. "Moral Implications and Effects of Legal Education." *Journal of Legal Education* 34 (1984): 190–204.

Shaffer, Thomas, and Robert Redmount. *Lawyers, Law Students, and People.* Colorado Springs, CO: Shepard's, 1977.

Shweder, Richard A., and Robert A. Levine, eds. *Culture Theory: Essays on Mind, Self, and Emotion.* New York: Cambridge University Press, 1984.

Silverstein, Michael. "Indexical Order and the Dialectics of Sociolinguistic Life." *Language and Communications* 23 (2003): 193–229.

———. "Language and the Culture of Gender: At the Intersection of Structure, Usage, and Ideology." In *Semiotic Mediation: Sociocultural and Psychological Perspectives,* ed. Elizabeth Mertz and Richard Parmentier, 219–259. New York: Academic Press, 1985.

———. "Language Structure and Linguistic Ideology." In *The Elements: A Parasession on Linguistic Units and Levels,* ed. P. Clyne et al., 193–247. Chicago: Chicago Linguistic Society, 1979.

———. "The Limits of Awareness." *Working Papers in Sociolinguistics* 84. Austin, Texas: Southwest Educational Development Laboratory, 1981.

———. "Metaforces of Power in Traditional Oratory." Lecture to Yale University Anthropology Department, 1981.

———. "Metapragmatic Discourse and Metapragmatic Function." In *Reflexive Language,* ed. John Lucy, 33–58. New York: Cambridge University Press, 1993.

———. "Monoglot 'Standard' in America." *Working Papers and Proceedings of the Center for Psychosocial Studies* 13. Chicago: Center for Psychosocial Studies, 1987.

———. "The Poetics of Politics: 'Theirs' and 'Ours.' " *Journal of Anthropological Research* 61 (2005): 1–24.

———. "The Secret Lives of Texts." In *Natural Histories of Discourse,* ed. Michael Silverstein and Greg Urban, 81–105. Chicago: University of Chicago Press, 1996.

———. "Shifters, Linguistic Categories, and Cultural Description." In *Meaning in Anthropology,* ed. Keith Basso and Henry Selby Jr., 11–55. Albuquerque: University of New Mexico Press, 1976.

———. "Translation, Transduction, Transformation: Skating 'Glossando' on Thin Semiotic Ice." In *Translating Cultures: Perspectives on Translation and Anthropology,* ed. Paula Rubel and Abraham Rosman, 75–105. New York: Oxford University Press, 2003.

———. "The Uses and Utility of Ideology." In *Language Ideologies: Practice and Theory,* ed. Bambi Schieffelin, Kathryn Woolard, and Paul Kroskrity, 123–125. Oxford: Oxford University Press, 1998.

———. "Whorfianism and the Linguistic Imagination of Nationality." In *Regimes of Language: Ideologies, Polities, and Identities,* ed. Paul Kroskrity, 85–138. Santa Fe, NM: School of American Research Press, 2000.

Silverstein, Michael, and Greg Urban. "The Natural History of Discourse." In *Natural Histories of Discourse,* ed. Michael Silverstein and Greg Urban, 1–17. Chicago: University of Chicago Press, 1996.

Smedley, Brian D., Hector Myers, and Shelly Harrell. "Minority-Status Stresses and the College Adjustment of Ethnic Minority Freshmen." *Journal of Higher Education* 64 (1993): 434–452.

Smith, Alfred. *Cognitive Styles in Law School.* Austin: University of Texas Press, 1979.

Solan, Lawrence. *The Language of Judges.* Chicago: University of Chicago Press, 1993.

Spelman, Elizabeth. *Inessential Woman: Problems of Exclusion in Feminist Thought.* Boston: Beacon Press, 1988.

Spradley, James. *Participant Observation.* Belmont, CA: Wadsworth, 1980.

Stanchi, Kathryn. "Resistance Is Futile: How Legal Writing Pedagogy Contributes to the Law's Marginalization of Outsider Voices." *Dickinson Law Review* 103 (1998): 7–57.

Starr, June, and Jane Collier, eds. *History and Power in the Study of Law: New Directions in Legal Anthropology*. Ithaca, NY: Cornell University Press, 1989.

Sternglaz, Sarah, and Shirley Lyberger-Ficek. "Sex Differences in Student-Teacher Interactions in the College Classroom." *Sex Roles* 3 (1977): 345–352.

Stevens, Robert. *Law School: Legal Education in America from the 1850s to the 1980s*. Chapel Hill: University of North Carolina Press, 1983.

Stone, Alan. "Legal Education on the Couch." *Harvard Law Review* 85 (1971): 392–442.

Stover, Robert V. *Making It and Breaking It: The Fate of Public Interest Commitment During Law School*. Ed. Howard Erlanger. Urbana: University of Illinois Press, 1989.

Street, Brian. *Literacy in Theory and Practice*. New York: Cambridge University Press, 1984.

Stropus, Ruta. "Mend It, Bend It, Extend It: The Fate of Traditional Law School Methodology in the 21st Century." *Loyola University-Chicago Law Journal* 27 (1996): 449–489.

Sunstein, Cass. *Legal Reasoning and Political Conflict*. Oxford: Oxford University Press, 1996.

Taber, Janet, Marguerite Grant, Mary Huser, Rise Norman, James Sutton, Clarence Wong, Louise Parker, and Claire Picard. "Gender, Legal Education, and the Legal Profession: An Empirical Study of Stanford Law Students and Graduates." *Stanford Law Review* 40 (1988): 1209–1297.

Tannen, Deborah. "Repetition in Conversation: Towards a Poetics of Talk." *Language* 63 (1987): 574–605.

———. "Waiting for the Mouse: Constructed Dialogue in Conversation." In *The Dialogic Emergence of Culture*, ed. D. Tedlock and B. Mannheim, 198–217. Urbana: University of Illinois Press, 1995.

Teich, Paul. "Research on American Law Teaching: Is There a Case against the Case System?" *Journal of Legal Education* 36 (1986): 167–188.

Teitelbaum, Lee, Antoinette Sedillo Lopez, and Jeffrey Jenkins. "Gender, Legal Education, and Legal Careers." *Journal of Legal Education* 41 (1991): 443–481.

Tharp, Roland. "Psychocultural Variables and Constants: Effects on Teaching and Learning in Schools." *American Psychologist* 44 (1989): 349–359.

Torres, Arturo Lopez, and Mary Kay Lundwall. "Moving beyond Langdell II: An Annotated Bibliography of Current Methods for Law Teaching." *Gonzaga Law Review* 35 (2000): 1–61.

Toulmin, Stephen. *The Uses of Argument*. Cambridge, UK: Cambridge University Press, 1958.

Travers, Max. "Understanding Talk in Legal Settings: What Law and Society Studies Can Learn from a Conversation Analyst." *Law & Social Inquiry* 31 (forthcoming).

Trubek, Louise. "Crossing Boundaries: Legal Education and the Challenge of a 'New Public Interest' Law." *Wisconsin Law Review* 2005 (2005): 455–477.

Trujillo, Carla M. "A Comparative Examination of Classroom Interactions between Professors and Minority and Non-Minority College Students." *American Educational Research Journal* 23 (1986): 629.

Tucker, Marilyn, Laurie Albright, and Patricia Busk. "Whatever Happened to the Class of 1983?" *Georgetown Law Journal* 78 (1989): 153–195.

Turner, Victor. *Dramas, Fields, and Metaphors: Symbolic Action in Human Society*. Ithaca, NY: Cornell University Press, 1974.

Turow, Scott. *One L*. New York: Penguin, 1977.

Unger, Roberto. *Law in Modern Society*. New York: Free Press, 1976.

Van Gennep, Arnold. *The Rites of Passage*. Chicago: University of Chicago Press, 1960.

Vitiello, Michael. "Professor Kingsfield: The Most Misunderstood Character in Literature." *Hofstra Law Review* 33 (2005): 955–1015.

Volpp, Leti. "(Mis)Identifying Culture: Asian Women and the 'Cultural Defense.'" *Harvard Women's Law Journal* 17 (1994): 57–101.

Vukowich, William. "The Lack of Practical Training in Law Schools." *Case Western Reserve Law Review* 23 (1971): 140–152.

Vygotsky, L. *The Collected Works of L. S. Vygotsky.* Vol. 1. Ed. R. W. Reiber and A. S. Carton. New York: Plenum Press, 1986.

Watson-Gegeo, Karen, and Sarah Nielsen. "Language Socialization in SLA." In *Handbook of Second Language Acquisition*, ed. Catherine Doughty and Michael Long, 155–177. New York: Basil Blackwell, 2003.

Weber, Max. *Economy and Society: An Outline of Interpretive Sociology.* New York: Bedminster Press, 1968.

Weinstein, Carol S. "The Classroom as a Social Context for Learning." *Annual Review of Psychology* 42 (1991): 493–525.

Weis, Lois. Introduction. In *Class, Race, and Gender in American Education*, ed. Lois Weis, 1–7. Albany: State University of New York Press, 1988.

Weiss, Catherine, and Louise Melling. "The Legal Education of Twenty Women." *Stanford Law Review* 40 (1988): 1299–1369.

Weissbourd, Bernard, and Elizabeth Mertz. "Rule-Centrism versus Legal Creativity: The Skewing of Legal Ideology through Language." *Law & Society Review* 19 (1985): 623–659.

Wertsch, James, ed. *Culture, Communication, and Cognition: Vygotskian Perspectives.* Cambridge, UK: Cambridge University Press, 1985.

———. *Vygotsky and the Social Formation of Mind.* Cambridge, MA: Harvard University Press, 1985.

White, G. Edward. *The Marshall Court and Cultural Change, 1815–1835.* New York: Oxford University Press, 1991.

———. "The Marshall Court and International Law: The Piracy Cases." *American Journal of International Law* 83 (1989): 727–735.

White, James Boyd. "Doctrine in a Vacuum: Reflections on What a Law School Ought (and Ought Not) to Be." *Journal of Legal Education* 35 (1986): 155–167.

———. *From Expectation to Experience: Essays on Law and Legal Education.* Ann Arbor: University of Michigan Press, 2000.

———. *Justice as Translation: An Essay in Cultural and Legal Criticism.* Chicago: University of Chicago Press, 1990.

———. *The Legal Imagination.* Chicago: University of Chicago Press, 1973.

———. *When Words Lose Their Meaning.* Chicago: University of Chicago Press, 1984.

Whorf, Benjamin Lee. *Language, Thought and Reality.* Boston: MIT Press, 1956.

Wightman, Linda F. *Women in Legal Education: A Comparison of the Law School Performance and Law School Experiences of Women and Men.* Newton, PA: Law School Admission Council, 1996.

Wilcox, Kathleen. "Differential Socialization in the Classroom: Implications for Equal Opportunity." In *Doing the Ethnography of Schooling: Educational Anthropology in Action*, ed. George Spindler, 268–309. New York: Holt, Rinehart, and Winston, 1982.

Wilkins, David. "A Systematic Response to Systematic Disadvantage." *Stanford Law Review* 57 (2005): 1915–1961.

Wilkins, David, and G. Mitu Gulati. "Why Are There So Few Black Lawyers in Corporate Law Firms? An Institutional Analysis." *California Law Review* 84 (1996): 493–625.

Williams, Patricia. *The Alchemy of Race and Rights: Diary of a Law Professor.* Cambridge, MA: Harvard University Press, 1991.

Wilson, Karen, and Sharon Levin. "The Sex-Based Disparity in Class Participation." *The Phoenix* (University of Chicago Law School student newspaper) (Nov. 26, 1991): 3.

Wilson, Lisa, and David Taylor. "Surveying Gender Bias at One Midwestern Law School." *American University Journal of Gender, Social Policy, and Law* 9 (2001): 251–284.

Wingate, Nancy. "Sexism in the Classroom." *Integrated Education* (Jan.–June 1984): 105–110.

Winter, Steven. *A Clearing in the Forest: Law, Life, and Mind.* Chicago: University of Chicago Press, 2001.

Woolard, Kathryn. "Language Ideology as a Field of Inquiry." In *Language Ideologies: Practice and Theory,* ed. Bambi Schieffelin, Kathryn Woolard, and Paul Kroskrity, 3–47. Oxford: Oxford University Press, 1998.

Woolard, Kathryn, and Bambi Schieffelin. "Language Ideology." *Annual Review of Anthropology* 23 (1994): 55–82.

Wortham, Stanton. "Linguistic Anthropology of Education: An Introduction." In *Linguistic Anthropology of Education,* ed. Stanton Wortham and Betsy Rymes, 1–29. Westport, CT: Prager, 2003.

Wortham, Stanton, and Betsy Rymes, eds. *Linguistic Anthropology of Education.* Westport, CT: Praeger, 2003.

Yale Law Women. *Yale Law School Faculty and Students Speak about Gender: A Report on Faculty-Student Relations at Yale Law School, 2001–2002.* Available at http://www.yale.edu/ylw/YLW%20Gender%20Report.pdf.

Yngvesson, Barbara. *Virtuous Citizens, Disruptive Subjects: Order and Complaint in a New England Court.* New York: Routledge, 1993.

Yon, Daniel. "Highlights and Overview of the History of Educational Ethnography." *Annual Review of Anthropology* 32 (2003): 411–429.

Yovel, Jonathan. "The Language beyond Law: Linguistic Performativity in Legal Context." SJD diss., Northwestern University, 1997.

———. "Rights and Rites: Initiation, Language and Performance in Law and Legal Education." *Stanford Agora* (2002): 3, available at http://lawschool.stanford.edu/agora/volume2/yovel.shml.

———. "What Is Contract Law 'About'? Speech Act Theory and a Critique of 'Skeletal Promises.' " *Northwestern University Law Review* 94 (2000): 937–961.

Zemans, Frances, and Victor Rosenblum. *The Making of a Public Profession.* Chicago: University of Chicago Press, 1981.

# INDEX

abstract/concrete language, 1, 5–6, 24, 27, 133–134, 212–214, 220–221, 230n.15
Amsterdam, Anthony, 274n.51
analogy, 5, 58–59, 61–62, 70–74, 146, 154, 201, 213–215, 217–218, 220–221, 274n.56
anaphora, 149–150
animator, 104, 107, 112, 126, 157, 246n.42
anthropological linguistics. *See* linguistic anthropology
Anyon, Jean, 233n.51, 234n.60
audience, 51, 148, 231n.29. *See also* participation
Austin, Regina, 211–212, 213, 269n.17
author, 59, 102, 104, 106, 107, 112, 126, 129, 246n.42
authority, 51, 91, 94–96, 129, 177, 215
　legal, 4, 61, 67, 75
　linguistic, 5, 77, 94, 166, 170
autonomy, 50–51, 229n.14, 234n.69
　of education, 22–26
　of language, 6, 23–24, 49–50, 152
　of law, 6, 238n.116
　semi-autonomous fields, 238n.116

backchannel, 34, 36–37, 146, 149, 240n.17, 255n.17
Baker, Brook, 214, 269nn.18–21, 274n.52
Bakhtin, Mikhail, 103, 231n.25, 246n.42
Banks, Taunya Lovell, 27, 178, 187, 237n.101, 260n.28, 262n.57
Bauman, Richard, 48, 232n.35, 241n.4, 243n.14
Bell, Derrick, Jr., 228n.9
Bourdieu, Pierre, 22–23, 25, 51, 233n.50, 234n.64, 234nn.71–72
Brenneis, Donald, 19, 231n.29, 232n.35, 233n.49, 238n.115, 239n.122, 271n.40, 274n.56
Briggs, Charles, 29, 48, 232n.35, 238nn.116–118, 241n.4, 243n.12
Bruner, Jerome, 274n.51
Burns, Robert, 220, 248n.60, 274n.51

Calhoun, Craig, 229n.14, 234n.63
case law genre, 5, 8–10, 13, 44, 46, 52–53, 59–64, 109, 170
Cazden, Courtney, 24, 176, 233n.59, 239nn.2–4, 260n.13
Chandler, Nahum, 230n.22

Chomsky, Noam, 272n.42
class. *See* social class
classroom, 222. *See also* education: legal;
    teaching: law
    dynamics, 16, 27, 31–32, 54–56, 175,
        177–178, 258n.36
    language, 3, 23–24, 30, 95
coherence (cohesion), 146–148, 151–155,
    158, 162–164, 167, 181, 214, 215,
    244n.30, 256n.20
Cole, Michael, 23, 233n.53
Collier, Jane, 227n.2, 238n.116
Collins, James, 23, 50, 51, 233n.51,
    233n.56, 233n.58, 234nn.62–63,
    234n.73, 234n.76, 239n.4, 246n.39,
    259n.10
Comaroff, Jean, 228n.6, 234n.68,
    238n.117, 241n.3
Comaroff, John, 227n.1, 234n.68,
    238n.117
commensurability, 214
conflict, 4–5. *See also* narrative: conflict
    stories
    social, 10–11, 29, 213
Conley, John, 29, 32–33, 137, 171, 173,
    227n.3, 228n.8, 235n.81, 237n.96,
    238nn.115–116, 239n.5, 239n.7,
    240n.16, 272n.43
Constable, Marianne, 217, 271n.37
context, 45–49, 173, 208–212
    acontextual context, 115, 129–130
    educational, 15, 49–50, 196
    institutional, 16, 19, 21, 23–25, 129,
        134, 220, 223, 242n.8, 265n.71,
        266n.86, 274n.56
    linguistic, 4, 18–20, 59, 231n.24,
        231n.28, 235n.76, 238n.106
    social, 4–6, 13, 18–20, 75–79, 115–
        120, 131–134, 176, 205–206, 216–
        218, 229n.14, 239n.122, 252nn.28–
        31
contextualization cues, 19, 207
conversation analysis, 35, 37, 240n.18,
    245n.32, 272n.43
Cook-Gumperz, Jenny, 24, 233n.59
Coombe, Rosemary, 238n.117
copy, 149
courtroom (trial) language, 29, 32, 106,
    135–137, 147, 170, 220, 235n.81,
    252n.35

creativity, 25
    indexicality and, 19–20, 232n.34
    legal, 232n.34
    linguistic, 20, 232n.36
Crenshaw, Kimberlé, 139, 209, 228n.9,
    236n.87, 253n.1
cross-examination, 145, 155
cultural dominance/invisibility, 1, 5–6, 25,
    132, 140, 202–203, 208, 213, 216,
    220–223, 226n.6, 228n.10
culture, 13, 17–22, 29, 73, 78, 88, 127,
    217–218, 233n.57, 234n.68, 239n.122,
    241n.3, 271n.40
Cunningham, Clark, 237n.96

Daicoff, Susan, 27, 237n.100, 277n.69
Danet, Brenda, 235n.81
decontextualization, 45, 48, 49, 243n.14
deictics, 103, 104, 251n.25
democratic values, 1, 3, 6, 15–16, 26, 47–
    48, 208, 220–223, 277n.66
denotational meaning, 45
Dezalay, Yves, 274n.53
dialogue, 4–5, 59, 81, 88, 90, 103, 106–
    112, 170, 211, 216, 246n.42, 251n.24
    dialogic self, 124–128, 131–136
    focused, 86, 89, 93, 192–194, 240n.11
    in short-exchange classrooms, 155–164
    unfocused (nonfocused), 86, 89,
        240n.11
dicta (*obiter dictum*), 28, 62
difference/similarity, 1, 13–15, 139–140,
    169, 208–209, 213–214, 229n.14
direct examination, 109, 145, 155,
    251n.25
direct quotation, 103–108, 110–113, 166,
    250n.16, 251nn.20–21. *See also*
    reported speech
discourse, 29, 211
    and education, 24–25, 181–182
    genres, 26, 28–29, 142–144, 220–221,
        241n.3 (*see also* case law genre;
        genres: legal)
    markers, 152, 248n.58, 256n.23
    structure, 20–21, 30, 143–144, 238n.106
Domínguez, Virginia, 239n.122
double edge (double character), 5–6, 16,
    101, 123–124, 133–134, 212–214,
    221, 226n.5, 229n.15
Duranti, Alessandro, 19, 231n.29, 232n.35

education, 22–25, 222
    college, 177–178, 185–186, 190, 208–
        209, 260n.26, 262nn.46–55
    elementary, 24, 54–56, 176–177, 185,
        190, 246n.39, 256n.21, 261nn.40–45,
        267n.92
    graduate, 51, 186, 188
    high school, 177, 185
    legal, 5, 26–30, 214
ellipsis, 150
emotion, 21, 27, 58, 95, 99, 120–128, 197,
    237n.100, 246n.41
empiricism, vii, 4, 12, 13, 29, 30, 31–35,
    237n.100. See also realism; sociolegal
    studies
entextualization, 45, 216, 242n.8,
    243nn.13–14
epistemology (worldview), 98, 223,
    245n.38
    capitalist (commodification), 6, 100,
        132–134, 205–206, 207, 212–214,
        230n.15
    cultural, 17–21, 23–24, 30
    legal, 3–6, 14, 67–69, 80, 95, 105, 110,
        131–136, 213–217, 226n.16, 226n.10,
        230n.15, 239n.121
    linguistic, 14, 17–25, 30, 131–132, 152,
        256nn.23–24
Erlanger, Howard, 236n.90, 250n.4,
    266n.84
essentializing, 140, 202, 208–211, 249n.8

facts. See legal facts
Felstiner, William, 29, 32, 227n.3, 227n.6,
    228n.8, 235n.81, 239n.6, 246n.41
filter. See language: as filter
Fineman, Martha, 15, 139, 228n.9,
    229nn.13–14, 253n.2
footing, 59, 104, 107, 109–110, 112, 126–
    127, 129–131, 135–137, 246n.42,
    251nn.24–25
Frohmann, Lisa, 33, 235n.81, 239n.8
Frug, Mary Jo, 228n.9, 269n.1

Gal, Susan, 20, 216, 232n.38
Garth, Bryant, 28, 238nn.110–111,
    253n.40, 258n.39, 274n.53
Gee, James, 24, 50, 51, 176, 233n.51,
    233n.59, 234nn.60–61, 260n.13
Geertz, Clifford, 238n.122, 239n.1

gender, 23, 33, 120, 208–209, 211
    gendered lives, 15, 229nn.13–14, 253n.2
    and language, 173
    and law, 229n.11, 238n.116
    and legal education, 4, 26, 202–203,
        236n.90, 263nn.59–66 (see also
        participation: and gender)
    and sex, 229n.12
genres, 19, 26, 29–30, 50, 142–144, 162,
    241n.3
    legal, 60, 77, 79, 210, 247n.43 (see also
        case law genre)
Goffman, Erving, 104, 233n.45, 246n.42
Goodale, Mark, 238n.117, 274n.53
Gooding, Susan, 239n.121, 240n.13,
    259n.5
Goodwin, Charles 19, 231n.29, 232n.35
Goody, Jack, 233n.52
grammar, 17–20, 63, 149, 230n.21,
    231n.27, 231n.30, 272n.42
Granfield, Robert, 210, 239n.123,
    250nn.1–2, 250n.5, 259n.2,
    264nn.66–67, 269n.10
Greenhouse, Carol, 29, 227nn.2–3,
    239n.121, 274n.55
Guinier, Lani, 27, 174, 187, 188, 237n.101,
    259n.1, 260n.31, 264n.67, 264n.70
Gulati, Mitu, 179, 259n.8, 260n.34,
    264n.66, 276n.64
Gumperz, John, 19, 231n.29, 232n.35

Hantzis, Catherine, 228n.9, 236n.87
Harris, Angela, 229n.12
Hastie, Reid, 250n.18
Heath, Shirley Brice, 1, 24, 225n.2,
    232n.37, 233n.51, 234n.62, 239n.2,
    239n.4
Hill, Jane, 232n.35
Hirsch, Susan, 29, 214, 216, 226n.6,
    227n.2, 234n.68, 235n.81, 238n.115,
    238n.118, 270n.22, 272n.43, 273n.48,
    274n.56
history, 13, 48–49, 63–64, 169, 238n.116,
    252n.36
    of legal education, 26–27, 235n.82,
        243n.22
holding (legal), 28, 62, 72–73, 80, 112
humor, 68–69, 116, 153, 154, 162–163,
    178, 181
hypotheticals, 65, 73–74, 77, 81, 108, 126

icons, 20, 59, 94, 216, 231n.31, 232n.38, 238n.106, 242n.10, 245n.38, 249n.64, 256n.24
identity, 29, 209–210, 239n.120, 277n.67
  initiate (initiand; law student), 21–22, 100, 115, 135–137, 233n.47
  legal professional, 122–123, 129–130, 237n.100, 246n.41
  and liminal state, 22, 233n.47
  social, 32, 239n.121
ideology, 96, 103, 104, 110, 116–120, 134, 137, 214–221. *See also* language: as filter
  implicit, 19–20, 98, 131, 214, 232n.34, 270n.24
  linguistic, 3–5, 19–21, 28, 95, 106, 108, 127, 131–137, 170, 214–220, 232n.37
  and pedagogy, 23, 179, 234nn. 67–69
  professional, 127–128, 134–137, 228n.7
  textual, 46, 49–50, 56–59, 62–64, 94–96, 214–216
indexicality, 25, 59, 94, 152, 215, 231n.31, 232n.39, 233n.43, 238n.106, 243n.16, 245n.38
indirect quotation, 103, 251n.21. *See also* reported speech
intersectionality, 139, 196, 202
intertextuality, 95–96, 107, 247n.47, 253n.48
Irvine, Judith, 20, 216, 232n.35, 232nn. 37–38

Jakobson, Roman, 18, 230n.23
Jefferson, Gail, 240n.15
justice, 5, 8, 11, 14, 16, 47, 58–59, 73, 77, 79, 98, 123–124, 213, 216, 228n.10, 245n.38, 271n.37

Kennedy, Duncan, 26, 27, 51, 228n.9, 235n.78, 235nn.81–82, 236n.87, 236n.91
Krauskopf, Joan, 187, 188, 260n.132, 263n.64
Krupnick, Catherine, 262n.48
Kurylowicz, Jerzy, 231n.26

Labov, William, 234n.62
Langdell, Christopher Columbus, 1, 26, 27, 219, 225n.1, 236n.88, 243n.22

language
  and education, 233n.59
  as filter, 5, 62–64, 75–76, 83, 94–96, 123–124, 131–137, 220, 226n.7, 239n.120, 247n.49, 250n.7
  and ideology, 5 (*see also* ideology: linguistic)
  structure, 5, 17–21, 127, 137
Larson, Jane, 230n.16
Lawrence, Charles, III, 228n.10
law schools, 38, 226n.16. *See also* education: legal; history: of legal education
  cultures of, 6, 173
  and indigenous caste system, 28, 142–143, 169–173, 179, 183, 188–189, 196, 198–199, 210–211, 222, 225n.3, 258nn.39–40, 276nn.63–64
law students, 11, 26–28, 37–38, 215, 226nn.15–16, 228n.10, 233n.47, 236n.90, 237n.98, 265n.72, 266n.84. *See also* identity: initiate
  perspectives of, 197–201
Lazarus-Black, Mindie, 227n.2, 234n.68, 235n.81, 239n.121, 274n.54
Leacock, Eleanor, 234n.70
lecture, 51, 57, 75, 86–89, 142–143, 164–169, 170
legal doctrine, 5, 57–59, 70–75, 82, 100–101, 113–116, 123–124, 169–170, 199, 201, 213–214, 227n.6, 229n.11, 235n.79, 236n.92, 248n.60, 252n.28
legal facts, 61, 65–74, 79–82, 145–146, 215
legal landscape, 105, 111, 126, 128–130
legal opinions, 26, 46, 52–54, 57–60, 63, 170, 242n.8. *See also* case law genre
legal persona, 97, 99–129, 135–137, 235n.78, 253n.50, 269n.13, 277n.69
legal procedure. *See* procedural history
legal profession/practice, 11–14, 27–28, 62, 98, 188, 215, 221, 223, 227n.6, 237n.100, 238n.109, 248n.63, 274n.56, 277n.69
legal reasoning, vii, 5–6, 13–14, 16, 26–28, 30, 41, 170, 217–219, 270n.24. *See also* education: legal; epistemology
Levi, Edward, 6, 26, 58, 63, 74, 226n.8, 235nn.78–79, 241n.1, 242n.11, 245n.36, 247n.50, 248n.60, 270n.24

linguistic anthropology, 3, 16–24, 29–30, 31–33, 82, 134, 215, 217–218, 231n.27, 233n.51, 245n.38, 271n.37, 273nn.48–49
literacy (literacies), 23–24, 49–50, 60, 233nn.52–56, 233nn.58–59
Lucy, John, 230n.20
Lugones, María, 209

Macaulay, Stewart (relational contract), 227n.4, 252n.29, 252n.32, 266n.84
MacKinnon, Catherine, 226n.10
Martin, Joanne, 28, 238nn.110–111, 253n.40, 258n.39
Maru, Olavi, 235n.82
Matoesian, Gregory, 29, 33, 104, 105, 110, 134, 216, 235n.81, 238nn.115–116, 239n.8, 240n.15, 248n.55, 250n.12, 250n.17, 250n.19, 252n.27, 256n.22, 256n.24, 272n.43
Matsuda, Mari, 228n.10
Matthews, Nancy, 240n.113
Maynard, Douglas, 235n.81
Mehan, Hugh, 24, 233n.51, 233n.59, 234n.62, 239n.2, 246n.41
Menkel-Meadow, Carrie, 228n.9, 236nn.87–88, 277n.69
Merry, Sally, 29, 33, 239nn.119–120, 239n.8, 269n.15, 271n.36, 274n.54
metalanguage, 29, 61, 88–89, 103, 152, 170, 214–217, 226n.7, 239n.120
metalinguistic discourse, 20–21, 80, 82–83, 154, 166, 232n.39
metalinguistic structure, 94–96, 98, 110, 157–158, 164, 223, 238n.106, 272n.42
    effect on awareness, 17–21, 134–135, 219, 228n.10, 231n.30, 232n.34
metapragmatic language, 107, 125, 130–133, 135, 152, 158, 214, 215, 238n.106, 243n.12, 272n.42
methodology, 4, 13, 23, 31–37, 239n.123, 239nn.9–14
metonymy, 218
Michaels, Sarah, 24, 176, 233n.51, 234n.59, 234n.60, 256n.21, 259n.10
Minow, Martha, 139, 235n.78, 253n.3
monologue, 109–110, 142, 147, 164, 170, 246n.42, 251n.24

Moore, Sally Falk, 238n.116
morality, 26–27, 29, 58, 76, 98, 120–128, 133, 135, 214, 220, 233n.49. See also norms; values

Nader, Laura, 238n.117, 274n.53
narrative, 54–59, 61, 79–82, 104, 145–155, 176, 231n.29, 233n.49, 233–234nn.59–61, 248n.57
    conflict stories, 5, 54, 94–96, 133, 242n.8
Njogu, Wamucii, 259n.5
norms, 15–16, 22, 170, 205, 214, 234n.59, 249n.3, 270nn.24–25. See also morality
Nourse, Victoria, 229n.11, 252n.37

O'Barr, William, 29, 32–33, 137, 171, 173, 227n.3, 228n.8, 235n.81, 238nn.115–116, 239n.5, 239n.7, 240n.16, 272n.43
Obiora, Leslye, 229n.12
Ochs, Elinor, 231n.31, 232n.40, 251n.26, 251n.33
oral argument (appellate), 109, 145, 170, 255n.13

pair-part structure (adjacency pairs), 36, 109, 112, 123–124, 134, 147–150, 170, 240n.18, 246n.42
    and turn-taking, 35–37, 162, 167
parallelism, 148–149, 162, 256n.20
Parmentier, Richard, 231n.24, 231n.31, 245n.38
participant observation, 31
participant structures, 32, 234n.59
participation, 174–197
    classroom, 154, 175–176
    and gender, 174–176, 185–197
    and race, 174–185
pedagogy, 26–28, 41, 50–51, 92, 95, 110, 111, 131, 155, 164, 174–175, 202–203, 210, 237n.98, 243n.22, 256n.24, 277n.66. See also education; schooling; teaching (teaching style)
Peirce, Charles S., 18, 230n.23, 245n.38
Pennington, Nancy, 250n.18
performance, 19, 47, 49, 51, 81, 232n.35, 241n.3, 252n.38
performative, 60, 215, 247n. 44

persona. *See* legal persona

Philips, Susan, 24, 29, 95–96, 134–136, 176, 214, 216, 233n.43, 233n.51, 234n.59, 235n.81, 238nn.114–115, 238n.118, 239n.123, 252n.35, 253n.48, 270n.24, 272n.43

poetic structure, 148–149, 233n.51

political oratory, 19, 231n.29, 245n.38

politics, 5, 29, 47–48, 95, 134, 245n.38

polylogue (polyphony), 158, 159, 163, 247n.42

polysemy, 96

Postone, Moishe, 133, 212, 226n.5, 229n.15, 253n.41, 269n.14

power, 6, 16, 30, 177, 220–223
   and language, 6, 29, 171–173, 231n.27, 238n.116, 271n.37, 272n.43
   and law, 106
   resistance to, 25, 124–125, 234n.68
   social, 24–25, 49–50, 60, 62, 101, 207–208, 213, 217–218, 271n.37

pragmatics, 48, 219, 231n.24, 232n.34, 243n.14. *See also* metalanguage; metapragmatic language

pragmatic structure, 218, 232n.34

pragmatic warrants, 58–59, 67, 77, 82, 89, 94–96

Prague School, 18, 230n.23, 231n.26

precedent, 46, 60–62, 242nn.9–10

presupposition, 20–21, 232n.34, 232n.36
   indexicality and, 20, 215

principal (footing), 104, 107, 112

procedural history, 57, 59, 60, 62, 69–70, 75

professors, 177
   law, 7, 33–34, 38–38, 171–173, 179, 181–183, 200, 241n.3

pronouns, 103, 108, 112, 115, 129–130, 251nn.24–25

propositional meaning, 18, 217. *See also* denotational meaning; reference; semantics; text: denotational

prosody (intonation), 151, 181, 188, 234n.61

psychology, 27, 237n.98, 237n.100

question-answer sequences, 36–37, 106, 108, 109, 148–149, 162, 240n.18, 252n.35. *See also* dialogue; pair-part structure (adjacency pairs)

quotation. *See* direct quotation; indirect quotation; reported speech

race, 15, 23, 26, 78, 119–120, 173, 202–203, 208–209, 211, 213–214, 234n.59, 239n.121, 249n.8, 277n.67
   "minority" students, 222, 225n.3, 240n.20, 259n.11, 260n.14, 275nn.59–67 (*see also* participation: and race)

reading, 52–56, 60–64, 83, 94–96, 99–100, 133–134, 169, 246n.40

realism, 114
   legal, 13, 219, 227nn.4–6; 228n.9
   new legal, 237n.96, 266n.84

recontextualization, 45–49, 52–54, 63, 242n.8, 243n.14, 252n.28

Redmount, Robert, 143, 173, 236n.88, 239n.123

reference, 32, 50, 94, 231n.24, 232n.34
   and ideology, 46–50, 63–64, 242n.10, 243n.13

repair, 126, 244n.30, 244n.32, 252n.35

repetition, 146–149, 163, 234n.61, 256nn.20–21

reported speech, 81, 88, 102–113, 153, 158, 162

resistance. *See* power: resistance to

Rhode, Deborah, 236n.87

role play, 65, 81, 82, 112, 126–127, 131–132, 254n.11, 257n.32

Rosen, Lawrence, 239n.122

Rosenblum, Victor, 27, 210, 225n.1, 236n.90, 238n.107, 238n.109, 258n.38, 269n.7

Sacks, Harvey, 240n.15

Sander, Richard, 179, 276nn.61–66

Sapir, Edward, 17–18, 230n.18, 230n.20, 230n.23

Sarat, Austin, 29, 32, 227n.3, 228n.8, 235n.81, 239n.6, 246n.41

Saussure, Ferdinand de, 18, 230n.20

Schegloff, Emanuel, 240n.15

Schieffelin, Bambi, 20, 21, 232n.37, 232n.40, 251n.26, 251nn.33–34

Schlegel, John Henry, 269n.1

schooling, 23–25, 49, 50, 60, 233nn.53–54, 234n. 72

Scollon, Ronald, 226n.7

Scollon, Suzanne, 226n.7
Scott, James, 234n.68
Scribner, Sylvia, 23, 233n.53
Searle, John, 232n.36
semantics, 46–50, 58, 231n.24, 232n.34. *See also* denotational meaning; reference
semantico-referential structure/content, 146–148, 164, 246n.38
semiotics, 73, 74, 95, 230n.24, 243n.13, 252n.28, 269n.13
Shaffer, Thomas, 143, 173, 236n.88, 239n.123
silence, 24, 176, 186, 188, 190, 202–203, 240n.19, 266n.84
Silverstein, Michael, 18, 20, 25, 45, 109–110, 215, 219–220, 225n.2, 228n.6, 229n.11, 230n.20, 230nn.22–23, 231n.25, 231n.27, 231nn.30–31, 232n.32, 232n.35, 232nn.36–37, 232n.39, 233n.43, 235n.76, 242n.8, 243n.13, 245n.38, 246n.42, 273n.49, 277n.68
similarity (sameness). *See* difference/similarity
social class, 24–25, 33, 51, 76, 133, 140, 174, 176, 177, 189, 221, 234nn.60–62, 234nn.64–65, 234n.69, 264n.70
socialization, 24, 34, 215
    linguistic, 14, 21–22, 29, 30, 232nn.40–42, 233n.49, 256n.21
    secondary, 21–22, 233n.43
sociolegal studies, 13, 227n.4, 227n.6
Sockloskie, Robert, 179
Socratic method, 26–28, 44, 50–59, 89–91, 142–155, 181, 196–197, 200–201, 219, 235nn.82–85, 236n.88, 236n.93, 238n.106, 239n.123, 239n.123, 243n.22, 254n.5
Solan, Lawrence, 235n.78
Stanchi, Kathryn, 237n.96
Starr, June, 227n.2
Stone, Alan, 27, 237nn.97–98, 239n.123
story. *See* narrative
Street, Brian, 23, 233n.55
syntax, 149, 231n.24

tag questions, 149
Tannen, Deborah, 250n.11, 255n.14

teaching (teaching style), 24, 38, 141–142, 167, 169–173, 192–197, 200–201
    law, 7–11, 26–28, 30, 34, 50–51, 236nn.83–85
text, 44–54, 215. *See also* contextualization cues; entextualization; ideology: textual; intertextuality; literacy (literacies)
    artifact, 45, 242nn.7–8, 242n.10, 243n.15
    authority of, 5, 46, 57–59, 94–96, 215 (*see also* authority)
    denotational, 45, 242n.8
    interactional, 45, 242n.8, 247n.48, 248n.62
    legal, 29
"thinking like a lawyer," 98–99
Toulmin, Stephen, 58, 245n.37
transduction, 273n.49, 277n.68
translation, 78, 83, 95, 107, 112, 131–132, 134, 207, 219–220, 223, 273n.46, 273n.49, 277n.68
Turner, Victor, 22, 231n.30, 233nn.45–37
turn-taking, 35, 37, 91–92, 159, 163, 168, 240n.18. *See also* dialogue; pair-part structure (adjacency pairs); question-answer sequences
    definition of turns, 35–37
Turow, Scott, 43, 68, 241n.1

uptake, 54–58, 142, 245n.32, 245n.33, 251n.24, 255n.19

values, 232n.42. *See also* morality; norms
Van Gennep, Arnold, 22, 233n.45, 233n.48
voice, 59, 103, 105, 108–113, 125–127, 129, 135–137, 166–167, 170–173, 203, 215–216, 246n.42, 251nn.20–25
Volpp, Leti, 226n.6
volunteered turns, 143, 159, 178, 186–190, 194–197, 265n.77
Vygotsky, Lev, 231n.25, 232n.42, 233n.57

warrants. *See* pragmatic warrants
Weissbourd, Bernard, 232n.32, 232n.34, 235n.77, 242n.10, 252n.39, 271n.41
White, James Boyd, 26, 27, 63, 218–219, 236n.92, 273nn.44–46

Whorf, Benjamin Lee, 17–18, 28, 230n.18, 230n.21
Wilkins, David, 63, 259n.8, 276n.63
Williams, Patricia, 26, 213, 217, 226n.13, 226n.14, 227n.3, 228n.9, 234n.69, 235n.78, 235n.81, 269n.16
Winter, Steven, 214, 217, 235n.78, 242n.11, 269n.17, 270n.24, 271n.38, 274n.56
Woolard, Kathryn, 20, 215, 232n.37, 271n.37

Wortham, Stanton, 25, 233n.51, 235n.76
writing, 3, 23–24, 28–29, 47–49, 62, 102–103, 129, 215–217, 242n.8, 243nn.13–15

Yngvesson, Barbara, 230n.15
Yovel, Jonathan, 214, 232n.36, 247n.44, 249n.3, 270n.25

Zemans, Frances, 27, 210, 225n.1, 236n.90, 238n.107, 238n.109, 258n.38, 269n.7

CPSIA information can be obtained at www.ICGtesting.com
Printed in the USA
BVOW031533101111

275684BV00004B/1/P

9 780195 183108